Lala's Story

LALA'S STORY

A Memoir of the Holocaust

LALA FISHMAN
AND STEVEN WEINGARTNER

NORTHWESTERN UNIVERSITY PRESS

Evanston, Illinois

Northwestern University Press
Evanston, Illinois 60208-4210

Second paperback printing 1999

Printed in the United States of America

ISBN 0-8101-1500-X

Library of Congress Cataloging-in-Publication Data

Fishman, Lala, 1922–
    Lala's story : a memoir of the Holocaust / Lala Fishman
and Steven Weingartner.
        p. cm. — (Jewish lives)
    ISBN 0-8101-1500-X (paper : alk. paper)
    1. Fishman, Lala, 1922– . 2. Jews—Ukraine—L'viv—
Biography. 3. Holocaust, Jewish (1939–1945)—Ukraine—
L'viv—Personal narratives. 4. L'viv (Ukraine)—Ethnic
relations. I. Weingartner, Steven. II. Title. III. Series.
DS135.U43F574 1998
940.53'18'092—dc21
[b]   97-36776
                                                        CIP

This book is dedicated to the sacred memory of my beloved parents, Olga and Ilya, my sister, Rysia, my grandmother Pesha, my grandfather Moses, and my aunts, uncles, and cousins who perished in the Second World War. May their descendants remember them always and know that they were once flesh and blood, drawing breath like the rest of us, living life in all its complexity, nurturing hopes and dreams for a future they never saw. We live in their future, and it is our solemn duty to ensure that they never disappear into our past.

May the Soul of the Deceased Be Bound Up in the Life Eternal

אנא תהיינה נפשותיהם צרורות בצרור החיים

This book is dedicated as well to the living: first and foremost to my dear husband, Morris; to my son, Eli, and his children, Lisa, Rebecca, and Jonathan; to my daughter Ora, her husband, Danny Munter, and their son, Jeremy; and to my daughter Abbey, her husband, Daron Romanek, and their children, Joshua, Michael, and Richard.

❀

Contents

❁

Foreword

At the end of the Second World War, Europe was swarming with hundreds of thousands of refugees, many of them survivors of Nazi concentration camps, all with no place to go and virtually no means of supporting themselves. Somehow, they had to be housed, fed, clothed, and otherwise cared for until they could be sorted out and resettled. Their welfare became the responsibility of the United Nations Relief and Rehabilitation Administration (UNRAA), which served as the umbrella agency under which numerous groups and organizations carried out the actual mission of helping these so-called Displaced Persons, or "DPs."

One of these organizations was the American Joint Distribution Committee. Established at the end of the First World War by American Jews and commonly known as the JDC, it was dedicated to aiding what remained of Europe's Jewish population after the fires of the Holocaust had finally been extinguished. I joined the JDC in the summer of 1946, leaving a rabbinical pulpit in Albany, New York, for a two-year posting to the displaced persons camps of Germany and Austria.

It was not my first trip to Europe. For several years before the war I had lived in Poland, studying at rabbinical seminaries (*yeshivoth*) in Łomża and Mir. But, of course, Europe was different now, changed by war. The Jews were different too. In prewar Poland, Jews tended to be quiet and respectful of authority. But no more. The cruelty they had experienced under Nazi rule had produced a "new Jewish type": bitter, angry, distrustful, truculent. Not surprisingly, they seemed

convinced that the Gentile world was determined to exterminate them. Even those who owed their lives to Gentiles felt
that way—although they had been hidden in the cellars and
attics of Gentile households, they spoke of being despoiled of
cash and precious jewelry by their rescuers. Their rancor, for
years held in check by the threat of death, was loosed at the
nearest available target: the UNRAA staff assigned to amelio-
rate their abject condition. I was often called upon to mediate
disputes between camp administrators and leaders chosen by
the DPs to represent their interests. I spent endless hours in
my office listening to complaints and allegations of mistreat-
ment: food rations were inadequate, medical care was poor,
housing was cramped—and why didn't we do something
about it right now?

I was sympathetic to their plight; I understood the reasons
for their behavior. Many of their complaints, to a greater or
lesser extent, were justified. And, after all, they had been
through hell. All had in some way been damaged by their
experiences; some had been broken. This I knew, and I tried
always to keep it in mind in my dealings with them. Even so,
they wore me out. Then, one morning, I was visited by someone as refreshing as all the others had been wearisome. Into
my office came a beautiful young woman with blond hair and
non-Semitic features. I gave her a quizzical look; I couldn't
figure out what this Gentile girl wanted from me. She smiled
at my evident confusion. She was, I would soon find out,
accustomed to people making such a mistake; in fact, she had
come to count on it. Introducing herself as Lala Weintraub,
she handed me her UNRAA card. The card identified her as a
resident of the Hasenecke camp for displaced Jews, which
was located near Kassel and under my jurisdiction. She then
presented documents from an uncle living in Perth Amboy,
New Jersey. I invited her to sit down and relax while I read
them. I was only too happy to spend this time with her. She
was pleasant, undemanding, and pretty—quite unlike the
typical visitor to my office.

She wanted to immigrate to America and thought the documents would help her achieve this goal. They were signed
by her uncle, Mr. Isadore Rosenwald, a U.S. Army veteran,

and they assured the government of the United States that he would assume full responsibility for the housing and care of his niece so that she would not become a public burden.

Her bearing and disposition conveyed such trust and candor that I felt it would be heartless of me to tell her that the United States had imposed severe limitations on Polish immigration. So I put the papers aside and joked that she did not need any guarantees from a relative to gain admission to the United States. "Forget about that," I said. "You can come to America as the bride of an American officer."

She laughed—a response I found amazing. She exhibited none of the trauma and guarded character of most victims of persecution. "You are a rose among thorns," I told her, quoting from King Solomon's Song of Songs in the Bible. She turned out to be much more than that. Two years later, she became my wife.

More than twenty years later, following intensive training in pastoral counseling, I was hired as a chaplain at Chicago-Read Mental Health Center, an Illinois state hospital for psychiatric patients. I was assigned to a treatment team along with other clinicians. One day at lunch in the hospital cafeteria, I sat with our team psychiatrists and a certain Dr. George Gruchowsky, a native of the Ukraine, to consult on the case of a Jewish patient suffering from paranoia. The patient was the son of Holocaust survivors, and I proposed that there might be a connection between his mental illness and the horrible experiences his parents had undergone. In the discussion that followed, Dr. Gruchowsky agreed that this was quite likely. After a while we started reminiscing about the war and its aftermath. I mentioned that my wife was from Lvov and that she, too, was a Holocaust survivor; she had managed to stay out of the camps by obtaining false documents that identified her as a Gentile. Upon hearing this, Dr. Gruchowsky chuckled. I stared at him. What, I wondered, was funny about surviving the Holocaust? It crossed my mind that many Ukrainians had collaborated with the Germans—was Dr. Gruchowsky one of them?

He was not. With great pride he explained that he was the

nephew of the Metropolitan Andreas Sheptytsky, wartime leader of the Ukrainian (Uniate) Catholic Church in Lvov — and a man who did much to help the Jews of Lvov after the city fell to the Germans in July 1941. "Your wife survived because of my uncle's role in the rescue of Jews," said Dr. Gruchowsky. He then informed me that his uncle, in addition to harboring Jews in his official residence and ordering his parishioners to refrain from violence against Jews, had instructed his clergymen to issue baptismal certificates and false documents to Jewish females. No doubt Lala got her documents as a result of Metropolitan Sheptytsky's directive.

My conversation with Dr. Gruchowsky made me realize that I had wrongly stereotyped Ukrainians as an entirely anti-Semitic people. I should add that Metropolitan Sheptytsky was not alone in his efforts to save Jews. There were many others like him, Polish and Ukrainian. I learned this from reading such books as Philip Friedman's *Roads to Extinction: Essays on the Holocaust;* Nechama Tec's *When Light Pierced the Darkness: Righteous Christians and the Polish Jews;* and Samuel and Pearl Oliner's *The Altruistic Personality.* But one of the best teachers in this regard was Lala herself. In the pages that follow, Lala has some harsh things to say about Gentiles. But she is also forthright, as usual, about the Gentiles who helped her. She is always the first to admit that she owes her life several times over to Poles and Ukrainians. And she has defended them, even to me. Once, shortly after the war, we were driving through Brooklyn, through neighborhoods where it seemed there were Catholic churches on every corner. At some point I made a disparaging remark about the Catholic Church's use of images — I think I said something to the effect that Catholics were idolatrous. Whereupon Lala upbraided me, noting that Catholics do not regard images as objects of worship but rather as a means for focusing their faith and piety. "They revere the images not because of what they are, but because of what they stand for," she said.

I have devoted a great deal of my life's work to establishing and maintaining friendly relations and mutual understanding between Jews and Christians. My career as a rabbi has been profoundly affected by the ecumenical spirit. Lala's life was saved by it. I thank God that this should be so.

Morris Fishman
Winter 1997

❖

Preface

Why did I wait until after my seventieth birthday to write this memoir of the Holocaust? The short explanation is that, until recently, I didn't have time for it. Early on, and for many years thereafter—decades, in fact—I had other things to keep me busy. When I came to the United States shortly after the war, my first priority was to adjust to the American way of life. It was no easy task. The biggest hurdle was language: I spoke English with a pronounced Polish accent that Americans sometimes found unintelligible and that always made me feel extremely self-conscious. What is more, my accent was a carryover from my European past, which I desperately wanted to put behind me. I wanted nothing more to do with my past: I tried to disown it. I didn't talk about it and I tried not to think about it; I wanted to focus on the present and the future. But the sound of my voice wouldn't let me forget where I was from, what I had been through. It was a very insistent reminder, and try as I might, I couldn't ignore it.

When my husband, Morris, became director of Hillel House at the University of Missouri in Columbia, I enrolled in a course in the school's speech department to learn how to lose my accent. I worked very hard at this, to the point where I would practice for hours in front of a mirror, speaking English and watching how my mouth formed the words. But to no avail. My vocal cords were by then nearly thirty years old and very set in their Polish-speaking ways. Then Eli, my oldest child, was born, and I became too busy with him to indulge in speech lessons. I still have a heavy accent; it is a legacy of my past, one of many that will not leave me.

Two more children followed Eli, my daughters Ora and Abbey, and I became busier still—so busy, as both a mother and a wife, that I had little time to think about anything other than the needs and concerns of my family. It was just as well; in a way, it was what I wanted. Marriage and motherhood accomplished what speech lessons could not: they pushed the memories of my childhood and life in Nazi-occupied Poland to the back of my mind, into a dark place that I visited only infrequently and finally not at all as the years went by.

But though I had effectively forgotten my past, my past had not forgotten me. In that dark place to which it had been relegated, it remained unaltered and intact, biding its time in silence, patiently waiting and watching for the right circumstances to reemerge and once again become a part of my conscious life. Then came the day when Abbey, my youngest child, went off to kindergarten. After that, every day during the week, my children were in school, Morris was at work, and I was alone in the house. But not really alone—I had company of sorts. Something inside me was stirring. At first, I didn't recognize what it was; I only knew that I was becoming increasingly restive and ever more dissatisfied with the way things were going. I did not understand what was happening to me, why I felt that way; after all, life was good. I loved my family, my husband made a better than decent living, we throve and prospered. And yet. . . .

And yet, I was in a bad state and getting worse. I realized that changes had to be made, or else . . . what? Again, I could not say. I just knew that I had to do something different, that I had to *be* someone different. For so many years I had been a mother to my children, a wife to my husband—who I was had been shaped and defined by what I was to my family. But was I not more than just a mother and a wife? Was I not still, at least in some small measure, the girl I had been in Poland, both before and during the war? I remembered that girl, but I could not locate her inside me. She was missing; she had gone without a word of good-bye, taking with her all the hopes and dreams of my childhood. And taking with her, too, the peace of mind that I had known before the war and should have had now.

As a child I had dreamed of becoming a fashion designer when I grew up. I now decided to pursue that dream, and thus, perhaps, find the cure for what was ailing me. So I enrolled in the Chicago Academy of Fine Arts, graduating four years later with a degree in interior design. For the next seventeen years, I worked part time as an interior designer, a profession that I greatly enjoyed, not least because it gave me back my sense of self—and the feeling that, at long last, I had a hand in determining who I was and would be. I had fulfilled the promise I had made to myself as a young girl, finally taking care of a critical piece of unfinished business.

But there remained more unfinished business—much more than I realized, and which professional achievement and satisfaction could not conclude. The past is real and does not die: its memory will be served. And so it was that, as the years went by, I began to think more and more about my past. Such thinking was involuntary on my part, and I knew that whatever caused it was somehow linked to my inner turmoil. My past was returning, clamoring for attention, demanding that I deal with it. I had no choice but to comply. But it hurt, and I wanted it to stop.

What a strange turn of events this was! Strange, because during the war, when the world seemed bent on destroying me, I had been completely at peace with myself. With death all around me, relentlessly seeking me, I somehow managed to convince myself that I would survive no matter what. This conviction was my armor and my shield, and it was my weapon: I defeated the Nazis with it. It had calmed me during my many moments of terror; it made me cool, decisive, and bold. Most important, it had given me a very strong sense of myself. I had known who I was and what I wanted. I wanted to survive. It was that simple; I had no extraneous concerns and no inner turmoil. On the surface, yes, I could be frightened nearly out of my wits. I could be as tense as coiled spring and anxious to the point of nervous collapse. But deep down inside, at the core of my being, where it really mattered, I was serene. It was a cold serenity, joyless and calculating—but it kept me alive.

One would think that I would have kept that serenity, that it would stay with me and grow in the absence of terror, becoming a warm and happy thing. But it didn't work that way. In America I was free and secure and comfortable, but I lacked the inner peace, the serenity of spirit, that I had possessed as a Jew on the run in occupied Poland.

This made no sense to me. It made sense to my husband, however. A clinical psychologist as well as an ordained rabbi, Morris understood exactly what I was going through, and why. Perhaps not coincidentally, I did not seek psychological counseling—I believed that I could solve my problem through my own efforts. In practice what this meant was simply ignoring the problem until it went away. Morris knew that I would solve nothing in this fashion, but he also knew that I would never talk things out on a psychiatrist's couch. As an alternative to therapy he suggested—gently but firmly, and often— that I write my memoirs of the war. In the beginning I rejected his suggestion. I was afraid that confronting the past, even by writing about it, would only cause me more pain. "Not so," he would say; on the contrary, it would surely alleviate my pain, if not do away with it altogether. He kept after me, with patience and persistence, but still I refused. Then, in about 1990, I "retired" from interior design work and found myself without anything to do or to keep my mind occupied. Morris pointed out that circumstances were ideal for writing my memoirs: "You owe it to yourself to write them," he would say, and finally I agreed with him. At any rate, I knew I owed myself *something*. You might say that I had an outstanding debt to myself. It was time, I realized, to pay up— and remembrance would be my currency.

Around that time Morris and I attended a dinner at the Ambassador East Hotel in Chicago where Abba Eban, the former Israeli ambassador to the United Nations, was guest of honor and keynote speaker. Seated at our table was Dr. Raya Shapiro, a psychiatrist and, we soon discovered, a Holocaust survivor. Raya, who recognized my Polish accent and figured that I might also be a survivor, struck up a conversation with us. We took an immediate liking to each other and, in the course of the evening, I recounted some of my wartime experiences. As it happened, Raya was then involved in a Yale University–sponsored project to interview Holocaust survivors on videotape. Remarking that she had never heard a story quite like mine — "and I have interviewed hundreds of survivors," she said — she asked whether I might be willing to go before the camera, with her asking the questions. I replied that I was willing and eager, and shortly thereafter Raya interviewed me in a building on the Northwestern University campus in Evanston, Illinois. The session lasted for more than two hours, and it had a powerful effect on both of us, leaving us in tears when we had finished.

After that interview I was on fire to write my memoirs. I wanted my children to know what had happened to me in the war and what I had done to survive; I wanted them to know that I was not just a survivor, not just a victim, but a fighter as well. I also wanted them to tell them about their family in Poland: they needed to learn what had happened to it and to be made aware of what a good family it was before so many of its members were killed. But writing in English was always, for me, a flawed enterprise; though I was literate and well educated, I wrote as I spoke, with a Polish accent. So I called my daughter Ora, a copywriter with an advertising agency in Los Angeles, and asked for her help. Ora was reluctant to take on the assignment — with good reason, as it turned out — but I was insistent, and she agreed to give it a try. Not long after that I was on a Los Angeles–bound jet, filling page after page of a legal tablet with musings that I would expand upon in forthcoming conversations with my daughter. And expand upon them I did, spending most of the next two weeks in a hotel room with Ora, talking to her (and into her tape recorder) about my life and experiences in Poland before and during the war. It was not a happy experience for either of us. Torrents of emotion were released in that room, more than either Ora or I could handle. We wept often and argued constantly, sometimes yelling at each other, always without really knowing why. Afterward, it occurred to me that the source of our friction was our love for each other: we were too close, we had too much history between us to deal objectively, as partners, with such an emotionally charged issue. The past, it turned out, not only hurt me, it hurt Ora as well.

Nevertheless, after I returned to our home in Skokie, Illinois, Ora began writing my story based on the tapes we made. She eventually produced a one-hundred-page manuscript, not long enough for publication, but an excellent first draft. She could go no further with it, however, for she was too busy caring for her son, Jeremy, and working as a freelance copywriter to research and write a manuscript of publishable length. Morris and I searched about for a writer, and, after consulting with several people in the publishing business, we were given Steven Weingartner's name.

Steve proved to be just the right person to expand Ora's manuscript into a full-fledged book. We spent more than two years at this task, Steve and I. Once or twice a week, Steve would drop by my house in Skokie, and we would sit at my dining room table for several hours with his tape recorder running while he questioned me about my family, my childhood, my war experiences, my experiences in the postwar period, my religious beliefs, my likes and dislikes, my political opinions, my views on child-rearing, the meaning of life—everything. Never, not even during the war, when I was jailed and brought before SS tribunals, had I been so thoroughly interrogated! Of course, it goes without saying that my sessions with Steve were more enjoyable than the others by a margin too wide to contemplate, much less measure. Funny thing about our conversations, though: at first, my past, previously so anxious to be heard, suddenly became shy about revealing itself. I had memory lapses; in many instances I was unable to recall the details of a key event or important episode. But Steve kept after me, probing at the gaps, asking the same questions over and over in different ways, thus coaxing the more reluctant parts of my memory out of a dark corner into the light of day. In this fashion we filled some thirty audiotapes. Steve transcribed the tapes, edited the transcriptions, researched the historical background—and then, working together, we began writing.

This book is the result of our efforts. It owes its existence to several people, and I would like to take this opportunity to acknowledge their contributions. First and foremost, I wish to thank my husband, Morris, whose encouragement and unwavering support provided both the impetus and the inspiration to write my memoirs.

I want to thank my daughter Ora, who had the courage and determination to sit down with me and explore a subject that was very painful for both of us. The manuscript she produced is truly the bedrock and the foundation on which this book was built.

I want to thank Steve Weingartner for being who he is and for helping to bring order to the chaos of my memories of the years 1939–45. I know that for Steve it was a work of love, with very little remuneration, and that is why I appreciate him and his work more than words can express.

I want to thank Dr. Raya Shapiro for really getting me started on this project and for being a good friend.

I want to thank my son Eli and my daughter Abbey for their encouragement, love, and, in Abbey's case, legal advice. With regard to the latter, I also want to thank Farley Weiss, attorney and grandson of my mother's cousin, Esther Weiss, who helped me with other legal aspects of the publishing business.

Last, but certainly not least, I want to thank Esther Weiss, who provided a wealth of information about our family and life in Russia before I was born. Esther passed away at age ninety-two, before this book was published, but her spirit lives on in this book, and she is remembered with love and affection by all who knew her.

Lala Fishman
July 1996

Lala's Story

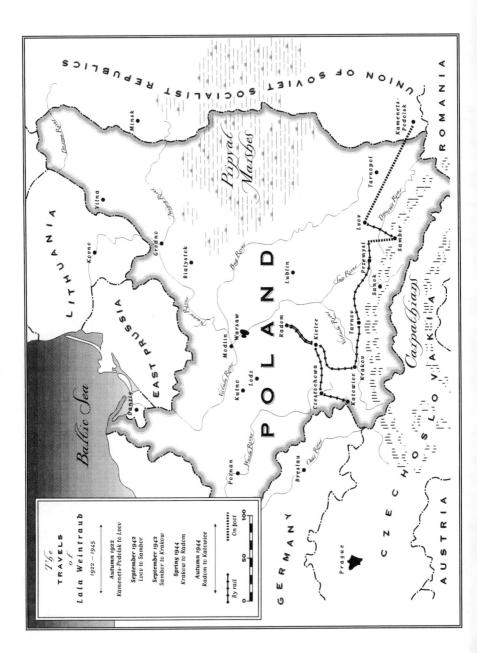

Katowice, 1945

Liberation from Nazi rule came stealthily to Katowice. It arrived on a cold winter night, while everyone was asleep, without any fanfare or fighting. One day the Germans were there; the next day they were gone. It happened that fast. I never saw them go. Nobody did. The hated enemy had fled under cover of darkness, sneaking away like back-alley thieves, leaving with what amounted to a whimper rather than the bang of combat.

The date was January 28, 1945. It was a Sunday, but not a day of rest, for there was no such thing in occupied Poland. I woke, as usual, at dawn and immediately got dressed for work, unaware that the Germans had departed. At the time I lived by myself in a single rented room of a two-flat apartment building located in the center of Katowice. An industrial city in Poland's Upper Silesia district, Katowice had been my home for the past ten months. Shortly after coming to the city, I had found employment as a secretary in the main office of a coal-mining company, and this was the job I was preparing myself for on that particular morning, the morning of our liberation.

Getting dressed didn't take long. My entire wardrobe consisted of one threadbare skirt, a blouse, and a sweater. After pulling on this meager ensemble, I fastened a slender chain around my neck, taking care to prominently display the attached silver crucifix on the outside of my sweater. Even though I was a Jew, I didn't think twice about wearing the Christian symbol. I wanted people to think I was a Christian, and this was one way to do it.

Another way was to change one's identity. This I had also done. My real name was Lala Weintraub, but in Katowice I was known as Urszula Krzyzanowska. That was the name on my *Kennkarte,* my identity card, a forgery I had obtained through connections with the Catholic Church. The Nazis had decreed that this all-important document was to be carried on your person at all times, and woe betide the individual who failed to produce it on demand. Arrest, imprisonment, torture, execution: this was the customary sequence of penalties inflicted on those caught without their identity card. The *Kennkarte* established who you were to inquiring supervisors, landlords, Polish policemen, SS troopers, and Gestapo agents; which is to say, it told them you weren't a Jew. Krzyzanowska, which translates as "cross," told them just that. It was a good Christian name, typically Polish, typically Catholic.

I tried my best to be everything it implied. This endeavor had required me to become something of an actress, playing the role of a character called Urszula Krzyzanowska. Judging by the results, I had proved an adept thespian. I think perhaps no actor or actress ever gave so convincing a performance—or played to so unforgiving an audience. But then, no actor or actress ever had my motivation to do so.

Fortunately, with my blond hair, blue eyes, and straight nose, I looked the part of a Gentile girl. (Actually, my eyes are bluish green; on some identification cards from the war they were listed as being blue, on others as green. Their color could change, depending, it seemed, on my mood, my surroundings, the color of my clothing. The Germans saw them as blue—perhaps because that is what they wanted to see. The point is—and it was, in that period, a very important point—my eyes weren't brown or black, as a Jew's eyes were "supposed" to be.) I could pass for a Pole; I could even pass for a German. The Germans might say that I had classic "Aryan" features. Some said that I was pretty. Maybe I was. So what? It was all a joke. Although, to be sure, there was nothing funny about it. I was no more an Aryan than any Jew with classic Mediterranean features. But the Germans and the Poles believed otherwise, and that was all that mattered. With luck, they would continue in their belief until the Nazis had been vanquished and it was not quite so dangerous to live openly as a Jew. With luck. This was the real key to staying alive. Without luck, my falsified documents, Aryan features, and acting ability would be of no avail. So far I had been very lucky. Then, on the morning of January 28, while I was getting dressed, someone began pounding on my door, and I thought my luck had finally run out.

The sound of that pounding ran through me like an electric shock, painful and paralyzing. Terror gripped my heart and for a few seconds I couldn't breathe. In wartime Poland such unexpected knocking, especially when it came at an odd hour, usually meant disaster, signaling a visit by the Nazis. I thought the jig was up, that the enemy had finally come to arrest me. Somehow the Germans had found me out; somehow they had discovered that I was not the Christian girl I pretended to be, but rather a Jew to be hunted down and murdered.

Yet even with these dreadful thoughts running through my mind, I moved to let them in. What else could I do? If I didn't let them in, they would batter the door down. Either way, they would get me. Either way, I was doomed. And so, certain that the worst was upon me, and nearly overcome by the horror of what was about to happen, I grasped the doorknob, turned it, and opened the door—only to discover that it was not the Germans, but rather my landlady, standing in the hallway.

A sense of relief washed over me. I could breathe again; my heart was beating again (although it was pounding harder and faster than the recent knocking on my door). I imagine I must have looked a fright, pale as a ghost, wide-eyed and stricken. If I did, however, my landlady didn't notice. She was too obviously excited to pay any attention to how I looked or felt. A middle-aged Pole with a normally subdued temperament, this woman was now grinning broadly and quivering with emotion.

"Urszula, the Germans are gone!" she blurted out. "They've left Katowice!"

At first I didn't know what to say; I couldn't say anything.

Stunned by this wonderful news, I merely stared at the landlady, while she grinned at me, waiting for my response. "I don't believe it," I finally told her, shaking her head. "I just don't believe it. I can't. It's too good to be true."

"But it *is* true, Urszula," the landlady insisted. "Believe me, I know it is!"

She didn't say how she knew. The source of her information might have been a BBC radio broadcast or a transmission by the Polish underground, which operated numerous clandestine radio stations. Then again, she might have gotten the news by word of mouth, which in those days was the primary means of mass communication in Poland. In either case, the news was plausible. And yet, I remained skeptical.

I glanced out my window. There were no Germans in the snow-covered street below. In fact, I hadn't seen any Germans in my neighborhood for over a week. But this told me nothing. The absence of Germans could be explained by their having taken up defensive positions on the city's outskirts. Thus, they would still be in control of the city, which would explain why the Russians, who were also, ominously, conspicuous by their absence, had so far failed to put in an appearance.

Nor did I think I would see the Russians anytime soon. The Germans were not the type to give up anything without a fight. The thunder of artillery on the eastern approaches of Katowice, audible for the past week or so, supported this view. The cannonading had drawn steadily nearer every day, indicating that the Germans, while losing ground, were bitterly contesting every step of the Soviet advance. Given the evidence of the guns, I was pretty sure the Germans would make the Red Army pay a bloody price for Katowice.

In any case, there was no way to authenticate the landlady's claim. I rejected it simply because the Germans had always been so strong, their tyranny so complete and ruthlessly dominating, that it was difficult to credit any report that had them beaten and on the run. And even if the landlady was right, even if the Germans really had quit the city, there was no guarantee that they might not soon return. This was a chilling prospect. Better to play it safe, I decided, and stick to my routine. So I went to work as if the Germans still ruled Katowice and were still the masters of my destiny.

My company's office was located a few blocks from my apartment, an easy walk when conditions were favorable. But conditions were not favorable that day. According to meteorological records, January 28 was the second day of a howling blizzard that dumped more than two feet of snow on Poland in a forty-eight-hour period. I have no memory of the storm, however. I can only reconstruct how it must have been for me, trudging along at the height of the blizzard, in bitter cold, lashed by wind and snow, pushing through deep snowdrifts on unshoveled sidewalks. I'm not sure why the storm made no lasting impression on me. I can only assume that I was preoccupied by more important matters. Namely, how to stay alive.

When I got to the office, I found everything there was business as usual. The entire staff (all of them Poles, including the managers) had shown up for work. I am sure that my coworkers had heard the news about the German withdrawal, but we did not discuss it among ourselves or even mention it to each other.

As usual, no Germans were on the premises. The Germans rarely visited the office and didn't interfere with the company's day-to-day operations so long as the government's coal production quotas were fulfilled. But the atmosphere was nonetheless heavy with their presence. This is no figure of speech. The heaviness in the air seemed quite real, like a huge weight on your shoulders. You could never forget about that weight because it was always bearing down on you with the full force of its mass. The substance of that weight, the element that gave it heft, was fear. I was always afraid of the Germans, of what they might do next. I was afraid from the moment I woke up to the moment I went to sleep; and I was afraid in my sleep, in the frightful nightmares where my fears were enacted.

This fear, I would venture to say, was an affliction shared by many, if not most, Poles. It had ravaged the population like a medieval pandemic, laying waste the spirit of its victims by undermining their courage and resolve. The net effect was the moral sickening and consequent transformation of a host of mostly decent people into weary, grim, and furtive creatures who suspected everyone around them of being spies and collaborators. For my part, I always wondered which of my coworkers was in the pay of the Gestapo, which would betray me to the authorities for any negative comment, no matter how trifling, I might make about the Germans.

My coworkers no doubt harbored the same fears and suspicions. As a Jew, however, I was doubly distrustful. The Germans offered rewards, usually a small sum of money, for information leading to the arrest of Jews. Sadly, the monetary incentive was not always necessary. Many Poles informed on Jews with no thought of financial gain, purely to vent their anti-Semitic hatred. I liked my coworkers. They were nice people. Probably none were collaborators; and, just as probably, none would turn in a fellow Pole for speaking ill of the Germans. But I was not a fellow Pole; I was a Jew. My coworkers did not know this, of course—but if they did, if they somehow discovered that I was Jewish, I was certain that some of them would not hesitate to denounce me.

Not all Poles were anti-Semitic. Many Poles were capable of joining Jews in common cause against the enemy. But at what price! The cost of resistance had been demonstrated the previous summer in Warsaw, where the Germans had ruthlessly crushed an uprising by the Polish underground, destroying the city and killing thousands in the process. It was no secret. The Germans had widely advertised their treatment of Warsaw for the purpose of discouraging revolt in other Polish cities.

In Katowice this purpose had been achieved. The population there was suitably cowed. My coworkers and I were typical in this regard. We spoke not at all about the war or any other subject that might get us in trouble if the wrong people overheard the conversation. We worked quietly and conscientiously, and when the day was over, we went straight home.

By then, however, it was apparent that the Germans were

truly gone. This was demonstrated in unequivocal fashion when, later that afternoon, Soviet troops marched into Katowice.

Many years later, I learned that the Russians had allowed the Germans to escape Katowice in order to spare that valuable industrial city the devastation of battle. This was why no fighting had occurred in the city, and why the Germans had disappeared so suddenly and, as it seemed to us, so mysteriously. Presented by their foe with an opportunity to save themselves, the Germans had bolted.

But although Katowice was physically untouched, its citizens had suffered devastation of a different sort. Brutalized by the long, cruel years of German occupation, they could scarcely find it in themselves to feel the joy the occasion warranted. In Western European cities, the arrival of Allied troops was greeted with hysterical acclaim, with frenzied cheering and wild capering as the triumphant armies paraded through the streets. There was none of that in Katowice. The Poles were in shock. They didn't know what to do; they didn't know how to be happy anymore.

And they were leery of the Russians. All were aware that Russian armies had come to Poland often in the past, not to liberate but to vanquish and subjugate. The Soviet government—which is to say, Joseph Stalin—had made all the proper noises about respecting Polish sovereignty, but promises made along those lines had a hollow ring. Few Poles could forget how, in mid-September 1939, while German armies were overrunning the western half of their country, the Soviets had invaded from the east, ostensibly to protect the Belorussian and Ukrainian minorities then residing in Poland—an explanation that elicited cynical laughter from the Poles, who recognized naked aggression when they saw it. Thus had the Soviets helped remove Poland from the map of Europe even as they acquired the buffer zone they had sought to establish between themselves and the expanding Third Reich. Now, in 1945, many Poles could be forgiven for thinking that the Russians were up to their old tricks, seizing Polish territory with every intention of holding on to it. The swastika had fallen, and the red star was ascendant. What Pole could say with any surety that they had not simply exchanged one emblem—and one conqueror—for another? The Soviets certainly looked like conquerors. The soldiers that entered Katowice in the next few days were a hard-bitten lot, stern-faced and steely-eyed, unimaginably filthy, and bristling with weapons. They wore fur caps with earflaps, quilted coats, thickly padded trousers tucked into high felt boots, and web gear festooned with grenades and ammunition pouches. Appearing stout and ungainly in their bulky winter clothing, with rifles and submachine guns slung over their shoulders, they tramped through the streets in seemingly endless columns, on either side of an interminable procession of tanks, armored cars, half-tracks, trucks, and tractor-towed artillery.

I especially remember the tanks, huge machines that clanked about like armor-plated monsters from the dinosaur age, their unmuffled engines roaring, exhaust pipes belching plumes of blue-black diesel smoke, steel treads grinding the pavement into a gravelly rubble. The earth trembled underfoot as they trundled by, and the throaty din of their engines was a palpable force that rattled the teeth and churned one's innards. When I saw those tanks, I heard and felt their strength and power. It was as if a light went off inside my head, and I realized that the Germans would return to Katowice no more.

The passage through the city of this mighty army lasted several days. It was an awesome spectacle, and the sight of it eventually jogged the Poles out of their benumbed state. Slowly the shock of events wore off, and people began to accept and appreciate their liberated circumstances. In the plazas and parks, in their apartments and houses and rented rooms, the citizens of Katowice finally allowed themselves a measure of rejoicing. Now and then, a few of the more exuberant Poles cheered and applauded their liberators, as people did in Western Europe. But, in general, their gaiety was muted, restrained, tinged with sorrow. They had gone through so much—five years of the Nazis, five years of war. Celebration did not come easy to them.

It certainly didn't come easy to me. For one thing, I couldn't shake the feeling that I was still under threat, that I still had to keep my guard up. The Soviet soldiers did not allay my fears; on the contrary, those fierce-visaged men scared me. Was a young woman safe around them? I didn't know, and I didn't care to find out.

I needn't have worried about the Soviets. I was never molested by any Soviet soldier. On the whole, the Soviets behaved correctly toward the Poles. In Germany, they would rape, pillage, and murder with vengeful abandon; but here, in Poland, such behavior was uncommon and usually punished when it occurred. But this was of little comfort to me. I simply could not overcome my misgivings toward anyone who wore a uniform and carried a gun. After all, it was men such as these, Russians as well as Germans, who were responsible for the extermination of my family.

So far as I knew, my father and mother, grandmother, sister, and all my aunts and uncles and cousins, nieces and nephews, had been murdered by the Nazis. And my brother, conscripted into the Red Army in 1940, was missing, presumably killed in action, another victim, it seemed, of men with guns. So, I thought, the people I had loved most in the world and who had most loved me were all dead.

Knowing that my family was dead made me feel as desolate as the ruins of a bombed-out building. But I did not experience the full extent of my desolation until a few days after the liberation, upon the occasion of dinner with a girlfriend and her family. The girl was the same age I was and, like me, she had lost her birth mother and father in the war. She had since been adopted by a young married couple with children of their own. Her foster parents were lovely people who were quite fond of me, as I was of them. They became a sort of surrogate family for me and, as a frequent visitor to their home, I knew that I could always count on them for a meal, companionship, and the nearest thing to parental love that I could hope to get at that stage in my life.

Dinner on that particular night was a happy event, full of conviviality and glad talk about the collapse of the Nazi regime in Poland. Afterward, as I walked home, the implications of Germany's impending defeat came to me in a flash, causing me to think: That's it, everything is all right, you don't have to run anymore, you don't have to be afraid. You're free. It was a glorious moment, almost blissful. Curiously, the weather, which had warmed up in the wake of the recent blizzard, was perfectly suited to my mood. The ice and snow were melting beneath my feet, inspiring pleasant visions of an early spring in a world at peace.

But the moment was fleeting, dispelled as soon as I returned to the solitude of my rented room. Once inside I sat on my bed and stared at the wall, darkly pondering my situation. At dinner I had felt as though I had belonged to my friend's family, but now I understood that I had been deluding myself, that I had no family. Moreover, with the war coming swiftly to an end, I had no purpose or direction either. During the war my only objective had been to survive. Well, I thought, I survived—so now what? What comes next? What should I do, where should I go? What in the name of God will become of me?

I had no answers to these questions, not even a clue. I felt all emptied out, fragmented, and utterly adrift. I was totally alone in the world, totally lost; I had no place to go and I hadn't the faintest idea where I would end up.

In the days following the liberation of Katowice, I would swing, pendulumlike, from euphoria to bottomless despair, finally stabilizing myself at a point midway between the two extremes. I accomplished this by clamping down on all thought and feeling with a ruthlessness the Nazis would have admired. My goal was to become emotionally anesthetized, to stop thinking and feeling altogether.

Of course, this was impossible. Though I devoted much strenuous effort to blanking out my mind, I brooded incessantly, and my prevailing mood was bleak and pensive. The problem of survival, once so acute, now more or less solved, had exacted an enormous toll on my psyche. The emotional bill had come due, and it seemed that I would pay it in the currency of depression.

My depression was manageable, however, and did not prevent me from functioning as before. I got up every morning, I went to work, and I did my job. In the evening I visited friends, after which I wandered aimlessly about the city, sometimes covering several miles before going home. While walking through residential neighborhoods in the early evening, I would look at the brightly lit windows of houses and apartments and imagine that each of these dwellings was home to a happy family. One family lives here, and here, and here, I would say to myself, pointing at each window in turn. And, if I could see inside, I would stop for a few minutes and watch from the sidewalk as parents and children talked, ate, laughed, and played with each other.

As I walked I had the sense of waking from a bad dream to a reality that was, if not worse than the dream itself, still a sad and tragic place. I had dreamed of war, and it was over; I had dreamed of family, and it was gone. Like Job's messenger, I alone had escaped. But, in escaping, I had ceased to be the same person I had been in 1939, when the Germans had invaded. I had changed, and the change had been grievous. That is why, upon returning to my room from my nocturnal ramblings, I would cry for hours on end, weeping for the family I no longer had, but also shedding tears for the girl I no longer was. My sorrow had been frozen inside for so many years and now, having finally melted, it was released in a flood of tears that would not stop.

One day while walking home from work, I saw a convoy of trucks from the Auschwitz concentration camp, which was located a few miles to the southwest of Katowice. Riding on the open back platform of each vehicle were a dozen or so former camp inmates, Jews whom the International Red Cross, in cooperation with the Red Army, were transporting to relief centers for medical care. Most of the passengers were men, the few women among them indicating by their scant numbers that the Germans had made the killing of Jewish women (and children) a top priority. Men and women alike were hideously emaciated and wan as cadavers, with their hair cropped close to the scalp and black-and-white striped uniforms hanging in soiled tatters from their starved bodies. The weakest ones sat on benches while the others stood, grasping the side panels of the truck or clinging to each other to steady themselves. All silently regarded the city around them, staring at everything and nothing with hollow eyes and insensate expressions.

Despite their wretched condition, the Jews aroused little sympathy in the Poles, who watched from the sidewalk as the trucks drove by.

"Look at those Yids," a woman near me snarled, her voice brimming with hatred. "Why do they get to ride in trucks when we have to walk?"

"Why didn't they get killed, too?" a man said, sounding disappointed.

"Too bad the Germans didn't kill them all," another man seconded.

I was enraged but not surprised by these remarks. It was no secret that some Poles were rabid anti-Semites who had gleefully welcomed the killing of Jews. A few had even participated in the butchery. One would have thought that these Poles, who had also suffered atrociously during the war, might feel solidarity with the Jews. But their malice could not be gainsaid. It was as virulent as a metastasizing cancer, spreading to the sidewalks of Katowice, where several Poles within earshot were upset that Hitler hadn't finished the job of obliterating European Jewry.

For my part, I suddenly wished that the Germans had obliterated more of the good citizens of Katowice. In that moment I was filled with a ferocious loathing for the Poles, all Poles, and a terrible frustration that they could still be a torment to the Jews. I cursed them under my breath, calling them stupid and miserable and corrupt, and I thought I was fully capable of shooting one or two of them myself if I could only get my hands on a gun.

The anti-Semitic Poles needn't have been too disappointed.

In January 1945, Poland's Jewish population was all but extinct. You didn't have to read a census report to know this. The evidence was everywhere to be seen; or, more precisely, it wasn't to be seen anywhere. The absence of Jews was readily apparent. Where once there had been many, now there were none. They had vanished from the streets and villages where they had lived for centuries. They had been carried off like puffs of smoke in the wind—as it turned out, a horrifyingly accurate description of their ultimate fate, actualized in the ovens and chimneys of the death camps.

Thus, I was only too aware that, in the company of the Auschwitz survivors I saw in Katowice, I had become a member of a very select group: I was a Polish Jew who had survived the war. But many years would pass before I learned just how select that group was. As the world now knows, the Nazis killed some six million Jews, a figure which then amounted to roughly 40 percent of the world's Jewish population. Of that number, three million came from Poland. In other words, Poland's resident Jewish population, which approached 3.5 million before the war, contributed half the total number of Jews—and 20 percent of world Jewry—to be murdered in what has come to be known as the Holocaust.

Simple arithmetic based on these numbers indicates that about five hundred thousand Jews should have been in Poland at war's end. But demographic records from that period reveal that this was not the case. Of those who survived, most had fled to other countries (particularly the Soviet Union) at the onset of war in 1939, or when the Germans invaded the Soviet Union in June 1941. Jews like myself who remained in Poland throughout the war were few and far between. By the spring of 1945, it is probable that I was one of only forty or fifty thousand still drawing breath on Polish soil.

Why did I survive? This is another question for which I have no simple answer. Much of the difficulty in answering it is due to my imperfect recollections of the war. The period spanned by the war years encompasses a jumble of experiences that I remember with a mixture of clarity and confusion.

Some events stand out in my memory while others hang back and are only dimly perceived. And even when I can recall an important incident, I may not be able to remember precisely when or where it happened.

My muddled memory is not only a function of age. It is not only attributable to the distancing effects of time. My experiences were incoherent to me even while they were happening. The problem here is not a flawed memory, but rather a flawed history. The war produced too much history, more history than any society, let alone any one person, could possibly retain. In consequence, remembrance is confounded with a superabundance of information and images, throwing into chaos the notions of time that provide the solid foundation upon which memories are built. For that reason, a small part of me believes that the war was too vast and terrible to be contained within the normal boundaries of time, occurring rather in a place outside of time, where linear chronology does not, indeed cannot, apply, and where cause and effect are hopelessly tangled. So, if I remember the war years imprecisely, and I do, it is not because I am confused, but rather because time itself, the time of war, was—and is—confused.

This I do remember, however: when the war began I was a sixteen-year-old girl named Clara Weintraub, nicknamed Lala, the eldest daughter of Ilya and Olga Weintraub. (My nickname, acquired as an infant, approximated the way my older brother Fima—himself only a toddler—mispronounced my first name.) Born into a moderately well-to-do family in what was then the Soviet Ukraine, I was raised in Lvov, to which my family had fled within days of my birth, and shortly after the Bolshevik takeover of that region.

In Poland as in Russia, my parents chose to assimilate, as much as it was possible for Jews to do, into mainstream society. They dwelled outside Lvov's old Jewish quarter in a religiously and ethnically mixed neighborhood of middle- and lower-middle-class professionals and had little contact with, and no affinity whatsoever for, the Orthodox Jewish community of that city.

Orthodox Judaism held no appeal for my parents. Like

most young assimilated Jews, my mother and father were altogether modern, bourgeois, and urban-cosmopolitan in their outlook. My father was a professional musician, the graduate of the prestigious Saint Petersburg Conservatory and a trained symphonic conductor who could play every instrument in the orchestra. He preferred the saxophone, however, and to earn a living he played that instrument as the head of jazz ensembles, swing bands, and orchestras that were invariably the featured entertainment in the chicest nightclubs of Lvov. My mother shared his taste in music and would often get dressed up in her most fashionable evening gown and go to the nightclubs to see him perform.

In Poland during the 1930s, jazz was regarded as racy and avant-garde, characteristics that placed all jazz musicians and their attendant aficionados firmly in the modernist camp. My father and mother embraced the modernist ethos, the very opposite of religious orthodoxy. Except for major religious holidays, which they observed less out of devotional principle and more as an excuse for a family get-together, they were largely uninvolved with their faith. They were secular Jews; that is, Jews, for the most part, in name and heritage only. They didn't even look Jewish; my father, like me, had blond hair. But, as they were soon to discover, name and heritage were enough to warrant a death sentence when the Germans came to Poland.

They never suspected that this would be the case. To be sure, they knew that Adolf Hitler and his Nazi followers hated the Jews; and they were aware as only Jews, even secular Jews, could be aware of such things that anti-Semitism was a contagion that had spread the length and breadth of Europe. But genocide? The possibility never entered their thoughts. Notwithstanding a long history of pogroms and persecutions, the idea of a systematized program for murdering the Jewish people in their entirety was simply unthinkable.

My family was cursed to live in a time and place when it was a capital crime to be a Jew. Most of my family members paid the ultimate penalty for that crime. I didn't. Maybe, as I have said, I was lucky. But had I been truly lucky, I would have never become embroiled in the Holocaust to begin with. So the issue of luck resolves itself in an ambiguity, with the good and the bad canceling each other out. I believe I outlasted the Nazi reign of terror because I loved life. This love gave me strength of mind and mettle, it made me obstinate and crafty, and it toughened my character and enabled me to use my Aryan looks, my brains, and my wiles to the utmost in furthering the cause of my survival. I further believe that such love, and what that love did for me, was a gift from God, but a gift that I received indirectly, through the intermediary offices of my beloved family—parents, siblings, grandparents, and ancestors going back to time immemorial. Because I credit my family for inculcating the moral and emotional wherewithal to resist the Nazi evil, it is to my family that I must now turn to show how it came to pass that a young Jewish girl, known to everyone but myself as Urszula Krzyzanowska, should be wandering the streets of Katowice at the end of World War II, alone and lonely, improbably but indisputably alive.

❖

Ukrainian Origins

Although I was raised in Poland and knew no other country until after the war, I actually began life as a citizen of the Soviet Ukraine. I was born on November 17, 1922, in Kamenets-Podolski, the principal city of Ukraine's Podolia region. Kamenets-Podolski is located in the southeast corner of what is now an independent nation, but which was then a recent and extremely restive addition to the newly incorporated Soviet Union. My father, Ilya Weintraub, and my mother, the former Olga Rosenwald, belonged to families that had lived in the Ukraine for hundreds of years but, in the manner of many educated Ukrainian Jews, spoke Russian as a first language and thought of themselves as Russian in culture and nationality.

I know little about the Rosenwalds and the Weintraubs. Much of the history of the two families is lost and can never be recovered—another legacy of the Holocaust. This is not a unique problem. In murdering the Jews, the Nazis murdered Jewish history as well: six million individual histories, along with the millions of family histories each executed Jew carried in his or her memory.

As for written records, such as birth and death certificates, marriage announcements, diaries, deeds, business contracts, official documents, even the inscriptions on cemetery headstones (as well as the headstones themselves)—they were destroyed whenever and wherever the Nazis came across them. That is why American Jews like myself who travel to the ancestral homelands of Eastern Europe in search of our roots often find little or no trace of our people. The areas of Jewish settlement, where communities rich in culture and venerable in tradition once throve, are no more; and except for the disintegrated bones of Holocaust victims buried in the soil of the Nazi killing grounds, the earth is barren of any Jewish presence.

To reconstruct their family histories, most American Jews must rely heavily on family legends and folk tales, passed down orally from one generation to the next. My primary link with the past was Esther Weiss, who was born in Kamenets-Podolski in 1900 to an older sister of my maternal grandfather, Moses Rosenwald. Two years before her death in 1994, I sat down with her at the home of her son and daughter-in-law, Maxi and Irene Weiss, in Phoenix, Arizona, and talked to her about our family. In our conversation, which I tape-recorded, she often spoke fondly of her Uncle Moses, or "Moshe," as she called him, using his Yiddish name. "My Uncle Moshe," she assured me, "was a brilliant man, a nice man, a good, kind man, and I loved him very much."

She knew him well, even as a child, because the two had grown up under the same roof. When Moses was only five years old, his mother died, and his father, being unable to care for Moses and his siblings (eight-year-old Sylvia; Rifka, six years old; Shimon, four), handed them over to Esther's mother, who raised them as her own. Of her parents' decision to adopt that brood, Esther said, "My mother and father weren't rich. My father made a living, but not so much. But they took them in without a second thought. And we had a lovely family. We were very happy, my Uncle Moshe and me."

In the Russian census of 1893, when Moses was in his early twenties, Kamenets-Podolski had a population of about forty thousand, of whom 50 percent were Jews. The most affluent part of Kamenets-Podolski, the so-called old city, was situated on an island in the Smotrich River and was connected to the suburbs on either bank by numerous bridges. For a description of the old city and other information about Kamenets-Podolski, I am indebted to an excellent book, *Kamenetz-*

Podolski: A Memorial to a Jewish Community Annihilated by the Nazis. According to Leon S. Blatman, editor of the book, the old city

had only stone houses of 2, 3, and 4 stories with stores and offices on the ground floor facing the streets. In the center of the old city were a few taller buildings of which the police station was the highest. Above the police station was a tower, serving as a lookout station for the fire department. The city clock, seen from quite a distance, was also housed in this tower. On both sides of these municipal buildings were small parks with benches for people to rest. These parks also served as the meeting place for tradesmen looking for jobs. Besides these little parks, the city had large parks, near the bridges; one known as the "New Boulevard" and the other as the "Old Boulevard." There was a third park, stretching from the new bridge to the [suburb of] Ruski-Folvarek and known as the "Path" (Dorojka). The suburbs were full of gardens and with the parks gave the city a picturesque, green appearance.*

The verdant aspect of Kamenets-Podolski is confirmed by Aunt Esther. "Ah, it was beautiful!" she exclaimed when I asked her what the city looked like. "It had tremendous trees and lovely gardens. Very nice. The Jewish people lived very nice, and there were a lot of people and a lot of business."

Among the major businesses in town, Blatman lists a beer brewery, several cigarette and tobacco factories, two plants for making seltzer water, two cotton factories, a number of flour mills, and an iron foundry. Some of these businesses were owned and operated by Jews. "The majority of Jews," observes Blatman, "were in business or in trades, the majority of Gentiles were their customers" (22). By and large, the Gentiles of Kamenets-Podolski and the surrounding region were govern-

---

Kamenetz-Podolski: A Memorial to a Jewish Community Annihilated by the Nazis, ed. Leon S. Blatman (New York: Sponsors of the Kamenets-Podolski Memorial Book, 1966), 17–18; hereafter cited by page number in the text.

ment employees, policemen and firemen, soldiers, teachers, priests, landowners, and peasants.

Blatman notes that Kamenets-Podolski, as the administrative center for Podolia, was home to the district governor, district and city courts, treasury and internal revenue departments, and the administrative offices of the city police and the Okhrana, the czarist secret police. The city also had an armory with barracks for a Cossack regiment and four infantry battalions.

Kamenets-Podolski also had its share of schools, hospitals, theaters, shops, retail stores, restaurants, and banks. Though Jews could not hold stock or management positions in the banks, they were allowed to assist the board of directors in an advisory capacity. The banks never granted loans to Jews, who responded to this ban by setting up their own cooperative banks and credit unions. The money these institutions lent went primarily to Jewish-owned businesses. They did not disburse cash to poor Jews, who turned to family and friends when money was needed to make ends meet. People like Esther's father, the well-to-do owner of four flour mills in the area—and a devoutly religious man who acknowledged and acted upon his moral obligation to help the poor—constituted a sort of ad hoc welfare system in the Russian-Jewish community.

"Anytime anyone needed something," Esther said of her father, "they came to him, and he helped. He never refused; he never said no."

He was frequently generous to a fault. Esther remembered how, on one such occasion, his sister came to their house to ask for money. The sister, a destitute widow and the mother of seven children, was weeping hysterically when she burst in through the kitchen door. She found Esther's mother preparing the midday meal; Esther's father, who had just returned from shul, was seated at the kitchen table reading the Bible. Seeing how distraught his sister was, Esther's father put down his Bible and invited her to sit next to him.

"My father," reported Esther, "helped her pick up her eyes. 'Oy vey,' he says, 'so what happened?'"

"I haven't got a piece of bread to feed my children!" the woman cried.

"Then," said Esther, "my papa—I remember like today, I was maybe four years old—he opened the drawer, and all the money he had, he gave to his sister."

Esther was dismayed. "As young as I was, I thought, he should give only a little bit; he should give half!"

"So," Esther continued, "I ran to my mother, who was cooking, and she heard what's going on between her husband and his sister. And she was very smart, my mother. She looked at me and said, 'Child, my dear child, she is your relative, and your father is the only one to help her. Nobody, no strangers can help her.'"

"That's the way my mother was," said Esther. "And Papa gave his sister money all the time. That was going on for years, not for one day!"

Much later, Esther's father offered the woman one hundred rubles to give to her eldest son. The boy's name was Morris, and he was in his late teens or early twenties—old enough to make his way in the world.

"It's time you should send the boy to America," Esther's father told his sister. "I heard that in America you can earn a mountain of money!"

Esther's aunt balked at the suggestion. Emigration was such a drastic step! "You really think I should?" she asked.

"Yes," replied Esther's father. "I'll give you the money; you send him."

Convinced, the aunt accepted the rubles. Shortly thereafter, Morris, his wallet bulging with his uncle's money, was bound for America.

Esther recalls that Morris was illiterate. Having never gone to school (her aunt couldn't afford the tuition), her cousin "couldn't even sign his own name."

But Morris did not let his lack of education hold him back. He was a young man on the make, intelligent if unlettered, and determined to succeed. And succeed he did, in New York City's garment industry. By 1932, when Esther arrived in America, he owned three factories, and conducted business from the lofty height of a seventh-floor office in a building on Fifty-Seventh Street.

"He had a lot of workers," recalled Esther, "And they used to make Persian lamb coats. He became the famous man for making and selling those coats." Upon saying this, Esther paused and smiled. "And," she added, "he became very rich."

Moses Rosenwald shared the entrepreneurial streak possessed by Esther's father and her cousin Morris. As an adult, he established himself as one of the most successful businessmen in Kamenets-Podolski and the Podolia region, eventually owning a tobacco company, a roller-skating rink, and a movie theater. The income generated by these enterprises made him a rich man, providing him with enough money to purchase a fine brick house in the old city. It was in that house that he and his wife Pesha raised their six children: Isadore, Olga, Motia, Yossi, Haika, and Nadia. And it was there, many years later, that Olga, as the wife of Ilya Weintraub, gave birth to my older brother Fima and me.

As Moses's wealth increased so, too, did his standing in the community. He further enhanced his prominence by becoming involved in local governmental affairs, although as a Jew he was forbidden from holding any formal post. (Official positions in the civil administration were reserved exclusively for Gentiles.) Family legend even has it that Alexander Kerensky, leader of the Provisional Government that briefly ruled Russia after the overthrow of Czar Nicholas II in 1917, once addressed a crowd from the second-story balcony of the Rosenwald house.

The visit by Kerensky may actually have occurred. But there is no truth to another family legend that had Moses acquainted with several ministers and advisors of the czar— "people close to the royal family," as Esther vaguely described them. This is an example of what is humorously known as "Jewish history," a euphemism for what is properly termed "pure fantasy." For one thing, the story has absolutely no basis in fact; not even a shred of evidence exists to support it.

For another, no matter what the extent of Moses's wealth, it is inconceivable that my grandfather, a Jew from a hinterland city like Kamenets-Podolski—which wasn't even connected by railroad to the rest of Russia until 1914—would be an intimate of highly placed functionaries in the czar's notoriously anti-Semitic court.

Perhaps this story is an outgrowth of the fame and respect accorded Moses by his Podolian business peers. It is possible to believe that these men, even the Gentiles, were sufficiently impressed by Moses to believe that his influence reached to the seat of national government in distant Saint Petersburg and to the innermost circles of the remote and powerful Russian monarch.

By all accounts, Moses had that kind of effect on people. I remember him as a big man, thick in middle age, yet nonetheless handsome. He was always outgoing, jolly, and irresistibly charming. You might say he was a real character, one who cultivated the image of a distinguished but dashing bon vivant by clothing himself in immaculately tailored suits, which were topped off by a broad-brimmed fedora worn at a rakish slant, "American-style." Yet for all his sartorial flamboyance, he was never overbearing or arrogant; on the contrary, he was a thoroughly likeable fellow, unflaggingly affable and tolerant, a man who approached life with gusto, humor, and style.

As Esther noted, Moses was a kind man—another trait he shared with Esther's father. As with Esther's father, the door to his house was always open to the needy. He regularly provided the penniless and the destitute with food, clothing, and money, all freely given, aiding Gentiles as well as Jews. For Moses, a person's religion was unimportant and irrelevant to the way you treated that person. He once told me that his attitude was, "If someone is poor, if someone is naked, if someone is barefoot, that person should be helped."

It was in the area of military service that Jews exercised a special claim on Moses's charity. Life in the Russian army was harsh for all of its soldiers, but more so for Jews, who were singled out for exceptional abuse by a blatantly anti-Semitic officer corps. Quite understandably, the parents of Jewish boys sought to keep their sons out of the army, and Moses did what he could for them.

In czarist Russia any man, even a Jew, could legally buy off his military obligation. But it took more than money to accomplish this. Political influence was also required. And political influence was something that Moses Rosenwald possessed in spades. Employing a mixture of arm-twisting congeniality and tactful diplomacy, he worked his connections, called in favors, spread his own money liberally around; he schmoozed minor officials, he buttered up low-level functionaries, he flattered the egos of petty bureaucrats—whatever it took to secure an exemption.

He also put the screws on wealthy Jews, compelling them to help their impoverished brethren. Esther recalls how rich people used to come to Moses to "see that their boys shouldn't go to the czar."

Moses would say to them, "If you pay for a poor boy, I'll take care of your boy." These supplicants invariably did as Moses asked.

"They had to pay up," says Esther, "because they didn't want their boys to go to the army and work for the czar. The rich people paid for the poor, and Moses got them both out. He didn't want to see a Yiddishe boy, no matter how poor, have to go in the army."

Moses's reluctance to provide cannon fodder for the czar applied as well to his son, Isadore. But instead of purchasing an exemption, Isadore avoided conscription by emigrating to America shortly before the outbreak of the First World War in August 1914. He settled in Perth Amboy, New Jersey, the first of the Rosenwalds to come to the United States. But not, his father hoped, the last—for Moses intended to move his entire family to these shores. His purpose was shaped by the belief that the good life and prosperity he enjoyed in Kamenets-Podolski would not continue indefinitely. Rather, he sensed a terrible disaster brewing for the Jews of Europe, one that would result in the spilling of more Jewish blood than in all the pogroms preceding it.

If Moses was prescient in this regard, he was not unique. Many Jews had forebodings of the coming Holocaust, even in a city as accommodating to Jewish businessmen as Kamenets-Podolski. They didn't have to look far to find portents of genocide; the history of the Ukraine was fraught with Jewish pogroms. The worst of these massacres prior to World War II were perpetrated during the Chmielnicki uprising of 1648–49, when Ukrainian peasants under the leadership of Bogdan Chmielnicki rebelled against the ruling Polish nobility. At the time, the Poles owned most of the land but did not live on it, instead leasing their sprawling estates to Jews, who ran the day-to-day operations of these holdings. In doing so, the Jews incurred the enmity of the fiercely nationalist-minded Ukrainian peasantry. Thus, while the rebellion started out as a reaction against Polish ownership of the land, it immediately degenerated into an anti-Jewish crusade, with Chmielnicki and his followers massacring over two hundred thousand Jews and razing nearly every Jewish settlement in the Ukraine before Polish forces suppressed the insurrection.

Interestingly, while the Ukrainians rampaged through the countryside, the fortified town of Kamenets-Podolski served as a safe haven for Jews. Up to ten thousand Jewish refugees were admitted within the city's guarded environs, where their residence was normally prohibited.

During the centuries that followed, the pogrom, or the threat of one, was a fact of life for Russian Jews. In Moses's lifetime, there were Ukrainian pogroms in 1881 and 1882, and again in the period from 1903 to 1906, which spanned the abortive October 1905 revolution against the czar. In 1905 alone, the Ukraine was the site of no fewer than 660 pogroms.

Kamenets-Podolski did not escape the violence. According to Blatman, "In Kamenetz-Podolski, where *Katzapi* (Russians from central regions) were seldom seen, quite a number of them suddenly appeared. During the market day the Katzapi started a riot inciting the peasants, who came to sell their products, to loot the stores and kill Jews. Most of the peasants hurriedly left the city for their homes in the nearby villages, the rest were chased by the local police" (28–29).

Esther's father encountered a group of about twelve peasants outside one of his flour mills. Esther says that "my father
knew all those goyim because they worked for him at the mill.
When he saw the goyim, the Gentiles who were his employees, that they are ready to rob and kill, he starts screaming,
'Get out! Get out! Don't come here! Get out!' To the goyim,
he yells this. They got scared and ran away. And that's how
my uncle saved the town!"

The First World War started on August 5, 1914. That very
afternoon, a Hungarian cavalry squadron crossed the Ukrainian frontier from Polish Galicia and advanced to the outskirts
of Kamenets-Podolski, where it halted to prepare for battle.
Rather than fight the Hungarians, the Russian troops gar-
risoned in the armory took to their heels, leaving the city's
mayor to confront the enemy. The Hungarians ordered the
city's immediate surrender, only to be rebuffed by the
doughty mayor. A three-hour artillery bombardment ensued,
after which the now-chastened mayor ran up the white flag.
The Hungarians did not occupy the city, however; instead,
they demanded an indemnity of one hundred thousand
rubles, or the equivalent of that amount in gold, silver, and
jewelry.

It was more than the citizens of Kamenets were able to
come up with. Hastily collecting their valuables and their
money, they gave what they had to the mayor, who fearfully
presented the deficient sum to the Hungarians. He was astonished to be told by the Hungarian commander to give everything back to the people of Kamenets-Podolski—a gift, the
commander announced, to commemorate the birthday of the
emperor Franz Josef of Austria, who had turned eighty-four
that day.

Blatman writes that the indemnity was collected "by a self-
appointed committee of prominent Jews" who went from
door to door for that purpose (33). Maybe Moses was one of
them. I don't know, for he never mentioned the incident to me.
My grandfather did not discuss his experiences in the First
World War. What I know about the war, about what happened
in Kamenets-Podolski, I learned mostly from books.

I learned, for example, that two days after the Hungarian cavalrymen rode into Kamenets-Podolski, they abandoned the city, retreating back across the frontier into Galicia with Russian forces in hot pursuit. Blatman says that when Russian troops marched into the city, they "mercilessly beat every Jew who happened to be in the street" (33). Was my grandfather one of those to be beaten up? Again, I have no way of knowing.

From 1915 through 1916, the fighting in Galicia ebbed and flowed across the Ukraine, occasionally sweeping over Kamenets-Podolski. In 1915, the Russian government ordered the evacuation of all high school faculties in Kamenets-Podolski to other cities, allowing their return in 1916. Russian defeats prompted the Grand Duke Nicholas, who held the Jews responsible for his country's military misfortunes, to drive them from their homes near the Galician front; and although most of the refugees were transported to the interior, tens of thousands ended up in Kamenets-Podolski, further swelling the Jewish population of the city to about one hundred thousand souls.

In the summer of 1916, General Aleksey Brusilov established his headquarters in Kamenets-Podolski to conduct the most successful Russian offensive of the war. He scored a great victory over the Austrians, but his army, like Russia itself, was spent by the effort. In March 1917, the tottering Romanov monarchy collapsed with the abdication of Czar Nicholas II. Authority passed to Kerensky's Provisional Government, which in turn was ousted by the Bolsheviks in the October Revolution.

Civil war broke out immediately after the Bolshevik putsch. Among the "White" forces that opposed the Bolsheviks were the Ukrainians, who in March 1917 colluded with the Germans to set up their own National Council, called the "Rada," under General Pavlo Skoropadsky. In January 1918, the Rada—which was controlled by the Germans—proclaimed sovereignty for the Ukraine, an act that provoked invasion by the Red Army. Ukrainian nationalists actually reached an accommodation with Jewish leaders, allowing Jews to elect delegates to the Rada and uniting with them to resist invasion by the Bolsheviks, as well as the armies of the newly constituted Polish state. But by July, the accord between Jews and Ukrainians broke down, and the pogroms began again in earnest.

The first of the pogroms was carried out in the spring of 1918, not by Ukrainians, but by Red Army units retreating before the Germans, whose forces continued to advance into Russia. However, the Soviets soon put a stop to the Red Army's depredations, no doubt at the instigation of Leon Trotsky, the top Red Army commander and himself a Jew. Eventually, Jews came to look favorably on the Red Army, with many Jews serving in its ranks—thereby further arousing the hatred of the Ukrainians.

Predictably, the Ukrainians committed the most savage pogroms. In the spring of 1918, Ukrainian army units retreating from Kiev massacred Jews in Berdichev, Zhitomir, and nearby towns. From late 1918 through 1919, Ukrainian Directory forces commanded by Simon Petliura—who established his headquarters in Kamenets-Podolski—earned considerable notoriety for murdering and terrorizing Jews. (The Directory had supplanted the now-defunct Rada, which had been turned out by the Germans in April 1918.) For example, on February 15 and 16, 1919, the Petliurists murdered 2,300 Jews in Proskurov and Feshtin (Gvardeiskoye). Tens of thousands more would be slaughtered under Petliura's aegis, with the result that, among Ukrainian Jews, Simon Petliura would acquire a reputation second only to Adolf Hitler in its fearsomeness.

In the summer of 1919, an anti-Bolshevik force under the Cossack leader, or "ataman," Grigoryev killed six thousand Jews in forty communities. In the autumn of 1919, Ukrainian Jews were further persecuted by White units commanded by General A. I. Denikin, whose troops were urged to "strike at the Jews and save Russia." In September, Denikin's men killed 1,500 Jews in Fastov. Another four thousand were killed by counterrevolutionary forces in Tetiev. "The anti-Jewish movement," observes the *Encyclopedia Judaica*, "set the total annihilation of the Jews as its objective and destroyed whole

townlets. Only the military weakness of the attackers prevented a holocaust of Ukrainian Jewry."*

During the Russian Civil War, Kamenets-Podolski was
ruled, on and off, by no fewer than three regimes: the Rada,
Petliura's Directory, and the Bolsheviks. The constant turmoil
of changing regimes made conditions appalling in the city. To
defend themselves, Jews took up arms and formed paramilitary units like the Haganah. In May 1919, when the Bolsheviks temporarily controlled the city, the Haganah joined with
Red Army units to repel Petliurist forces advancing from
Galicia. The Jews and their Bolshevik allies were defeated and
the Petliurists captured the city, unleashing pogroms that
claimed seventy-two lives in June, and another fifty-two
in July.

In 1921, the Soviets reasserted their authority over the
Ukraine. By then, some 162 pogroms had occurred in fifty-
two towns in Podolia, and over 3,700 Jews had been
butchered. In the Ukraine as a whole, more than 1,200
pogroms in 530 communities had killed a total of a hundred
thousand Jews. Hundreds of thousands more had been
wounded, uprooted from their homes, and otherwise hound-
ed and harried to the limits of extinction. The *Encyclopedia
Judaica* reports that "small Jewish settlements in the villages
were destroyed and completely abandoned. Refugees from
the villages and the townlets streamed into the larger towns of
the region and Odessa. Many crossed the borders into
Bessarabia and Poland. Typhus and famine also devastated the
Jewish population."†

The pogroms ceased under Soviet rule, but the misery of
the Jews continued. Many Jews now began to look for a way
out of the Ukraine, with over three hundred thousand eventually fleeing the region.

Family legend has it that, in mid-March 1917, my grandfa-

Encyclopedia Judaica, vol. 13 (Jerusalem: Keter Publishing, 1971), s.v.
"pogroms."

†Ibid., s.v. "Podolia."

ther and mother took a train to Petrograd on the occasion of my mother's seventeenth birthday. It was on this trip that Olga was said to have met Ilya Weintraub, her future husband and my father, after attending a birthday-eve performance by the student symphony orchestra of the city's renowned musical conservatory.

This, I think, is another instance of "Jewish history." It is hard to believe that they would have undertaken such a journey, given the events that were transpiring in and around Petrograd in March of that year. My mother's birthday was on March 18; three days earlier, Nicholas II had been forced to abdicate while en route to Petrograd from Russian army headquarters at Mogilev. Even before his abdication, however, it was anarchy and not the czar that reigned in Russia; the government had ceased to function, the army was falling apart, and the nation was racked by revolutionary turmoil. The countryside swarmed with armed men—soldiers, deserters, bandits—while the cities starved and were torn by riots. February and March saw the collapse of law and order in Petrograd, where rioters demanding bread were joined by Cossacks and regular army troops in pitched battles with the local police, who were unable to quell the disturbances despite killing hundreds. By March 18, the city was in a revolutionary uproar—hardly an atmosphere conducive to travel between Kamenets-Podolski and Petrograd, much less concert-going in the city itself.

I can only speculate, but I believe they went to Petrograd in 1916. Even then, the journey would have been difficult, what with the war raging not too far distant in Russia's western provinces. For that reason, I doubt that Moses and Olga ventured to Petrograd merely to celebrate my mother's birthday. Perhaps Moses had some pressing business in the capital and had availed himself of the opportunity to show his daughter what a real city looked like. He might also have had another objective: to play matchmaker for Olga and Ilya.

The only thing I know for certain about the episode is that it did indeed result in Olga and Ilya meeting each other. Ilya Weintraub, a twenty-one-year-old student at the conservatory, was conducting the orchestra; tall, with blond hair and blue eyes, looking resplendent in his elegant, quasi-military school uniform, he cut quite the dashing figure on the podium. My mother was smitten. After the concert, she begged Moses to take her backstage to be introduced to the golden-haired conductor. Moses did so, and Olga and Ilya gazed on each other for the first time.

By all reports, Ilya was equally smitten. As well he should have been. My mother was a beautiful girl, with black hair and hazel eyes set in striking contrast to her porcelain skin. She had delicate features, long, tapered fingers, and perfect teeth that seemed to sparkle when she smiled; and she carried herself with a swanlike grace as alluring as it was appealing. Moreover, she was a modern girl for her time and place, one perfectly suited to a man like Ilya.

My mother inherited her modernist sensibilities from two sources: her father and the movies. She worked as a cashier in Moses's movie theater, which played all the most popular films from Europe and America, and this gave her the opportunity to become an avid cinema buff. The world outside Kamenets-Podolski—that is, the motion-picture rendering of that world—fascinated and enthralled her both as a teenager and, later, as an adult. I remember her to have been a great fan of Marlene Dietrich and Jean Harlow—sophisticated, cosmopolitan women with whom she felt she had much in common.

Olga most definitely did not take after her mother, Pesha. My grandmother was the traditionalist in the family. Being devoutly religious, she went to temple, prayed often, lit the Shabbat candles, and kept a scrupulously kosher board. Her conservative nature might have caused her to be somewhat taken aback when she heard that Ilya Weintraub, purveyor of risqué American music, had proposed marriage to her daughter within a week of their meeting (my father had popped the question to Olga before she left Petrograd); nevertheless, Pesha approved the match.

It goes without saying that Moses also approved of the match between Olga and Ilya—otherwise, there would have been no marriage. His easygoing acceptance of their lightning romance and its outcome has made me suspicious of his part in the whole affair. It would have been just like my grandfather, a consummate handler and behind-the-scenes wheeler-dealer, to have arranged that "accidental" meeting between his daughter and her husband-to-be. Most assuredly, he would not have permitted Olga to consort with, much less marry, Ilya Weintraub until he had thoroughly checked into the young man's background. Nor would he have given Ilya the nod to marry after a whirlwind courtship lasting less than a week unless he knew beforehand that my father was an upstanding fellow, from a good family, with prospects and potential.

Esther believes that Olga and Ilya were not total strangers when they had their face-to-face encounter backstage in Petrograd. "In the old country," she told me, "there used to be a man who introduced. A *shadchan*. It was this person, a *shadchan*, who introduced Golda [Olga] to Lusha [Ilya]."

This is probably what happened. But I want to believe the story of a first-time meeting in Petrograd, with Moses slyly and gently manipulating the two youngsters into place—in effect, performing the duties of a *shadchan* for his daughter. In any case, Ilya and Olga did fall in love with each other. And they continued to love each other throughout their tragically shortened lives.

Their wedding was a big event in Kamenets-Podolski, all the more so because it brought a small measure of happiness to the war-ravaged city. So that all might share his joy on the occasion, Moses invited the general public (Gentiles as well as Jews) to participate in the festivities. All during the week of the wedding, tables groaning with food were set out in front of his house, and everyone was urged to stop by and eat and drink as much as their stomachs could hold.

For a wedding present, Moses gave Ilya and Olga ownership of his tobacco factory and movie theater. But Ilya didn't come to the wedding empty-handed. His father, Abraham Weintraub, owned a fabric store, a flour mill, and a vineyard in the nearby town of Dunajec. All these businesses were profitable, providing Abraham Weintraub with the means to send his son to music school in the nation's capital.

I never met Abraham Weintraub. In fact, other than my father's two sisters, Yunia and Nenya, I never met anyone else from his family, and I rarely heard my father talk about his relatives. Ilya was estranged from his father, both physically and emotionally, and so far as I know he never made an attempt to heal the rift between them. Abraham Weintraub was an Orthodox Jew, unassimilated, bearded, and pious. He apparently looked askance at his son's interest in jazz music, which he regarded as a frivolous and nearly blasphemous pursuit. By the same token, Ilya was indifferent toward religion, and as a young man had chafed against his father's strict Orthodox outlook and customs. It was an instance of youthful rebellion that developed into a permanent condition, forever unresolved.

After November 1918 and the end of the First World War, Moses traveled frequently between America and Kamenets-Podolski. In Perth Amboy, he and Isadore worked hard to prepare the way financially for emigration by the entire family. With his father providing the capital, Isadore opened a market stall where he sold pots and pans, dried fruits, and sundry items; meanwhile, Moses started up an import-export business. Moses couldn't get everyone out of Russia all at once, and besides, he wasn't fully committed to leaving Kamenets-Podolski. In the opening stages of the Russian Civil War, he thought that the Bolsheviks would be defeated, in which case he would have been content to remain in Russia, or least maintain a home there. But he also wanted to be ready to get out if the Bolsheviks triumphed and their governance of the country turned out to be as bad as Moses thought it could be.

Isadore was now an American citizen, a status he had attained by virtue of his service in the United States Army in the First World War. He had gone into the army willingly, for he recognized that military service would both smooth and hasten the naturalization process, which otherwise might have taken several years to complete. Nevertheless, it seems ironic that Isadore left Kamenets-Podolski in part to stay out of a Russian uniform, only to become a soldier soon after arriving in America.

He paid a high price for his enlistment. Assigned to an infantry unit in the American Expeditionary Forces, he was promptly shipped overseas to France to fight the Germans in the trenches of the Western Front. While engaged in battle, his lungs were seared by mustard gas, and in consequence he suffered all his life from chronic asthma. But he figured that his asthma, which was not too severe, was a price well worth paying for the precious commodity of American citizenship.

Isadore's younger brother, Motia, never made it to America. After the war Motia moved to Berlin, where jobs were more plentiful than in Kamenets-Podolski. He found employment as a coal-mining engineer, a position that carried with it the glittering promise of future affluence. But it was not to be. One day while inspecting a mine shaft, an overhead beam fell and crushed his arm. His doctors judged his limb to be irreparably damaged and counseled immediate amputation as the only viable treatment. Motia was horrified. He had come to Berlin to spread his wings, not to have them clipped! And so, blinded by his youthful inability to imagine his own death, he stubbornly rejected the advice of his physicians, instead gambling that he would recover in reasonably good form. Poor, obstinate Motia, it was a wager he lost. The inevitable gangrene set in, swiftly killing him when the poison in his arm spread throughout his system.

Motia's death came as a terrible blow to his parents and siblings. But their sorrow was somewhat ameliorated when, on April 23, 1919, my brother Fima was born. Fima was reportedly a strong, solid baby. And a good thing, too, for he had entered life in a world beset by war, revolution, and indiscriminate slaughter—conditions that were especially prevalent in the Ukraine and bound to get considerably worse before they got better.

The Bolshevik victory over counterrevolutionary forces

brought an end to large-scale warfare in the region. But no sooner had the communists established themselves in the Ukraine than they began to make trouble for private businessmen. Esther says that when the Bolsheviks came to Kamenets-Podolski, "the first thing they did was put inspectors in every one of my father's flour mills. You couldn't take out a pound of flour without them knowing. And my father, he used to come home from shul and sit and cry, 'They rob me, they rob me!' Because the inspectors wouldn't let you take out a single pound of flour!"

Moses coped with this situation as best he could, optimistically holding to the belief that Bolshevik rule could not last. And if they did stay in power—well, he had his businesses in America to fall back on. He was playing both sides of the fence and making a tidy profit in the bargain.

The Bolsheviks knew exactly what Moses was doing, and they were not amused. In due course, they determined to put a stop to his activities.

I was born in my grandfather's house on November 17, 1922. Only hours before my life began, while my mother was in labor, Bolshevik soldiers came to the house to arrest my grandfather. The Bolsheviks finally felt secure enough to make their move against the bourgeois elements in Kamenets-Podolski, and Moses Rosenwald was one of those who ranked high on their enemies list. Hustled from his home under armed guard, he was taken to the police station for interrogation and God knows what else. He was not even allowed to be at home for the birth of his granddaughter, so anxious were the Bolsheviks to clap him behind bars.

Pesha was inconsolable. The happiness she might have felt over my birth was erased by concern for Moses; instead of rejoicing at the new addition to her family, she spent the night praying fervently for her husband's salvation.

Her prayers were answered the next day. My grandfather's deliverance was engineered by none other than the good citizens of Kamenets-Podolski—the selfsame people who had so often in the past benefited from his generosity and friendship.

Even as he was being hauled into prison, news of his arrest was spreading around the town, provoking outrage against the Bolshevik authorities. In the morning, a large crowd assembled before the prison, clamoring for his release. The Red Army soldiers posted at the door looked out at that sea of angry faces, which included Christians as well as Jews, and responded to this threat by leveling their rifles at them. It looked as if they were going to open fire when voices in the crowd called out for calm.

"Don't shoot!" someone shouted. "We've come in peace."

"We don't want any trouble," yelled another man.

The soldiers hesitated. "What do you want, then?" one of them shouted back at the crowd.

The question elicited a chorus of demands to set Moses Rosenwald free. The people told the soldiers that they loved Moses, that he was a man who had never let anyone in Kamenets-Podolski go hungry or cold. At this juncture, the soldiers cautiously lowered their weapons. The hell with it, they probably thought; just because people were making a lot of noise was no reason to massacre them. Besides, the crowd made sense. This Moses Rosenwald, whoever he was, sounded like a decent fellow; surely he deserved a fair hearing.

Amazingly, a fair hearing is exactly what he got. It would not have been out of character for the Bolsheviks to summarily execute Moses, thereby demonstrating who was boss in Russia. Several indiscriminately aimed rifle volleys to disperse the crowd might then have followed. A few years hence, the Bolsheviks would use such methods to collectivize the Ukraine and eradicate the kulaks, at a cost of ten million dead. But not on that day. The Bolsheviks recognized that their writ was not completely extended over the Ukraine, that it was still necessary to win the hearts and minds of the people before they could begin killing them. Therefore, the Bolshevik authorities, hearkening to the message and mood of the crowd, let Moses go.

The Bolsheviks must have felt chagrined to give in to these rowdy Ukrainians. More than that, they must have been infuriated. The Bolsheviks could not stand to be thwarted. But they were nothing if not devious. They knew how to restrain themselves, how to bide their time and hide their anger until the opportunity for getting even presented itself. One can easily imagine them smiling at the populace even as they plotted their revenge. Someday soon, they must have thought, these people will pay in blood for defying us. And Moses Rosenwald will be among the first to bleed.

Of course, Moses was well aware that the Bolsheviks were not yet finished with him. He understood that once the situation in the Kamenets-Podolski had stabilized, the Bolsheviks would grind him into the dirt. Naturally, he did not intend to give them the satisfaction. But he, too, would have to exercise some restraint.

Walking out of the police station, he waded into the crowd, accepting the congratulations of the people, shaking hands and thanking them for their support. He moved slowly and deliberately, to show the Bolsheviks that he had no cause to hasten. But once he had gotten to where the Bolsheviks could not see him, he made a dash for his house.

His appearance there came as a great relief to everyone, especially Pesha. But her relief swiftly turned to dismay when her husband announced to family members and servants alike that they were leaving Kamenets-Podolski.

"Pack up everything we can carry," he ordered. "We're going to Poland tonight."

"Poland?" cried Pesha. "Tonight? But why so soon?"

"We mustn't be here when the Bolsheviks come for me again," he said. He was under no illusions that his freedom was permanent. "If they take us, we'll all be sent to Siberia."

He told Pesha to get her jewelry. "Bring it all to me," he commanded. "Your diamonds, your rings, your silver bracelets, your emeralds and rubies—everything."

Reluctantly, she fetched these things. Moses wrapped the valuables in a cloth and hid the package behind a loose brick in one wall of the house.

"Why don't we bring the jewelry with us?" asked Pesha.

"And what if we run into a Bolshevik patrol?" countered Moses. "They'll search us, find our jewels, and rob us. No, better to leave them here. That way, we'll have something to start over with when we return."

Pesha didn't like the sound of this. "We may not be able to return," she observed.

"Don't talk that way!" Moses snapped. "Communism will fail, and when it does, people will beg businessmen like me to come back!"

Moses was an optimist. He was also right—the fall of Communism and the resurgence of private enterprise in Russia would certainly occur. But he foresaw this happening within months, whereas nearly seventy years elapsed before his prophecy was fulfilled.

Despite my grandfather's sense of urgency, the family did not flee that night. Evidently, Moses decided to risk staying for a few days more in order to get his affairs in order and prepare the family for the hazardous journey that lay ahead of it. Meanwhile, the Bolsheviks confiscated his tobacco factory, movie theater, and skating rink. Within a week, they had ruined him. He owned his house and nothing more. And there was no telling how much longer this property would remain in his possession.

Esther recalls that Moses, with typical bravado, hosted a farewell get-together for his friends on the night we absconded to Poland. Moses and his cronies were playing cards when a late-arriving guest informed Moses that the Bolsheviks had issued a second warrant for his arrest. They intended to serve the warrant the next day. Upon hearing this, says Esther, Moses jumped up from the table, exclaiming, "They'll never get me again!"

A few hours later, the Rosenwalds and Weintraubs left Russia forever. (Esther and her family, however, remained in Kamenets-Podolski until 1927.) The escape party consisted of my grandparents, my mother and father, Fima, Uncle Yossi, Aunts Haika and Nadia, Nadia's son Marcus, two or three servants, and, of course, myself. I was transported in the arms of a servant, since my mother was still too weak from childbirth to carry me.

After an arduous cross-country trek, the family reached

the Polish frontier. It was still dark. On the Russian side of the border, Red Army soldiers in guard towers trained searchlight beams on the no-man's-land that separated the two countries. When a searchlight beam swept across our group, Moses indicated that we should make a run for it. Just then I started to cry.

The servant carrying me stuffed a blanket into my mouth to muffle the sound of my voice. But he botched the effort, and I wailed even louder. Panicking, the servant gagged me so hard with the blanket that I began to suffocate. Fima saw what the servant was doing and, thinking that he was trying to murder me, kicked the man and hollered at him to stop. The servant removed the blanket, and I screamed at the top of my lungs. The soldiers in the guard towers heard me and, pointing the searchlight in our direction, shouted at us to halt. Instead of halting, however, we sprinted for the border. The guards shot at us, but nobody was hit, and we made it safely across no-man's-land onto Polish soil.

We continued on to Lvov, where my grandfather knew people who could help us. Probably he had contacted someone in advance as part of his plan to escape Kamenets-Podolski. I don't know where we spent the next few nights—possibly with one of my grandfather's friends or business associates. A few days later, Moses rented a room at 6 Piekarska Street. The room was very small, quite unlike our big brick house in Kamenets-Podolski. But the adults all realized that, however cramped their quarters, they were much better off in Poland than in Russia. And they would remain so for the next seventeen years.

❧

Lvov Childhood

L vov is nestled in a valley on the river Peltew at the foot of a
hill called Wysoki Zamek, or "High Castle." From 1772
to 1918, the city was ruled by the Austro-Hungarian Empire
(when it was known as Lemberg). It was ceded to Poland
upon the conclusion of the First World War. In the interwar
period, Poles constituted a majority in the city, with Ukrainians predominant in the surrounding countryside. Like all
Polish cities, Lvov also had a venerable Jewish quarter, populated almost exclusively by Orthodox Jews.

In 1910, close to one hundred thousand Jews lived in Lvov,
mainly in the Jewish quarter. Due to the influx of refugees
from the Soviet Union, the number of Jews had increased to
110,000 by 1939. In that year, Jews constituted a third of
Lvov's population of 340,000—after Warsaw and Łódź, it had
the largest Jewish community in Poland. A great many of
them were Orthodox. They were something of a mystery to
me; I had almost no contact with them and rarely encountered them on the streets. Until the Germans came to the city
in June 1941, I never saw the "Lyczakowska," as the Jewish
quarter was known, and was only vaguely aware that, in rela-
tion to where we lived, it was located somewhere behind the
city's Opera House.

I have extremely fond memories of the Lvov of my childhood. It was a pretty city with an improbably harmonious
blend of architectural styles, including the medieval, baroque,
romantic, neoclassical, Italianate, and modern. Within its
environs, one could find narrow cobblestoned streets that

meandered through quiet neighborhoods, and wide boulevards and bustling plazas that were lined with chic cafés, nightclubs, and stores. The city was further graced by lovely parks and municipal gardens with ponds swarming with ducks, acres of manicured lawns, and hundreds of huge, shade-giving oak trees. In my mind, however, Lvov's most characteristic feature were its ornate apartment buildings, most of them of eighteenth-century construction, with elaborate wrought-iron filigree on their balconies and entrance gates, and roofs covered over with red terra-cotta tiles.

Our first residence was in an ethnically mixed neighborhood where Jews and Gentiles lived side by side without incident or any apparent enmity. I recall very little from the Piekarska Street period. I remember playing with dolls and my pet cat. I remember Christmas in a year I can't recall; I saw a Christmas tree in a neighbor's window and asked my parents if I could become a Christian so I could have a Christmas tree too. I also remember how, that same winter, we burned Russian ruble notes in our stove to keep warm. Apparently, Moses had smuggled a quantity of paper rubles out of Russia in the vain hope that he could convert them to Polish zlotys. By then, this currency, which had been printed during the reign of the czar, was completely worthless as a medium of exchange, having been repudiated by the Bolsheviks. It was good as fuel for the fire and nothing more.

Immediately upon our arrival in Lvov, my father was confronted with the difficult task of finding a job in a foreign country whose language he spoke only haltingly. Fortunately, he possessed a marketable skill: he was a talented musician, especially when it came to playing the saxophone. With one or more of his saxophones in tow, he made the rounds of Lvov's nightclubs, seeking to hook up with one of the many jazz bands that performed in those establishments.

Moses, ever the raconteur and man-about-town, was favorably disposed to Ilya's musical aspirations, but Pesha regarded them with unconcealed scorn. She didn't like jazz and she looked askance at the musicians who played it. She called her son-in-law a "klezmer" and wished aloud that he would find honest work. In response, my father would smile tactfully and, just as tactfully, ignore her. He soon got himself hired by a band, working full time and earning enough money to support his family. In doing so, he became something of a local celebrity to the young adults of Lvov. In the 1920s, jazz was the music of the hour; this was the "jazz age," and my father was an integral part of it in Lvov's cosmopolitan milieu.

My father did not, however, fit the popular image of a jazz-age musician. He was not the kind of wild and reckless character one might encounter in contemporary literature about that era. Far from it. He was, rather, a man of calm demeanor and proper manners. He was also a strict disciplinarian with an unrelenting work ethic. Since he worked nights, he would have been fully justified in sleeping late in the mornings and lounging about the apartment in the afternoons. But such behavior went against his grain. Instead, he got up early every day and practiced on his saxophone for at least two hours before breakfast. He practiced in the kitchen so as not to disturb the rest of the family, playing the scales up and down, over and over again.

My father was as strict with Fima and me as he was with himself. He did not tolerate idleness and sloth. We could not just sit around and stare into space, as kids so often do; we always had to be doing something, anything, either reading a book and thereby improving our minds—my father's chief concern—or engaged in some physical activity that he endorsed. Daydreaming was not tolerated. "Don't waste your time," my father would say, and if we knew what was good for us, we would get moving in a hurry.

My father was especially firm with Fima, a rough and tumble boy with a willful personality and a mind of his own. Fima was assigned myriad chores to keep him out of trouble and, not incidentally, to inculcate the twin virtues of discipline and hard work. One of Fima's chores was to carry my father's saxophone case to the nightclubs where his band was performing. Sometimes Fima had to lug two saxophone cases, one in each hand—a heavy burden for a young boy. But with these responsibilities came certain freedoms. When, as a teenager, he went out at night with his friends, he could stay out as late as he wanted and come home any time without fear of reproach. My father trusted him to behave well, and Fima rewarded this trust with exemplary conduct.

My father went easier on me because I was a girl. For the same reason, however, my range of activities was narrowly circumscribed. When going out with my friends or on a date, I was told to come home at a certain hour, and if I was so much as one minute late, I would find my father waiting up for me, demanding to know where I had been, what I had been doing, and why I had failed to meet my curfew.

Sometimes I wanted to break free of these restrictions. I would feel rebellious and impatient, just like the children of today. But unlike today's children, I didn't dare complain or talk back to my father. Neither did Fima. Instead, I might simply balk at my parents' commands. My father dealt with such passive protests summarily, with a curt order to do as I was told. My mother preferred a more subtle approach: bribery. If, for example, I had an appointment with the den-tist—always an unpleasant experience that I sought to avoid—she would soften me up by taking me to Shirley Temple or Deanna Durbin movies. Her tactic usually worked. I loved those actresses, to the extent that I was willing to endure the torments of the dentist's chair if only I could see one of their movies afterward.

My brother and I were always busy. School, of course, occupied the main part of the day. I attended a private Jewish girls school, wearing a prim navy blue dress for a uniform. Fima went to a public school, but he also wore a navy blue uniform, one with silver buttons, and a hat with a visor in front, like soldiers wore.

School let out for both of us at two o'clock in the afternoon, and we would return home for the main meal of the day. The entire family would gather around a big table in the living room (we didn't have a separate dining room) and while we ate my father would ask Fima and me questions about what we had done in school that day. After the midday meal we would all rest for about an hour, and then I would go out again, either to the home of my language tutor for a private French lesson, or to a nearby dance studio where I was enrolled in a ballet class. In the late afternoon, Fima and I had to do our schoolwork before we were allowed to play with our friends. To reward us for completing our assignments, my mother served us hot cocoa and little cakes. In the evenings, my father helped with whatever schoolwork problems we couldn't solve. "Did any of the teachers call on you?" he would ask us. "Did you know the answers?" And if we hadn't known the answers, he would go over the questions with us.

The weekends were more relaxed, but even then my father usually found something for us to do. On Sunday afternoons, he often took us to a matinee performance at the Opera House by a childrens' theater company that was in residence there.

The Opera House still stands, having survived the Second World War relatively unscathed. It is situated on a large cobblestoned piazza with a garden in the center. In the interwar period, the piazza had cafés, boutiques, newspaper kiosks, candy stores, and tobacco shops around it. The Opera House resembles the cathedral in St. Mark's Square in Venice. Like the Venetian edifice, every nook and cranny of the rooftop and exterior facade is adorned with winged angels, gargoyles, and statues.

At the conclusion of a performance in this magnificent building, we would stroll about the piazza among the many other Lvovians who were also walking about in the fresh air and sunshine. My father always wore an expensive suit, custom-made in England, that consisted of a houndstooth jacket, a white shirt, and brown trousers. It was the only suit he owned besides his tuxedo, which he wore when he played with his band. We called his tuxedo his "smoking jacket" because he was a "smoking hot" jazz musician. An impeccable dresser, my father justified the purchase of his expensive suit with the half-flippant, half-serious remark, "I'm too poor to buy cheap clothes."

I enjoyed the childrens' theater plays immensely. They were invariably entertaining, yet also challenging to our developing intellects. They examined important issues and big ideas in a language and format children could readily grasp, but without condescending to their young audience. My favorite play was *Pyr Gynt*. I remember how, in one scene, the entire stage was empty except for a plain, bare stairway. Then the actor who played Pyr Gynt appeared onstage and ascended the first step. "Who am I?" he asked, and in reply a stentorian voice from the wings called out, "You are yourself!" Pyr went up another step, asked the same question—and received the same booming answer. This action and its accompanying dialogue were repeated, step by step, until Pyr disappeared into the darkness at the top of the stairs.

Afterward, while ambling around the piazza, my father asked us if we understood what all this meant. We said that we did not.

"Then I'll explain it to you," my father said. "When the man goes up the stairs, he is actually going to a higher place in the world. He is going to God. And it is God who speaks to him, telling him that, no matter what you do or where you go in life, you are a unique person, and you have to be true to yourself."

This little drama, coupled with my father's interpretation, left a deep and lasting impression on me. It taught me that I was a unique individual, created by God and bound to God, with a distinct identity that, being God-given, was worth preserving. It was a message I would take to heart and that would sustain me during the years of the Nazi terror.

Whenever we talked about the plays, my father found a way of turning the conversation to subjects like morality, ethics, and how one should live his or her life. "When you work, work hard," he would say. "Always try to do your best. If you're a scholar, be the best scholar. If you're a plumber, be the best plumber."

He believed that character was fate. "You're just a little

girl," he would tell me, "but you're never too young to develop character. You have intelligence and you can use it. I can't make you act intelligently. What you do with your mind, with your education, that's something you have to accomplish all by yourself. But that's how you build character."

My father often emphasized how irrelevant money could be to living a good life. "You might think that having a lot of money automatically guarantees happiness. But it doesn't. A rich man with no character has nothing. He will be bored; he will have nothing to do. He will be miserable. Happiness comes from within, from the self—from your character."

In the late 1920s, we moved out of the cramped flat on Piekarska Street to take up residence in an apartment building at 51 Zyblikiewicza Street. Our family occupied two large apartments on the third floor of the building, which was a beautiful old structure with an ornate front door and balconies overlooking an interior courtyard. In one apartment lived the Weintraubs: my mother and father, Fima, and myself. Next door were the Rosenwalds: my grandmother and grandfather, Aunt Haika, and Uncle Yossi. (By then Aunt Nadia, her husband, and their son Marcus had moved to Warsaw.)

The building was located near the citadel where several Polish army units were billeted. On many weekends, the army units went out on field maneuvers, and if we stood on our balcony or left the windows open, we could clearly hear the sound of galloping horses and marching soldiers, and the boom of artillery and the crack of rifle fire as the troops took target practice.

Our new neighborhood, like the one we had moved out of, was ethnically diverse, with Jews and Gentiles, and Poles, Russians, and Ukrainians living together in harmony. A lawyer lived in one of our building's second-floor apartments; a doctor lived just across the street. We got along well enough with the Gentiles, but we didn't socialize with them. A few polite words of greeting usually marked the extent of our dealings with each other.

My parents didn't socialize with Polish Jews either. There was no friction between Polish and Russian Jews, but little effort was made by either group to get to know the other. My parents kept to their own kind, Russian immigrants who had fled Bolshevik oppression.

A Russian Jew named Petia lived in our building's first-floor apartment. A pharmacist by trade, Petia was far more interested in politics and current events than the drugs he dispensed. Often, in the evening, he came to our apartment to talk about the news of the day with my father, who delighted in such conversations, being himself very much interested in international affairs. Petia was a bachelor in his forties. He was, to put it bluntly, a slob. He always wore the same navy pinstriped suit with a wrinkled white shirt and a jacket spotted with food stains. He wore the jacket draped over his shoulder like a cape—a ridiculously aristocratic affectation that was made all the more preposterous by the garment's soiled fabric. A cigarette was usually dangling from his lips, and his teeth had the brown and yellow tint of a heavy smoker. He had bulging green eyes that were always bloodshot. His salt-and-pepper hair was cropped close to the scalp, giving him a pinheaded look, and his sallow cheeks bristled with stray salt-and-pepper whiskers he had missed when shaving.

In today's parlance, Petia would be called a nerd. All the children in the neighborhood made fun of him to his face because he acted and looked so goofy. Even my parents, who were fond of Petia, thought him a somewhat ridiculous figure. But my father enjoyed talking with him because he was intelligent and highly educated. The two men amused each other, and they joked and laughed a lot when they were together. In actuality, however, Petia was a Gloomy Gus, extremely pessimistic, particularly with regard to the future of Jews in Europe. After Hitler came to power, Petia often prophesied a Jewish apocalypse if Germany and the Nazis continued on their present course. My father did not share this view and always pooh-poohed Petia's dire predictions. His bleak outlook, my father thought, was consistent with the man's generally depressed emotional state and in no way reflected an ability to accurately foretell the future.

Petia was by no means the only visitor to our home. The apartment was a cheerful, bustling place, enlivened by the near-constant comings and goings of good friends. The latter were always displaced Russians like ourselves, people who had formed ad hoc immigrant communities in the Polish cities where they had settled after the Bolshevik takeover. Our doors were always open to these people, and they dropped by whenever they felt moved to do so—which was often!

My mother's friends usually came over in the early afternoon for what could be described as the Russian equivalent of English high tea. An accomplished dessert cook, my mother would set out tea and all manner of tasty sweets—tortes, tortes with *poziomki* (small strawberries), sugar cookies, mandel bread, and kugel. She displayed these delicacies on the marble slab of a black mahogany breakfront, her most prized piece of furniture. On either side of the slab were cabinets with inlaid-glass doors where she kept her best china; beneath it were drawers where the bathroom linens and bedding were stored, and behind it was a big mirror with a beveled surface.

The breakfront was the centerpiece of the living room and thus the center of our household. Both Fima and I slept in the living room in beds placed on either side of a tall oven with a surface of glazed tiles. In the middle of the room stood a large table where we sat to eat meals, do homework, listen to the radio, and socialize with guests.

Around five in the afternoon, at the end of the workday, the men would begin to show up. While the women chatted in the kitchen, my father and his friends would gather in the living room, standing and sitting around our dinner table to listen to radio news broadcasts and discuss the issues of the day. As they sipped tea and nibbled on pastries—provided at regular intervals by my mother—they would talk about Communism and Fascism, what was going on in Germany and the Soviet Union, the Zionist movement, whether it was better and more desirable to emigrate to Palestine or America, Polish attitudes toward Jews, and what seemed a hundred other topics, all of them having something to do with politics and current events. These gabfests always started out on an even note but invariably heated up as the evening wore on. Quiet conversations would explode into noisy arguments which saw one participant or the other jumping up from his chair to pace across the room and make loud pronouncements punctuated with a great deal of gesturing and finger-wagging. But for all the passion and vehemence with which they put forth their views, there was no animosity; these men were close friends who thoroughly enjoyed the intellectual give-and-take their verbal sparring matches entailed.

Though I listened in on their conversations, very little of what they said made an impression on me. I just wasn't interested in politics and current events. Naturally, nobody asked for my opinion. Nor did I offer one. It would have been terribly inappropriate for me to speak in that company, and it would have angered my parents had I done so. I was just a child, which meant that I was supposed to be seen, not heard. It was just as well. I really had nothing to say. Which was why I was always relieved when our guests went home, usually around nine o'clock. Finally, I could go to bed. Not that I didn't enjoy having the grown-ups in our apartment. I found them endlessly entertaining. But I was looking forward to a busy day on the morrow—classes, French or ballet lessons, studying—and I needed to get to sleep.

My grandmother, Pesha, did not attend these get-togethers, preferring instead to spend the evenings in her apartment, either cooking or praying. Fima and I found her piety a bit odd, even forbidding, but not so her culinary propensities. These we greatly appreciated, especially when they resulted in mouth-watering desserts, as was often the case. When Fima and I went across the hallway to pay her a visit, we could always expect to be served plenty of homemade cookies and kugel. I think that the secret ingredient that made these confections so delicious was the love with which they were made. Dear, sweet, quiet Pesha, her love of family was second only to her love of God. She lived for her family and her religion, deriving immeasurable joy and contentedness from both.

Of all the family members who lived in those two apartments, I was closest to my Aunt Haika. Only ten years older than me, Haika was the big sister I never had. I idolized her. She was very pretty, jovial, and outgoing, and, not incidentally, very popular with the boys. Every weekend, it seemed, a young man none of us had ever seen before came clomping up the stairs to knock on the door of her apartment. I was fascinated by this whole process, and by the way Haika handled herself. When she got ready to go out on a date, I would sit in her room and watch as she got dressed and put on her makeup, all the while telling myself that when I grew up I would be just like her. She often wore fancy store-bought dresses that Moses, who doted on her, had sent from America. I envied her at such moments, for I wanted to wear store-bought American dresses, too.

Haika had something else I coveted: a leather-bound journal that she used as a diary, writing down her personal thoughts and drawing pictures in pen and ink on its blank pages. Once, when she was out of the house, I cut out all the drawings and took them to my room. Possessing Haika's drawings, I felt, would make me more like her. I soon learned that this only made her cross with me. When Haika discovered the theft of her drawings, she immediately guessed that I was the culprit, and severely reprimanded me for my misdeed. Ashamed and distraught that I had provoked my beloved aunt, I fetched the drawings and gave them back to her, apologizing profusely as I handed them over. But Haika was not mollified by my show of contrition. She was not about to let me off the hook that easily: she meant to teach me a lesson by staying cross with me for a few days. But she could not pull it off. She was too sweet-tempered to harbor a grudge—she couldn't even pretend to be angry. After a few hours, we were pals again, talking and laughing as before.

The dresses my grandfather sent Haika from America, along with sundry other items, often represented the only communication we'd had from Moses in months. Since leaving Kamenets-Podolski, Moses had traveled to America every year, staying for six months or more at a time to build up the

business interests he had developed in partnership with
Isadore. Moses worked hard at this task, but he had a rough
go of it and achieved only limited success. In the end, he
failed in his ultimate goal to bring his family to America, with
tragic consequences for everyone. He strove tirelessly, even
valiantly, to realize his dreams, but he could not overcome the
many negative factors arrayed against him. And therein lies a
sad tale.

When Moses was in America, he lived with Isadore and
Isadore's wife, Hilda, in their apartment in Perth Amboy,
New Jersey. Moses depended on Isadore for financial assis-
tance, having little money and few valuables he could convert
into cash. Most of his tangible wealth—diamonds, jewelry,
and the like—had been left behind in the house in Kamenets-
Podolski, never to be retrieved.

Isadore and Hilda were somewhat better off than Moses,
but they, too, were struggling to get by. Consequently, Hilda
bitterly resented Moses. In their straitened circumstances, she
insisted, not without justification, that they were in no position to help anyone, not even Isadore's father—despite the
fact that Moses was in business with Isadore and therefore
entitled to a some measure of their joint earnings.

My Aunt Esther, who emigrated to America in the early
1930s, remembers that "Srulik," as Isadore was nicknamed,
did what he could for his father. But Isadore's money problems and Hilda's attitude made for a difficult situation that
was never resolved. Esther felt that Moses was unfairly treated: "My uncle," she said, "deserved to be treated like a mensch,
because he was always a *grosser* man, he was a good man, and
he helped everybody."

Among those he had helped were a number of Jewish boys
from Kamenets-Podolski. These were the same youths who
had dodged service in the Russian army because of his efforts.
One was Esther's cousin Morris, but there were many others.
In the 1930s, they were grown men, and several had, like
Morris, emigrated to America and were doing quite well for
themselves. Moses sought out each man and asked him not
for charity but for a job. Every one of these men, Morris
included, turned him down. They had owed him a debt of

gratitude and much more, but they gave him nothing in return.

In desperation, Moses turned to his sisters for help. At that time, Moses had two sisters living in America, Esther's mother and his younger sister, Rifka. Esther's mother very much loved the brother she had raised as a son and gave him whatever extra money she had. This was never much, for she and her husband were impoverished. By contrast, Rifka was fairly well-off; her husband owned and operated a dry goods store and various other properties. But for reasons that remain obscure, Rifka and Moses were not on friendly terms. So Moses received little help from her.

Depressed by these goings-on, Moses would sometimes drop by Esther's apartment seeking companionship and solace. "He used to come to me," Esther recalls, "and he was crying—my uncle, the *grosser* man, crying like a baby. He had no money. He left his fortune in Russia. He couldn't bring his wife and children to America. He couldn't do anything because he didn't have money. And I was very poor because my husband only made seven dollars a week. But I always gave him lunch, or breakfast, or something. This I could do, at least. I could give him a good meal. And he was telling me all the stories, that he left a fortune in Russia. Oh, I felt so bad!"

Moses didn't want his family in Poland to know that he was having such a hard time in America. He didn't want us to worry about him. That is why he sent us presents. We were supposed to think that, if he could afford to purchase dresses and other frivolous items, he must be doing just fine.

During his infrequent return trips to Lvov, he always put on a brave front for his family. I can almost see him now, swaggering down the boulevards of Lvov, dressed to the nines in an immaculately tailored suit complete with overcoat and silk scarf, wearing his broad-brimmed fedora jauntily aslant, grinning broadly as he twirled a walking stick capped with a gold or silver knob. He positively radiated confidence, making you think that he could succeed at anything he tried, that if anyone had the Midas touch, he was that person.

In the evenings, we would all sit around his dinner table

and listen, enthralled, as he regaled us with stories about America and the opportunities that awaited us there. "America is a golden land," he would tell us. "Even the Jews have it good there."

"You mean there is no anti-Semitism in America?" a family member would ask.

"Of course there is," he would reply. "But it's not so bad. Not like here. Over there, everyone can make a better life for themselves, and for their children."

My father took all this with the proverbial grain of salt. Nevertheless, he shared his father-in-law's desire to emigrate to America. Like Moses, he believed that the Jews of Europe faced a bleak future. America was the only place to be. But he understood that he would have to wait his turn to get there. Moses had it all worked out. First, when he was able—which is to say, when he had enough money—he would bring Pesha to America. Following her, Haika would come over, then Nadia and Marcus, and finally the Weintraubs. Moses supposed that it would take several years and a lot of money to implement this plan. But he was certain that it would all come to pass. And so was my father, who took English lessons in anticipation of the day.

Although hatred for the Jews and the violence it often generated supplied one of the chief reasons to emigrate (another, of course, was the desire to better one's condition), I never saw or experienced any anti-Semitic incidents while I was growing up. Not that I was unaware of such occurrences. I knew that gangs of Polish thugs sometimes made forays into the Jewish quarter of the city to beat up on any Orthodox men they came across. The Poles had no trouble finding victims: the latter were made instantly recognizable by their beards and sidelocks, objects of scorn and disgust that aroused an unreasoning fury in their attackers.

No thugs ever bothered me, however. For one thing, I didn't look Jewish, which protected me from harassment on the streets. Moreover, as a student at a private Jewish girls school, I was fortunate in being effectively removed from the anti-Semitism in Polish society. There were Christian girls enrolled in my school, but they had no hostility toward Jews. The mere fact of their presence indicated that they were tolerant of, and perhaps even in sympathy with, the Jews who lived among them.

My brother Fima, however, has a different story to tell. Fima attended a public school where most students, and teachers as well, were Christian Poles or Ukrainians. They tended to dislike Jews and were openly hostile to the school's dozen or so Jewish students. As if being a Jew weren't bad enough, Fima was further handicapped by his imperfect grasp of the Polish language, which he spoke with a pronounced Russian accent. This was tantamount to waving a red flag in front of his teachers and classmates, who were not at all fond of Russians, whom they regarded as traditional enemies and frequent oppressors.

The bigotry of his teachers did not concern Fima overmuch. The quality of his schoolwork was such that no teacher, however anti-Semitic, could justify giving him anything other than the high grades he deserved. Classroom sessions could get unpleasant but were not intolerable since, on the whole, the teachers stayed aloof from their students, be they Christian or Jew. It was in the schoolyard where real trouble occurred. There, Fima often got in fistfights with his Christian classmates.

They had their hands full. Fima was strong, tough, and fearless. A superb athlete, he excelled at soccer, to the degree that, when he was eighteen or nineteen, he earned a starting position on a semiprofessional team in Lvov that normally excluded Jews from its roster. His talent for the game was matched by his abilities as a bare-knuckled pugilist. In that capacity, he often demonstrated that his innate athleticism had advantages not limited to sporting events. In countless schoolyard brawls, his opponents discovered that they had picked a fight with a Jew who was both willing and able to defend himself. Fima was no shrinking Jew from the shtetl; he was no pacifist. He may have suffered some cuts and scrapes in the process of proving this to his would-be tormentors, but he sent more than a few boys home with bloody noses and second thoughts about picking on the "Yids."

In 1931, we were blessed by the birth of my sister Rysia. I was nine years old when she was born and very much excited and fascinated by this new and wondrous addition to our family. She was a beautiful baby with golden hair and flawless features, and I remember studying her while she lay in her crib and thinking that she looked like a perfect little doll that God had brought to life to make us all happy.

By then my father was earning a decent if still modest income as the leader of a jazz band. His band usually played at one of two nightclubs, the Bistro and the Café de la Paix. My parents rarely took me to the clubs when I was a child. I think I went two or three times at most. This was a real treat for me. My parents didn't think it appropriate to bring a child to the clubs, even though these establishments were really quite tame. The Café de la Paix, for instance, was a charming place that one entered by ascending a red-carpeted stairway with mirrors on either side of a long hallway. On the upper level, there was a foyer with a cloakroom, and beyond that was the main room, which had tables, a stage for the band, and a spacious dance floor.

When Rysia got older and could be left in the care of Pesha or Haika, my mother would go to the clubs to watch my father perform. She would put on her makeup for the occasion and wear her finest evening gown, a black satin dress that dramatically accentuated her porcelain-complected skin. Never was her beauty more evident than when she wore that dress. Over her shoulders she draped two fox furs that made her seem impossibly elegant, like a Hollywood movie star. Normally I found those furs, with their little fox heads and beady marble eyes, to be bizarre and somewhat frightening; but my mother wore them with a panache that made me forget how weird it was to have a couple of dead animals looped around one's neck.

My mother went to the clubs with woman friends, and they all sat at a table near the stage and drank coffee while my father and his band performed. When the night was over, my parents walked home together, Ilya with one arm around Olga's waist, the other carrying his saxophone case.

As a teenager, I was free to go out at night and to go to the clubs if I so desired. One evening, shortly after I had turned fifteen, I went to the Café de la Paix with a group of friends. My father was onstage with his band when we crowded into the place. He was busy playing a bouncy tune on his saxophone, but our entrance did not escape his attention. What a look he gave me! There was surprise and concern in his face, but also a stern warning. The warning was intended for both myself and my companions—particularly the boys.

Although well aware of his gaze and the message it conveyed, I pretended not to notice him. My father didn't quit playing his saxophone, but his eyes followed us intently as we made our way across the room to a table, and he kept me under constant surveillance. When one of the boys in my group stood and invited me to dance, my father's brow wrinkled into a frown. And when I got up from my chair and allowed the boy to lead me by the hand out onto the dance floor—well, my father stared so hard at me that I thought his eyes might pop out of his head!

I knew what was going on in his mind. He was watching to make sure I didn't dance too close to my partner, that no hanky-panky was committed. I was mortified by his scrutiny. But I kept dancing, and my father kept playing the saxophone. We were two very stubborn people. Neither of us gave in easily to pressure.

This episode was fairly typical of my social life. I didn't have many dates with just one boy. None of my girlfriends did. We generally chummed around in groups, boys and girls together. However, any boy who wanted to keep sole company with me first had to pass muster with my father, who insisted that my companion be enrolled in school. And he insisted that when I became of marriageable age only college graduates or, better still, professional men would be allowed to pay court to me. Doctors and attorneys would make acceptable suitors, but not salesmen, artists, or, heaven forbid, musicians like my father. I was absolutely forbidden to even consider dating (much less marrying) such men, who were judged to be unreliable, feckless, and incapable of making a decent living during economic downturns.

On my evenings out, I was required to return home no later than eight o'clock. This was an inalterable law, and one that I thought to be unnecessarily strict. As I grew older I became more vocal about my lack of freedom, often protesting that I was a prisoner in my own apartment. My father turned a deaf ear to my complaints except to say that he would not even consider a later curfew. Though he was very stern with me during these exchanges, I sensed that he was really quite amused by my adolescent histrionics. A smile seemed to be playing about the corners of his mouth, which indicated that he was not taking me at all seriously. I realized that, in his eyes, I was just a silly teenager. His attitude was maddening, the more so because it obviously reflected the love and affection he felt for me. I did not want his love and affection just then, and I certainly did not want him to find me amusing. I wanted his respect; I wanted him to let me stay out late! But he remained unyielding on this score. And so, frustrated and angered by his obdurate stance, I would burst into tears and seek sympathy in the arms of my mother or grandmother.

"Why won't he let me stay out longer?" I would wail. "Why does he have to be so strict?"

"He's just trying to protect you," my mother would murmur soothingly.

"Protect me from what?" was my rejoinder. "What's everyone so afraid of?"

"Pretty girls have to be especially careful in this world," my mother replied.

"Men will want to take advantage of you," my grandmother would add.

Most of my schoolmates and friends were Polish Jews. Unlike my parents and their fellow Russian émigrés, the children of Russian and Polish Jews mixed easily and unself-consciously. My circle of friends also included a German Jewish girl and several Catholic girls, who were enrolled in my school. I spoke Polish in school and with my friends; however, I still considered myself a Russian since that was the language spoken at home.

On summer weekends and evenings when the weather was nice, we would all stroll up and down Akademicka Street, a wide thoroughfare bordered by tall trees and a number of pleasant sidewalk cafés. After promenading for a while, we might go dancing at a nightclub, or meet at a friend's house to talk and play games until it was time to go home. The relationship between the sexes was casual but chaste. Playing spin the bottle was our idea of racy entertainment. Even that innocent game was almost too racy for us.

You could say that I was a typical teenage girl, uncomplicated, self-involved (as are all teenagers), and happy. I lived totally in the present; I never thought about tomorrow. And I steered clear of any activity that smacked of serious purpose.

Fima was far different from me in this regard. The violent anti-Semitism he sometimes experienced in school had politicized him to the extent that he became an earnest and energetic convert to the Zionist cause. The unalterable hatred directed at him by a few of his Christian classmates had convinced him of the need for Jews to secure a homeland of their own in British-ruled Palestine. As this goal constituted the very heart and soul of Zionist philosophy, it was only natural that he would join, at age thirteen, the Zionist youth organization called Hanoar Hatzioni.

The organization was composed of Jewish boys and girls ranging in age from thirteen to eighteen. These were the children of assimilated Jewish parents; Orthodox Jewish teenagers had their own, separate, Zionist group. The basic purpose of Hanoar Hatzioni was to prepare young Jews for emigration to Palestine to achieve the Zionist goal of creating a Jewish homeland in the same region once dominated by the ancient kingdom of Israel. Zionist values and the ethos of Jewish settlers in Palestine were inculcated at weekly meetings, where members studied the Hebrew language and Jewish history, sang Palestinian songs, and danced the dances then in vogue among Jewish settlers in Palestine. The songs and dances were taught by an eighteen-year-old boy from Lvov who had lived on and gone to school at a Zionist settlement, then returned to Lvov to impart what he had learned from the experience to other teenagers.

My brother rose quickly in the ranks of the movement. When he was thirteen years old, he became a leader of his *kvutza,* or age group, which was known as the Wolves. As such, he wore a quasi-military uniform to his group meetings, thus anticipating a future in which the wearing of uniforms would figure prominently. At his invitation, I once attended a new members' meeting to see what Hanoar Hatzioni was all about. For the first hour or so of the meeting, we sang and danced the hora until we were too exhausted to put one foot in front of the other. This was followed by an induction ceremony for the new members. After that, and just before the meeting broke up, Fima paraded the Zionist flag and led us in the singing of the "Hatikvah," the Zionist anthem (later to become the national anthem of Israel). As we sang, Fima stood ramrod-straight and unmoving, holding the flagpole with both hands and gazing with distant solemnity at a point above and behind the assemblage. All eyes were on him, including my own. I was struck by how he handsome he looked in his uniform, how noble and proud it made *kvutza* leader Fima feel to be the standard-bearer of his people.

Fima had wanted to recruit me to Hanoar Hatzioni; that was why he had invited me to the meeting. But I disappointed him. I was in sympathy with his Zionist convictions, but not enough to become an activist. I attended one or two more meetings after that, and then I quit going. Political movements were just not my cup of tea. But to this day, any time I hear the "Hatikvah" played or sung, I picture Fima at that meeting, standing there so proudly with the staff bearing the Zionist flag grasped firmly in his hands.

Notwithstanding its nationalistic allure, Zionism did not enjoy widespread popularity among the Jews of Eastern

Europe. Most Jews who were inclined to emigrate chose America over Palestine as their destination of choice. My father was one such Jew. Although he approved of Fima's involvement in Hanoar Hatzioni, he had no real intention of ever moving the family to Palestine. America, the new Jewish Promised Land, was always his preferred goal.

I remember seeing a photograph of my father, taken in the late 1930s, posing with the five saxophones he had collected through the years—a bass sax, two baritones, a soprano, and an alto. They had all been purchased in America by Isadore with money my father had sent him for that purpose. The instruments were then shipped to our apartment, or my grandfather brought them home after one of his overseas business trips. In the photograph, the saxophones are arranged in a curve on the kitchen table, behind which stands my father, smiling at the camera with an expression of almost childlike delight. Those instruments were his pride and joy and, along with his expensive suit, one of the few extravagances he allowed himself. He derived much pleasure from them. I think they represented America to him: America, birthplace of jazz, land of vibrant music and people, a safe haven for the Jews of Europe—and, he fervently hoped, a future home for his family as well.

That picture was taken in the final days before the storm broke. In my father's smile, there is no hint of concern that another world war was in the offing, a war in which European Jews would be targeted for special treatment by the Germans. Yet concerned he most definitely was. Both my father and grandfather understood the situation well enough. They saw that Europe was hurtling toward the brink of an abyss, and that this rush to catastrophe was gaining momentum as the decade drew to a close. But their efforts to get the family out of Poland were frustrated by several factors, principally America's restrictive immigration policies, but also by money problems and the tangle of domestic and professional exigencies and simple day-to-day distractions that making a living and raising a family necessarily entail.

It is also possible that they misjudged the speed with which the situation in Europe was deteriorating. I cannot fault them for this. They were good men who loved their family and desired peace and bore no ill will toward anyone. Such men do not easily imagine war even when war is imminent. Perhaps if Lvov had been a bad place to live, they would have tried harder and done whatever was necessary to emigrate at an earlier date. Perhaps then they would have emigrated to the first country that would accept them rather than waiting for the United States to let them in. But life in Lvov was reasonably comfortable and this deceived them into thinking that time was on their side.

Ironically, my Aunt Esther was more fortunate in that she had stayed behind in Kamenets-Podolski, where conditions had worsened precipitously since the Communist takeover. In the aftermath of the Russian Civil War, Soviet rule in the Ukraine became increasingly harsh as the Moscow government sought to take control of the region's farms and agricultural output. The brutal measures employed to achieve this aim provoked much hostility among the Ukrainians, who were naturally unwilling to let the Communists expropriate their lands and livelihood. Their recalcitrance brought the wrath of Stalin down on their heads to the tune of ten million deaths in the late 1920s and early 1930s. But by then Esther and her family had escaped that country, immigrating not to the United States, but to Mexico.

They decided to leave the Ukraine in 1927 because, as Esther told me, "It was impossible to be in Russia. The Russians were bad. They were very mean. They tried to kill the Jewish people." They wanted to go to America, where her older brother, Jake Peltz, a naturalized American citizen, already lived. Esther wrote Jake a letter in which she asked him to send her at once the documents their mother and father needed to immigrate. This was done, and soon thereafter, Esther's parents embarked on the long journey to the United States. "I pushed them out of Kamenets," she recalled, indicating in that statement both her parents' reluctance to leave and her unswerving determination to make them go.

But Esther could not accompany them. Only the parents of American citizens were allowed to immigrate; siblings and other relatives were denied entrance visas. In desperation, Esther applied for, and received, permission to enter Mexico, which was more open to immigration. "So I took charge; I was the one to work on it," said Esther. "My brother-in-law, my sister's husband, and I, we handled the details of the journey. There were three families in all. My husband and I, and my two-year-old son, Aaron. And my sister, she had two babies, with her husband, Mo Schleimer. And then I had another brother, Chaim, and his wife and their child, Hanchela, a little girl. So my cousin and my brother-in-law and myself, we made out all the papers. We were supposed to leave on a Sunday. But that Thursday, my sister-in-law — Chaim's wife — came and cried that it's too far for her to go to Mexico. She didn't want to go. My poor brother had to stay in Russia with her and their child. But the rest of us left for Mexico."

They went to Mexico City, the home of a thriving Jewish émigré community complete with an Orthodox rabbi and a Jewish school noted for its academic excellence. Esther's husband, a former grammar school principal in Kamenets-Podolski, accepted a similar post at the school, which eventually boasted an enrollment of over four hundred students.

The amenities and consolations of a close-knit Jewish community were not, however, sufficient to make Esther feel any less a stranger in what seemed a very strange land. She was an Eastern European Jew in a nation populated largely by devout Catholics of mixed Indian and Hispanic blood, and she recognized that she would forever be an outsider among them. Thus, although she was thankful to Mexico for its tolerant policy toward Jews, she never really liked the country, nor did she intend her stay there to be anything other than temporary. She only wanted to join her parents and brother in America.

In 1930, she got in touch with her mother's cousin, who owned a farm in New Jersey. She prevailed upon this man to act as their American sponsor by putting herself and her husband to work on his farm. He filled out the requisite documents in which he stated that he would give them both jobs, then sent the paperwork to the American consul in Mexico City. Esther's husband received his papers, but no documents for Esther and their son ever arrived; somehow, they had gotten lost in transit. Consequently, the consul could not issue these two the visas they needed to immigrate.

They learned of their plight when they went to the consul's office to pick up the documents. Esther's husband gallantly refused to leave Mexico without his wife and child; Esther was adamant that he should go. Once in America, she told him, he would be better able to resolve this problem and obtain their visas. The consul concurred with this view. "In a couple of weeks you'll be settled," he said to her husband, "and then your wife and child can join you."

But it was not to be as easy as all that. Two years would pass before Esther and her son gained entry into the United States. She was reunited with her husband in New York City in 1932, at the height of the Depression. They lived in a tenement with Esther's parents and her older brother, who in the interim had been stricken with some sort of fatal and lingering disease. They were very poor. Esther's husband was their chief means of support, and as I mentioned earlier, he earned a mere seven dollars per week—a pathetically small amount even in those days. (Apparently, for unknown reasons, her mother's cousin had not given them a job on his farm.) "We had a very hard time," Esther recalled, "but we didn't give up. I worked and I did everything I could think of to keep our heads above water."

Three months after she arrived in New York City, Esther's father suggested that she approach another cousin, Morris, to ask him for a job. This was the same cousin whose journey to America had been financed by Moses Rosenwald, and who had subsequently made a killing in the garment industry. Perhaps Esther could persuade Morris to employ her in one of the three factories he owned, at a job sewing together the Persian lamb coats that had made him a rich man.

Esther, a proud and self-reliant young woman, was cool to

this idea. She was willing to take any job, no matter how demeaning the work might be; but she did not want to give Morris the satisfaction of coming to him with her hat in hand, as it were, like some beggar off the street. It would be just like Morris to send her packing with words of scorn and condescension. Her cousin's rise to wealth and prominence in the New York garment industry had caused him to become very much taken with himself, to the point where he no longer cared to associate with his poorer relations from Kamenets-Podolski. He was of a type that appeared in every immigrant community, the nouveau-riche businessman who believes that he is better than his fellow countrymen solely because he is better off. Blinded by this conceit, he could not see that he was nothing more than a parvenu who revealed his vulgarian tendencies in the contempt with which he regarded his family members and in his churlish reluctance to help them in any way.

It goes without saying that Morris was tightfisted about his money and could not easily be persuaded to disburse even the smallest sums to his impoverished kin. He had conveniently forgotten or chosen to forget that his present affluence and generally favorable circumstances had been made possible by the one hundred rubles that Moses had thrust on him back in Russia to start him on his way. Of course, Morris had never repaid his benefactor nor had he ever shown any inclination to help Moses in kind now that my grandfather was struggling to get by. Esther's husband instructed her to make an issue of this when she presented herself before Morris. "You tell Morris, if he isn't going to pay Moses back, the least he can do is give you a job."

And that is what Esther did. It was a nervy, not to mention insolent, tactic, but it worked. She must have caught Morris on a day when he felt guilty about his familial misanthropy and miserliness and was seeking to make amends for it; or, maybe he just needed another healthy body to operate a sewing machine in one of his factories. The important thing is, he put Esther on his payroll, and from then on life for her and her family improved at a slow but steady rate.

I met Esther's father and mother for the first time in 1948, when I came to New York City with my husband. They were living with Esther; both were in their nineties, and I remember that they spent most of their waking hours sitting at the kitchen table, praying and reciting psalms. Now and then they would stop to eat one or two bread rolls with a glass of warm milk, after which they would return to their prayers and their religious readings. They were a precious couple, the more so because they had escaped entirely the monstrous events in Europe. They had only the vaguest notion of what had happened to the European Jews, and I envied them their ignorance. They died old and in peace with their family around them, their faith intact, and their personal histories innocent of the Nazis' genocidal evil. I envied them for that, too.

Returning home from school one day in 1936, I flounced breezily into the kitchen only to be brought up short by the sight of my mother and grandmother weeping and moaning. Choking back a sob, my mother told me that her father had died several days ago in America. Notification of his death had arrived only that morning in the form of a telegram sent by Isadore. The telegram informed us that he had died of a heart attack, but there were no further details. A few weeks later, we received a letter from my uncle in which he told us that Moses had suddenly collapsed and died in a street in New York City while rushing from one business appointment to another.

At the time, Moses and Isadore jointly owned a small candy shop. It was not a successful enterprise. They worked many long hours at it and exhausted themselves in the effort, but even so managed to turn only the barest of profits. With the economy prostrate, the odds were stacked against them. Moses was sixty-five years old when he fell lifeless to the pavement of that New York street. The cause of death was officially listed as heart failure, but we all knew better: what had really killed him were the cumulative pressures and anxieties of trying to make enough money during the Depression to get his family out of Poland before the onset of war.

Isadore handled the funeral arrangements, which had long since been completed and carried out by the time his telegram reached us in Lvov. Moses Rosenwald's final resting place was a Jewish cemetery in Perth Amboy, New Jersey. He was an old man who should have spent his twilight years in the comfort of an easy chair bouncing grandchildren on his knee, but he had taken it upon himself to save his family instead. His exertions on his family's behalf had been unceasing and diligent and were thus entirely valiant. He had worked and worried himself into an early grave knowing that he had failed to accomplish his mission. I think this knowledge coupled with his presentiment of war and what it would entail for European Jews had killed him as surely as any rifle bullet or the inhalation of Zyklon-B fumes in the gas chambers of the Nazi death camps.

We were all saddened by my grandfather's death, none more so than Pesha, who now had to get used to the idea that she would never see her beloved husband again. Moses was dead and buried in a faraway land, and this was something that was very difficult for her to accept or even comprehend. He had been the dynamic center of her existence, and the abrupt and unanticipated manner by which he was removed from that position was a cruel blow from which she could not readily recover. His distant demise and quick interment had denied her the necessary catharsis and sense of closure a funeral normally provides. She could not stand over his casket to say good-bye to him, nor could she visit, or even visualize, his grave site—small but significant consolations that might have comforted her immeasurably in her hour of grief. And yet, she endured. After her initial tears, she inwardly mourned his passing for many weeks with a sorrowing but stoic dignity that was quite in keeping with her character. She had reserves of emotional strength, not the least of which were invested in her family, that would enable her to survive the loss, even though she would never quite get over it.

I, too, was upset about my grandfather's death, but I was even more disturbed by my mother's immediate reaction to it. To find her sobbing in the kitchen . . . this had rocked the foundations of my very sheltered universe. For once, my mother was thinking only of herself; for once, her husband and children were not paramount in her thoughts. I saw her then as the daughter she had been to Moses, as a little girl who loved and missed her father. It was a profoundly dislocating experience, one that made me feel as if the end of the world had come.

It wasn't the end of the world, but it was the beginning of the end—and my father clearly perceived this. In his own thoughtful way, he was deeply distressed by my grandfather's death. He knew that Moses was the only family member who could obtain the documents we needed to immigrate to America. The lengthy immigration process required its participants to satisfy various regulations (chiefly those involving quota restrictions) before the documents granting entry into the United States could be issued. From the standpoint of the government, this was an undertaking for which Moses alone, as the head of the family, was legally qualified. But Moses was dead; so, too, were my father's hopes and aspirations for making a new life for our family in America.

Now my father began to cast about for another escape route. For the first time, he seriously considered the possibility of immigrating to Palestine. In 1937 and 1938, he explored the Palestine option through a series of letters he wrote to friends and relatives—cousins, mostly—who lived in that region. He wanted to get us out of Europe as soon as possible, and he felt that permission to immigrate to America would come too late to save his family from what he knew was coming.

In his letters he queried his friends and relatives about the quality and character of life in Palestine, and asked for their help in securing permission to immigrate from the British government (which then ruled Palestine under a League of Nations mandate). They advised my father that, at present, Palestine was a dangerous and difficult place to live, so he and his family would be far better off staying in Lvov.

Discouraged by their replies, my father decided against Palestine. Fima and I knew nothing of his decision. My father had kept us ignorant of the whole affair. I believe his secretiveness stemmed from a desire to spare us any trauma connected with leaving (or not leaving) Lvov, and because the idea of immigrating to Palestine never really appealed to him. I only found out about his abortive scheme after the war. My informant was Fima, who learned about it from one of my father's prewar correspondents, Mr. Lemberg. Both Fima and I were astonished by this information: we had always thought that our father was dead set on going to America and nowhere else.

So, our family was stuck in Lvov, at least for the time being. Our lives went on uneventfully, and from my standpoint everything seemed just fine. My father's musical career—and our family's financial well-being—improved markedly when he was elected president of the Lvov chapter of the musicians' union. One of my father's duties as president was to apportion jobs to union members and thereby keep Lvov's nightclubs supplied with musicians and bands. When a nightclub manager wanted to hire a jazz combo, or when a musician was looking for work, they came to my father, and he saw to it that their needs were met. Naturally, he saw to it that his own needs were met as well. As head of the union, he made sure that he was employed on a regular basis, allocating plum jobs at Lvov's ritziest clubs to his own band.

Not that he was getting rich. Even steadily employed musicians like my father earned yearly incomes that placed them securely—and, it seemed, inextricably—in the lower middle class. We were always struggling to get by. And whatever extra money my father managed to save after the bills were paid, he put toward schooling for Fima and me. He was determined to send us to college or trade school, even if that meant spending every last zloty he earned. Our continued education was his top priority, even more important to him than our family's immigration to America. I had long aspired to be a fashion designer and was constantly inventing and drawing up women's outfits that would, I hoped, one day be acclaimed as the epitome of haute couture on the runways of

Paris. My father encouraged me in this pursuit; my goal was his goal as well, he told me, and he vowed that he would do everything within his power to help me achieve it. Thus, in my final year of high school (we called it a lyceum), he promised to finance my professional studies at a design school in the French capital, which was also the fashion capital of the world.

I was elated by his promise, for I knew that he would make good on it—my father's word was gold. It confirmed beyond the shadow of a doubt what I already knew: that he believed in me and had respect for my talents and abilities. Knowing this gave me confidence in myself and reinforced a growing conviction that my ambitions, whatever they might be and however far-fetched, were fully attainable.

With regard to career aspirations, my father had made similar assurances to Fima. But my brother, who wanted to study architecture at a public academy in Lvov, was denied entry to that institution because he was a Jew. Instead, he applied to a private trade school in the town of Jaroslav, located some forty miles west of Lvov, that offered an extensive course of study in house and building construction. The school accepted him, and as the summer of 1939 drew to a close, he was eagerly anticipating the start of the fall semester and all the attendant joys of living away from home for the first time in his life.

As for other members of our family—well, life went on for them, too. In Warsaw, Aunt Nadia had divorced her husband and gotten remarried to a man named Broder. I recall that the family was mildly scandalized by her divorce, a rare occurrence in 1930s Poland, and therefore not to be treated lightly as it is today. It was particularly difficult for the women involved, who were henceforth regarded as "damaged goods" by the community bluenoses. But being concerned for Nadia's welfare and desiring nothing more than her happiness, we were glad when she married Broder, who seemed a decent sort.

Nadia wasn't the only one of my aunts who was unlucky at love. In 1938, Haika was dating Mr. Zuckerman, a civil engineer from Vilnius. This Zuckerman (I forget his first name) was not only well educated, smart, and successful, he was also quite handsome; and, being several years older than Haika, he possessed an air of maturity and charm that further enhanced his attractiveness in Haika's adoring eyes. But Zuckerman, who often professed to be equally fond of Haika, nevertheless proved a laggardly swain who was in no great hurry to stand beneath the wedding canopy. His courtship of Haika dragged on and on, which of course only made Haika crazier for him. Thus, when he finally proposed to her, she said yes with no hesitation whatsoever.

Plans for the nuptials soon proceeded apace, with Pesha using the money Moses had bequeathed to her in his will to purchase an expensive trousseau that included a new bed, linens, curtains, and handmade lace pillowcases. These things made me green with envy for Haika, and also curious—or should I say excited?—about what marriage truly entailed. In the weeks prior to the wedding I was a frequent visitor to Haika's room, where the two of us subjected her dowry to close scrutiny, which was accomplished amid a good deal of embarrassed giggling as we contemplated her new bed and what she and husband would do with it.

My grandmother was pleased with the match and felt that Moses would have approved of Zuckerman and given the bride and groom his unconditional blessing. She was also relieved that Haika, her youngest child, had found a husband who would provide for her after she, Pesha, was gone. This had been Pesha's chief concern in the aftermath of Moses's death. Unfortunately, it was to remain her concern for several years to come. A few days before the wedding, Zuckerman disappeared from Lvov. He left suddenly, without a word of farewell to Haika. Two or three weeks later, we learned from mutual friends that he had gotten cold feet about getting married and had gone back to Vilnius.

Of course, Haika was heartbroken. Several friends and family members advised her to get on a train to Vilnius and find the reluctant groom. Perhaps, they said, he could be persuaded to go through with the wedding. To Haika's everlasting credit, she dismissed this advice out of hand. She had a job in Lvov and she had her pride, and she wanted to keep them both, even if that meant giving up on Zuckerman.

Our family subsequently hushed up Haika's matrimonial debacle, and to spare her feelings any further hurt, Zuckerman became a nonperson, never again to be mentioned within the confines of our two apartments. Later, during the war, Haika fell in love with and married another man in Lvov. For a short time, then, she experienced a modicum of happiness with a man of her choosing—until the Germans killed both of them.

Fima graduated from high school in June 1939. His commencement ceremony featured an address by the school principal. "This is the last time we will see each other together," the principal told the assembled students. "You will receive your diploma, and then you will begin to make your way in life. You may go far away, to another country, you may go to war—who knows? The important thing to remember is, from now on you will be an adult. And, as an adult, you will be the master of your destiny. And nobody else but you can say what your destiny will be."

Fima had told me that it was all he could do to keep from laughing at the man; his speech was the most ridiculous thing Fima had ever heard. "You idiot," he had thought, "what's all this talk about going places? I'm going to stay in Poland for the rest of my life."

Some three months later, in the final week of August, my friends and I were sitting around a table at the Café de la Paix, discussing the latest developments on the international scene. On August 23, Germany and the Soviet Union had announced the signing of a nonaggression pact, after which Hitler had made ominous gestures toward Poland. The Führer was threatening military action if Poland did not recognize Germany's claim to the city of Danzig and the narrow corridor of Polish territory dividing East Prussia from Germany proper. He had repeatedly asserted that the area in dispute belonged to Germany and that Poland must immediately renounce sovereignty over it if war was to be avoided. Of course, war could not be avoided even if Poland acceded to his demands, because his real intent, in addition to regaining Danzig and the corridor, was to accomplish the destruction of the Polish state. But no one outside Germany realized this, or would admit to it if they did, preferring to believe that a peaceful resolution to the dispute was still attainable. A flurry of diplomatic activity had failed to defuse the crisis, and Lvov was all abuzz with rumors of German troop movements on the Polish frontier and talk of mobilizing the Polish army.

With peace slipping away by the hour, we sat around that table, my friends and I, and tried to imagine what the pending war would be like and how it would affect us. Because we hadn't the faintest idea of the nature of war, our conjectures were naive, foolish, and profoundly superficial. I remember one girl saying, "You know, during a war there is never enough to eat. Food is scarce. If we go to war, I bet we won't even have salt to put on our eggs."

Her words greatly troubled me. Visions of tasteless omelets floated into my thoughts. How, I wondered, can you eat eggs without salt? I told myself that this was impossible, that saltless eggs were inedible.

And so, on the eve of World War II, what I feared most about the future was the negative impact that war would have on my breakfasts.

❊

War

The war began for me, as for the rest of Poland, early in the morning on Friday, September 1, 1939. My brother and I were asleep in our beds, beside the tile oven in the living room, when antiaircraft artillery and machine guns positioned somewhere nearby opened fire. Awakened by the racket, my brother and I sat up and looked at each other. The time was about 7:00 A.M. Just then, my mother came out of her bedroom to get me up for school.

She hadn't come for Fima, however. My brother should have been in Jaroslav getting ready to attend technical school, which would be starting its autumn semester the following Monday. But our father, who had been following the escalating crisis between Poland and Germany with growing unease, had insisted that Fima stay in Lvov because he did not want his son to be separated from the family if and when the Germans invaded. So Fima could have slept late had events not conspired to rouse him from his slumber.

Curiously, and despite all the saber rattling of the past week, neither my brother nor I thought the gunfire signaled the outbreak of hostilities. We simply did not know what to make of it.

"What's happening?" I asked my mother.

"Oh, that's just the troops over at the citadel," my mother replied in casual tone. "They're on maneuvers, I suppose—just practicing."

The records show that the first German bombers did not appear over Lvov until about 9:00. It is conceivable, however, that the Polish gun crews had spotted and fired on a German reconnaissance plane that had overflown the city in advance of the bombers. Or perhaps they were jittery and had mistaken a flock of birds for the anticipated German aircraft, or had seen in the clouds phantom planes conjured up by their own anxieties. In any case, I clearly remember that the shooting, if not the bombing, started while I was still in bed.

The soldiers at the citadel must have been very nervous, since by then they would have been told by their officers that German army units had crossed the frontier in force sometime around dawn. But we didn't know this and were therefore unconcerned about the gunfire. My mother's explanation was the logical one, and I didn't give the matter any further thought. After all, I had more important things on my mind—such as the clothes I would wear to school that day.

A few minutes later, while I was getting dressed, my father came into the living room and turned on the radio, tuning it to a news broadcast, which announced that Poland had been invaded by the Germans. My father frowned and shook his head. "That's it," he muttered. "Now we're at war."

The first German bombers appeared in the clear blue sky above Lvov a few hours later. We were not warned of their approach—no sirens blared, no church bells rang, no announcements were made on the radio. (Ironically, the radio had been playing military marches and other martial music, a ploy by the government to prepare us psychologically for the rigors of war.) All of a sudden, they were directly overhead, their motors thrumming like a swarm of angry bees. In the next instant, I heard the whistle of falling bombs, then a chain of explosions somewhere on the other side of the city. A few seconds later, the Polish troops at the citadel began banging away at the attacking planes with every weapon at their disposal.

At the sound of the detonations, my father, Fima, and I made a dash for the balcony. That lofty perch was situated three stories above the courtyard at the rear of the building, and it afforded a panoramic view of the city. Grasping the balcony's iron filigree railing with one hand, shielding our eyes with the other, we gazed at the part of the city that was under attack. The target area, which was several miles from our building, was already in flames and marked by billowing clouds of black smoke.

My father scanned the sky above the smoke clouds. "There they are!" he shouted, pointing in that direction. "I see them!" I saw them too, dozens of black cruciform shapes cruising many thousands of feet over Lvov in a perfect V-formation, like a flock of geese. They were twin-engine aircraft, and they looked very small because they were high and far away. I do not recall seeing any Stukas, the soon-to-be notorious dive-bombers with the gull wings and fixed landing gear. The planes flew straight and level, droning across the city with an unhurried and haughty indifference to the hostile fire from the citadel. Clearly, they were well out of range of the Polish ack-ack guns, as evidenced by the dirty puffs of shell bursts that blossomed ineffectually in the empty sky beneath them.

The bombers appeared to be moving in slow motion, almost on the verge of stalling—an optical illusion enhanced by the precision and unwavering adherence to formation with which they executed their attack. As I watched the planes, the bombs came tumbling from their belly bays and wings, then plummeted shrieking to the earth, where they burst with a flash that was followed a second later by a resonant thud—ka-boom!—that made the balcony shake. Each blast threw up chunks of concrete and masonry, red roofing tiles, slabs of street and sidewalk pavement, and other assorted debris. There were many bombs detonating in rapid succession, like a string of firecrackers, and the sudden brilliant light of their multiple booming explosions made me think of hundreds of camera flashbulbs popping off.

During the raid the balcony trembled without letup, but my father stayed put because he was fascinated by the Luftwaffe's aerial onslaught. Also, I think he wanted to see whether the planes would turn our way and attack our neighborhood. He kept pointing at the sky, saying things like, "Look where the planes are going," or, "There they are," and "Here come some more." He did not order us off the balcony. He permitted us to watch the raid, probably because he was so absorbed in the goings-on that it did not occur to him that we should seek shelter.

Overall, the air raid had been a frightening experience, but also, I must admit, quite thrilling as well. It had been foolish of us to watch the raid from the balcony, where we could easily have been killed by a direct hit or even a near miss from a bomb, or mowed down by strafing aircraft, or mortally wounded by spent bullets and antiaircraft shell fragments. But we were ignorant of these dangers because we were new to war and because the government had neglected to tell us what to do or expect in the event of a German attack.

At last, the planes had disgorged all their bombs, whereupon they turned in unison and headed west to their bases in Germany. We went back into the living room and peered out of the window that overlooked the street in front of our building. On the street and its adjacent sidewalks, hundreds of people were running this way and that in confusion and panic, their faces twisted with fear. Women were screaming and men were yelling while cars and trucks sped by, horns blaring and tires screeching as they swerved and braked frantically to avoid hitting anyone. It was if the entire population of Lvov had gone stark raving mad.

One of our neighbors, an elderly woman, had certainly come unhinged. Leaving her apartment, she staggered outside and began walking around aimlessly below our window, wringing her hands and moaning, "What will we do now, what will we do?" She was so distraught that I thought she might be in real physical pain, and her skin had a ghastly pallor, as if the blood had been drained from her body.

Someone began pounding on our door. Then we heard Petia bellowing, "It's war! It's war! Let me in, we're at war!"

My father, smiling faintly, opened the door. Petia, wearing his inevitable rumpled blue suit and a ferocious frown, barged in without a word of greeting. Even now, in the aftermath of a German air raid, I found him an altogether ludicrous figure, one who somehow reminded me of a cartoon character. This morning he was more agitated than usual, more manic, as tense as a coiled spring. But there was also something of an "I-told-you-so" smugness to his demeanor. The war that he had long predicted was now upon us, and he took a kind of grim satisfaction in having been confirmed in his self-appointed role as a prophet of doom. He knew that his friends regarded him as a buffoon, but with the advent of war, he felt vindicated as a sage and serious man whose prognostications were to be heeded.

My father invited Petia to sit at the kitchen table. Soon the two men were engaged in an intense conversation about the air raid and the German invasion. In the next hour, several more neighbors dropped by to discuss the war. Our apartment was filled with people who, like Petia, were very tense and worried. They all wanted to find out what was happening, but their only reliable source of news—the radio—was of no help to them. Around midmorning—ten o'clock, I believe it was—President Ignacy Mościcki addressed the populace, acknowledging what his fellow citizens already knew: that Germany had attacked Poland and that a state of war existed between the two nations. But he said nothing about the battles that were no doubt being fought on the frontier even as he spoke.

Unlike the adults, I was not alarmed by the onset of war. On the contrary, I found it rather exciting. Better still, it gave me an excuse to cut school. This was my parents' idea. "We want you to stay home today," they said, and who was I to argue? I was to have an impromptu holiday, and I had the war to thank for it!

It was also a holiday of sorts for my parents and their friends, who did not go to work, but instead stayed at our apartment, talking and listening to the radio. They were not sure that this was the right thing to do, and they debated the matter endlessly, trying to decide whether it would be better and more patriotic of them to report to their jobs or stay at home and thereby keep the streets clear for use by the Polish army. They got no help or advice from the government or any of the local authorities. Nobody came on the radio to tell us what to do; evidently no civil defense plans had been drawn up, or if such plans did exist, they were neither implemented nor communicated to the populace.

We later found out that some of the German aircraft in that

first raid had dropped their bombs in the neighborhood of Krotka and Grodecka Streets, killing dozens of civilians—including women and children—and blowing up a number of houses. So the Germans had not restricted their attacks to military installations, but had also gone after the city's residential quarter and the people who lived there. This was terror bombing pure and simple, and it had been quite methodical and deliberate; there was nothing accidental about the way the enemy planes had worked over their targets.

The German bombers returned at midday and at least two more times during the afternoon. I cannot be certain about the exact number of raids that day, but I do remember that the enemy squadrons attacked the city repeatedly and with what seemed a great many planes in each raid. In the second raid and in all subsequent attacks, the planes flew much lower, often zooming down at rooftop level to drop their bombs and to spray the streets with machine-gun bullets. As before, there were two-engine bombers, but these were joined by those awful bent-wing Stukas, which plummeted down on the city in nearly vertical power dives with their sirens screaming. The Stukas had been equipped with fire-engine sirens to make their attacks all the more fearsome, and the sound they made as they swooped down was terrifying. They fell upon us shrieking like savage birds of prey, an impression enhanced by their fixed landing gear, which reminded me of the outstretched talons of an eagle.

Fima vividly remembers the Stukas. He once told me that he has a mental picture of walking on a sidewalk with my father when the Stukas came. He recalls that the attack occurred around noon, which would make it the second air raid, and he thinks that he and Father were on their way home from some errand, possibly to purchase groceries. Of course, the attack came without warning; once again, no sirens heralded the enemy's approach. One moment, all was quiet; the next, the air was filled with the crescendoing drone of diving Stukas, the shriek of their sirens, the earsplitting blast of exploding bombs.

For a few seconds, my brother and father did not move, but

stood as if rooted to the sidewalk, gazing up at the German planes, rather like deer crossing a highway who freeze at the center stripe and stare glassy-eyed into the headlights of an oncoming automobile. They were momentarily paralyzed, not with fright, but with astonishment and no little fascination at the violence that had descended on them. The novelty of the first air raid had not worn off, and there was something strangely captivating about the noise and tumult of this attack. They were still so new to all this and were thus susceptible to the dire enchantments of modern war, to the machinery and the pyrotechnics and the din.

But not for long. In the next instant, they came to their senses. "Run!" yelled my father, and run they most certainly did, joining countless other Lvovians who had also been caught in the open when the raid began. Fima recalls that people were stampeding blindly in every direction, shouting a one-word refrain: "War! War! War!" He and Father took cover in the doorway of an apartment building, crouching low and pressing hard against the closed door with their arms thrown over their heads to shield themselves from bomb blasts and lethal gusts of shrapnel and debris. The bombs were exploding all around them, causing the ground to heave beneath their feet, and Fima was thinking that his death was at hand when the planes departed as suddenly as they had appeared.

When the planes were gone, they emerged from the doorway and made their way home through streets that were choked with the rubble of blown-up buildings and pitted with bomb craters. Everywhere Fima looked he saw the mangled corpses of children and adults strewn about like broken dolls in pools of bright red blood. Several blocks from our apartment, they encountered a cavalry squadron with horse-drawn artillery clattering through the shattered streets. With regimental guidons snapping on their lances and sabers hanging from their saddles, these mounted troops provided a piquant and anachronistic counterpoint to the technological prowess embodied in the aircraft of the German Luftwaffe; and the irony inherent in that scene was not lost on my father. They were a noble and stirring sight, to be sure, but also a pathetic one to a realist like my father, who understood well that horse cavalry would not stand a chance against an enemy equipped with machines like the Stuka. According to Fima, my father watched with a sad smile as the Polish cavalrymen galloped past, then shook his head and said, "The Germans have so many airplanes, so many bombs. This war cannot last very long."

The German aircraft had dropped incendiary bombs as well as high-explosive bombs, and the fires they started burned all night and into the next day. Destroyed or damaged in the raids of September 1 were rows of houses and apartment buildings on Peiracki Square, Toakrzewski Street, Rue du Marechal Foch, Zimorowicz Street, and Krtoka Street. A hospital had been hit by a bomb and dozens of patients killed and wounded. In all, it was said that several hundred casualties had been inflicted in the raids.

At night the fires from the burning buildings lit the sky with an eerie crimson glow and filled the air with eye-stinging smoke and the coarse reek of incinerated wood, fabric, and flesh. I did not know it at the time, but have since learned, that in some quarters there was no water with which to douse the fires, as many of the water mains had burst during the raids. I also learned that the city's electric power station was hit and a number of gas lines were ruptured, with the result that several neighborhoods had no electricity or gas for their stoves and hot water heaters.[*] Fortunately, our building was not hit in these early raids, and no bombs fell anywhere near it.

After that first day of war, I remember above all else that everything was in chaos, that the city services were in disarray, that people were terribly frightened and confused. Nobody was ready for the war, and people did not know what was expected of them and what they were supposed to do during

---

[*]My source for all this is Stefan Szende's *The Promise Hitler Kept* (New York: Roy Publishers, 1945), 9–16. The author, a Jew, lived in Lvov from 1939 to 1943, when he escaped to Sweden and wrote his memoir.

an air raid. But they quickly acquired such knowledge if they hoped to stay alive.

Their education was provided courtesy of the Luftwaffe, which gave us a crash course in war by attacking us every day, several times a day. By the end of the second day of the conflict, my family members and I were seasoned veterans of this brand of warfare and fairly adept at the procedures one employed to survive it. We had shed our naïveté and with it much of the fascination that had previously characterized our reaction to the raids. No longer did we stand on our balcony gawking at the German planes as they dropped their bombs and strafed our city. Instead, we sought shelter in the cellar of our building at the first indication that a raid was in progress.

The virtual nonexistence of an organized civil defense network guaranteed that there was rarely any warning of an impending raid. The German bombers announced their arrival with the drone of their engines and the sound of exploding bombs. The instant we heard the planes, everyone would start running around and shouting all at once, "Go to the shelter, go to the shelter!" And we would scramble down the stairs to the cellar, almost tripping and falling over each other in our haste to get there before a bomb landed on the building and killed us all.

The cellar was a dank, dark space with bare brick walls and a low ceiling that forced the taller men to stoop while they were standing. What little light there was in the place came from outside through tiny windows set near the ceiling at ground level (Either the cellar wasn't wired for electricity, or the electrical outlets were broken.) The floor was supposedly made of concrete, but we couldn't be certain of this because it was covered with a thick layer of dirt. The cellar wasn't designed to protect us from bombs, and a direct hit on our building would no doubt have collapsed the structure on our heads and buried us alive. But we had nowhere else to go and it was better than no shelter at all.

Typically, as many as thirty people representing five families were crowded into the cellar during a raid. As the cellar was not roomy enough to accommodate so many people in any sort of comfort, we found ourselves standing or sitting lit-erally cheek by jowl with each other. In these circumstances of forced intimacy, the atmosphere in the cellar quickly be-came oppressively hot and humid from the presence of so many bodies in such close confinement. The stagnant air was also fouled by bad breath and the pungent stench of body odor produced by the potent chemistry of sweat and fear.

People rarely spoke with one another while the raids were under way. In particular, the adults were too upset to engage in idle chatter, much less purposeful conversation. Instead, we stared at the floor or gazed vacantly at the walls and tried not to think about what was happening. It was most desirable to become lost in thought, or better still to simply blank out your mind and have no thoughts at all. But this was difficult, if not downright impossible, because the ambient sounds of the raid, although muffled by the walls of the building, were distinctly audible in the cellar. Like it or not, we couldn't help but hear those sounds: the droning planes, whistling bombs, explosions, the ponderous rhythmic pounding of ack-ack guns, and the staccato rattle of machine guns.

With each bomb explosion, the ground quaked, the build-ing above us shook, and bits of dirt and plaster sprinkled down on us from the ceiling. Sometimes we looked up at the ceiling and tried to determine whether the whistling bombs were going to hit us. We strained our ears to follow the bombs in their downward flight, tracking their descent with mount-ing anxiety, our muscles tensed for the inevitable impact. In our thoughts we tried to deflect each bomb from its path, silently telling the bombs to go away, as if we could use the power of our minds to stop them.

The old people among us—men and women in their fifties, sixties, and up—were especially devastated by the onset of war. During a raid, they would often become extremely dis-traught and begin weeping, wringing their hands, and moan-ing, just like the neighbor lady outside our window on the war's first day. My grandmother was more stoic than most. Instead of raising a fuss, she would pray silently and fervently, with her eyes shut tight and her lips moving as she pleaded for our deliverance. Her absolute conviction in the efficacy of prayer and her steadfast faith in God's mercy were very impressive, and I thought that because she was so devout her prayers would surely be answered.

Each raid seemed to last hours, although it probably went on for no more than twenty or thirty minutes at most. No "all-clear" siren signaled the end of a raid; we knew the Germans had finished bombing the city only when the explosions had stopped, the antiaircraft guns went silent, and the sound of the droning planes had faded into the distance. Even then, we would stay in the cellar for a few minutes just to make sure that the raid was really over. If the world outside remained quiet, we would go to our apartments to inspect the damage, if any, to our homes and await the next raid.

Waiting for the German planes to return was a nerve-racking experience, almost as hard to endure as the raids themselves. Adding to our worries were the food shortages that occurred almost immediately upon the outbreak of war. In the first two or three days of the war, the women of Lvov had made a run on all the food shops, clearing the shelves and market stalls of all edible goods. The depleted stocks could not be adequately replenished in the days and weeks that followed due to the fact that only small quantities of food— meat, grain, vegetables, milk—were getting through to the city. The fighting in the west and the resultant congestion on the roads (which were jammed with refugees fleeing the advancing Germans), combined with Luftwaffe attacks on railroads and road junctions, had effectively interdicted the transport of foodstuffs from the farms in the countryside to the urban areas. As a result, the people of Lvov, as well the other big Polish cities, were forced to go out on a daily hunt for scarce provisions. After every raid, the streets would be filled with people running to the nearest shops and markets to purchase whatever food they might find and then hasten back to their homes before the next attack.

These scrounging expeditions yielded progressively fewer acquisitions. After the fourth or fifth day of war, most of the food shops had closed. The lack of food soon preyed upon our minds, even at the height of the air raids. Hunkered down in our cellar, with bombs overhead exploding one after the other, all we could think about was where and how we would get enough to eat. As far as I was concerned, the food situation was the most bothersome aspect of the war—and never mind the bombs that were killing people by the scores and reducing Lvov to a smoking ruin!

So this was how we spent the next few days: dashing down the stairs to our cellar to wait out the air raids, listening for the next raid to come; searching for food. After about a week of this, my father began going to work again, and Rysia and I began going to school. Life, after all, had to go on: my father had to make a living, and my sister and I had to get an education. Fima, however, was at loose ends; his education was put on indefinite hold when, in the war's second week, the Germans captured Jaroslav. So he made himself useful around the apartment by helping my mother and father.

We all went about our business as best we could. My father played with his band in the cafés and nightclubs, and he administered the affairs of the musicians' union. His principal activity was finding jobs for the many musicians who were out of work because the cafés where they were employed had been demolished in an air raid. Some of these musicians tried to get special consideration by offering bribes of money or food, but my father always refused these inducements. He was a decent and honest man who was simply incapable of using the circumstances of war to take advantage of people. He figured that the war had unleashed enough evil on the world without his adding to it by accepting payoffs. I was more pragmatic. When he told us that he had turned down money from an unemployed musician, I would think, Why doesn't he just take it?

Coming home from school could be something of an ordeal. German planes usually attacked the city in the afternoon, right about when school let out, and it seemed that I was always getting caught out on the street in the raids. When that happened, I would run from door to door, pressing my face against the doors as the bombs whistled down and exploded around me. During one raid, I ran home only to find the front door of the apartment building locked. I pounded furiously on the door and cried out for someone to let me in as the ground was heaving beneath my feet and I was being buffeted by shock waves from nearby bomb blasts. "Help me!" I shouted above the noise. "Please, someone, help me!" Suddenly, I heard someone fumbling with the lock, and the handle turned and the door swung open. My father was standing in the foyer.

"My God, you're here!" he exclaimed. "I'm so glad!" Then he grabbed me by the hand and more or less dragged me down to the cellar.

Later, it occurred to me that my father had been the only person in the cellar to brave the exploding bombs when he realized that someone—not necessarily his daughter—was trying to get into the building. His courage at such moments was typical—and something I always took for granted.

At school, the teachers and students had to contend with the daily air raids just like everyone else. The school had its own shelter, and it was much better constructed than our cellar at home: it was clean, with exposed concrete floors like a finished basement. Because my fellow students and I were young, we adapted readily to the routine of class work interrupted by air raids; we thought it was no big deal to run to the shelter, then return to our classrooms and resume our studies as if this were the most normal way to live.

While we were in the school shelter, we talked about the war, wondering what would happen, when it would end, and when the food supplies would return to their former abundant state. Despite all that had happened thus far, we were not overly concerned about the war. I just couldn't get too worked up about it. Although I was annoyed by the food shortages and frightened by the air raids, I still felt very secure. I knew that my parents would take care of me. Whatever happened, I knew that I would be with them, and that they would see to it that I was safe and that everything turned out all right. I believed in them, and I never doubted that they were capable of protecting me from harm and evil.

The adults, including my parents, were not nearly so san-
guine about our prospects. They understood that their world
was coming to an end and that soon their lives would be radi-
cally changed, probably for the worse. In the shelter, they
passed the time by speculating on what the future would
bring. The uncertainty of what lay ahead of them was maddening and made them anxious and despondent. "What's
going to happen to us?" they would say, and, "How come the
Americans don't help us?" They wanted the Americans to
intervene in this war just as they had in the First World War.
The failure of the Americans to get involved perplexed and
frustrated them. How could the United States stand aside and
allow the Germans to conquer Poland? And where were the
French and British, Poland's nominal allies, who had so far
taken no offensive action against the Germans? These were
just some of the questions the adults asked as German planes
pulverized the city.

Children and teenagers like myself adjusted more readily to
the hardships of war because we were too young, ignorant,
and inexperienced to really understand what was going on or
to guess at what might lie ahead of us. After a while, for me,
the war became more an exercise in boredom and discomfort
than danger and death. I hated being cooped up in our
cramped foul-smelling cellar, where there was nothing to do
except sit around and listen to the adults moan and kvetch. It
almost made me want to go outside where the bombs were
falling. I was scared of the bombs, but I did not think that I
would be killed because I was seventeen years old and felt
immortal. No one at that age really believes that he or she will
die. And since I did not think I would die, I could not see the
war for what it was and what it might do to me. I viewed the
war as a movie melodrama that would surely turn out all right
in the end.

There were moments of levity, even during the most violent
raids. As always, the source of our humor was Petia. The poor
man did not bear up well under the bombing. To his credit, he
made no pretense of courage nor did he try to conceal his
cowardice from the rest of us. At the drone of approaching
aircraft, he would come completely unglued and run down

the stairs to the cellar, waving his arms over his head and shouting unintelligibly, bowling over anyone, including women and children, who got in his way. This was something new for me: I had never seen an adult behave so badly. If my parents had acted thus, I would have been profoundly shaken, but this was Petia, and the sight of him going all to pieces with such clownish flair was not only entirely in keeping with his character but also quite comical.

His cowardice was like a goad to the kids in the building, and we teased him mercilessly for it. The object was to work him into a thoroughly craven state, and we usually succeeded. At the start of a raid, we would yell, "Petia, the bombs are falling, the bombs are falling right on top of us!" Petia would bray like an anguished donkey and pull his soiled suit jacket over his head, as if the fabric could shield him. We would then laugh so hard that our knees went weak and it was all we could do to make it to the cellar without collapsing in a heap.

The raids were also the cause of an incident that struck me as merely odd at the time but in retrospect seems funny. The incident involved the owner of the building, a German Jew in his mid-seventies who had lost the use of his legs as a result of some unexplained accident or illness. He had been confined to a wheelchair ever since we had known him, and he lived in an apartment on the second floor with his daughter, her husband, and their little girl. My family's relations with the man were decidedly cool. Like many German Jews, he was a snob who considered himself superior to Russian Jews. Naturally, my parents resented him. They were civil to the man and he was polite to them, but always there was an undercurrent of restrained enmity in their encounters. Everyone who lived in the building catered to his every whim, primarily because he was our landlord, but also because he was handicapped and we felt obligated to help the man even though we disliked him.

I don't know how the owner managed to get himself to the cellar during the first few air raids. Perhaps his daughter and son-in-law, aided by one or more of his tenants, lifted him up, wheelchair and all, and carried him down to the cellar. But one day when the German planes came, he did something quite extraordinary. He was sitting in the hallway at the top of the cellar stairs when the bombs began exploding a few blocks away. As it happened, there was nobody around to carry him to the cellar, so he stood up from his wheelchair and ran down the stairs with all the agility of an Olympic sprinter.

How we all stared at him when he joined us in the cellar! We were flabbergasted! We didn't know what to say; we didn't know whether to laugh or congratulate him for having regained the use of his legs. We wondered whether he had been faking paralysis all this time, and if so, to what end. Perhaps he had suffered from some sort of hysterical paralysis, which made him think his legs were dysfunctional, and the air raid had provided a form of shock therapy that cured him of his psychological problems. Nobody said anything to him; whatever comments or questions were forming on our lips remained unsaid, cut off by the defiant, challenging way he glared at back us. It was if he were daring us to say something about his former handicap and his "miraculous" recovery. Nobody was willing to take him up on that dare because he had the power to evict us. So we kept our mouths shut and stared at him while he glared at us.

The term *blitzkrieg* (lightning war) is always used to describe the Polish campaign, and rightly so. The Germans moved with amazing speed to destroy the Polish forces opposing them. Even so, it wasn't until the first week of October that the fighting altogether ceased. In Lvov, the war lasted a mere seventeen days, yet this seemed a very long time to me. The interminable nature of those seventeen days was attributable to the countless air raids and the underground existence the raids imposed on us. We practically lived in the cellar, where the passage of time seemed considerably slowed by the isolating confinement and tedium of that place. Recognizing that the cellar was to be our home away from home for however many weeks it took for the Germans to conquer Poland, my father brought a cot down from the apartment so that my mother could at least lie down and get some rest. There really wasn't any room for the cot, but nobody objected to it, and our neighbors crowded closer together to allow my father to set it up.

As the war progressed, we tried to follow what was happening by listening to radio news broadcasts and reading the newspapers. The reports were always sketchy, inaccurate, or deliberately misleading, as the government did not want to us to know what was really going on. In the first week of the war, all kinds of outlandish and conflicting rumors were flying about; stories of catastrophic Polish defeats competed with tales of great Polish victories. Lacking any solid news about the fighting, most Poles with whom I was acquainted were confident that our forces would beat the Germans quickly and handily. "We're going to push them back, all the way back to Germany," I remember them saying. "We're going to teach those Germans a lesson they'll never forget."

Jews like my parents and their friends doubted that the Poles had anything to teach the Germans about war. The frequent and bloody pogroms that Slavs and Teutons alike had perpetrated against the Jews over the course of centuries had made the latter fatalistic about the prospects of resisting an armed foe. So often had European Jews been defeated and slaughtered that they could hardly think otherwise. And yet for a brief spell my parents and their friends believed, or tried to believe, that the Polish army would prevail, despite the punishment the Luftwaffe was daily administering to Lvov and other Polish cities.

Hindsight has shown us that Poland was doomed from the start, that the Polish army didn't stand a chance against the Germans. Any belief to the contrary now seems either stupid or crazy, or both. Yet, at the time, the idea that the Poles could win the war was not so far-fetched. Hadn't a Polish army triumphed over invading Russian Bolsheviks at the Battle of Warsaw in 1920? And might they not achieve the same results against the Germans? It seemed reasonable to think that they would.

The Poles were a proud and patriotic people who were imbued with a fighting spirit and a willingness and determination to defend their nation against its enemies. But their pride and patriotism had blinded them to the reality of the situation: by the end of the second day of the war, the Luftwaffe had established air supremacy over Poland and was attacking at will cities, railways, road junctions, military convoys, and troop concentration areas. The damage inflicted on the nation's infrastructure disrupted mobilization; with the road and rail transport system in ruins, army reserves summoned to duty were prevented from reaching their assembly depots. Meanwhile, German ground forces raced across the Polish countryside. By September 8, German forces had broken through Polish defenses on every front, capturing Łódź and advancing to the outskirts of Warsaw. The Germans laid siege to the capital the next day. Farther south, the Germans took Kraków on the sixth, crossed the River San near Przemyśl on the tenth, captured Radom on the eleventh, and drove past Przemyśl ninety miles east toward Lvov, seizing the Zboiska Heights just north of the city on the thirteenth.

Throughout the campaign, the Poles fought bravely, but to no avail. Outgunned, outmoded, and, above all, outmaneuvered by fast-moving German mechanized forces, the Polish field armies reeled back in disarray. One after the other, Polish formations were cut off, enveloped, and annihilated. In Lvov there were unconfirmed reports that German panzer divisions had advanced deep into the interior, east of the Vistula River and Warsaw, and that the Polish army had been routed everywhere. People talked about this all the time until I was certain it must be true. But the magnitude of defeat remained unknown until about the second week of the war, when a flood of refugees from the west started pouring into Lvov. The refugees had actually begun showing up on the second day of the war. At that point, I was comforted by their presence. It meant that adults older and smarter than myself considered Lvov a safe haven, a place the Germans would never take.

In the beginning, the refugees came singly and in small groups, then by the hundreds, then by the thousands. Their numbers increased day by day, hour by hour. Within a week, the streets were flooded with people heading east to escape the onrushing Germans. Many came on foot, pushing baby carriages and wheelbarrows, pulling small carts, lugging suitcases, wearing bulging knapsacks on their backs. The wheelbarrows and carts were loaded with bedding and luggage, and children were often perched on top. Clearly, their journey had not been an easy one: their eyes held the wild, confused look of hunted animals; their unwashed faces were drawn with fatigue and fear; their clothes were rumpled and dirty; they were literally stumbling with exhaustion. The luckier refugees rode in automobiles with suitcases and steamer trunks tied to the roof with twine, or in horse-drawn wagons piled high with luggage and large pieces of furniture such as bed frames, mattresses, and the like.

Throughout the first three weeks of September, endless columns of refugees wended slowly through the streets with the somber stateliness of a religious procession. The street we lived on was thronged with people filing by at all hours of the day and night. Individually the refugees were silent, but collectively they made a soft, murmuring sound that reminded me of a herd of gently lowing cattle. That sound was punctuated by shouts, the wailing of infants, gunning automobile motors, honking horns, grinding gearshifts. When the German bombs began to fall, there were screams as well. Those poor people were particularly vulnerable to air attacks: they had no place to hide, no cellars where they might seek shelter, and they suffered many casualties as a result.

One day, when I came home from school, I stood at the front window of our apartment and gazed at the refugee column in the street below. I was chewing absentmindedly on my lunch—a slice of black bread with sugar sprinkled on it—and I remember thinking that it tasted very good. It was all I would have to eat that day, but at least I would not go hungry. In that respect, I knew that I was significantly better off than many of the refugees, who had little or no food at all and almost no likelihood that they could obtain any in a city where the grocery stores and markets had long since been emptied out and closed down.

Most of the refugees passed through the city, but thousands

remained in Lvov, camping out in the parks and along the riverbanks, sleeping on the streets and sidewalks, and in doorways, churches, synagogues, schools, public buildings — wherever they could find an open spot to lie down without someone chasing them off. In the second week of the war, the entire city lost its electric power, making it impossible to listen to the radio for war news or to run the presses that printed the newspapers. But the mere presence of the refugees told us everything we needed to know about the course of the war.

The refugees themselves were also a source of news. They gave harrowing accounts of their experiences on the road, where they were bombed and strafed relentlessly by low-flying German aircraft, and they described the shattered state of the Polish army units they had come across. Many of the refugees were Jews from Kraków and Poznań, and when we talked to them, we learned of the horrible things the Germans were doing to our people — how they were rounding up Jews in the ghettos and villages and massacring them with machine guns.

Terrified by these reports, many citizens of Lvov packed up their belongings and joined the shambling refugees in their weary exodus to the east. Their destinations varied; some went to the homes of relatives who lived in rural areas, while others fled into the forests to wait until the fighting stopped and it was safe to return to the city. A large number of people intended to cross the eastern frontier into the Soviet Union, where it was thought that the Russians would welcome their Slav brethren — be they Christians or Jews — with open arms.

Going to Russia seemed like a good idea to me, as I was convinced that the Germans would take Lvov. But when I suggested this course of action to my father, he flatly rejected it. He had once been a refugee when he had escaped with the family from Kamenets-Podolski, and he understood well the perils involved. He told us that it was better to stay put in the familiar environs of Lvov and see how events unfolded. For one thing, he said, there was no telling what sort of reception the Russians would give us. For another, the trek to Russia would be difficult and hazardous; in the countryside, food would be scarce, and we would be totally at the mercy of the predatory German dive-bombers.

Fima was unfazed by these arguments. He didn't mind taking risks. As the German forces closed swiftly on Lvov, he met often with his friends to discuss the situation and what they should do about it. Several of his friends decided that they would leave the city and head south, crossing the frontier into Czechoslovakia, Romania, or Hungary. Fima was eager to go with them and he told my father that this was what he wanted to do. My father wouldn't hear of it. "You're not going anywhere," he told Fima. "What will happen to us will happen to you. I won't permit the family to be separated!"

Needless to say, Fima remained in Lvov. His friends left the city without him. Long after the war was over, Fima found out that they were all killed before they reached the border.

Shortly after capturing the Zboiska Heights on September 13, the Germans encircled Lvov, closing off all avenues of escape from the city. Like it or not, we were staying in Lvov. The Germans then began bombarding the city with heavy artillery. The air raids continued, so that now we were being bombed and shelled at the same time. This combined air and artillery bombardment was tremendously destructive, yet somehow our building was not hit. But the danger from exploding shells was so great that the authorities closed my school, and I soon found myself spending most of my waking hours in the cellar with my family and neighbors.

The artillery bombardment prepared the way for German infantry of the elite First Mountain Division, supported by tanks, to launch the first of a series of violent assaults on the city. But the troops of the Polish garrison commanded by General Langner put up a tough fight, repulsing every attack the Germans threw at them. The Polish troops were assisted by civilian volunteers, including women and children, who dug trenches and tore up paving stones and trolley tracks to erect barricades in the streets. In some instances, the civilians even took up arms against the invaders, fighting side by side with regular army troops. Among the civilian fighters were schoolboys and members of Lvov's Jewish socialist bund. It was said that a band of Polish and Jewish schoolboys jumped on top of German tanks and set them afire with Molotov cocktails. Thus the Germans had accomplished the near-impossible: they had united Polish Christians and Jews in a common cause!

On September 19, the Germans broke through Polish defenses in the north and west sector of the city, advancing past the slaughterhouse district to the banks of the Upper Grodecka River, only a mile or so from our building. By midday, German patrols had pushed into the city center, and the fall of Lvov seemed imminent. But at the very last minute, we were saved from German conquest by none other than the Soviet Red Army.

※

Occupied by the Russians

In the third week of the war, we heard that the Red Army had invaded Poland from the east. The Soviets crossed the frontier on September 17, but I don't recall learning about the invasion until a few days after it occurred. It was an astounding development, and no one knew quite what to make of it. Some people were elated by the news because they thought the Russians had come to help us fight the Germans; others, like the ever-cynical Petia, scoffed at the idea that the Soviets had acted with Poland's best interests in mind. These doubters believed that the Russians, running true to historical form, were simply trying to grab as much Polish territory as they could before the Germans completely overran the country.

The leaders of the Polish government had no illusions about the Soviet intervention and fled to Romania the next day. Meanwhile, as Soviet armies advanced across eastern Poland, the Germans stepped up their efforts to capture Lvov. On or about September 22, the shooting stopped and an eerie silence fell over the city. We emerged from the cellar to discover that the city's garrison had capitulated to the Germans, probably because the Polish soldiers hated the idea of surrendering to the opportunistic Russian Communists. But the Germans had no sooner accepted the garrison's surrender than they handed the city over to the Russians and began withdrawing their forces to the west.

My parents were naturally quite happy that it was the Russians rather than the Germans who had taken possession of Lvov. Being Jews, they were afraid of the Germans, whereas they were merely apprehensive about the Russians. They knew that in the Soviet Union anti-Semitism was officially banned. Jews were supposedly accorded full rights as citizens and treated just like everyone else. Thus, it was reasonable to assume that the Soviets would institute the same policy of tolerance toward Jews in Poland. Besides, my parents were Russians by birth and upbringing who still spoke Russian at home and counted Russian immigrants as their only friends. They were perhaps still Russian in spirit and as such were comfortable with the idea that Russians, even Soviet Russians, would be ruling Lvov.

It seemed to me that most Polish Gentiles also preferred the Russians to the Germans as being the lesser of two great evils. The Poles hated the Soviet regime and regarded the Russian invasion an act of treachery, a stab in the back. But at least the Russians were Slavs, and therefore people the Poles understood and felt they could work with.

Small wonder, then, that when the Red Army entered the city, it was a gala event and the cause of much rejoicing by the populace. Thousands of Lvovians turned out to greet the Soviet troops. I watched the spectacle of their entry with some girlfriends while my father went off somewhere with Fima and Rysia to watch it as well. The Soviets marched in columns down one of the city's main thoroughfares, and the people who thronged the sidewalks clapped and shouted Polish hosannas while pretty girls skipped and capered alongside the soldiers, tossing flowers to them and strewing blossoms at their feet. Most of the Soviet troops were infantrymen who strode vigorously by with their arms swinging and their jackboots clomping on the pavement; but there were also officers on horseback, horse-drawn artillery, and a few tanks and trucks. The majority of the soldiers seemed to be boys my own age, and they were grinning as only boys can when pretty girls welcome them with an abundance of flowers and affection.

I was not one of those flower girls. They were cavorting like barefoot maidens in a pagan fertility rite, and I was somewhat taken aback by their antics. I was no prude and I did not think their behavior wrong, but it was really beyond me to carry on like that in public. So I did not dance alongside the Russians, and I did not cheer and applaud them either. But like so many others, I was glad that they had come.

After a while my girlfriends and I strolled over to another one of the main boulevards where we often promenaded on the weekends. At one corner we found several tanks parked in the middle of the intersection with the Russian crewmen lounging in the sun on the decks and turrets of their machines. We approached the tanks because we were curious to see Russian soldiers up close, and when the crewmen saw us coming, they jumped down off their machines to flirt and talk with us. They were polite and personable young men who smiled constantly and seemed eager for us to like them. A crowd soon formed around our little group, and the Poles began asking them all sorts of questions. The Russians answered the Poles with unfailing courtesy, even though some of the questions were intended to provoke them and offend their socialist sensibilities.

"Why did you come to Poland?" a man asked.

"To protect you from the Germans," came the amiable reply.

"Do you have any bread?" asked another man. Bread had been scarce since the war began and was therefore a frequent topic of conversation.

"Oh, sure, we have truckloads of bread!" one of the crewmen declared. His tone was ebullient, almost boastful—you could see that he was fairly bursting with pride in Mother Russia's agricultural productivity.

"Do you have any sugar?" a woman called out.

"Yes, yes, truckloads of sugar!" the Russian assured her.

"But when will we see these trucks?"

"Soon, soon! They're on the way," said the Russian. "Sugar is coming, bread is coming—in a few days, comrades, you'll have plenty of everything!"

"What about culture?" shouted one wag. "Is culture coming, too?"

The Poles began to snicker. But the Russian did not realize

that his interlocutor was baiting him. "Yes, certainly," he said ingenuously. "Plenty of culture is coming."

More snickering. The crowd was fairly vibrating with suppressed mirth. It ran through us like an electric current. You could sense that people were about to explode. I know I was. I wanted so much to laugh—I could hardly control myself. I bit my lip and glanced around at my friends and saw that they were shaking from the effort to hold their laughter in check.

"You mean to tell me that there really *is* culture in Russia?" the wag said slyly.

And, of course, the Russian said, "Yes, truckloads of culture!"

That was the last straw. Everyone in the crowd began laughing uproariously at the Russian soldier. For a moment the soldier and his comrades looked at us with confused expressions. Then they began laughing too. They were so naive and gullible that they did not realize we were making fun of them. They thought we were laughing because we were so happy that the Soviet Union would be providing us with truckloads of bread, sugar, and culture.

The Russian soldiers also told us that Stalin would make our lives "sweet." They actually said that. They said, "You can pray to God to give you candy, but you won't get any. Candy will not fall from heaven. But if you pray to Stalin for candy—boom! The candy will come down!" Whereupon they reached into bags and tossed handfuls of candy high into the air so that it fell on the crowd.

What a commotion that caused! Adults laughed as their children, squealing with delight, scurried this way and that to pick the candy up off the ground.

The Sovietization of Lvov began at once. The next day the Russians began posting big signs on kiosks and the walls of buildings informing us that the schools would be reopened, that we should all go back to work, that foodstuffs were coming soon. The city was bedecked with red flags emblazoned with the Soviet hammer-and-sickle emblem and banners bearing Soviet slogans in Polish, Ukrainian, and Yiddish. Huge portraits of Stalin and Lenin, as well as Voroshilov, Molotov, and Kalinin, were hung from the sides of buildings.

Meanwhile, the war continued to rage in western Poland. The Germans had laid siege to Warsaw, and we could not communicate with my Aunt Nadia and my cousin Marcus, who were trapped in the city. As it turned out, we would never hear from them again.

Warsaw surrendered to the Germans on September 27. Two days later, Germany and the Soviet Union signed a treaty of friendship and announced their intention to divide Poland between them. By October 3, all organized resistance in Poland had ceased—and so, too, had the existence of Poland as a sovereign nation.

Later that month the Soviets held an election in which the inhabitants of Western Ukraine—a region that included Lvov—were to decide whether they want to be incorporated into the Ukrainian Soviet Socialist Republic. Of course, the election was rigged and the outcome was never in doubt. On November 1, the region was formally annexed by the Ukrainian Republic. Russian was made the official language over Polish, Soviet passports were issued, and we all became citizens of the Soviet Union.

My parents were cautiously optimistic about our new status. They thought the Soviet government might look favorably on Russian Jews who had immigrated to Poland to the extent that it might grant us permission to move back to Kamenets-Podolski. With immigration to America now a virtual impossibility, my father was toying with the idea of returning to that town and perhaps reclaiming some of the property we had once owned there. It was true that we were bourgeois expatriates who had run away from the Bolsheviks and this was unquestionably a black mark against our family name. But as a union leader, hence a representative of the "working man," my father thought he had something in common with the Communists, who had always championed the cause of the workers. Maybe, he thought, his affinity with the Communists would earn us special consideration if and when we decided to relocate to Kamenets-Podolski.

It was all a pipe dream but it did not seem so at the time. The Russians were (and are) a likeable people and at first the Communist system did not seem as bad as we had been led to think. A policy of overt friendliness and fraternization governed all their initial contacts with the citizens of Lvov. In a determined attempt to convince us that Communism was the best of all possible worlds, the Russians shipped large quantities of butter, milk, and meat to the city. They established a decent minimum wage for unskilled labor and put people to work repairing buildings damaged in the war and clearing the rubble from the streets.

Most important, however, was the fact that the Soviets had kept the Germans out of Lvov. When Britain and France had declared war on Germany, I thought they would help Poland by attacking Germany. But their armies had remained idle while Poland was being overrun. The British and the French had been worthless as allies. At least the Russians had done something. So I didn't much care that Poland had lost the war or that our part of Poland had been absorbed by the Soviet Union. Better to be conquered by the Russians than the Germans, I told myself.

A few days after the Russians occupied Lvov, all kinds of things began to disappear—things like wristwatches, clocks, children's toys, and cheap trinkets of every sort. The Russians did not have consumer goods like this in their own country and they desperately wanted them. But they didn't steal the items they coveted. They bought them from the Poles, who sold the items at exorbitant prices.

Many Poles duped the Russian soldiers into purchasing broken wristwatches. A Pole would approach a prospective customer, hold out a broken wristwatch, and say, "You see this watch? Look, look, it's a good watch. I'll give you a special price for it." Having never seen a wristwatch, the soldier would not know that it was broken. So he would hand over the money and become the extremely proud owner of a wristwatch that would never keep time for him.

Such ignorance was very typical of the Russian soldiers. They tended to be very backward and unsophisticated. Russian civilians were no different. In the coming months, hundreds of Russian administrators moved to Lvov with their families to manage the factories and business the Soviets had seized; they commandeered the best apartments with running water and toilets, but they often did not know how to use these modern conveniences. They kept live pigs tethered in the bathtubs, and washed beets, radishes, and carrots in the toilets while using chamber pots or outhouses to perform their bodily functions.

Millinery shopkeepers took advantage of Russian women by passing off black nightgowns as formal evening dresses! The shopkeepers would tell them that these garments were the epitome of haute couture, the sort of finery that every well-heeled Parisian socialite was wearing this year to the theater or ballet. The women were easy prey. They had never before encountered a high-pressure sales pitch and thus lacked "buyer beware" savvy. And they didn't know the difference between a nightgown and a formal dress because they had never seen either. But they did know that they wanted to look as good as any capitalist woman in the decadent West, and it became common to see Russian women wearing these bedroom garments in the nightclubs, acting as if they were sophisticated and smartly attired. My friends and I—in fact, all Poles—could hardly believe what we saw. We laughed at these women behind their backs and thought: How could they be so stupid?

Throughout the autumn and into the winter, Lvov was invaded and occupied not only by the Russians but also by a ragtag army of refugees from the German-occupied zone. My brother (who was now attending a technical school in Lvov) met one of them, Roma Steinbeck, and began dating her. From Roma and other refugees, Fima heard about the conduct of the Germans toward the civilian populace. Some of the refugees had encouraging news. They told Fima that, overall, German army troops had behaved correctly. But other refugees told him that the Germans were massacring Jews in villages throughout western Poland.

Our family gave shelter to dozens of refugees. My mother and father knew what it was like to be on the run and felt duty-bound to take these people in. At night the front room of our apartment was often crowded with refugees sleeping on the wood floor. In the morning and evenings, we fed them as best we could, and my mother spent most of her waking hours cooking meals and baking bread for them.

Once, when we were running short of food, my mother somehow managed to contact our Uncle Herman, who owned a farm near Borszców, a small rural town just outside Lvov. Herman was a robust, ruddy-faced man with iron-gray hair. His wife had died before the war, leaving him to raise a son and daughter on his own. I did not know him very well, since he rarely visited us in Lvov. My mother asked him to send food, and he did so at once, sending the supplies to Lvov by train. Fima and my Uncle Yossi, a big, strong man who lived in Lvov, hired a small horse-drawn cart and drove to the train station to fetch the supplies. They got gunnysacks of flour, sacks filled with potatoes, half a pig, and several cured geese. They brought these foodstuffs home, and immediately my mother set to work cooking them. Much to the revulsion of Pesha, my mother made fat from the pig and used this in cooking various other dishes.

I don't remember much about the refugees who stayed with us. Usually they came and went before I got to know them or even learned their names. Their faces are a blur. Our apartment was nothing more than a way station for people heading east into Russia. However, I do remember clearly a young Jewish couple, a husband and wife from Poznań who were named, coincidentally, Poznanski. They had a one-year-old baby girl, and because the child was so young, my mother gave them a room of their own to stay in, with their own bed.

Mrs. Poznanski came from a wealthy family, and I believe she gave money to my parents to help cover the cost of feeding so many refugees. She and her husband had impeccable manners; they were both articulate and obviously well educated, and they were always stylishly dressed in expensive clothes.

Needless to say the Poznanskis worried a great deal about their infant daughter and what might become of her. Mr. Poznanski especially felt responsible for the safety and well-being of his family. But it was no longer in his power to protect his wife and child or to provide for them. He fretted constantly about his family's predicament and tried to puzzle a way out of it, and soon enough the anxieties of the former endeavor combined with the frustrations of the latter to take a physical toll on him. In the short time the Poznanskis stayed with us, his black hair turned gray at the temples, and you could see white whiskers in his beard in the morning before he shaved.

The Poznanskis lived with us for several months. The Russians were deporting the majority of refugees to the east, to camps in Siberia or Central Asia, but not the Poznanskis. Thanks to the efforts of my mother and father, who notified the authorities that the Poznanskis were permanently ensconced in our apartment, they were granted resident status and with it permission to stay in the city for as long as they wanted. Eventually, the Poznanskis went to another city in Poland to live with friends or relatives. I never saw them again.

I'm not quite sure how the refugees learned that we were taking people in. I believe my parents put the word out through Jewish community organizations—all the people who stayed with us were Jews—which steered the refugees to our door. People came to our apartment in droves, but my parents never turned anyone away, no matter how crowded it got. Later, after Fima was drafted into the Red Army, I asked my parents why they had inconvenienced our lives by giving so many refugees a place to sleep. My mother reminded me that Fima was in the army and might some day need to seek help from strangers. Therefore, we should help strangers in the hope that our good deeds might be repaid in kind to her son. "Cast your bread on the water," she would say, "and you get bread back."

The refugees told my parents many frightening stories about what the Germans were doing to Jews in western Poland. They said, for instance, that the Germans were killing all the Jews in many of the big-city ghettos.

My father refused to believe these stories. "Oh, no," he

told his guests, "the situation over there can't be as bad as you say. You know how it is—people exaggerate. Someone could tell you a story about a person getting killed, and the story makes the rounds, and after a while the death of that one person is turned into a massacre. When a story gets repeated so many times, it grows in the retelling."

Occasionally the refugees would become angry with my father for not believing them. "You're wrong!" they would shout. "It's true, it's all true—we swear to God it is!"

"Well, maybe," my father would say. "Of course the Germans are arresting Jews. I'm sure of that. But I don't think they intend to kill us. They'll put us in ghettos, just like others have done to us in the past."

My father seemed to think that getting put in a ghetto wasn't so bad. But as I sat there silently listening to the adults argue with each other, I made up my mind that I would never let the Germans put me in a ghetto. Instinctively, I was preparing myself for the worst; perhaps deep down I believed the stories the refugees were telling my father.

One day in late November, our doorbell rang and I opened the door. In the hall stood a heavyset woman about fifty years old with large dark eyes and a handsome face with a peasant's ruddy complexion. She was wearing a voluminous Russian peasant dress and a babushka scarf tied under her chin. I stared at her, tongue-tied: I didn't know who she was. Another refugee, perhaps?

"Hello," I finally said, speaking in Polish.

She smiled. "Hello," she replied in Russian. "Is this where Ilya Weintraub lives?"

Switching to Russian, I said that Ilya Weintraub was my father, and he did indeed live here.

"May I see him, please?"

I ran to get my father, who was in the kitchen reading a newspaper. "There's a woman at the door," I said. "She wants to talk to you."

"Who is it?" he asked me.

"A big woman who looks like a Russian peasant."

My father gave me a bemused look and got up from his chair and went to the door. When he saw the woman and she saw him, they both let out a joyful cry and fell into each other's arms. In the next instant, they were weeping and kissing each other repeatedly on the cheeks and stroking each other's hair.

The woman was Yunia, my father's long-lost older sister. She was married to a non-Jew, a tank officer in the Red Army, and, she told us, when her husband's unit was transferred to Lvov, she had come with him. They had arrived in Lvov a few days ago.

My father and Yunia exchanged news about their other sister, Nenya, and their younger brother, Chaim. Nenya and Chaim both lived in the Soviet Union, in Dunajec. Chaim was in ill health. I tried to remember what this man looked like. I had never seen him in person, only in photographs. The pictures showed a man who resembled my father, but who was darker complected, with dark hair and brown eyes. My father did not seem at all perturbed by the news about his brother's health, and he did not seem interested in news about Nenya either. I think he was estranged from his siblings. They, like his parents, were very traditional, very religious, which set them apart from my father, the jazz musician, the secular Jew.

Yunia, however, was very concerned about us. In the Soviet Union, she had been told that everyone in Poland was poor. Poland was a capitalist country and capitalism was, of course, a failure, and therefore we were all living a hand-to-mouth existence. Yunia visited us many times after that, and she always brought something for our apartment—knick-knacks and trinkets, and sometimes sugar. Most memorably, she brought us a family heirloom: a beautiful old goose-down quilt that my mother and father had left behind in my grandfather's house in Kamenets-Podolski.

Yunia was very nice, and so was her husband—even though he was a member of the Communist Party. Our family had an unspoken rule not to discuss his Communist Party affiliation, and whenever I inadvertently mentioned it, my parents put their fingers to their lips and shushed me. They told me that the less said about such things, the better; after all, we were "White Russians," members of the bourgeoisie, while Yunia's husband was most definitely a Red Russian and therefore nominally our class enemy.

During the Russian occupation, friends of my parents were constantly dropping by our apartment to talk politics and play cards. I would listen to the adults, eat some of the cakes, and drink a cup or two of the tea my mother set out for them, but I wasn't allowed to participate in their conversations. In their view, I was still a child, even though I was eighteen years old. If and when I did venture an opinion, they would swiftly cut me off by saying, "You don't know what we're talking about. Go sit over there and be quiet."

One of my parents' friends and most frequent visitors was Mr. Lewandowski, a Russian Jewish émigré. He was an architect and a very handsome man, tall and slim, with blue eyes. My mother once asked him if he would give me a job, and he readily agreed to hire me as a secretary. But before I could start working for him, I would have to learn how to type in Russian on a typewriter with Cyrillic keys.

I could already speak and read Russian, but I did not know how to use a Russian typewriter. So I took a night-school course in Cyrillic typing. The course lasted one month. At home I practiced every night on a diagram of a Cyrillic typewriter keyboard because we could not afford a real typewriter. Finally, when I graduated from the typing course, I started working at Mr. Lewandowski's office.

My job was to type up project descriptions that were written in Russian by the architects he employed. This was easy— my practice sessions on the faux Cyrillic keyboard had prepared me well for the real thing. The only hard part of my job was putting up with Mr. Lewandowski. I quickly discovered that my boss was not the same polite and cultivated man who came to our apartment to play cards and discuss politics. He was rude to me in a way I had never before experienced. By then my body was fully developed, more so than most girls my age, and Mr. Lewandowski took great pleasure in noting this fact. He often made lewd comments about me to his male colleagues, and he always made sure that I heard them. Then they would all laugh and leer at me.

I was shocked and astonished by Mr. Lewandowski's behavior. After all, I thought, he had children of his own, he was a friend of my parents, and he was old enough to be my father! How, then, could he have the temerity and bad manners to talk about me as if I were a girl of loose morals? Nowadays, his conduct would be termed "sexual harassment" and he would get in all kinds of trouble for it; but in Poland in 1939 a man could speak and act as he pleased around his female employees. I dealt with the situation by ignoring him and pretending that I did not hear what he said about me. It thus became obvious to him that I did not appreciate his smutty remarks and after a few weeks he quit making them. I never told my parents about his behavior, in part because I was too embarrassed to say anything, but also because in those days a girl just did not talk sexual matters over with her mother and father.

I had no further trouble with Mr. Lewandowski. I worked for him in the afternoons and on weekends and attended school in the mornings. This was my routine until the spring of 1940, when I graduated from Gymnasium (high school) and went to work for Mr. Lewandowski full time.

My job was not what I wanted to be doing at this stage in my life. I still had dreams of attending fashion school in Paris. Of course, this was impossible while the war continued and the Germans occupied France. But I believed that the war would soon end and everything would go back to normal, allowing me to fulfill my dream. I could have gone to school in Poland, at little expense to my family, because the Russians had made university education free. But my father wasn't that keen on my going to college, not while the war made life so unsettled.

I wasn't that keen on going to school, either. Not in Poland, at any rate. It had to be Paris or nothing. In the meantime, I wanted to work, even if that meant working for Mr. Lewandowski.

Actually, the job with Mr. Lewandowski was fine once he

stopped harassing me. It got me out of the apartment and provided me with a little spending money. Very little—I gave most of what I earned to my father, but he allowed me to keep a certain amount for my own use. Once on the way home, I passed by a woman's clothing shop that had silk stockings on display in the window, and I immediately went inside and bought a pair. They were my first silk stockings, and when I got home and put them on I was thrilled by how grown-up they made me feel.

These stockings were the only pair I would own until the war was over. In the dark years that were soon to come, during times of flight and persecution, I would somehow manage to hold on to those stockings, mending them over and over again until they had all but fallen apart.

Soviet rule became markedly less tolerant, and tolerable, as time went on. The Russians expropriated major industries and organized medium-sized enterprises into cooperatives. Small businesses like the nightclubs where my father worked were allowed to remain in private hands but were heavily taxed. Farms were collectivized and churches and synagogues were closed down outright or taxed into penury. There were mass arrests of so-called undesirable elements: Polish intellectuals, clergy, businessmen, civil servants, landowners, government functionaries, demobilized soldiers, and, of course, refugees.

At one point Yunia brought us news, obtained from her husband, that Soviet authorities were aware that our family had fled Kamenets-Podolski in 1921. This was unsettling news. My father became concerned that we would be labeled undesirables, arrested, and sent to Siberia.

My father asked Yunia for help. She spoke to her husband, and he somehow arranged for us to stay in Lvov. My parents were greatly relieved. They thought that deportation into deep Russia was the worst thing that could happen to us. They never imagined that deportation could have been our family's salvation.

In December, Fima became a soldier in the Red Army. One

Sunday morning, he left the apartment on some sort of errand, and when he got outside he found that one wall of our building was covered with a big poster announcing in Russian characters that all young men in Lvov henceforth "had the privilege and the honor to join the Red Army." The poster said that service in the army was strictly voluntary. But at the bottom of the poster, in smaller type, was a paragraph stating ominously that any man who failed to present himself to the local Red Army recruitment office "would be dealt with accordingly."

Fima went back upstairs to tell my father about the poster. My father came down to read it, and when he had finished, he was momentarily silent. He understood what "dealt with accordingly" meant. Then he looked at Fima and said, "You don't have a choice in the matter. You have to go."

My father wasn't happy about this, but there was nothing he could do. He knew that if Fima refused to report he would be arrested. The one positive note in all this was the statement on the poster that said any young man who came forward voluntarily could choose which branch of the armed forces he wanted to serve in.

Fima went over to the recruitment office that same morning. Immediately after he signed the enlistment papers, his head was completely shaved. Then he was taken before a group of officers who asked him what he wanted to do in the military. Fima had an answer at the ready. Like so many young men of that era, he was enthralled with airplanes and aviation. Moreover, like so many young men, he had romantic notions about aviation both as a profession and as a way of meeting beautiful women. Such notions were confirmed and reinforced by the way aviators were portrayed in books and movies. On the silver screen, in particular, the men who flew planes were always shown to be glamorous and enormously attractive to the opposite sex. They were inevitably dashing figures, reckless and bold, lovers in equal measure of women and a good fight. Theirs was an image, a way of life, that Fima found irresistibly appealing—even though it wasn't precisely true. But it was true enough. In the 1930s, aviators were considered a special breed simply because aviation itself was still very much an emerging field of endeavor. So Fima told the Russian officers that he wanted to be a pilot, preferably a fighter pilot.

The Soviet officers were agreeable to this and told him that he would be enrolled in pilot training school upon his formal induction. Fima was thrilled! Knowing that he would be a pilot almost made him forget the humiliation of a shaved head. He practically ran home, he was so excited.

When he walked into our apartment, we were all shocked by his appearance. My mother and grandmother began to cry. I cried too. The women of the family could not stand to see this handsome boy made to look like a convict. Fima grinned and told us not to worry. "I'm going to be a pilot!" he blurted happily.

His announcement did not have the desired effect. My father exploded. "What did you do?" he roared. "What did you tell the Russians?"

"That I want to be a pilot," Fima said in a small voice.

"There will be no pilots in my family!" shouted my father. Then he grabbed Fima by his collar and said, "You're coming with me."

"Where are we going?" Fima managed to ask as my father dragged him to the door.

"Back to the recruitment office," my father replied. "We're going to have a little talk with the Russians."

When they got to the recruitment office, my father went up to the officer in charge and told him that his son had made a mistake, that he did not really want to be a pilot. Fima hung his head in embarrassment. The Russian officers laughed at his discomfiture—they found the whole situation quite amusing.

"And what branch of the service does your son really prefer?" the Russian officer asked with a wry smile.

"Why, artillery, of course," said my father.

"Artillery!" Turning to Fima, the Russian officer said, "You're sure about this? You're sure you don't want to be a pilot?"

Fima looked at my father, who frowned at him. Fima nodded to the Russian officer. "Yes," he said meekly.

"Then artillery it shall be!" the Russian officer declared.

Later, when Fima asked my father why he had chosen artillery, he was told that "with the artillery, you'll be at least twenty-five miles behind the front lines in a war. The artillery is always in the rear."

My father was wrong about the artillery's positioning. But he was right in his instincts. On the first few days of the war between Russia and Germany, most of the Soviet air force was destroyed. Thousands of pilots and air crew were killed. But my brother was on the ground, training to be an artillery officer just outside Leningrad.

Fima has told me that the Russian officers at the recruitment office were decent fellows. They acceded to my father's wishes because they respected the relationship between father and son. So Fima was assigned to the artillery and then sent home to await further orders. One or two days later, he received a letter instructing him to report for induction into the Red Army. The letter told him what clothes to bring, and that he would be transported by train to some undisclosed destination.

The morning of his departure was not a pleasant one. Once again all the women in the family, myself included, were weeping as Fima packed his belongings. He tried to ease our fears by making light of the situation, cracking jokes about how he was going to be a brave soldier and a good Communist for Stalin. My mother was not consoled. She was literally sick to her stomach at the idea of losing him to the Red Army.

After a while we all went with Fima to the induction center. There he was just one of hundreds of boys with shaved heads. They all looked self-conscious, embarrassed, and scared. They were a pitiful sight. Fima and his fellow draftees were "disinfected"—they had to take off all their civilian clothes, which were washed and deloused with chemical powder. Then they were given Red Army uniforms to wear. Much later, when Fima's civilian clothes were returned to him, he found that they had shrunk so much that he could no longer wear them.

After disinfection, the inductees waited around for several hours. Finally, they formed columns and marched through the streets to the train station. We followed them, and there was another wait of several hours before the train arrived. When the train showed up, army officers loaded the boys into boxcars, each of which had two rows of shelves constructed along the length of the car for sleeping. My mother stood next to the car that Fima had boarded and watched the train leave the station, bound for a training center on the outskirts of Leningrad. As the train pulled out, Fima stood by a window and waved at us. It was a poignant farewell at the time; today, in retrospect, it seems tragic as well, for although he could not know it then, he would never see his parents and youngest sister again.

Fima left a girlfriend behind when he went into the army. Her name was Mila, and she was a pretty girl with big green eyes, long brown hair, and a bright smile. Mila was very intelligent, and I liked her, but she was something of a perfectionist—everything had to be just so for her. I did not associate with her before the war except when I accompanied Fima on visits to her apartment, where she lived with her parents and younger brother. Her family was struggling to get by and they lived simply and frugally. Their apartment was tidy and clean, and Mila, who could not afford new clothes, spent much of her spare time patching and mending the clothes she had.

Mila and Fima were very much in love with each other, but for some reason she did not come down to the train station to see him off. This was unfortunate, since Fima would never see her again, either. But I would soon be spending a great deal of time with her.

Fima's departure wrought a profound change in my parents. My mother was never the same again. She became melancholy and had trouble sleeping. She lost her appetite and with it a great deal of weight, becoming so thin that we worried about her health.

My father became more religious. In the past my grandmother might urge him to go to the synagogue for the High Holidays, and he would refuse, telling her bluntly, "Don't bother me with that." But after Fima went into the army, he began to pray on a daily basis. He said his prayers every night on the kitchen balcony. He would sway forward and back with his eyes tightly shut and beseech God in a soft voice to keep his son out of harm's way.

Becoming a soldier almost certainly saved Fima's life. I know that Fima had two friends who refused to answer the call to duty in the Red Army. Somehow these friends evaded the draft and remained in Lvov. They were brothers, the sons of a dentist. They were killed in 1941, when the Germans came to Lvov.

Shortly after the Russians came to Lvov, a bakery was opened in a storefront on the ground floor of our apartment building. It was there on a warm spring day in 1940 that I met Marcel. I was waiting in line to buy bread and Marcel was standing behind me. I looked him over and liked what I saw: lean body, dark blond hair, oval face, baby-blue eyes. He was of average height, and I guessed that he was in his early twenties.

We struck up a conversation, which is to say, we flirted with each other. He asked where I lived, and when I told him "Right here in this building," he said he was surprised that I had to wait in line just like everyone else. He told me that he was from Kraków. He said he was a Jew and that he had run away from Kraków because "the Germans are killing everybody there." His father had owned a jewelry store and had been murdered by the Germans.

I asked Marcel if he had found a place to live in Lvov. "Not yet," he said. But he was hungry and wanted to get something to eat before he went looking for a room.

I told him that he could stay with my family. "My father has taken in so many refugees, he won't notice one more."

We went upstairs to our apartment and I introduced Marcel to my parents. They liked him at once and invited him to stay. He lived with us for over a year, sleeping in a room just off the kitchen that had served the previous tenants as quarters for an au-pair girl. He was a congenial young man, funny, modest, and unfailingly optimistic. Everybody liked him. My grandmother and Haika often had him over to their apartment for tea and cakes, and sometimes supper as well. He went back and forth between the two apartments as if he were one of us, a member of the family.

Of course, I had a heavy crush on him. My parents must have been aware of this. But they had the good sense not to make a fuss about it. They trusted me and they trusted Marcel, and so they did not interfere with us in any way.

I know that Marcel was attracted to me. But not as passionately as I was to him. I never thought of marrying him—I just wanted to be with him, all the time. I vowed that I would follow him to the ends of the earth, and I almost did.

Marcel did not have a job. But he always had money and was able to pay a portion of the rent and buy groceries for the family. Probably he had escaped to Lvov with some of his father's diamonds and was selling them on the black market. But I never asked him about this and he never told me. I wasn't interested in where he got his money. I was only interested in winning his affection.

One night I went into his alcove and sat next to him on his bed. He began to kiss me. He was wearing an undershirt but no trousers—just a pair of boxer shorts. I pushed him away, saying, "You can't kiss me, you don't have any pants on!" I knew that I had to put a stop to things right then and there, or something might happen—something we would both regret.

Marcel was a gentlemen, and he did stop. Then he put on his pants, and that was that. But it certainly wasn't the end of our romance. We were always sneaking around, kissing each other and "making out" when my parents weren't in the apartment.

My romance with Marcel ended abruptly in the autumn of 1940, when four NKVD policemen came to our apartment and arrested him. Because he was a refugee from the west, he had been declared an "undesirable element" and was to be deported to Russia. I don't know how the Russians learned that he was living with us, but I suspect that he was denounced by our janitor, a closet anti-Semite who was now openly expressing his hatred for the building's Jewish tenants.

The NKVD men came to our apartment at night while my father was working at a nightclub. My mother and I watched helplessly as they took Marcel out the door and down the stairs. They held him by his arms, and though they weren't rough with him, they made it clear that they weren't going to let him break free and run away. Suddenly I realized that the love of my life was leaving forever. "I'm going with him!" I told my mother.

My mother looked stricken. "No, don't!" she cried. "Lala, stay here!"

But by then I was already gone, flying down the stairs in pursuit of my love.

They put Marcel into a truck that was filled with other refugees who were standing or sitting on benches. I told the Russians that I was a refugee too, and they believed me. Why shouldn't they? Who would be crazy enough to say you were a refugee when you weren't?

A young girl in love, that's who.

We were driven to the railway station where we boarded a train that was filled with deportees. We sat in a train compartment all night and waited for the train to leave. It was cold and the train was unheated and we snuggled against each other for warmth. Throughout the night, Marcel urged me to leave.

"Lala, go home," he said. "The Russians want me; they don't want you."

"No," I said adamantly. "Wherever you go, I'm going with you."

"But I don't know where they're taking me."

"I don't care."

"It could be someplace terrible."

"I still don't care. I just want to be with you."

Marcel shrugged resignedly. He knew that I was determined to stay with him and that nothing he said could get me to leave his side. He didn't know what to do. And he was scared—his face was pale with fear. Poor Marcel, his fear only endeared him to me all the more.

Morning came and still the train remained in the station. As we sat there waiting for the train to leave, someone opened the door to our compartment. It was my father! He had gone slowly and methodically through the train, opening the doors of each compartment to see who was inside. He was very angry. I had never seen him as angry as he was then. He grabbed me by the arm.

"Get up!" he barked, jerking me to my feet. "We're going home."

I said nothing. I was too surprised and intimidated to speak. My father never so much as glanced at Marcel. But Marcel rose from his seat and said, "Go on, Lala. Go with your father."

As if I had a choice. But I don't think my father was angry with Marcel. On the contrary, I am sure that he would have taken Marcel with him if that had been possible. But it wasn't.

My father led me by the hand through the train yard. It was now important to avoid an encounter with Russian soldiers, who would surely think that we were refugees and interpret our flight from the train as an attempt to escape the deportation to which we had been condemned, whereupon they would arrest us and there would be hell to pay. So, instead of exiting through the train station, where soldiers were standing guard, we scurried across the tracks and down a flight of concrete steps. Then we ducked under a boxcar, scrambling between the wheels in the cinders on our hands and knees. On the other side of the boxcar, we broke into a run with my father holding my hand and pulling me behind him.

We emerged from the train yard onto a side street. There we slowed to a walk, my father still holding my hand. His face was taut with anger. Throughout all this I hadn't uttered a word of protest, because I thought my father might hit me if I did. He was that angry and his anger frightened me. He was

not physically abusive and he did not believe in corporal punishment, but just then he seemed capable of anything, including violence to his daughter. He only spoke to me once the
whole way home, through lips that were so tightly drawn and
with his jaw so firmly and furiously set that I could hardly
understand him. "I don't know why you'd want to go to
Siberia," he muttered, "when we're going to be returning
soon to Kamenets-Podolski."

Part of me, the part that was a child, felt guilty because I
had dared to disobey my father. But the young woman in me
was filled with a desperation that came from being forcibly
separated from the man she loved.

When we got home I burst into tears. Now it was my turn
to get angry. I knew that I would never see Marcel again. I
also felt that I was no more than a possession of my father's, a
piece of chattel who could be pulled out of a train yard or any
other public place and dragged around whenever and wherever my father wanted to take me. I had no independence, no
freedom—I had to obey him.

I went to bed without eating and cried on my pillow. I
didn't want to talk to anyone, but my mother came to me
anyway and tried to console me. She felt sorry for me. She
was happy that I had come home, but she knew what I was
going through; she knew that I was in pain because I had lost
my first love. Holding me in her arms, she soothed me by
saying, "Don't worry, Lala, it'll be all right, you'll see. Someday you'll find somebody special, I promise."

Ever since Fima's induction into the Red Army, my father
had written him at least one letter every week. In June of
1941, he wrote to say that he had obtained a travel permit and
would be visiting Fima in August. At that time Fima was stationed just outside Leningrad at the Red Army Heavy
Artillery Academy, where he had completed ten months of a
two-year officer training course.

Fima was thrilled by this news. He was proud to be an
officer trainee and he very much wanted my father to see
what he had become, to see that he was a grown man and a

soldier and not the shaven-headed teenaged boy who had left Lvov over a year ago. He wanted to brag a little about how much money he was making as an officer trainee—he earned a good salary by Soviet standards—and he wanted to show off his smart new uniform and the shiny leather boots that went with it. But he never got the chance. On June 22, my father's travel plans were permanently aborted by the German invasion of the Soviet Union.

❁

The Germans Invade Again

The Germans invaded the Soviet Union on the morning of June 22. The attack took everybody by surprise, Poles and Russians alike. Many people had thought that war between Germany and the Soviet Union was inevitable, but no one dreamed that it would come so soon or so unexpectedly.

In Lvov it was 1939 all over again. Once again we were rudely awakened to the fact of war by droning aircraft, whistling bombs, and explosions.

Being seasoned veterans of air raids, we knew exactly what to do. And what not to do. This time, there was no watching the raid from our balcony. Immediately upon hearing the boom of exploding bombs, we dashed down to the cellar, where we waited out the raid in the company of our neighbors.

Most of us endured the bombing in stoic silence. But not Petia. Running true to form, Petia ranted on and on about the Nazis, crying, "They're going to kill us; they're going to kill us all!"

The Luftwaffe was typically relentless in its efforts to reduce Lvov to a pile of smoking rubble. German planes attacked the city repeatedly that day and every day in the week that followed. Nor did our building escape the bombing unscathed, as it did in 1939. On the second or third day of the German invasion, a bomb hit our building in the interior courtyard, just across from our kitchen balcony. In the cellar we tracked the bomb's descent with our ears, listening intently and with mounting alarm as the whistling grew swiftly nearer and louder. Upon impact, there was a roaring sound, the whole building shook, and plaster rained from the ceiling. We were all very frightened, and several women screamed and began weeping hysterically.

After the raid was over, we all rushed up to the courtyard to inspect the damage and to see whether our homes were still intact. We found that the bomb had blown away a section of the building's outer wall and had destroyed the apartment behind it. The apartment was the home of a Jewish family, a young lawyer who, along with his wife and small daughter, had been in the cellar with us during the raid. They had lost just about everything they owned and were naturally quite devastated. That same day they took what they could from the ruins of their apartment and left Lvov, joining the refugees who were fleeing the city by the thousands.

There were several air raids on that first day of the Russo-German war, and many more in the days that followed. Now whenever the Luftwaffe attacked sirens went off all over the city. Sometimes the sirens began their mournful howl before the planes arrived overhead, but more often than not the bombs were already bursting when the warning sounded. The German airfields were so close to Lvov that their planes could cover the short distance to the city before the Soviet air defense net detected them. And we knew that if their airfields were close, their armies were probably closer.

In one raid a bomb blew up the residential building across the street from our apartment, killing and wounding several occupants as well as a number of unfortunate passersby. After the raid I went outside to survey the carnage, the likes of which I had never seen before. It was horrendous. Bodies were strewn about the street, and among the dead was a girl I knew from school. She was sprawled on her back with her eyes wide open and her long hair spread out around her head in a pool of blood. I felt so sorry for her, but also queasy, for the sight of all that blood had sickened me. But there was more to it than that. To see her lying dead on the pavement was to undergo a kind of revelation, one that showed me an aspect of reality I had never before experienced and that, moreover, was totally beyond my ken. Death, terrible and mysterious, had revealed itself to me in the now-lifeless form of someone I had known, a young girl just like me, and I did not know what to make of it except to think: if she can die, so can I.

At night my parents and their friends gathered in the front room of our apartment to talk about the war and listen to radio news broadcasts. Everyone was extremely worried by what they heard. The Germans were thrusting across Poland and the Red Army seemed powerless to stop them.

"What shall we do?" my mother once asked my father.

"We'll just have to make the best of every situation, whatever comes," he answered. He said this in a calm voice, but his troubled expression and anxious, preoccupied manner spoke volumes about how he really felt.

The Russians began to flee Lvov. Tanks and trucks trundled through the streets, heading east, accompanied by columns of bedraggled infantry. With them went the Russian civilians who had moved to the city after the Soviet invasion of 1939. These included civil servants, government administrators, factory managers, and business professionals, all with their families in tow. Most escaped by train or in army trucks provided for that purpose, but some—the privileged few, the Communist elite—drove off in automobiles filled to overflowing with people and luggage. Around June 24, the Russian architects at Mr. Lewandowski's office left. When I showed up for work, Mr. Lewandowski told me that the office was closed; I might as well go home, he said, for I no longer had a job. It was just as well: the city was without gas, electricity, and water, and no business could operate under such circumstances.

The German onslaught reached Lvov at the end of the month. On the morning of June 29, an air raid sent us down to the cellar, and we stayed there the entire day. As the hours dragged by, the atmosphere in the cellar became increasingly unpleasant. Women and children cried and moaned, men complained incessantly about the incompetence of the Red

Army, and Petia, naturally, ranted about the Germans. There was no fresh air because the windows were all closed and it was a hot summer day. The stink of body odor was so strong that one could hardly breathe without gagging.

The Germans pulverized the city throughout the morning with bombs and artillery fire. Toward noon the din of explosions was punctuated by the sputter of small arms fire nearby. Despite what this portended, I wanted to leave the cellar at once, for I was sick and tired of the tedium, the foul smells, and the incessant lamentations of my neighbors. I was sitting on the cellar stairs when I was suddenly impelled to get up and move around. Without thinking, I leaped to my feet, went over to a window, and boosted myself up for a look outside. There I saw Soviet and German soldiers fighting no more than twenty feet from my window. There were about four or five Russians fighting as many Germans, and they were surging to and fro across my field of vision, charging and countercharging and lunging at each other with bayonet-tipped rifles. Then shots rang out. I ducked down and did not dare lift my head to the window for the rest of the day.

We stayed in the shelter until after dark. As night fell the fighting gradually slackened and then ceased altogether. It got very quiet outside, and we took this as a sign that it was safe to leave our shelter. We went upstairs to our apartment, and my mother prepared a meager dinner of black bread and tea. Several of our neighbors stopped by to rehash the day's events. We stayed indoors and kept the window shades closed and hoped for the best. Two days later, when we finally ventured out of our apartment, we would find that the building's facade was pocked with bullet holes from the skirmish I had witnessed.

We hoped for the best, but we got the worst. The next day we watched from our window as the Germans entered Lvov. They passed through the street in tanks, half-tracks, and trucks, and in columns of marching infantry. My first impression of them was, oddly enough, a favorable one. The German soldiers looked more cultured and civilized than the Russians; they were cleaner, better groomed, and healthier in appearance. They looked as if they came from towns and cities rather than rural villages; they did not look like peasants. They seemed middle-class and professional, businesslike and competent—the sort of men who would behave correctly, with bourgeois rectitude and in accord with their Christian moral precepts.

I was not afraid of them or of anything as long as I was with my mother and father. I knew my parents would protect me, so I did not worry about what could happen.

My parents were terribly distraught, however. They must have realized that the arrival of the Germans was the beginning of the end. "Thank God Fima is gone," they would say to me. "Thank God the Red Army took him away from here. This is a blessing, and we must be thankful for it."

We could also be thankful that the German soldiers we saw that day were front-line combat troops. Their motorized units drove through the city almost without stopping in their haste to catch up with and destroy the retreating Soviet forces. As an army in pursuit of a beaten enemy, they were too busy to deal with the civilian populace. They left us alone and we stayed out of their way, and nothing much happened—at least in our neighborhood.

It was a different story in the Jewish quarter, where mobs of Ukrainians were said to be running wild, slaughtering Jews while the Germans looked the other way. The German invasion came as a godsend to the Ukrainians, who hated the Jews and were none too fond of the Poles and Russians, either. They welcomed the Germans as liberators in the mistaken belief that Hitler would allow them to form an independent Ukrainian state; in the meantime, they were using what they thought would be a brief interregnum of German rule as opportunity to give free rein to their anti-Semitic impulses. In consequence, some four thousand Jews were killed in the first week of the German occupation.

Toward the end of July, German authorities in Lvov set up a Jewish administrative body, known as the Judenrat, to help them govern the Jewish community and to ensure that their plans for that community were efficiently carried out. These plans were implemented in stages and were varied in their immediate objectives, but they all served to make life increasingly difficult for us. And they all shared the same long-term goal of destroying the Jews of Lvov.

I will not enumerate in detail the measures employed by the Germans to accomplish this aim. Nor will I provide a comprehensive history of the Holocaust as it unfolded in Lvov and wherever else I journeyed during the war. I am not interested in writing Holocaust history, but rather in presenting my experience of that history—in revealing the Holocaust as seen through the eyes of a young girl who survived it. From that perspective, the annihilation of European Jewry was an episodic affair, a set of steadily worsening circumstances underscored by despair and fear, permeated and intensified by physical suffering, and punctuated by localized acts of brutal oppression, horrifying violence, and sudden, savage murder.

This is what I remember. For the first few days of the German occupation, we stayed in our apartment—a sensible precaution, considering the bloodbath the Ukrainians were perpetrating in the Jewish district. Three or four days later, the Germans dispersed the rioting mobs and restored order to the city. A period of relative calm ensued during which Jews ventured cautiously from their dwellings to purchase food and other necessities.

In the middle of July, notices were posted on kiosks and building walls ordering every Polish Jew to wear a white armband with a blue Jewish star on it when going out in public. The *opaska*, as the armband was called in Polish, also had to be worn by Jews who had converted to Christianity, and by Christians with Jewish ancestors three generations removed. The penalty for being caught in public without one's armband was death, with execution frequently occurring on the spot.

My parents briefly entertained the notion that we did not have to wear the armbands because we were *staatlos*—that is, stateless people, citizens of neither Poland nor the Soviet Union, and thus, technically, not Polish Jews (my parents never had become naturalized Polish citizens after fleeing Kamenets-Podolski). But my father wisely never put this matter to the test. He realized that the Germans did not care whether or not we were Polish Jews. The point was, we were Jews. We would wear the armbands—or die.

Though I did not say so, it seemed to me that we would die in any case. Even then I knew the Germans had ordered us to wear the armbands for one reason, and one reason only: they were singling us out for murder.

At the end of July, Ukrainian mobs once again rampaged through the Jewish community, this time to avenge the death of their hero Simon Petliura, who had been murdered in Paris on July 28, 1926, by a Jewish assassin. The Petliura pogrom lasted several days and claimed some two thousand Jewish lives, yet I had no idea that it was going on. Lvov is a fairly big city, and, aside from word of mouth, we had no means of obtaining news about what was happening several miles away in the Jewish district. There were no telephones, no radios, and no newspapers to keep us abreast of current events. Every apartment building was an island unto itself, cut off from the rest of the world. All hell could be breaking loose one block over and we would not know it.

This ignorance gave me a false sense of security. I knew that conditions for Jews in Lvov were bad, but I did not know how bad. And though I heard plenty of atrocity stories, I ignored them. I just closed my eyes and ears to events and pretended as if they weren't happening.

At length, the Germans, deciding that nothing further could be gained by allowing the Ukrainians to run amok, again brought the rampaging mobs to heel. The Germans then established the Judenrat and, on August 1, announced the incorporation of Eastern Galicia, including the city of "Lvov/Lemberg," into what was known as the Government-General of Poland. The entire region was henceforth a protectorate of the German Reich rather than an independent nation, a development that thoroughly outraged the Ukrainians. Not surprisingly, the Ukrainians directed most of their anger at the Jews, thus upholding the ancient tradition of scapegoating Jews for whatever had gone wrong in their own lives.

As the summer wore on, we found it increasingly difficult

to obtain food and other essentials. Jews were forbidden to purchase groceries and medicine—and just about everything else—in shops other than those with signs that said "For Jews Only." These shops were few and far between, and the amount of foodstuffs we could purchase from them was limited to what was, in effect, a starvation ration. Nor could we turn to Uncle Herman for help, as we had done during the Soviet occupation. Herman had disappeared from his farm, having gone into hiding with his children, and we did not know where they were holed up, or even whether they were still alive.

We solved our food procurement problem by letting my sister Rysia do the shopping for us. Rysia was nine years old, cute as a button, and very Aryan in appearance, with a turned-up nose, bright blue eyes, a fair complexion, and golden hair arranged in long braids, "Gretchen braids," we called them. She was a buoyantly happy child with a little-girl prettiness and an irresistible charm that made people smile just to look at her. Moreover, she was imbued with an innocence so profound as to make her seem incapable of any deception whatsoever, which was fortunate, since deception was exactly what we required of her.

I cannot fathom the desperation that compelled my parents to place their youngest daughter in mortal peril, but I can well understand the necessity for doing so. The fact is, Rysia represented the only viable alternative to starvation. So my mother and father dressed her in a starchy white Polish peasant dress with flower patterns (but no *opaska*), hung a wicker basket on her slender arm, gave her money with which to make her purchases; then, after admonishing her to put on a pleasant face, they sent this adorable sprite skipping forth into the evil streets of German-occupied Lvov.

Rysia was a willing and excellent player of this most dangerous of games. She went from shop to shop, chatting it up with the Polish shopkeepers, modestly accepting myriad compliments about her beauty, occasionally bestowing a sweet smile on a hardened SS trooper who could not help smiling back at this elfin paragon of Teutonic comeliness. She never got caught and she always returned with the groceries, whereupon we would hug and kiss her and shower her with the praise she so richly deserved. In such moments, she beamed at us, basking joyfully in all the love and attention she was getting and never for an instant indicating that she realized how close to death she had come. I believe, however, that she understood the precarious nature of her undertaking; and for that reason, I believe, she relished it. Dear, brave Rysia, she viewed each shopping trip as an adventure, at once exciting and fun. Beyond that, it made her feel important and grown-up to be making such a critical contribution to the family's welfare.

Like Rysia, I wore peasant dresses and arranged my hair in Gretchen braids. And because I was also blond and blue-eyed, I could pass myself off as a Pole. But I could not go shopping because I was a reasonably attractive teenage girl and therefore much too conspicuous. All it would take was one German soldier demanding to see my identification papers as a pretext for meeting me. If that happened I would probably be dead before the end of the day. Quite honestly, Rysia was the right person for the role. I did not possess her ingenuousness or exuberance, prerequisites for shopping success. The dangers outside our apartment made me serious and somber—traits not exactly conducive to winning the confidence of Polish shopkeepers or to convincing German soldiers that I had no cause to fear them. Though I was capable of bravery, I was not fearless, and I was not reckless either. The streets were never safe, and I let that fact guide my behavior. When I was walking around, I smiled blandly, looked at the ground, and avoided making eye contact with everyone, especially the Germans, and most especially the SS troopers. I did not greatly fear the regular soldiers; they usually had nothing to do with the Jews. But the SS men terrified me. I always walked by them with my heart pounding. They were in Lvov for one reason: to kill Jews.

In the first months of the German occupation, neighbors and friends of my parents continued as before to visit our apartment to discuss the situation in Lvov. The men would do most of the talking, while the women sat beside them, weeping softly. My mother served them tea, but nothing to eat—we did not have any extra food to give them. The adults would trade information and swap rumors, which were mostly concerned with the imminent outbreak of an *Aktion* (action)— the German equivalent of a pogrom. The adults also talked about America. They wondered why America would not help us, why President Roosevelt would not declare war on Germany and put an end to Hitler and the murderous Nazi regime.

Some of the adults were cautiously optimistic, believing that the Germans would desist in their persecution of the Jews and allow life in Poland to return to some semblance of normality. They figured that the actions could not continue forever since they were too disruptive to the economy, of which the Jews were such an integral part. My father was not one of these optimists. By now he was persuaded that the Germans were killing Jews wholesale and that they were not about to quit doing so however much the economy suffered. The situation made him very angry, the more so because there was really nothing he could do about it.

Petia was in a constant panic. His most dire predictions were coming true. He would say that we were all going to die, that the optimists were blind, stupid fools, that the Germans were going to murder every single Jew in Lvov, in Poland, in all of Europe. Many of the adults agreed with him, but not me; I still had my whole life ahead of me and was determined that I would somehow survive.

In the late summer or early fall, word got around that any Jew who was employed would be reasonably safe from arrest. There was much truth to this, at least in the early stages of the occupation. Being employed meant that you would be issued an *Arbeitkarte,* or work card, which soon became among the most valuable possessions a Jew could own. The work card identified your place of employment and was to be carried on your person day and night in the event that you were caught up in an action. This could happen without warning anytime, anywhere. You might be strolling down the sidewalk in a peaceful neighborhood, one where there were no Germans or Ukrainians in sight, when suddenly trucks would pull up beside you and slam on their brakes. In the next instant, SS troopers and Ukrainian militiamen would jump out of the trucks and fan out on the double to stop anyone wearing a Jewish armband and demand to see his or her work card. If you could come up with one, they would usually let you go; if you couldn't, it meant that you were unemployed, and you would be hustled aboard a truck for a trip to a labor camp, or worse.

Sometimes the Germans and their henchmen would stop everybody in the immediate vicinity, even those who weren't wearing armbands, and demand to see their *Kennkarte,* or identification card. This established one's identity as a Jew or a Gentile, and if it turned out that you were the latter, you would also be sent on your way. But if you didn't have an identification card, or had one which revealed that you were a Jew—and a Jew who wasn't wearing an armband, no less— then you might as well start saying your prayers, and quickly, for in most such cases there would be precious little time left to you before your captors beat you to death or put a bullet in your head.

Even if you did have a valid work card, you might still be arrested; or you might be beaten, shot, or strung up on the nearest lamppost. There were no guarantees. You could be arrested or killed because an SS trooper did not like your looks, or because a Ukrainian militiamen was feeling irritable that day. Did the militiaman's wife deny him sex the night before? Had he been humiliated or made to feel inadequate by a girlfriend or his male peers? Or was he brimming with anti-Semitic hatreds which had been stirred to a boiling froth by German propaganda and incitements to violence and which he was only too eager to express? Whatever the case, an action afforded him the opportunity and the excuse to vent his anger and frustrations on the Jews, even Jews with work cards.

Nevertheless, a work card was a much sought-after item because it did offer some protection from arrest. Needless to say, everybody looked for work, any kind of work. My father was lucky in this regard. He had lost his job as president of the musicians' union, which had been disbanded, and as a Jew he was no longer permitted to work as a musician in the nightclubs. But after registering with the Judenrat's labor department, he was able to get a job as a night watchman at a Luftwaffe uniform and clothing warehouse located downtown. Coincidentally, Uncle Yossi was also hired by the Luftwaffe to work as a janitor and handyman in a factory, also located downtown, that was used to clean and repair underwear for air force personnel. This menial job was quite a reversal of fortune for Yossi, who had previously been employed as a building engineer. But he was glad to be gainfully employed and, equally important, to have a work card attesting to that fact.

Working for the Germans was a cruel irony for my father, but he tried to be philosophical about it. "If you can't change the way things are," he would say, "you have to make the best of the situation. And that's what I'm doing."

I remember once how Petia upbraided my father about his job, saying that he was aiding and abetting the enemy of his people. "You're working for Hitler!" he said. "You're working for the man who wants to kill us all!"

"I have responsibilities to my family," my father countered. "And this is the best I can do."

"You call that the best?" Petia said in mocking tone. "Watching over Hitler's *gatskis* [underwear] is the best you can do?"

"Yes, it is," my father calmly replied. "For now."

"Then God help us!"

"Perhaps He will," my father said. "One can only hope."

My father knew that working for the Luftwaffe was better, far better, than having no job at all. He thought his job may even have been better than most jobs, because the Germans might exempt their Jewish employees from arrest, whereas a Jew who worked for a Polish firm was still liable to be arrested at any time. This was really wishful thinking on his part, as the Germans made no promises to protect their Jewish employees. But a person has to believe in something. A person must have hope. And my father still had hope, although it was rapidly fading.

One day Yossi came by our apartment after work and told me that his factory was hiring seamstresses. Up until then I had been confined to the apartment to avoid being arrested in a Nazi dragnet. But the next day, I ventured outside and, fearful that I might at any moment be swept up in an action, I hurried over to the factory to apply for the job.

The man who processed my application was the director of the factory, a middle-aged German with thinning blond hair and a potbelly. Although technically an officer in the Luftwaffe, he wore a civilian's navy blue suit jacket and charcoal gray trousers. He had probably been a businessman in private life and was only nominally a member of the Luftwaffe, an entrepreneur who had been absorbed into the German military to manage one of the many enterprises it had acquired and operated as part of a burgeoning industrial empire. Judging by his noticeably dispassionate attitude toward me and the other Jewish women he supervised, it is possible that he was not even a Nazi. During my interview with him, I stood in front of his desk and answered various questions about my background, which included identifying myself as a Jew. I spoke in a respectful tone, trying to strike a balance between meekness and assertiveness—the Germans hated too much of both in underlings—while doing my utmost to conceal the anxiety I felt. The director conducted the interview in a brisk, professional manner, filling out forms as we talked, and though he was not friendly, he was not hostile either. At one point, he asked whether I knew how to operate a sewing machine with a foot treadle. I told him that I did, which was a lie. But I knew that I could figure out how to work a sewing machine simply because my life depended on my doing so.

I was hired on the spot and sent to work in a room with about twenty other girls, all of them Jewish. That same day I received my work card, and I knew that I would be safe for a little while.

It wasn't a bad job by the standards of occupied Lvov. I worked five days a week from eight in the morning to about four in the afternoon, and though we did not take any breaks, we were allowed to eat whatever food we might have—perhaps a slice of bread and a piece of onion—while seated at our machines. Most of us went without meals, however, because we had no food to spare for lunch.

The job even provided us with a small wage, which was based on a quota system. We had to sew, patch, and repair a certain number of undershirts and underpants every day, and if we fulfilled our quota—which was not hard to do—we were paid what amounted to a few pennies.

The director was a decent sort to the extent that he did not abuse us in any way. The same was true of his codirector, a German girl who performed double-duty as his mistress. They lived together in an apartment in the factory, and a more unattractive couple you would be hard-pressed to find. The girl, who was several years younger than the director, had buck teeth, dirty blond hair, and a scrawny figure whose bony angularity was accentuated in a most unflattering way by the severe cut of the navy suit jacket she also wore. Both she and her portly paramour always had their faces scrubbed so clean that their skin virtually shone from the astringent soap they no doubt used; and of course she did not wear any makeup whatsoever, not even a hint of lipstick or blush to soften the lines of her stern features. They struck me as a pair of cold fish, and it was impossible to imagine them as being romantically linked and otherwise doing what lovers normally do, but for all their lack of personal charm they nevertheless treated us fairly and were never harsh or brutal to us.

Every hour or so the director and his mistress walked through the shop, coming up behind us to look over our shoulders and inspect our work. They rarely said anything to us because we were, after all, Jewish *Untermenschen*, a lower form of human being, and therefore people who were not worthy of casual discourse with members of the master race. Nor did we say anything to them, but instead worked diligently on our machines as they walked back and forth behind us.

We were permitted to talk among ourselves, however, and we did so incessantly. Having arranged our sewing machines in a circle to facilitate conversation, we gossiped, told jokes, and gabbed about boys, food, movies, and the like. Our German supervisors did not mind our talking so long as we got our work done. Our topics were innocuous; even when the director and his mistress had left the room and returned to the office they shared, we did not dare talk about politics, or the war, or anything having to do with the German occupation.

At the beginning of October, signs were posted all over Lvov proclaiming the establishment of a Jewish residential area in the north and northwest part of the city. This area, which would eventually evolve into a bona fide ghetto, encompassed Lvov's Jewish quarter plus working-class neighborhoods that were home to Polish and Ukrainian Gentiles, that is, all of the Zamarstynowska and Zniesienie districts, and part of the Kleparow district. The same posters ordered Jews throughout the city to move to the residential area within the month and gave resident Gentiles until January to seek lodging elsewhere, preferably in the homes that the displaced Jews had recently been forced to abandon.

My father, in company with thousands of other Jews, immediately went out and rented a room for us in the Jewish district. Movement into the designated area started almost at once, and in the weeks that followed, one became accustomed to the sight of Jews walking through the streets carrying suitcases and assorted bundles and packages, or pulling handcarts piled high with their luggage and other belongings.

We immediately made preparations to join them, even though the deadline for relocating wouldn't expire for another three weeks. All the adults felt a sense of urgency about leaving, but my mother was especially anxious to go. She didn't want to be in our apartment on 51 Zyblikiewicza Street if and when the Nazis came to evict us, a prospect that terrified her. I argued with her about this, telling her that we should stay put for a while, that we should wait and see what was going to happen in the Jewish district.

"We can't wait," my mother said. "We have to go now. We have to obey the Germans."

But I did not want to obey the Germans. "I am not going

to the ghetto!" I exclaimed. "The ghetto is a trap! The ghetto is death! I won't go there!"

In response to this outburst, my parents just shrugged and shook their heads. "Well, we'll see about that," they said. "You'll go, just like everyone else." They did not take me seriously.

In the next day or so, my family packed our best clothes and most valuable possessions in a steamer trunk, the one my grandfather had used on his trips back and forth between America and Poland; then my father and Yossi carted the trunk to what was to be our new home.

By then I had made up my mind to stay out of the Jewish district no matter what my family did. I had no idea where I would go or what I would do, and I didn't care. I was on the brink of open rebellion against my parents. This was something new for me. I had never before defied my parents on any important matter; I had never really contemplated it. But no more. Suddenly I saw my parents not as all-knowing adults but as fallible people who could make mistakes and who had no power to influence the course of their lives or the lives of their children. The Nazis had all the power, and Hitler was their almighty god, the lord of life and death in Europe. I began to feel that I could not depend on my parents to protect me from that monster. My sense of security, of being a little girl safe at home in the care of my parents, was fast becoming a thing of the past. I realized that I needed to assert myself, to do what I felt was right.

The Germans had said nothing yet about turning the Jewish residential area into a true ghetto, by erecting walls and barbed-wire fences around it and closing it off from the rest of the city. They had yet to restrict movement in and out of the residential area. But I knew that all this would occur soon enough. First, the Germans would concentrate the Jews in the residential area, then they would seal it, and then they would kill us. It was all quite obvious to me. And because it was so obvious, my intuition was practically screaming at me to stay out of the Jewish area. I decided that I would rather die than move to that area, which was tantamount to walking into a trap. In our neighborhood we *might* be killed, whereas in the Jewish area, it seemed to me, we would *certainly* be killed.

I reached this decision on my own, without consulting anyone in my family. I did not discuss it with my father and mother because I did not want to further upset them or get into another argument. And I certainly did not talk about it with my friends and coworkers at the underwear factory. They could not be trusted, even if they were Jews. A Jew could sell you out to the Nazis just as easily as a Pole or a Ukrainian. People were desperate, afraid of their own shadows, and in their desperation and fear they were liable to turn on you in an instant if by doing so they thought they could increase their own chances for survival.

The Jewish police were, I thought, proof of this. Officially known as the *Ordnungsdienst* (Order Service), the Jewish police were young men recruited locally to serve as a sort of intermediary constabulary force between the Jews of Lvov and their Nazi overlords. They wore caps and yellow armbands, both with the Star of David on them, and they were armed with rubber truncheons, which they did not hesitate to use on their fellow Jews. Although nominally charged with maintaining order in the Jewish community, they were also employed as instruments of repression. In this capacity they were usually involved in the actions, helping SS troops and Ukrainian militiamen in their efforts to round up Jews for deportation to the labor camps and, later, to the death camps as well.

They had their work cut out for them. Throughout the autumn, there were actions aplenty to keep them busy. Most of the actions were small in scale, consisting of the arrest of a dozen or so men and women in whichever neighborhood the Germans had targeted for the day. The actions were undertaken mainly to stock the labor camps, where the high death toll created a constant need for replacement workers. But there were also actions carried out to loot Jewish households of their furniture, actions to enforce payment of a twenty-million-ruble tax (the equivalent of four million dollars in 1939) imposed on the Jewish community to finance the repair and reconstruction of the city's war-damaged infrastructure, and actions to evict Jews from desirable neighborhoods and buildings. And, of course, there were actions that were undertaken for the sole purpose of harassing, tormenting, and killing Jews.

Sometimes, when I was coming home from work, I came across an action in progress. SS troops, aided by their minions in the Ukrainian militia and the Jewish police, would be seizing people on the street and sidewalks, demanding to see their papers, roughing them up, punching them with their fists and hitting them with truncheons, and shoving and dragging them to trucks, then kicking them as they climbed aboard for transport to a prison or a labor camp. Somehow I always managed to avoid arrest. When I was certain that no one was looking, I would quickly slip off my armband and stuff it in a pocket or in my purse; then I would walk straight through the action, minding my own business, looking neither to the left nor the right at the tumult and violence on either side. I never walked or ran away from an action, because to do so would have called attention to the fact that I was Jewish and trying to escape arrest. I behaved as if I were confronted by a snarling dog. If you run from a dog, he'll chase you. But if you act confident, as if you know what you're doing, he won't attack you.

It did not hurt my chances that I had braided blond hair and wore a white peasant dress like so many Polish girls. But the real key to walking through an action without getting arrested was self-confidence. That, and a certain ability to shut down your rational functions, to blank out your thoughts, to operate on pure instinct. I don't know where or how I acquired this ability. Perhaps it was a gift from God. But this I do know: I was good at it. And it usually kept me out of trouble. Usually, but not always.

The order to move to the ghetto set in motion an action that was wider in scope, more violent, and more prolonged than its predecessors. It was during this action that I went into the Jewish district for the first and only time, and in doing so witnessed scenes of hitherto unimagined horror.

This is what happened. Despite the German order, and despite my parents' concern about obeying it promptly, we did not vacate our apartment. Having deposited our luggage in the rented room in the Jewish district, my family had made no further preparations to leave. Fearing, as I did, what a move to the district might entail, the adults had decided to adopt the "wait and see" approach that I had so vehemently counseled. For the time being, we would neither quit our apartment nor give up our room in the Jewish district; rather, we would lie low and watch how the situation developed before committing ourselves to one course of action or the other. This approach seemed the correct one when after a few days nobody in authority had come around to evict us.

We were lucky, for many Jews had in fact been rousted from their homes, and of these, many had been murdered in the streets while en route to the Jewish district. The Germans and Ukrainians killed Jews for sport, not because the Nazis had specifically mandated their annihilation; the Final Solution had yet to be made official policy (this would happen in January 1942, as a result of the infamous Wansee Conference). And what a sport they made of it, gleefully beating Jews to death, or shooting them down, or stringing them up from the nearest available lamppost or balcony railing.

I can only assume that the Germans did not raid our apartment because there were too many Jews in Lvov to keep them busy. The Germans were discovering that, due to the influx of refugees from the west and the surrounding countryside, Lvov's Jewish population was much bigger than they had originally thought. They were also finding out that it was one thing to order the Jews to move and quite another to make them all obey the order. When Jews like my parents simply dug in their heels and refused to leave their homes, there was little the Germans could do about it except to go to each household and drag its occupants out. This was a difficult undertaking, and the Germans temporarily lacked the manpower to do it. Eventually, the sheer number of Jews defeated the Germans' attempt to resettle them. The deadline for resettlement came and went, and still many Jews, including my family, remained outside the Jewish district. At which point, the ever-practical Germans, having wearied of the effort, called a halt to the whole operation. Satisfied that they had managed to concentrate a significant portion of the Jewish population in a constricted area, the Germans issued a proclamation informing Jews who had not moved that they could continue to live in their homes until they received notice to the contrary.

So we stayed in our apartment and waited on events, hoping all the while that such notice would never come. One day during this period, our janitor, Wacław, appeared at our door along with another man. Although the latter was a Pole, he was wearing the tattered remnants of a Red Army uniform. My father did not let them in, and the three men stood in the doorway conversing in low voices, like conspirators hatching a plot. Meanwhile, my mother and I hovered in the background, trying unsuccessfully to make out what was being said.

Wacław and his companion left a few minutes later. When they were gone, my father called a meeting of the family. My grandmother, Uncle Yossi, and Aunt Haika were summoned from the apartment next door, joining my mother, my sister, and me in our living room to hear what my father had to say. He had incredible news: according to Wacław's companion, Fima was alive and well and in hiding somewhere just outside Lvov. The man claimed to have served in Fima's artillery battery, which had been shattered in battle with the Germans up on the Finnish frontier. But rather than surrender to the invaders, as most of the men in their unit had done, they had both gone into hiding. Traveling mostly at night, keeping to the fields and forests while avoiding roads and towns, they had slowly made their way back to Poland without getting caught. A few days ago they had reached the outskirts of Lvov, and Fima had sent the man into the city to make contact with us.

The man told my father that Fima wished to come home but could not do so without money and civilian clothes to wear. The man said that he would take these things to Fima, but only if my father rewarded him for his troubles. The man named his price and my father agreed to pay it, but not right away as the clothes and the money weren't handy. Could the man come back that evening? The man said he could, admonishing my father to have the clothes and the money ready when he returned.

The news that Fima was alive, coupled with the possibility that he might soon be reunited with us, caused the women in the family to burst into tears of joy. But our celebration was tempered by the understanding that the man may have been stringing us along. Our tears subsided, we dried our eyes, and we began to soberly assess the situation. It was entirely possible, we realized, that Fima was not outside Lvov, and that our informant had invented a cock-and-bull story to con us out of our money. Haika, for one, flatly believed that the man was lying, and my father and grandmother had their doubts. "How can we know whether the man is telling the truth?" my father asked. "How can we be sure?"

My mother, who was almost frantic at the prospect of getting Fima back, would not permit any equivocation on my father's part. Bursting into tears again, she told my father, "We can't know, but we have to take that chance! We have to give that man whatever he asks for! If we don't, we'll be left wondering whether we abandoned Fima when he needed us to help him."

The debate went on for a while, but eventually it was my mother's view that prevailed. It did not take much to persuade us. We knew we were grasping at straws, but no matter—we all wanted to believe that Fima was nearby and that an outlay of money and clothes would bring him home to us.

That settled, the next order of business was to fetch Fima's clothes. I was elected for the job because I was the only member of our family who had a chance of passing in and out of the Jewish district without getting arrested. My sister was too young; my mother, aunt, and grandmother were too old; and my father and Yossi, being men, were too obvious.

I put on my coat and got ready to leave. Everyone was calm—no anxious words of warning from my father, no weeping by my mother, no hysterics from Haika and Pesha. They all assumed that I would make it to the Jewish district safely and return without incident. Perhaps the adults were worried, but I did not notice it.

I, too, was calm. Although not eager to go into the Jewish district, I was not afraid either. I went to and from work every day and was accustomed to the danger in the streets. I understood the risk involved and accepted it because I wanted to help my brother. What I could not accept was the idea that I might be killed or harmed by the Nazis. Even in the autumn of 1941—even after two years of war and four months of German occupation with all its attendant cruelties, bloodshed, and deprivations—this seemed inconceivable to me. I was nineteen years old, and like so many young men and women I had an irrational faith in my own invincibility. I like to think that such faith was a form of courage, but I also know that it was due in large measure to my callow nature. I was brave, but I was also ignorant.

I did not intend to wear an armband, or even take one with me. I was wearing a peasant dress, my hair was in braids—I looked like a Gentile girl, and I did not want to spoil my disguise. But just as I was about to walk out the door my mother handed me an armband. I took it and put it in my purse. Then my mother gave me some practical advice: "Look for Fima's good clothes," she said. "His nice gray suit, his dress shoes, and his white shirt."

It took me over an hour to walk from my apartment to the Jewish district. It was a fine autumn day, warm and blustery, with the sun shining brightly and the air suffused by a hazy glow. Windblown dust and scraps of newspaper skittered through the streets and alleys. Nothing happened to me on the way and I saw no atrocities or arrests. Just before I reached the entrance to the Jewish district, I ducked into a doorway, took my armband out of my purse, and slipped it on over my coat sleeve.

The Jewish district had not yet been walled off from the rest of the city—that would come later. The Peltewna Street viaduct was the most heavily trafficked route into the district, and there were German and Ukrainian troops posted on it. But the district had no formal entrance, and it was thus still possible to move freely in and out at any point along its periphery.

I entered on an unguarded side street. Once inside I began to look for Lyczakowska Street, where the house with our new apartment was located. I had no idea where it was. The district was swarming with Ukrainian militiamen and blue-jacketed Jewish policemen. Always one of the poorer areas of the city, the district had become even more impoverished due to the influx of homeless Jews from other neighborhoods in Lvov as well as the surrounding countryside. There were hundreds, perhaps thousands of Jews milling around, toting suitcases and bundles of clothing, pushing and pulling handcarts and baby carriages as they made their way to their new homes. Entire families, destitute and with no place to go, crouched in doorways—fathers, mothers, grandparents, and children, pressed together for warmth, watching the passersby with hollow, expressionless eyes. I approached a Jewish policeman and asked him for directions to Lyczakowska Street. He told me how to get there, and I soon arrived at my destination.

The house was a two-story structure situated in a residential neighborhood among other houses and small apartment buildings. It had a yard bounded by a low picket fence with a gate, and the front door was bustling with people coming and going. I opened the gate and went into the yard, thinking that in better times the house must have been a nice place to live. But not anymore. These were bad times, and when I went inside the house, I found that it had changed accordingly.

There were perhaps a dozen rooms in the house, and each room was now home to one or more families. People who were moving into the house crowded the hallway and the staircase leading to the second floor. I asked a man where I might find the Weintraubs' room. He told me that it was just off the kitchen. I walked down the hall past several rooms, all with their doors wide open. The rooms were unheated and the people inside were huddled together, using their combined body heat to ward off the cold. Every room seemed to have its complement of the aged and the infirm, all of them moaning, wailing, and sobbing—an awful sound that made me want to put my hands to my ears to shut it out. Better still, I thought, I could just turn around and walk right back out the door. I resisted the impulse by reminding myself that Fima was depending on me. For his sake, I would stay and do what was required of me.

I continued on down the hall. Glancing into one room, I saw an old woman wearing a black babushka scarf over her head and a black shawl draped over her thin shoulders. She was seated on a chair in the corner of the room, and she was rocking back and forth, weeping and keening in a loud voice. She was the most pathetic person I had ever seen, and as I looked at her, I began to feel as if the walls were closing in on me.

The door to our room was unlocked, and I went in. Our steamer trunk was there, but when I opened the lid, I found it empty. The contents had been rifled, almost certainly by the inhabitants of the house. I suppose I could have gone around from room to room in search of our stolen belongings, but I did not think this would do me any good. Whoever had stolen our clothes had probably sold them on the black market or exchanged them for food. Besides, I could not stay in that house one minute longer. The atmosphere was heavy with misery and sorrow, and I had a very powerful feeling that I must leave at once or I would be suffocated by it. I told myself: That's it, there's nothing you can do; now get out of here. And so I left.

I had not been in the house more than a few minutes, and I had said nothing to anyone except to ask directions to our room. I felt very different from the people in there, and not only because most of them appeared to be old fashioned, tra-ditional-minded Jews. I felt no affinity to them because I could sense that they were all going to die. They had submit-ted to their fate and in doing so had condemned themselves to death. But I was determined to live; I would never submit, and I would not be a victim!

Once outside I walked quickly away from the house. My only thought was to get out of the Jewish district as fast as my feet could take me, but without breaking into a run. By now it was late afternoon; the sun was still shining and the air still had a hazy autumnal glow. In the house I had felt as if I were going to be sick to my stomach, but the cool fresh air on my face revived me somewhat and made me feel better. Then I entered a large piazza and came to an abrupt halt, brought up short by a scene more shocking by far than in the house on Lyczakowska Street.

At the far end of the piazza, about a block away, five men had been hung by their necks from the first-floor balcony of a residential apartment building. They were Jews, as evidenced by the Star of David armbands on their sleeves; they had their hands tied behind their backs and the ropes that had strangled them were fastened to the balcony's iron railing. Several SS men stood on the balcony above them; clearly, these were the executioners, and it seemed likely that they had dispatched their victims by simply flinging them off that makeshift scaffold. Having performed this task, they were alternately chatting casually with each other and leaning out over the railing to appraise their handiwork. On the sidewalk just beneath the balcony stood a second group of SS men as well as about a dozen civilian onlookers, all gazing up silently at the hanged men.

For a moment I was petrified with horror and fright. In the next instant, panic washed over me and I was seized by a desperate urge to run away. Then I gave myself a little shake, thus regaining my composure and my self-control. In one quick motion, I surreptitiously slipped off my armband and stuffed it back into my purse. For a second I thought of throwing the armband away but decided against this. With bowed head and lowered eyes, I hurried out of the piazza onto a side street, and as I walked away from that place, I told myself that I was invisible, that nobody could see me, that I would certainly escape because I was hidden from view.

As soon I got home, I gave my parents a full account of my trip. My father listened quietly, almost without comment. The news that Fima's clothes had been stolen elicited a resigned shrug, as if he had expected all along that something like this would happen. When I described the scene in the piazza, he shook his head with a despairing but distracted air. I realized that he wasn't paying attention to me; he was thinking about Fima. His concern for Fima was such that he was barely cognizant of what I had been through, of the horror and danger to which I had been exposed. I know now that he blamed himself for not being able to do more to help Fima. He felt that he had failed his son as both a man and a father, and though he was certainly mistaken in this regard, neither his family members nor his friends could ever say anything to persuade him otherwise.

My mother, for her part, began weeping when I told her about the theft of Fima's clothes. Without these clothes, she thought, Fima would not be able to come home. This was a cruel blow to the hopes that Wacław's companion had raised in her. "Now what?" she said, between sobs, to no one in particular. "What shall we do now?"

My mother scarcely acknowledged that I had just had a close brush with death in the form of an SS execution squad. She was more worried about her son than me. But I could not fault her for this, since I, too, was worried about Fima.

Wacław and his companion showed up again after dark. My father explained that although he did not have Fima's clothes, he had the money the stranger had asked for. My father then handed over a thick wad of banknotes to the stranger, who quickly counted the money. But after pocketing the money, the stranger said it was not enough and demanded my father's wristwatch as well. Without argument or hesitation, my father unfastened his wristwatch and gave it to the man. This concluded the transaction, and the two men left.

Then we waited. And waited. And waited some more. My mother, sick with anxiety, lay down on the sofa; my grandmother sat beside her, stroking her hair, holding her hands, saying comforting words to her. Meanwhile, my father paced about the room like a caged lion. Haika, Yossi, Rysia, and I sat around the kitchen table. We waited, we stared at each other, we looked up at the kitchen clock, we stared at each other. We waited in silence—no one wanted to talk. The hours crawled by.

At some point Pesha spoke up and said what we all knew to be true. "You know that man was lying," she told my father.

"He played us for fools. He took our money, and he'll never come back."

"Maybe, maybe not," my father said in toneless voice, as if he did not have the energy or conviction to contradict her.

"And you know that Fima isn't coming back, either."

My father said nothing. My mother wept.

We waited. Nine o'clock came and went. Then ten o'clock, then eleven o'clock. Still no Fima. At midnight my grandmother sadly rose from her chair and went back to her apartment without saying a word in parting. A few minutes later Haika and Yossi followed her. Then my father stood, took my mother by the hand, raised her up off the sofa, and led her weeping to their bedroom. It was over. Fima was not coming home.

And what of Fima? My brother was attending artillery school in Leningrad when the Germans invaded. His training program was cut short and he was commissioned a second lieutenant in the artillery. Shortly thereafter he was posted to a fortified area in the vicinity of Vyborg in the province of Karelia, which the Soviet Union had wrested from Finland in the Winter War of 1939–40. There he assumed command of a battery of four 155mm guns and 120 men.

My brother was now officially known as Yephim Vinogradov. Although this is the Russian equivalent of Fima Weintraub, it sounds like a Gentile name—which was the whole point. The Soviet high command had authorized the name change for Fima and for any other Polish Jew who wished to pass himself off as a Gentile. It was a precautionary measure taken with the understanding that, in the event of capture by the Germans, a Polish Jewish name would earn the bearer immediate execution; moreover, the Germans would probably track down the soldier's family in Poland and kill all his family members as well.

It was appropriate for Fima to have a Russian name, for he was a genuinely loyal Red Army soldier. He was not, however, a believing Communist. Marxist theories and ideology had been drummed into his head as part of his training regimen, but he did not subscribe to any of it. Of course, he pretended to be an enthusiastic Communist because if he did not he would be sent to a labor camp in Siberia.

Fima's artillery battery was situated in a lovely pine and birch forest. His sector was quiet; elsewhere the Finns had gone on the offensive to recover territory lost to the Soviets in the Winter War, but not here, not yet. However, despite the peacefulness and pleasant scenery, Fima was miserable. Aware that the Germans had captured Lvov, he was tremendously worried about his family. Plus, the forest was infested by mosquitoes. In the evening the tea and turnip soup that normally constituted the final meal of the day was swimming with mosquitoes, depriving the soldiers of whatever pleasure they might otherwise have gained from their food. Making matters worse was the determination of these insects to feast upon the soldiers as well, a problem that continued into the night, with the soldiers wrapping shirts around their faces, leaving only their noses exposed for breathing, to avoid being bitten as they lay sleeping—or trying to sleep—on their cots.

The mosquitoes were more than just an annoyance, however. As carriers of malaria, they accounted for much sickness and several deaths. Other diseases and ailments were rife; dysentery and pneumonia, for example, claimed a number of victims. Morale accordingly plummeted and inevitably some men deserted to the Finns as a way out of their predicament and, not incidentally, as an escape from Soviet domination as well. Most of the deserters were Ukrainians who had been conscripted into the Red Army and were not at all fond of the Russians and bitterly resented Soviet rule of their homeland. Fima, himself a displaced Ukrainian, was sympathetic to their views. But, being a steadfast soldier, he would not even entertain the thought of desertion.

There was another consideration, however. The men who went over to the Finns were Christians, and Fima was a Jew. His Russian name might conceal this fact, but then again it might not. He did not want to take the chance. While the Finns might not treat him badly, the Germans would. And Finland was an ally of Germany.

When the Finns finally attacked his position, it was late autumn and the forest was blanketed with a deep layer of snow. Aided by German air and ground units, the Finns struck with overwhelming force and quickly penetrated the Soviet defenses in the Vyborg sector. Such was the speed and fury of the Finnish onslaught that Fima never had time to get his guns into action. The front had collapsed and the thunder of battle was rolling toward them at a rapid pace. Less than an hour after the initial assault, and with the battery in danger of being overrun, Fima and his men were ordered to abandon their equipment and withdraw. It was an order they were only too happy to obey. Having never once fired their guns in anger, they plunged into the forest on foot, intent on putting as much distance as they could between themselves and the enemy.

Fima and his men pushed through the snow toward Leningrad with the main body of the Finnish army in hot pursuit. As they made their way through the forest, Finnish irregulars harassed them with sniper fire from camouflaged blinds set high in the branches of the trees. Nicknamed "kookushka" (cuckoo bird), the snipers were uniformly excellent marksmen who exacted a steadily mounting toll in killed and wounded.

Most of the casualties were suffered when the Soviets crossed a clearing. There wasn't much Fima and his men could do in retaliation. So adept were the Finns at the art of concealment that they made themselves virtually invisible to their victims. Their bullets seemed to come out of the forest from everywhere and nowhere at once, with the reverberations from each shot foiling any attempt to pinpoint by sound the direction whence they came. About all the Soviets could do was collect their wounded and get out of there before another man was hit. The dead, of course, were left behind.

In the afternoon Fima halted his men at the edge of a clearing to catch their breath and take stock of their situation. None relished the prospect of crossing the open ground, but they realized that cross it they must if they wanted to outdistance their pursuers. Fima sent a scout into the clearing to reconnoiter. When the scout reached the center of the clearing, a shot rang out and the man fell lifeless to the ground.

Fima was certain that the sniper was hidden in a certain

clump of trees, but he was not about to send another scout into the clearing to find out. Instead, he ordered each man in his unit to pick a tree and watch it closely. In the meantime, he dispatched a runner to the headquarters unit which was following along a few hundred yards to the rear. Traveling with that unit, he knew, were several Finn prisoners. The runner fetched one of the prisoners and brought him to Fima.

Fima ordered the Finn to take off his clothes and put on a Red Army uniform. Then Fima took the Finn to the edge of the clearing. "This way," he said, giving the man a little shove in the back. "Go home!"

The Finn took a few tentative steps into the clearing. Suddenly a shot rang out. The Finn pitched forward, killed by one of his countrymen.

"Where did that shot come from?" Fima shouted. "Which tree?"

No answer. Not one of his men had spotted the sniper. Fima ordered a machine gun to be set up. At his command, the gunner methodically raked each tree in the suspicious clump of trees from bottom to top, walking the spray of bullets from the trunk up into the branches. Suddenly a body fell from one of the trees, dropping about ten feet into the soft snow piled at the base. The kookushka had been shot from his nest.

There were now three bodies strewn in the clearing. The sight of them lying in the snow, perhaps wounded and suffering, goaded the unit's medic into action. A man of humane instincts, the medic jumped up and, without waiting for orders from Fima, dashed into the clearing to see if he could help the stricken men. He knelt by the sniper and as he did so the latter suddenly rose up and fatally stabbed him with a knife.

When the Russians saw this, they went berserk. Howling with rage, they charged into the clearing, ignoring Fima's orders to halt. They were uncontrollable. Grabbing the wounded sniper, they pulled off the hood of his parka and the woolen scarf that masked his face—only to discover that the kookushka was not a man, but rather a teenaged girl wearing a Finnish army uniform. Fima yelled at his men to leave her alone, but still they ignored him; and when Fima tried to physically restrain them, they pushed him aside. The girl had murdered the unsuspecting medic while he was trying to save her life—in their view an act of treachery so atrocious that it demanded an atrocity in return. The medic had shown her compassion, but they would not. And so, in a wrathful frenzy they stripped her naked, shoved a grenade between her legs, and blew her to pieces.

Having avenged their medic, the soldiers submitted once again to Fima's authority. Fima said and did nothing to punish his men for ignoring his commands, much less for their barbarous behavior. He certainly did not condone what his men had done to the Finnish girl, but he had neither the time nor the inclination to dwell on the incident. By then he had witnessed many hideous deeds and deaths, and these had hardened him to the sight of bloodshed even when it was so viciously accomplished. To be sure, the girl's fate was a cruel one, but she had brought it on herself. She was a kookushka, and if she did not deserve to be blasted apart by a hand grenade, she did deserve to die for killing the man who had tried to help her. Anyway, she was dead, and that was that. What mattered to Fima now was getting his men moving before the Finns caught up with them.

They continued on toward Leningrad. The next day they were ambushed while crossing another clearing. Fima and his men began running to the tree line. Just as Fima reached the trees, a Finnish soldier popped up from the underbrush directly in front of him. The Finn had a rifle with a bayonet pointed directly at Fima's heart. He lunged and Fima parried the thrust with the barrel of his submachine gun. He then loosed a burst at the Finn and cut him down.

Fima began running again. But he did not get very far, for suddenly he felt dizzy and weak. He also felt a sharp pain in his left side, just above the hip. He stopped and touched his coat over the sore spot. The coat was wet and when he held his hand up he saw that it was covered with blood. It was then he realized that he had deflected the Finn's bayonet away from his heart only to have it stab him in the side.

Fima began screaming for help. A medic patched him up—

the wound was deep but not fatal—and he was taken to an aid station. There he was tended to by a nurse named Zoya, a pretty Russian girl with flaxen hair and large green eyes that Fima found irresistibly appealing. Zoya was equally attracted to Fima, and the two fell instantly in love. When, a few days later, Fima was evacuated to Leningrad, Zoya somehow got herself assigned to his hospital. With Zoya caring for Fima, their romance blossomed and they talked about getting married. Army regulations, however, forbade marriage during wartime, forcing them to put their wedding plans on hold. "Just tell me you'll marry me after the war, and I'll be happy," Zoya said. Fima promised her he would. Zoya was ecstatic. So much did she love Fima that she pronounced herself willing and eager to accompany him to Lvov when the war was over.

At the time, however, it seemed unlikely that they would ever get out of Leningrad. The Germans had almost surrounded the city and were subjecting it to daily artillery bombardments and air raids. Worse, few supplies were getting through from the rest of the Soviet Union. The siege of Leningrad was under way and soon people there would be dying by the thousands.

Fima's experiences in Karelia were harrowing indeed. He had seen much carnage, he had killed a man, and he had been painfully wounded. Then he was hospitalized in a besieged city where the inhabitants were slowly starving to death. Yet for all that he was better off than his family in Lvov. He was a soldier and therefore able to fight those who wished to kill him. In Lvov we could not fight. We were a conquered people, and we were at the mercy of the Germans. Which meant that we were as good as dead, for the Germans had no mercy at all.

Yet they could not kill Lvov's Jews all at once. There were too many of us. So they killed us in dribs and drabs, beating to death one or two here, hanging five or six there, shooting a couple of dozen elsewhere. Those of us who survived knew that our days were numbered. We felt as if the proverbial sword of Damocles was suspended over each of our heads by a very slender thread. The fear and uncertainty as we waited for that thread to be cut pressed in on one's thoughts like vise grips. Every day the pressure mounted because every day more Jews were killed, which meant that fewer Jews remained, so your own odds for survival had diminished.

Many broke under the strain. Some fell apart quickly and completely, others slowly and gradually. My mother was one of the latter. Over and above the general misery and danger of life in Lvov, it was Fima's continued absence after the visit from Wacław and his mysterious companion that precipitated her slide into the abyss of mental collapse. From that day forward, she became progressively more depressed and withdrawn. She hardly troubled herself to eat. Already thin, she now became gaunt, her features haggard and careworn; she rarely spoke . . . and never smiled.

There was little my father could do to ease her agony of mind. She thus presented him with yet another example of his inability to protect and provide for his family. He dealt with the situation in typically stoic fashion. "We have no choice," he would tell me, "except to do the best we can."

I was not satisfied with this tactic, and I am certain that he wasn't either. The best we could do was not good enough to keep the Germans from killing us, and he knew it. Nor could he conceal the fact that he was deeply troubled by our prospects. He constantly racked his brains for a way out of our predicament, and in doing so he became distant, pensive, and fretful.

At length he hit upon a scheme to get me out of Lvov by marrying me off to a Polish man, a Gentile my father knew either through his work at the Luftwaffe building or from his days as a nightclub entertainer. I am unsure as to whether my father approached this man on my behalf or whether the man had sought out my father. What I do know is that the man had seen me somewhere and had found me sufficiently attractive to agree to marry me without a dowry or any other form of compensation. He told my father that he would take me to Warsaw and obtain Aryan identification papers for me. My father and mother readily assented to this proposal and a date was set for my departure.

This all transpired without my knowledge. My father deliberately kept me in the dark about his plan until the appointed day, thereby hoping to present me with what amounted to a matrimonial fait accompli. He told me about my "wedding" only hours before it was to occur. I was stunned. I could hardly believe that my parents would on such short notice send me away with a Gentile, one whose bed I would soon be forced to share. They were treating me as if I were mere property, something that could be bartered away, and I resented them for it.

Aware that my personal sovereignty was at stake, I indignantly informed my father that I had no intention of leaving home as the bride of a Catholic Pole. My father, his face flushed with anger, shot back that I had no say in the matter. Just then a knock on the door announced the arrival of my husband-to-be. I flew to the door and put my eye to the peephole. Standing in the hall was a pudgy young man with a round face. Without saying another word, I ran into the bathroom and locked the door.

My parents let the man into our apartment. Then, while he waited in the living room, both my father and mother came to the bathroom door. My mother asked me to come out. I refused. My father tried a more forceful approach.

"Open up, Lala!" he bellowed, pounding on the door. "Come out of there right this instant!"

"No!" I shouted. "I won't open the door, I won't come out—and I won't marry that man!"

"Do as I say!"

I sat on the toilet, put my head in my hands, and began sobbing. "No!" I cried. "Go away! Just go away and leave me alone!"

They did. I heard my father thank the man for coming and apologize for my behavior. Then the man left. Fearing a trick, I stayed in the bathroom for at least another hour. Finally, my mother came to the door and spoke to me in a soft, soothing voice. "Lala, you can come out now. He's gone."

I trusted my mother. I knew she would not lie to me. Nevertheless, I opened the door tentatively, ready to slam it shut at the first sign of betrayal. I poked my head out of the bathroom and looked around. The pudgy young man was indeed gone. I hesitantly emerged from the bathroom, glad that I had forestalled my unwanted nuptials but fearful that my father would punish me for defying him.

To my surprise, he neither punished nor reproached me. He wasn't even angry anymore. "Well," he said, shrugging, "that's that, I suppose. You don't want to go off with this man, so we might just as well forget about him."

Would I have gone to Warsaw with that man if he had been handsome rather than homely? Perhaps. But I don't think so. Even in the midst of war, I yearned for a romantic love affair with a dashing young man who would sweep me off my feet and steal my heart away. More than that, however, I wasn't ready to get married, and I wasn't ready to leave my parents. I still felt secure with them and believed that they would somehow shield me from all the bad things that were happening to the Jews.

I realize now that my parents' boundless love for me lay behind their decision to give me up to a stranger, and a Gentile at that. Thousands of years ago in Egypt, the mother of Moses had cast her son adrift in the Nile when Pharaoh's soldiers came to butcher the Hebrew children. In the same spirit, my parents had arranged for me to marry a Pole. They were only trying to save my life before the Nazis slaughtered all the Jews in Lvov.

Around the same time I rejected my Polish suitor, I became acquainted with a boy about my age who possessed all the attributes I sought in a member of the opposite sex. He was smart, friendly, courteous, and modest. More important, he was physically attractive—tall, slim, with flaxen hair and blue eyes. He was exactly the type I had in mind when I pictured myself falling in love, the very incarnation of my romantic fantasies. There was only one problem. He was a German soldier.

I remember very little about him. I know that he was a private in the regular army, not the SS, and I know that he visited our apartment two or three times at most. But his name, his background, where and how we met—I have forgotten all of it. It seems to me that this is no ordinary memory lapse. Whenever I reflect on the episode my thoughts become suspiciously vague, as if a part of me is deliberately trying to obscure my view of the past. Yet, while all I see when I look back is veiled by an amnesic mist, I see things nonetheless: images now and then emerge and resolve themselves into sharp focus. And what strange and astonishing images they turn out to be.

I see myself in the kitchen with the German soldier. We are standing next to the kitchen table, facing each other, separated by perhaps five or six feet—just far enough apart to maintain a semblance of propriety, but just close enough to hint at the possibility of future intimacy. We are chatting each other up, talking about nothing in particular with the feigned nonchalance that invariably signifies real interest. I see that we are smiling, occasionally laughing; we are both bashful and self-conscious, but we are enjoying ourselves; we definitely like each other—we are definitely flirting.

I see my mother come into the kitchen. She stops and stares at us for a moment, taking in the scene, her gaze shifting back and forth between the German boy and me. Then, with a worried but determined expression, she steps between us and politely but firmly tells the boy that he must go. She informs him that we have family business to conduct and that his continued presence would be inappropriate. The boy looks puzzled, a bit hurt, somewhat disappointed, but he leaves quietly, without protest, bidding us a cordial farewell as he goes out the door.

That was the last I saw of him. I cannot say much more about him except that I think he must have been an extraordinary person. He knew that I was a Jew, but this did not prevent him from striking up a flirtatious yet mannerly relationship with me. I do not recall him ever once uttering an anti-Semitic comment, nor did he indicate in any way that he was in accord with Nazi policies toward the Jews. Nor did he mention what was happening to the Jews of Lvov. Our conversations were frothy and innocuous as we indulged in the amiably superficial small talk of a budding relationship. But actions truly speak louder than words, and his actions were unfailingly commendable. He treated me with respect, and he was deferential to my mother, hardly the sort of behavior one might expect from a Jew-hating member of the so-called master race. My God, when my mother had ordered him from our apartment, he could have killed her then and there! He could have killed all of us, or denounced us to the Gestapo. In fact, he was obliged by Nazi law to do so—a Jew who had the temerity to give orders to a German had to be eliminated. Moreover, merely by consorting with us, the German boy was committing a crime for which severe penalties had been mandated. But he was no killer. And, clearly, he was not a Nazi: not a good Nazi, at any rate. He was a good German, though— one of the few I encountered during the entire war. Which is why, if I can't quite remember him, I can never forget him, either.

One day Haika's husband failed to come home from work. This could only mean one thing: he had been arrested. That night my parents, sister, and I listened from the living room of our apartment as, next door, Haika went hysterical with grief. She wailed for hours over the disappearance of her man, and there was nothing anyone could do or say to make her stop. The other women in the family also wept, though we did so quietly; and, in my case, the tears were shed more out of a sense of obligation and in the interests of family solidarity than as a genuine expression of sorrow. I truly pitied my aunt, but not with the earnestness and empathy of my mother and grandmother. I made a conscious effort to pull back and distance myself emotionally from Haika's anguish and despair. A callous indifference to the suffering of others even when they were close family members was my only defense against the Nazis. Thus, so far as I was concerned, the disappearance of Haika's husband was just one more tragedy among many. Better him than my father, I thought; better him than me.

Of course, we did not go out looking for her husband. That would have been tantamount to committing suicide. He was gone, and we just had to accept that fact.

Shortly thereafter, Uncle Yossi vanished without a trace. A

few days later, it was my father's turn. He went to work and did not come home. We told ourselves—we wanted to believe—that he had been press-ganged into a labor battalion. The Germans were constantly grabbing men off the street for this purpose. But my father should have been exempt from arrest by virtue of his employment with the Luftwaffe, as verified by his *Arbeitkarte*. The Germans had made a mistake. And when the Germans made mistakes, they usually tried to correct them: it was in their nature to do so. We were counting on this cultural trait to secure my father's release. He would show them his *Arbeitkarte*, and they would let him return to his job with the Luftwaffe. That is what we told ourselves. Of course, he would have shown them his *Arbeitkarte* the moment he was arrested—and it had done him no good. But we didn't want to think about that. And we didn't want to admit to our fear that what had befallen him was far worse than mere conscription into a labor battalion.

My father's disappearance was a calamity for me, for my family. All my life he had been our rock and bulwark, a pillar of masculine strength and authority—a person I had looked up to as a guardian, a provider, and a mentor. He was a source of courage and comfort, and I loved him very much—but not as much, I knew, as he loved me. Now he was gone. I could not imagine how we would get by without him. But, again, I kept my feelings to myself. I had to hold them in, or else become hysterical like Haika. And if I became hysterical, there would be no stopping it; I would never regain control of myself. I would go crazy and then I would die.

Fortunately, I had become adept at suppressing my emotions. I had a lot of experience in this regard, and experience had been a great teacher. I lived that way every waking minute: my feelings concealed, held in check. Inside a storm was raging, but outwardly I appeared calm—very serious perhaps, constantly frowning, but calm.

My mother did not have this ability. The disappearance of my father, on top of everything else that had happened, devastated her beyond all hope of recovery. If Fima's continued absence had been the beginning of the end for her, this was the

end—the end of her existence as the loving wife of Ilya Weintraub, the end of her life as a mother who could care for her
children, the end of the vital young woman who had gone to
nightclubs dressed in chic black evening gowns to listen to her
husband's band play American jazz. Unable to cope with the
situation, the poor woman went to bed and stayed there for
nearly two weeks. At first she refused all nourishment and
would have starved herself had it not been for my grandmother. Hovering over my mother's bed, Pesha begged her to eat.

"If you don't eat, you'll get sick and die," Pesha told her.

"I don't care," my mother would reply in a toneless voice.

"Think about your children," admonished Pesha. "What
will they do if you die? What will Ilya do if he comes home
and finds you dead?"

Finally, after much pleading and remonstrating, Pesha persuaded my mother to leave her bed and eat. As before, she ate
sparingly—barely enough to sustain herself. Food did not
interest her, for she had lost her will to live. She became
addled and childlike in her behavior, almost as if she had suffered a brain-damaging blow to the head. Her physical condition continued to deteriorate. Just forty-two years old at the
time, she had the white hair and haggard features of an older
woman. She barely looked younger than her mother.

It was about this time that she somehow chipped one of her
front teeth. Of course, we could not have the tooth capped, as
dentists and physicians were not permitted to treat Jews. So
the tooth remained chipped, which only served to accentuate
the ruin of her once beautiful countenance. No amount of
emotional distancing could alleviate the pain and sadness I felt
for her when I saw how that broken tooth changed her
appearance.

With my father gone and my mother mentally unbalanced,
I wondered how much worse things could get for my family
and, not least, for myself. The answer came a few days later
when I was arrested by the Nazis.

It happened after work. I was walking home on Akademicka Street when I was stopped by three SS soldiers, two wear-

ing helmets and armed with bayonet-tipped rifles, and the third, an officer, wearing a peaked cap and a holstered pistol on his belt. The officer demanded to see my *Kennkarte* and *Arbeitkarte*. I was scared, but took some comfort in knowing that my documents were legitimate, having been issued by the proper agencies and bearing all the necessary signatures and stamps. And although the documents identified me as a Jew, they also attested to the fact that I was gainfully employed and therefore not an "anti-social element." I was a useful and functioning cog in the repressive machinery of Nazi governance and my papers were, as the Germans were fond of saying, *in ordnung*—in order.

So I pulled the papers from my pocketbook and handed them over. As I did I was filled with misgivings because my papers were my most valuable possessions, and even though they were meant exactly for the situation in which I now found myself, I was loath to part with them. I had come to think of my papers as talismans imbued with magical properties that would ward off any harm directed at me. Sometimes, when I was walking around, I clutched them in my pocket like a small child will grasp a favorite blanket for the sense of security it gives her. In doing so, I felt a similar sense of security that arose from the silly notion that they were working powerful and protective spells on my behalf.

On this occasion, however, their enchantments proved no match for the Nazis' dark sorceries. The officer studied my papers for a moment, then handed them back to me. Relieved, I put them in my pocketbook, expecting to be told that I could go. Much to my dismay, the officer informed me that I was under arrest.

"Come with me," he barked.

They marched me to a police station located a few blocks away on Akademicka. Flanked by the two soldiers, I followed the officer with my head meekly bowed and my stomach churning. At the police station, I was put in a large room with several dozen girls, all around my age. The room was guarded by blue-uniformed Ukrainian militiamen, who watched us impassively as we milled around and tried to figure out what was going on. I was filled with dread. All the girls were: you could see it in their faces. It gave them a horrified and haunted look, as if they were gazing into a pit of nightmares from which they could not turn away. I did not talk to anyone, but I listened in on several conversations, all conducted in murmured voices to avoid provoking a reprimand—or worse—from the Ukrainians. I overheard one girl explaining to another why we had been arrested.

"The Germans are rounding up young women all over Lvov," she said.

"What for?" asked her companion.

"They're looking for Jewish girls who don't have jobs—the ones from rich families, who can afford to purchase counterfeit identification papers on the black market."

After about an hour, the Ukrainians herded us outside to a large truck that had pulled up in front of the police station. At their command we clambered onto the back of the vehicle. When the loading process was complete, we stood packed together like tinned herrings. The engine started and the truck lurched forward, and we were on our way. The truck trundled through downtown Lvov, swaying precipitously as it rounded corners. We swayed with it, grabbing the vehicle's side panels and each other for support. The sun was going down, and I thought of my mother and how worried she would be that I had not yet come home from work. None of us had been told where we were being taken, but as we jounced along there was some talk that we were bound for a place called the Janowska Camp.

I was vaguely familiar with that name. I recalled that a friend of the family had said that it was a labor camp for Jews and that my father might have been taken there after his arrest. My mother had desperately wanted to believe that this was true. I did not know what to believe, and in the absence of any hard information I had not given the camp any further thought.

But now I did, especially after our truck swung onto Janowska Street and headed west out of the city center, bumping over the tram tracks that were partially embedded in the pavement. Emerging from the residential district, with the city cemetery on our right, I noticed that the west side of the cemetery, which before the war had encompassed the Jewish section, was now hidden from view by a high concrete wall. The wall ran alongside the road for a distance of several blocks and was topped with barbed wire. On the far side of the wall stood watchtowers manned by soldiers equipped with searchlights and armed with machine guns.

German guards for Jewish graves? Not likely. Clearly, the Jewish section of the cemetery was no more. I would soon discover that it had been converted to another use—but one not entirely dissimilar from its original purpose, insofar as it was a place of death for most of the Jews who ended up there.

Just past the Kleparow train station, where the Lvov-Tarnopol-Kiev line crossed Janowska Street, the tram tracks veered off the road toward the wall. The truck turned with the tracks, which terminated in front of a portico built of two rectangular concrete columns roofed by a concrete slab. Affixed to the top of each column was a huge metal statue of a German eagle with widespread wings, perched on a swastika. Posted on one of the columns was a sign bearing the inscription *Zwangsarbeits-Lager der SS* (Forced Labor Camp of the SS).

The address was 123 Janowska Street, formerly the site of textile factory owned by a Jewish concern. Upon capturing Lvov in the summer of 1941, the Germans had razed the factory and eradicated the cemetery's Jewish section to construct the Janowska Camp. The camp had been conceived as an SS-operated industrial complex with a workforce composed of slaves. To a large degree, it was still functioning in this capacity when I arrived there. Housed within its walls were two firms that manufactured uniforms and armaments. But Janowska had also evolved quickly into an extermination camp where, eventually, upward of a quarter of a million Jews were murdered or otherwise went to their deaths.

The truck slowed and shifted gears and we rolled through the gate between two sentry kiosks. We continued on past several buildings to a second gate over which was posted a sign that told us *Arbeit Macht Frei* (Work Brings Freedom).

We went through this gate and stopped in the middle of a broad parade ground bordered by rows of barracks.

Several German soldiers stomped up beside the truck. "*Raus, raus!*" they shouted, waving us down from the vehicle.

We scrambled in twos and threes off the back of the truck, jumping to the packed earth of the parade ground in a welter of flailing arms and legs, flapping coattails, swinging braids of hair. We were virtually falling all over each other, so hastily did we make that leap. Gesturing with their rifles, the soldiers formed us into a group and ordered us to stay put, but to have our papers ready. Their officers were going to check our papers, but not just yet. At the moment the officers were occupied with a large group that had arrived before us, which numbered perhaps two hundred men, women, and children.

While the Germans busied themselves with this group, I took stock of my surroundings. What I saw left me breathless with horror. The parade ground and the lanes between the barracks were strewn with corpses. Since the war began in 1939, I had seen more than my share of dead bodies, but never so many as this, never so many in one place. There must have been dozens of them, scattered all over like swatted flies. Nor was any attempt being made to collect them for burial. They lay where they had fallen, with the living stepping over or around them as if they weren't even there.

Nearby, the Germans were dividing the first group into several smaller groups organized on the basis of age, sex, and the validity of their papers. In doing so, they brutally snatched children and babies from the arms of their mothers and fathers. Older children holding hands with their parents were also yanked away. Naturally, the children did not want to be separated from their parents nor the parents from their children. The result was mass hysteria, with parents and children screaming, howling, and sobbing. In response, the Germans slapped and shoved the children, and hit and clubbed the adults with their fists and rifle butts. I gaped at the Germans in stunned disbelief. Even then, after all the cruelties the Germans had visited upon the Jews of Lvov, I could still be shocked and astounded by their barbaric behavior.

I toyed with the idea of making a run for it. And, as if they had read my thoughts, the soldiers who ringed our group warned us not to move. "If you do, you're dead," growled one of the soldiers. He jerked a thumb toward the corpses on the parade ground. "Just like them."

The Germans finished checking the documents of the first group. All but one of the smaller groups were then led off into the heart of the camp. The people in the group that remained, we heard the Germans say, were those with valid documents. They were to be released. The Germans were going to give them a ride back to the police station on Akademicka Street.

Now it was my group's turn. Four SS officers approached us, strutting like peacocks in their perfectly tailored uniforms, as if they were just so pleased with themselves, so proud of their ability to mistreat and kill defenseless Jewish children and adults. They began checking our papers with businesslike dispatch. The girls that failed the test were sent off in one direction, while those who passed were directed to join the people left over from the first group.

I was standing in the middle of my group, surrounded by the other girls. It was getting dark, and I was almost too terrified to think clearly. In a few minutes an SS officer would be checking my papers. I felt like a cornered animal. I had to do something, and do it soon. But what could I do?

Go.

A voice inside my head. A "still small voice," like the one that spoke to Elijah, speaking to me.

Go. Go now.

It was not my voice. It did not sound like me. It was a different person, someone I did not know: maybe a man, maybe a woman. But it was real. It was audible—I literally heard it. And it spoke from inside my head.

Go now, Lala. Go away from here.

I took a deep breath. Then I began to move toward the front of my group. I weaved my way through the throng, gently pushing some of the girls aside to make a path for myself. None of the girls protested my action—I don't think they even noticed me. They were too busy worrying about their papers and whether they would pass muster with the Germans.

Just like that, I found myself in the front rank of my group. On either side of me, the German officers were examining documents and curtly asking questions of the girls who owned them. In the open ground beyond stood two or three soldiers, and beyond them was the group that had been given permission to go home. I hesitated.

GO NOW!

I held my *Kennkarte* straight out before me at shoulder height and stepped forth from my group. Then I began walking slowly but purposefully toward the other group. My heart was in my mouth as I went past the soldiers with my *Kennkarte* held high. I did not so much as glance in their direction. I flashed my *Kennkarte* at them, but as I did I looked straight ahead and kept walking. Out of the corner of my eye, I saw them staring at me. I just kept walking. I expected at any moment to hear them yelling at me to halt. But they said nothing. I took a few more steps and found myself standing with the people who had been released.

How was it that I was able to get away so easily from my group? In the first place, there was a great deal of noise and chaos on the parade ground, and these served to partially mask my movements. What with the way people were being sent off with this group or that, it must have been difficult for the Germans to keep track of everyone and to make sure they were all headed in the right direction. It was to my benefit as well that the officers had their noses buried in the documents they were scrutinizing. Consequently, they did not see me walk away from my group. Thus, when the soldiers standing guard saw me heading toward the other group, they could only assume that I had been given leave to do so by their commanders. It never occurred to them that I would be acting on my own volition.

It helped that I was a well-dressed young woman with Aryan looks. Because of my appearance, the soldiers were disposed to be sympathetic to me. But it was more important that I had acted like I knew what I was doing. The Germans of that era were, I think, preconditioned to respond favorably to such behavior.

Then, too, there was the Voice. I will not try explain this

phenomenon. Call it a hallucination, if you wish; call it thought, or fantasy, or imagination. Or call it God. Whatever it was—whoever it might have been—it had saved my life.

After a while a truck pulled up to take our group back into Lvov. It was late at night. I did not talk to the other passengers the whole way back. We were dropped off outside the Akademicka Street police station. I stood there, not sure what to do next. I couldn't stay there, but I was afraid to walk home for fear of getting arrested again. A young Ukrainian militiaman was standing guard outside the police station. I had an idea. I went up to the boy and asked him to take me home. I told him that I would somehow find a way to pay him if he did. The boy looked at me and saw that I was distraught. He looked up and down the street, then looked at me again and nodded. "All right," he said, "don't worry; I'll walk home with you."

He told me to lead the way; he would follow close behind with his rifle and bayonet pointed at my back. That way, he said, any Germans we encountered would think that he had arrested me and was taking me to the police station.

So this is how I went home to my family's apartment, walking through the darkened streets of Lvov with a Ukrainian militiaman all but prodding me in the backside with his bayonet. When we arrived at my building, I invited the boy inside. As I opened the door to our apartment, my mother came running up to see who it was. When she saw me, she burst into tears. I went inside and the militiaman came in after me. My mother gasped when she saw him, and I hastened to tell her that everything was all right, that he meant us no harm. I explained that I had been arrested and then released, and that the Ukrainian boy had escorted me home. I didn't go into the details of my brief incarceration in the Janowska Camp; the whole story would have to wait until later. First, we had to do something about the Ukrainian boy.

I asked my mother if she could give him something to eat. This was the only way I could think to pay him, since we had no money.

"Of course," my mother said. She gestured toward the dining-room table. "Please, sit down!"

The Ukrainian boy propped his rifle against the wall and seated himself at the table. My mother prepared some hot grits and milk—the only food we had—and served it to him in a cereal bowl. The boy ate silently, ravenously. We watched him eat. He seemed incredibly hungry. Nobody said anything. When his bowl was empty, he pushed his chair back, stood, fetched his rifle, and left. The whole time he had been in our apartment, he never said a word. He didn't even say good-bye, and he never told me his name.

A few days after my escape from the Janowska Camp, we received a letter in the mail from my father, the first communication from him since his disappearance. It came as a great surprise, the more so because its return address was the Janowska Camp. He wrote that he was taken there after his arrest and had been held there ever since. This, according to my mother, who showed me the letter but wouldn't let me read it. "He goes on to say, 'I saw our daughter Lala in the camp a few nights ago,'" my mother said, reading aloud. "'She was in a group of new arrivals.'"

"What else does he say?" I asked.

My mother skimmed through the letter. "He wants us to send him a food package. He says the Germans aren't giving him enough to eat."

"What else?"

But my mother wouldn't tell me. Her eyes brimming with tears, she said that the rest of what he wrote was meant for her alone. Perhaps the letter contained a declaration of his undying love for her—the parting words of a man who was doomed and knew it.

What he didn't know, evidently, was that I had been released from the camp, which is why he told my mother that he had seen me. No doubt he had written the letter thinking that she was desperate for news of my whereabouts.

His letter had a strange effect on me. The strange thing about it was, it did not affect me much at all. I did not feel either happy that he was alive or sad that he was in the Janowska Camp. I did not feel anything. I was numb. I could not cry. I did not have time to cry. I suddenly realized that, with my father in the Janowska Camp, I was responsible for my mother and Rysia, and that I must do whatever I could to ensure their survival.

My mother told me that we would send my father whatever food we had, as he had requested. We would do this even if it meant our going hungry for a day or two. I was fully prepared to make such a sacrifice, but, recalling my recent experiences at the camp, I wondered aloud how we would get the package to my father.

"Don't you worry," my mother told me. "I'll take care of it."

And she did. She put together a small parcel of food and arranged to have it delivered. Though I do not know the method of delivery, I assume it involved one of the slave labor gangs that worked in the city by day, only to return to the camp at night. The labor gangs were normally guarded by a couple of bored Ukrainian militiamen who did not much care what their prisoners said or did on the march back to the camp so long as all were present and accounted for when the roll was taken inside the gate. Once outside the camp, a laborer might hand a letter to a civilian passerby and ask that person to mail it. Anyone at all sympathetic to the prisoner's plight would see to it that the letter was mailed. I am sure this was how my father's letter reached us.

Sometimes Poles who worked in the camp, or the Ukrainian guards themselves, would perform messenger service for the Jewish prisoners—for a price, of course.

Incidentally, this delivery system also worked in reverse. It was possible to slip a package or a letter to one of the laborers accompanied by a whispered plea to deliver it to the person for whom it was intended. My mother might have asked one of my father's friends to do this, or she might have done it herself.

I have often thought about what my father was doing in the camp when he saw me. He must have been working with a labor gang, and he must have been very close to my group to have recognized me at night, in the midst of all those people. He would have wanted to shout my name, but could not—he knew that the Germans would shoot the two of us as punishment for his unauthorized utterance. He could only watch in silence as the girls in my group had their papers inspected. Did he see me walk away from my group and board the truck that took me back to Lvov? There was no mention of this in his letter, but maybe he did. I hope so. I hope he had the satisfaction of seeing his daughter escape that place of death and misery. But I cannot know what he saw because he did not escape. In circumstances unknown to me, the Shoah claimed him and left me with nothing but a memory of the good man who had been my father.

Shortly thereafter the Germans took my grandmother.

She was arrested on a warm spring day when the sun was shining and the streets seemed quiet—which is to say, when the Germans were not conducting any major actions or otherwise seriously harassing the citizens of Lvov. I was at work and so was Haika. My mother, weary of being cooped up in our apartment, took note of the apparent lack of activity and judged that streets were safe enough for her and Rysia to risk going out for a breath of fresh air. Pesha, who had come to our apartment to visit with my mother, decided to stay there until they returned.

They strolled around for several hours. When they came home, Pesha was gone. My mother went next door, thinking that Pesha would be there. She wasn't, and my mother, now growing alarmed, went back outside to look for her. She walked up and down the block but did not find Pesha. Growing frantic, she went to Wacław's apartment and began pounding on his door. When Wacław opened the door, she tearfully asked him if he knew what had happened to Pesha.

He did. The Germans, he said, had just completed a sudden, brief action on our street. He said that several SS men had entered our apartment and that they had found Pesha hiding in the alcove underneath the window bench in the living room. The SS men had dragged her out of her apartment and tossed her into a truck with several other Jews, and had then driven off.

Haika came home from work at about three o'clock. When she learned that her mother had been arrested, she, too, became frantic. Like my mother, she went outside to search for Pesha—and that was the end of her. She never returned.

I came home at about six o'clock. My mother told me what had happened and pointed out Pesha's hiding place to me. I noted that the apartment's furnishings were undisturbed—everything was neat and in its place. I found this most curious. The place should have been a mess, with broken and overturned furniture. The Germans should have torn the place apart in their search for Pesha. The fact that they had not suggested that they knew exactly where to look for her.

I smelled a rat, and I was fairly certain that its name was Wacław. It was easy for me to believe that our scruffy anti-Semitic janitor had something to do with my grandmother's arrest—that he had betrayed Pesha to the Germans by leading them to her hiding place. But I had no proof of this. And my mother said that Wacław had recounted Pesha's arrest in a matter-of-fact tone, expressing neither sympathy nor delight. Perhaps he was merely indifferent to the fate of his Jewish tenants. As evidence of this, there were no more raids on our building. So, obviously, Wacław did not report us to the Germans. But I am equally sure that he was not at all troubled by the arrest of my aunt and grandmother.

So now the Weintraub family was reduced to three people: my mother, Rysia, and myself. A few days later, we were joined by Mila, Fima's former girlfriend. She showed up at our door without prior notice, her beautiful green eyes red from weeping.

"Mila!" I exclaimed when I opened the door. "This is a surprise!" I had been out of touch with her since before the German invasion and was somewhat taken aback to find her standing in the hallway. But I was glad to see her—even though she was in a bad way.

"Please, Lala, can I come in?" she sobbed.

"Of course you can." I took her by the arm and gently pulled her into our apartment. "But what's wrong?"

"I'm all alone," Mila cried. "I have no one."

"What about your parents?" I asked, though I had a pretty

good idea what the answer would be. "And your brother?" "Gone," came the expected reply. "Taken by the Nazis." "Listen," I told her. "You can stay with us. Whatever happens to us happens to you as well. We'll be like a family."

Mila moved in with us then and there. She came with the clothes on her back and nothing more. Everything she owned, all her personal belongings, she had left behind in her family's apartment, where she dared not go for even a minute out of fear that the Germans would find her there.

Not that my mother and I had much more in the way of material possessions. By then we had little to offer Mila aside from the companionship she so very much desired. We were utterly impoverished: the wages I earned as a seamstress were our sole source of income (Mila did not have a job at the time) and not nearly enough to support four people. Food was getting increasingly scarce and expensive, and we realized that we somehow had to make more money or we would soon starve.

My mother temporarily solved the problem by selling off the furniture in our apartment and my grandmother's apartment. These were among her most prized possessions, attractive pieces that would have commanded a high price in peacetime. Instead, she got almost nothing for them. For instance, my mother sold our lovely black mahogany breakfront for a single loaf of bread! The man who purchased it was Wacław, who perpetrated this swindle without displaying so much as a flicker of bad conscience. He came to our apartment, put the bread on the dining-room table, and carried the breakfront downstairs to his apartment. My mother watched with a wounded look as he took it away—the breakfront had stood, both literally and figuratively, at the center of our lives, and its loss was all too symbolic of the destruction of our home and the family that had lived there. I was very angry with Wacław for the way he had taken advantage of us. But I said nothing, for I knew that we were in no position to haggle. It was, as they say, a buyer's market. And the bread would taste good.

On the night of August 9–10, hundreds of German troops and Ukrainian militiamen stormed into the Jewish quarter to launch what has since been called the "Big Action." This action lasted through August 23 and claimed the lives of some fifty thousand Jews. Many were killed outright, shot on the spot whenever and wherever the Germans or their Ukrainian thugs found them. Others were taken to Janowska and mowed down en masse in a sand quarry situated at the rear of the camp. A third category of victims comprised those who were shipped to Bełżec to be asphyxiated in the camp's recently built gas chambers.

I learned all this after the war. I wasn't aware of the action while it was under way because it did not reach into our neighborhood. But our turn was coming. Toward the end of August, either shortly before or just after the Big Action was completed, notices were posted on the walls and kiosks of Lvov proclaiming the establishment of a ghetto, to be created by sealing off the Jewish quarter and prohibiting all unauthorized movement between that area and the rest of the city. The same notices also ordered all Jews then residing in the Lvov's Gentile sectors to relocate to the newly formed ghetto no later than September 8. Any Jew found to be dwelling outside the closed ghetto after that date would be put to death. There would be no exceptions to this rule: not even Jews with valid working papers would be spared.

When I read these notices, I understood at once what they really meant and ultimately entailed. The message was, in a very real sense, the handwriting on the wall; as such, it was both a warning to all Jews as well as a judgment against them. Even the dullest intellect could grasp what the Germans were up to. They wanted to finish us off—a job that could be done faster and easier when we were all in one place, gathered together in the ghetto.

It was time to leave Lvov. And I knew that it was up to me to find a way out. My father was gone and my mother was emotionally prostrate and unable to think clearly. I would have to think and act as the head of our family.

I remember thinking that I had a very clear view of the situation. I was unwilling to compromise for anything less than life itself. I could see that, although I was basically a decent person, I was also headstrong and sometimes selfish. But it was my headstrong and selfish nature that gave me the will to carry on and do whatever was necessary to survive. Decency played a very small role in all this. Decency was a feeble weapon to use against the Germans.

Mila also felt as I did. When I broached the idea of leaving to her, she enthusiastically endorsed it. We immediately began to formulate a plan. The success of the plan hinged on fulfilling two requirements: obtaining "Aryan papers," counterfeit documents that identified us as Poles; and learning how to pass ourselves off as Polish Catholics. We straightaway embarked upon a crash course in Catholic prayer and ritual. Our instructors were sympathetic Gentiles, boys and girls around my age. Several of them had been friends of Fima; now they were my friends too. Occasionally, they dropped by the apartment to drink tea and talk about the war and finally to help transform us into believable if not believing Catholics.

Mila and I didn't need too much help, however. We had grown up in a predominately Catholic society and were familiar with many aspects of the Christian faith. Catholicism was a ubiquitous presence in both Polish civil and private life; it permeated the air you breathed and you could not fill your lungs without absorbing some portion of the Catholic ethos. Our friends taught us how to genuflect and make the sign of the cross with a convincing display of piety. They provided us with copies of the catechism, and we memorized all the material therein. They also gave us silver crucifixes to wear on chains around our necks, just like the ones every Gentile in Poland seemed to wear. I secretly resolved, however, that although I would attend mass and kneel and appear to pray like a Catholic, I would not take Holy Communion. I would go through all the motions of being a Catholic save this one; and when I prayed, I would make up my own prayer, silently asking God for his aid and protection. I meant no disrespect to the Catholic Church and Christians by these actions. Rather, I felt that it would be both sacriligious and blasphemous for me to do otherwise. I believed that for a Jew to willingly accept what Catholics believed was literally the body and blood of

Christ would be a sin, an insult both to my Jewish heritage and to the Christians who were doing so much—and placing themselves in such danger—on my behalf.

At any rate, Mila and I engaged in our Christian studies with the diligence of nuns preparing to take their vows, and I daresay that before long we could have gone into any church in Poland and played the role of devout Catholics without arousing any suspicions whatsoever among the genuine Christians. Sadly, the same could not be said for my mother and sister. Rysia was just nine years old, and therefore too young to learn Catholic rites and prayers, much less comprehend the urgent necessity for doing so. And my mother, devastated by grief, had undergone what amounted to a nervous breakdown and was incapable of the intense effort that even a false conversion to Catholicism demanded from her.

Nevertheless, we pressed forward with the scheme. Getting Aryan papers would have to be our next step. But how? This problem was solved when some of Fima's friends brought a Catholic boy named Staszek to the apartment for one of our evening get-togethers. Staszek had been told about our plans and wanted to help. He mentioned that he could get four blank birth certificates (*metrycas*) from his parish priest. He was extremely good-natured and he liked Mila and me very much, and was sympathetic to our plight.

I must say that before the war I would not have had a friend like Staszek. But the war had changed human relationships. While throwing up barriers between people, it was also tearing them down. Now I was part of a group that included Gentiles and Jews, united in friendship and a mutual hatred of the Germans.

Staszek got us the birth certificates. As payment, we gave him a piece of furniture he could sell on the black market. We filled out the certificates with false names but with our actual birthdays. I decided that my name would be Urszula Krzyzanowska. It is a very Christian name. My mother, Mila, and Rysia each took a different name. We did not want to appear in any way related—an important consideration if one of us was arrested. At the bottom of each document was a blank line where the parish priest was supposed to sign his name. I thought up a likely name for the priest and then, wielding my pen with a flourish, signed it on all the documents in bold, sweeping letters.

With the September 8 deadline drawing near, we began to liquidate whatever assets we still had. Of course, by then we did not have much. Mila and I sold most of our possessions to our friends. These were people we could trust. They would not notify the authorities that I belonged to the remnant of a Jewish family that was trying to collect enough money to flee Lvov. So we kept our prices low. Nevertheless, we raised enough money to cover our traveling expenses, if only for a few days.

We could not sell everything, however. Among the items we did not get rid of were various household furnishings, bedding, linens, cookware, crockery, china, silverware, and such. There was no way we could take these with us—we would just have to leave these behind in the apartment. This troubled my mother. She was worried that looters would break in and make off with our belongings. So she asked Wacław to keep an eye on the apartment and its contents in our absence. She told him that he could use our possessions while we were gone, but that he would have to give them back upon our return. Naturally, Wacław was amenable to this arrangement. I think my mother had actually convinced herself that Wacław would keep his end of the bargain, and that we would come back after the war was over to find our home more or less intact. I harbored no such illusions. Wacław, I thought, would be hawking our possessions on the black market almost as soon as we had walked out the door. Not that this bothered me. By then I did not give a fig for material possessions. All that mattered to me was survival.

I quit my job with the Luftwaffe about a week before we left. Of course, I did not tell my boss I was quitting. That would have been suicidal of me. I just stopped going to work. I knew my boss would think I was ill and would not immediately notify the authorities. After about two weeks, he would inform the SS of my absence. But by then I would be long gone from Lvov.

The night before we left, we each packed a small overnight

bag with an extra change of clothes, some toiletries, and our all-important Catholic prayer books. My mother then went to her closet and got out our bedding and bathroom linens. She spread these things out on her bed and began counting them. Perplexed, I watched her for a moment without saying anything.

"Mother, what are you doing?" I finally asked.

"Counting our sheets and towels," she answered. "And the pillowcases, too."

"I can see that," I said, growing impatient. "But why?"

"When we come back, I'll count them again. And then we'll know whether Wacław took anything."

When she told me this, I became very angry with her. The Germans were breathing down our necks and this was all she could think about! It seemed so pedantic of her, so foolish and irrational.

"Are you crazy?" I exploded. "How can you be concerned about a few sheets at a time like this?"

My mother gave me a hurt look, like a rebuked child about to cry. She began to stammer something in reply, but I cut her off.

"Put them down!" I shouted. "Just put them down, and forget about them!"

She meekly obeyed my order and left the bedroom, obviously stunned by my outburst. I, too, was somewhat taken aback—I could scarcely believe what I had done. Never before had I dared speak so harshly to my mother. But I did not feel guilty about this. The circumstances warranted such unprecedented measures. So I gave the incident no further thought. But I knew what it signified. By submitting passively to my authority, my mother had confirmed my already-assumed role as head of the family.

September 7, the day of our departure, finally arrived. It was a beautiful late summer day, hot and sunny. We had earlier decided that our destination was to be Sanok, a small town located southwest of Lvov near the juncture of what is now Poland's border with Slovakia and Ukraine. Our friends had told us about this town. One or two of them either came from Sanok or had family there. They recommended it to us because it was an out-of-the-way place where few Jews lived and there wasn't much going on.

It sounded good to me—few Jews meant minimal SS activity, so it would be relatively safe. We didn't know anybody in Sanok, but we were told that this would not be a problem if people thought we were Christians. I imagined how it would be for us. Posing as Catholics, we would find a place to live, and Mila and I would both get jobs. While Mila and I worked, my mother would stay at home and take care of Rysia; or, if conditions were truly favorable, we would enroll Rysia in school. And that's how we would live until the Germans were defeated and the war ended.

That morning we divided up our money, vowing to spend none of it except to buy train tickets and food. I should say that food was not a major concern. We were too keyed up to think about eating. All we could think about was getting out of Lvov. We hung the crucial silver crucifixes around our necks. Then Mila, Rysia, and I donned cotton summer dresses of the type usually worn by Polish peasant girls. They had flower-print patterns, gathered skirts, wide bodices, and puffy sleeves. My mother wore a skirt and blouse that belonged to me—in the past few months she had lost so much weight that she could wear my clothes. Mila had bleached her hair with peroxide and now she arranged her newly golden tresses into Gretchen braids, piled on her head. Dressed as she was with her green eyes and braided blond hair, she looked the very ideal of Slavic beauty. I also braided my hair, and Rysia's as well, and piled the braids on our heads. Little Rysia with her turned-up nose, blue eyes, and golden hair that was even lighter than my own looked more Aryan than many German girls and could easily have duped even the most suspicious-minded SS man into thinking that the blood flowing through her veins was 100 percent Teutonic.

My mother's features did not have the pronounced Semitic cast depicted in Nazi propaganda, but her hair and her eyes were black, and her coloring was somewhat darker than that of the average Pole. These traits were not exclusive to Jews. Plenty of Gentiles had them too. But they suggested a Mediterranean ancestry, and this alone was sufficient to provoke any conscientious Nazi into checking her papers. I shuddered to think what she would do if this happened. Her new false papers identified her as a Polish Catholic. They were quite convincing, but I could not say the same for her. She remained unfamiliar with the Catholic catechism and she had failed to memorize any Christian prayers. Her genuflections were clumsy and she made the sign of the cross ineptly. If put to the test of being a Christian, she would certainly fail. I could just picture the scene: an SS man demanding that she prove her faith by praying aloud, and my mother, dropping to her knees, making some fumbling gesture with her hands, unable to speak. After which she would be taken away and shot.

There was nothing we could do at this late date to make my mother more Gentile in her appearance and behavior. So we decided that she would pose as Rysia's nanny rather than her mother. We also decided to split into pairs; we would travel separately, pretending not to know each other. I would be with Mila, my mother with Rysia. The two pairs would stay close, but not too close. And we agreed that if one pair was detained by the Germans, the other would keep going.

A few minutes later we were walking down Zyblikiewicza Street to the local tram stop. We left an apartment building that was nearly empty of tenants. All the Jews who had lived there, the Weintraubs on the third floor, the Posnanskis on the first floor, Petia and his sister on the second floor, were gone.

We took the tram to the train station, Mila and I riding at the opposite end of the car from my mother and sister. We went into the station separately, we purchased our tickets separately, and we waited for the train separately. The lobby was jammed with people, mostly peasant families returning to the countryside after coming to the city to sell milk, bread, and other produce from their farms. I remember how the women tied the ends of their shawls together to form a pouch. They slung the shawls over their shoulders and loaded the pouch with their belongings, which in many cases included infant children.

Mila and I blended easily into that crowd. So did my sister. My mother was rather more conspicuous, but even so nobody seemed to notice her. Fortunately, there were only a few soldiers present and they were not checking papers.

When the train to Sanok arrived, we boarded the same car but, again, sat at opposite ends. As the train pulled out of the station, I thought, so far so good. I was relieved to be leaving Lvov, even though I had lived there all my life. I was looking forward to starting anew in Sanok as Urszula Krzyzanowska, Christian girl. I knew that we were still in danger, but I thought that we escaped the worst of it. However, as they say in Yiddish, *Mensch tracht, und Gott lacht* (Man plans, and God laughs).

I couldn't know that our troubles were just beginning.

❁

Arrest in Sambor

The journey was uneventful at the outset. It was to occur in two stages. From Lvov we were to go to the town of Sambor, where we would change trains to continue on to Sanok. On the way to Sambor, the train chugged through the Polish (now Ukrainian) hinterland, past tiny rural villages set amid vast fields of wheat grown tall and golden in the late summer sun. Despite the crush of people in our compartment, the side-to-side rocking of the car and the rhythmic clacking of the wheels on the rails had a marvelously soothing effect on my badly frayed nerves. Equally calming was the bucolic landscape. I saw farmers working in the fields, preparing their crops for harvest; I saw barnyards where stout women scattered grain to flocks of manically fluttering chickens and swatted enormously fat pigs with twig switches; I saw cattle clustered around feed racks and water troughs, or resting in the shade of one of the few trees to be found in this otherwise wide-open landscape; I saw horse-drawn carts piled high with hay trundling along dirt roads. The countryside seemed untouched by war. It was all a far cry from Lvov, racked by the violence and oppression of the German occupation.

As we neared Sambor, however, a commotion arose in the train itself. Somehow a rumor had gotten started that the Germans were awaiting our arrival at the Sambor station. "The Gestapo is at Sambor," I heard people say. "They're going to arrest everyone." The rumor passed from one person to the next as fast as it could be spoken, spreading through the crowded compartments like a wind-driven prairie fire.

The passengers all became quite agitated. Although most of them were Catholic peasants and therefore in no particular danger of being arrested, they were nevertheless frightened by the prospect of any encounter with the Germans.

We pulled into Sambor station in the late afternoon. As the train slowed to a halt, I looked out a window to see if the rumor was accurate. It was. On the platform perhaps two dozen SS men stood watching the train with impassive but alert expressions. The moment the train stopped, they sprang into action, rushing to the doors of each car and shouting at the passengers to get out. In a panic to obey them, the passengers stampeded for the exits. As we tumbled out of the car, the SS men shoved us with their hands and rifle butts in order to direct our movement. "Go over there!" they bellowed, gesturing toward the street just beyond the station platform. "Be quick about it!"

It was plain that the Germans were conducting this round-up to find Jews who were fleeing Lvov. I do not know whether they had specific information that there were Jews on the train or whether they simply assumed this. In any case, they were not at all concerned about who they detained. They took into custody almost everyone on the train regardless of the obvious fact that the majority were Poles. They did not demand to see our papers. Clearly, they intended to sort out the Jews from the Gentiles at their leisure in some other place.

We were hustled out of the station to the street, where we were ordered to sit down on the cobblestoned surface and wait. Mila and I sought out my mother and Rysia, and we sat on the curb beside them. It hardly mattered to me that in doing so I might reveal to the Germans that we were a family. Under the circumstances, staying apart and pretending not to know each other seemed a pointless ruse. Also, we looked as if we belonged together. Though we did not appear to be Jewish, we bore little resemblance to the peasants around us. We lacked their ruddy complexions and rough features. We were not wearing knapsacks and bundles filled with food and produce to sell in the city. We were not plump like so many of the peasant women, and we were not wearing babushka scarves over our heads as these women were. Everything about us said that we were urban bourgeois Poles. This was not a crime. It was not even a reason to be arrested. But it did make us stand out among the peasants in that crowd. And the mere fact of standing out could have unpleasant consequences.

For the time being, however, the Germans took no notice of us. They were still too busy rounding up passengers from our train. The passengers were being herded from the station platform to the street in a dense mass with the Germans running back and forth alongside it, shouting and gesticulating with their rifles. As I watched this operation, an odd thing happened. Right before my eyes, the Germans seemed to metamorphose into ravening wolves. I mean this literally. What I saw were not human beings but creatures in uniform with savage lupine faces. Like wolves, they barked and snapped at the heels of their hapless prey; and, like wolves, they actually curled their lips and bared sharp vicious teeth when they shouted.

It was an ugly and terrifying sight—really a kind of hallucination, I suppose. It passed in an instant. But it had done something to me. Suddenly I felt overwhelmed. For more than a year, those beasts in uniform had hunted and bullied and threatened me. Now it seemed that they had finally run me to ground. The chase had exhausted me. And like any animal brought to bay by predators, I was made frightened and frantic by what I knew would be coming next.

My mother, seeing how distraught I was, put her arms around me, and, without saying anything, gathered me to her bosom. In trying to comfort me, however, she inadvertently made me feel worse. In the past, whenever I had been upset about something, she would hug me thus, and I would lay my head against her soft ample bosom and feel sheltered and secure. But not now. Her bosom was no longer soft and ample, and I found no shelter or security in her embrace. She could not help me—she could not even help herself. We were surrounded by SS men, and I had little hope that they would let us go or that we could slip away from them as I had walked away from the doomed group at the Janowska Camp. I realized then that although she was trying her best to protect me, it was no longer within her power to do so. It is a tragic and devastating thing to see a parent reduced to ineffectuality, and I reacted accordingly: I broke down and cried. I felt so sorry for her, all the more so because she thought she could still reassure me with her touch. I could see that she was scared and confused—she could not comprehend our situation—and the look on her face as she struggled to make sense of it broke my heart.

In that look, I saw the end of the world I had known as a child. I thought about the time I was fired from a secretarial job for arguing with my supervisor. I had come home weeping tears of shame and humiliation but was unable to tell my father what had happened because I knew he would be angry with me. He would have reproached me for my contrary behavior, saying that I had nobody to blame but myself for losing my job. And he would have been right. But I did not want to hear this from him. So I went to my mother instead. I expected sympathy and solace from her, and that was exactly what I got. In a halting voice choked by sobs, I told her about my dismissal, and when I was finished she held me tight and said, "Don't be sad, Lala, everything will be all right." Her gentle love had soothed me and eased my pain. In the world of my childhood, her love was a healing force no misery could withstand. But that world was no more.

At length the roundup of train passengers ceased. The Germans had detained approximately two dozen people, all sitting on the curb next to us or standing on the sidewalk. From there we were herded at bayonet point along Sambor's one main street to a two-story brick building located a few blocks from the train station. This building had the look of a government edifice of some sort, perhaps the town hall or a regional courthouse, which it must have been before the war. But since the German conquest of eastern Poland, the SS had taken it over and adapted it for the usual purpose of harrowing Jews and other innocent people.

Once inside we were relieved of our identification papers

and marched up a staircase to the second floor. At the top of the stairs, we were halted in a circular vestibule to be assigned to the cells where we would be held pending an "interview" with the SS. Mila and I were put in one cell, and my mother and Rysia were put in a cell across the hall.

Each cell was tiny, measuring about ten feet in length and six feet in width. The door was made of wood, not metal as one might expect, indicating that the place had not been built to house prisoners over the long term. However, the single barred window in the outer wall told us that we were prisoners nonetheless and that we would not be going anywhere for the time being. The only furnishings were two unframed mattresses made of burlap stuffed with straw and a bucket for a toilet. Realizing that there was nothing for me to do except wait for the inevitable summons from our captors, I threw myself down on this rough bed and immediately fell fast asleep. Night had fallen and I was very tired, and sleep was a form of escape which barred windows and bolted doors could not prevent.

I slept soundly, without dreaming. The next morning I was awakened by the golden rays of the sun streaming in through the window bars. I got up and, out of curiosity, went to the door and tested it. To my surprise I found that it was unlocked. I opened the door and stepped cautiously into the vestibule. There were no guards around. Evidently the Germans were not overly concerned about escape attempts. And rightly so, for there was no getting by the guards who were posted at the bottom of the stairs and at the building's main entrance.

But there was no one to stop me from going across the hall to my mother's cell, and that is what I did. I found my mother and sister both sitting on the floor on their burlap palettes. As I entered the cell, Rysia turned and gazed at me with an innocent expression. My heart sank and I nearly burst into tears over her appearance. My precious little sister's sweet, beautiful face was covered with ugly red blotches where she had been bitten by the bedbugs that infested her mattress. Even so, she didn't seem upset or in any great discomfort. As she looked at me with her big blue eyes, she scratched idly at the bite marks—they were no more than minor irritations to her. But, oh, how they hurt me! Rysia's face had always been without blemish; she had had a perfect peaches-and-cream complexion that would have been the envy of any fashion model or movie star. To see her features marred by those blotches disturbed me as much as anything did in the war. I wanted to cry, but did not. Instead, I reached for Rysia and pulled her to me, hugging her tight to my body as I kissed her ravaged cheeks.

It did not occur to me then that I was imitating my mother, hugging Rysia just as my mother had hugged me the previous day. But I was well aware that this was really a gesture of futility, which expressed not only my love for my sister, but also the realization that love was all had I had to give her—and that this was no defense against the Germans.

While I embraced Rysia, my mother ignored us to rummage through her belongings (the Germans had let us keep our overnight bags). I asked her what she was doing. "Looking for my toothbrush," she mumbled in a distracted tone. "I have to brush my teeth; I have to brush them right now."

At the moment this was her sole concern, and it obsessed her to the exclusion of all else. Our arrest and imprisonment, Rysia's ravaged face, my own distress—she was oblivious to all of it. She went through the same few articles of clothing over and over again, shaking them out and inspecting the folds for the elusive toothbrush. She never found it. But then, finding it was not really the point of her search. In truth, there was no point—unless, I suppose, it was to keep what was left of her mind occupied. I did not even try to help her, for I knew that she was beyond help.

After a while I returned to my own cell. I could not stand to be with my mother and sister any longer; it was too depressing. I knew that it was up to me to take care of them. But I also knew I was powerless to do so.

All I could do now was wait for the guards to come. I sat on my mattress and stared into space and tried not to think. Mila likewise sat on her mattress and did not speak. The minutes ticked by. I became at once bored and anxious, an improbable and emotionally abrasive combination. Boredom and anxiety do not mix: one part of me felt leaden and apathetic, and wanted to continue staring into space; another part was agitated and restive, and wanted to get up and walk around. Finally, the latter won out. Unable to hold still any longer, I stood and looked out the window. Across the street I saw a young Polish girl about my age swinging breezily down the sidewalk in the bright morning sun. She was wearing a flower-print peasant dress like the one I wore; and, like me, she had blond hair arranged in Gretchen braids. She was smiling, and this coupled with her bouncy stride told me that here was a girl who still had it in her to feel happy. I gazed at her with envy and bewilderment. She was just like me, except that she was free. I thought, what is going on here? Why is she free, and I am behind bars? Why can't I walk around Sambor with a sprightly step and a lighthearted smile? What did I ever do in my life to deserve persecution and imprisonment?

Of course, I knew the answer to these questions: I was a Jew. But that was really no answer at all, at least not one that I could understand. I thought, I am just a young girl like that girl outside. I have never done anything to harm anyone. Yet the world wants to destroy me. It made no sense whatsoever.

The cell door suddenly flew open and a heavyset woman guard, wearing a uniform and speaking in German, ordered us out into the vestibule. Mila and I emerged from the cell, and the woman guard, frowning impressively, indicated with an impatient gesture that we were to go down the stairs in front of her. As Mila and I descended the staircase, I silently rehearsed the Christian prayers I had memorized. On the ground floor the woman guard ushered us into a small room with a desk, behind which sat two SS officers. Then she left, closing the door behind her.

We stood before the two Germans with our heads slightly bowed, staring at the floor. They regarded us for a few seconds with that arrogant, self-important air so typical of German officers. Then one of the SS men got up and came around the desk and planted himself in front of me. Leaning forward until his face was only inches from my own, he shouted, "Are you a Jew?"

I raised my head and looked him squarely in the eye. "No!" I exclaimed.

"Liar!" And with that he reared back and smacked me across my face with his open hand. So hard did he strike me that I was driven to my knees and saw stars. One of my front teeth was knocked loose and I was bleeding slightly from the inside of my mouth. The pain had been like an explosion inside my head, and for a moment I thought that I would pass out because of it. But somehow I managed to remain conscious.

As I knelt there on the floor, I heard the other SS man say to his companion, "Wait a minute! What are you doing? What's wrong with you? Maybe they aren't Jewish!"

"We are not," I insisted. "Check our papers if you don't believe me."

"The papers may be false," said the man who hit me.

The SS man seated behind the desk conceded that false papers were indeed a possibility. But there was another way we could prove the validity of our claim: by demonstrating that we were Christians.

And so, instead of beating or interrogating us, they ordered Mila to her knees beside me and commanded us to pray as only Catholic Christians knew how. We did, reciting one prayer after the other and all the while crossing ourselves with saintly fervor.

Finally, the two Germans had heard enough. They told us to stop and stand up. We had convinced them that we were Christians.

As we got to our feet, I wondered about the nature of these men. Their behavior was incomprehensible to me. What sort of a man would hit a woman? I asked myself. Only a very cowardly one, I thought, only a man who is not really a man at all, but a beast.

They were not finished with us. They took us into another, larger room, where we joined by several other young girls who had preceded us in the interrogation process. The SS men ordered all of us to strip down to our brassieres and panties. When we had taken off our outer garments and were standing before them in nothing but our underwear, the Germans made us form a circle and march around the room. They stood outside the circle and, as we paraded before them, they appraised us dispassionately like cattle buyers at a livestock show. Finally, they told us to stop and get dressed. All of the girls were then dismissed from the room except for Mila and me. "You two stay," one of the SS men said.

As soon as the other girls were gone, the demeanor of the SS men underwent a sudden transformation. Where before they had been cruel and aloof, they were now friendly and polite. Grinning broadly, they asked if we'd be interested in joining them after work, at the house they shared, for a drink and some conversation. Of course, we smiled and nodded enthusiastically and said yes, that sounded just fine. As if we could refuse them. As if one of them had not punched me to the floor within the past hour.

We asked them where their house was located.

"It's just across the street," one of them said. They told us the address. "Go on in—the door is unlocked. Make yourself at home. We'll be along in a little while, after we're finished here."

Still grinning, the two SS men walked us to the door of the building and handed us our papers and belongings. They pointed out their house. "That's it over there."

We walked down the steps of the building and started in the direction of the house. The SS men went back into the building. In the next instant, Mila and I veered away from their house and scurried into a cornfield that bordered the main street of Sambor.

We did not really know where we were going when we entered the cornfield. We were in a kind of trance, moving instinctively, without thinking. We plunged into the field and picked our way down the rows between the cornstalks, which were taller than we were and heavy with ripening ears of corn. And they provided concealment: if someone had been watching from the town, he would have seen us step into the field and disappear immediately and totally from view.

The field was vast, extending several miles across the flat Polish countryside. We walked through it aimlessly and without any sense of the direction in which we were headed. All that mattered to us was getting away from Sambor, to put as much distance as we could, as fast as we could, between ourselves and the town.

We walked and walked. It was a magnificent day, the kind of day that makes you want to thank God that you are alive to experience it. The sun was a radiant gold medallion in an azure sky populated by fleecy little clouds; the air was silky-soft and warm, and a mild breeze wafted playfully across the field, stirring the cornstalks with its feathery touch. There was something magical about it, and I remember falling into a peaceful dreamlike state, becoming suddenly and dramatically aware of the beauty of the world around us. The sky was so blue! The air was so clean and fresh! Birds were singing, bees hummed and buzzed, butterflies flitted this way and that. I could smell the ripeness of the corn and the rich fecundity of the soil in which it grew. I felt intoxicated and euphoric; I was under an enchantment, utterly captivated and happily stupefied by the overwhelming splendor of God's creation. I thought to myself, life can be so good, so sweet, so ravishingly beautiful.

But in the next instant, I thought that it could be horrible as well, especially if you were Jewish. This made no sense to me. What kind of world is this, I wondered, where beauty and horror could exist simultaneously—where I could meander through a lovely field of corn on a gorgeous summer day while so many people were at this very moment being tortured and murdered in the dungeons and labor camps of the Third Reich? It was perverse, it was absurd, and it was desperately wrong. For this situation to exist, there had to be something askew in the order of things, something so far out of whack as to render itself incomprehensible to any reasonable person.

At this point I hardly gave a thought to my mother and sister. Not that I had any illusion as to what lay in store for them. They would undergo a perfunctory examination in which it would swiftly be determined that they were Jews, and two especially "useless" Jews at that: a little girl and an aging woman who had lost her mind. And what then? Would they be physically abused, as I was? Would they be beaten and then shot within the confines of the jailhouse, or taken to the outskirts of Sambor and shot at the edge of some mass grave recently dug for that purpose? Or would they be sent back to Lvov and the Janowska Camp, where death was also a virtual certainty?

Such possibilities were too terrible too contemplate, so I pushed them from my thoughts. I could not allow myself to dwell on the fate of my mother and sister, for to do so would distract me from my purpose and, ultimately, destroy my resolve to stay alive. Concern for them was an indulgence, a luxury I could not then afford. They were as good as dead, and well I knew it. Their destiny was fixed, and no amount of concern on my part would change that. But my destiny was still very much an open-ended thing. I could still affect its outcome by my own actions. I intended to do whatever was necessary to survive, even if this meant banishing them from my thoughts and emotions and relegating them, for the present, to some backwater province of memory without grieving for them or even pausing to mourn their passing.

Having done so, I felt curiously liberated. The burden of responsibility, of caring for my mother and Rysia, of always being the one who had to figure out what to do, had been lifted from my shoulders. What a relief this was! I was on my own, and I looked forward to taking care of no one but myself, of being responsible to no one but myself. I found the prospect exhilarating. Now, it was just myself against the Germans, a challenge I was more than ready to take on. All the teenage rebelliousness that I had once harbored toward my father and mother I now transferred over to the Germans; I would rebel against them, and since I owed them nothing in the way of respect, since I did not love them as I had loved my parents—on the contrary, I now hated them with a passion, even more than they hated Jews—there would be no limits to my rebellion. I could go as far as I wanted with it, and in doing so, I would be freer than I had ever been in my life.

Nor did I then fear the consequences of rebellion. Like most teenaged boys and girls, I felt invincible, indestructible, even immortal. I could not imagine my own death, and because I could not imagine it, I deemed it an impossibility. I was confident that I could, that I *would,* prevail over the Germans.

I had good reason to think so. Hadn't we outwitted the Germans in Sambor? We had! I thought about those two SS men, and laughed. First, they had thought they could frighten and intimidate us into confessing that we were Jews. Then, they had thought they could charm us into joining them for some after-hours hanky-panky in their bachelor pad. It was incredible—they had really thought that Mila and I would go across the street and wait for them!

I knew why they had chosen us over the other girls: because we were attractive and we weren't peasants. The latter must have been obvious to them—our manner of speaking and general comportment were dead giveaways of an urban, middle-class background. This was probably more important to them than our physical appearance, inasmuch as they were products of either a middle-class or aristocratic upbringing. (I am assuming this; they didn't come across as peasants.) Presumably, this meant that we had things in common with them, namely an education, an ability to carry on a moderately interesting conversation, and, they must have hoped, a more liberal attitude toward sex than one might normally find among the conservative Catholic peasantry. Hence, their invitation.

What fools they were! What a pleasure it was to disappoint them!

Sometimes I think it would have been amusing to see the look on their faces when they entered their house, expecting to have all kinds of naughty fun with us, only to find that we had stood them up. But then I think of my mother and Rysia, and my sense of amusement dies. We may have outsmarted those two Germans, but in the process I lost my dear mother and sister, whom I never saw again.

We walked hour after hour, mile after mile through one sun-drenched field after another. We were blessedly alone and saw no one the whole day. We did not think about where we were going; we went wherever our feet took us, plodding along like migrating cattle, dumb and phlegmatic. And, like cattle, we grazed haphazardly on the vegetation in our path, picking and munching on whichever crops were ripe and reasonably fit to be eaten raw. Mostly we ate kohlrabies and radishes, which were hardly what one would term "energy food," but which nonetheless proved sufficient to keep us moving and our hunger at bay. Food was not the source of our energy that day. Our bodies were fueled by that potent and nearly pathological mixture of adrenaline and soaring elation engendered by a close but inconclusive encounter with death. We were in a fever of ecstasy, impelled and animated and sustained by our miraculously achieved survival, by a sense of being alive and free that was so profound as to be almost unbearable. We understood that we were totally on our own, beholden to no one, responsible for nobody but ourselves; we were utterly liberated from human bonds. It was a heady feeling. Even though we were afraid of the Germans, even though I had lost my mother and sister, I could not help but feel exhilarated by our circumstances.

Finally, though, as the day waned, so, too, did our strength. The sun was low on the horizon and the light was beginning to fade when we suddenly realized how exhausted we were. We began to cast about for a place to sleep. We walked a little farther and emerged from a cornfield into a clearing in the middle of which stood a small thatched-roof hut. We made straight for that dwelling without hesitation or discussion and without giving any thought to the dangers that might be lurking there. We went up to the door and gave it three or four hard raps, then stepped back and waited for a response.

The door was opened by a man and a woman who appeared to be in their late forties or early fifties. It was hard to tell—they were peasant farmers, and like so many people who worked outdoors, their features were weathered, making them look older than their years. The woman wore the inevitable babushka scarf, and she looked at us with twinkling eyes and a friendly but slightly bemused smile, as if to say that she was pleased to see us even though she did not know who we were. She was about to say something but we spoke first, blurting out in unison that we were "politically sought," a euphemism that meant we were on the run from the Germans. We had been walking all day, we told her, and we needed a safe place to spend the night; could they perhaps shelter us for the night?

Now, the Poles are an intensely patriotic people with a proud tradition of resistance against invaders, of whom there have been many in their long and violent history. To say that we were politically sought was to imply that we were somehow involved in such resistance and thus patriots of the highest order. Inasmuch as Poles virtually imbibe love of country with their mother's milk, it was only natural that these two rustics whose home and privacy we had intruded upon would be eager to take us in, even though in doing so they would be placing their own lives at risk. If the Germans discovered that they were harboring fugitives, they would be executed. But neither the woman nor her husband were daunted by this prospect. "Please," they said, motioning us inside, "come in. We would be glad to have you stay with us."

No doubt they assumed we were associated with the Armia Krajowa ("Home Army," or AK), the military arm of the Polish government-in-exile, which was based in London throughout the war. The Home Army was the largest of several organized resistance groups operating in occupied Poland. It had been conducting a guerrilla war against the Germans since the 1939 invasion, despite ruthless measures by the occupiers to suppress and eradicate it. These measures included savage reprisals against the civilian population in areas where the Home Army was active. If, for example, a Home Army unit tore up some railroad tracks, set off a bomb in a café frequented by German soldiers, or assassinated a German government worker or Polish collaborator, it was the civilians in the immediate vicinity who paid the price. Mass shootings and deportation to labor camps were standard penalties for actions by the Home Army (or any other resistance group).

Even so, the mostly young men and women of the Home Army were looked upon as heroes. This worked to our advantage. Mila and I did not want to disabuse our hosts of the notion that we were resistance fighters. And, of course, we were not about to tell them that we were Jews. Patriotism was not necessarily incompatible with anti-Semitism: this kindly old couple might hate Jews and Germans with equal fervor. So we let them think we were good Catholic girls.

We went inside. Their home consisted of one big room with two beds on opposite sides and a table in the middle. The room was tidy and immaculate, with spotless white walls and a rough but well-scrubbed wooden floor. Despite the presence of the extra bed, they appeared to be childless, as there were no children on the premises. They sat us down at their table and fed us a meal of hot milk and warm pumpernickel bread. It wasn't much, but Mila and I were famished, and it seemed like a feast. The bread was indescribably delicious. Rarely before or since has food tasted so good to me as it did then. The passage of years has not diminished this feeling. Today, more than half a century after the fact, I would be hard-pressed to name a meal as savory and satisfying as that simple repast—the taste of which I can still experience just by thinking about it.

When we had finished the meal, the peasant couple, seeing how tired we were—we were both nodding in weariness over our empty plates—made up one of their beds. Mila and I stripped down to our underwear and, after saying good-night to our hosts, crawled in under the covers. The sheets were clean and cool; they felt marvelous. But I didn't have much time to enjoy them, at least not consciously, for I fell asleep almost as soon as my head touched the pillow.

We slept soundly and woke early the next morning feeling refreshed and ready to get on with our journey. But where to go? After being served another appetizing meal of hot milk and warm pumpernickel bread, we went out behind the house into the couple's garden to consider our next move. We sat on chairs and tried to formulate a plan but were unable to do so. We were really at a loss. As we were pondering our dilemma, an extraordinary thing happened. Without warning two men came around the corner of the house and walked right up to us. Mila and I stared at them in wide-eyed alarm but said nothing.

The men were in their mid-thirties—one short, one tall—and they looked like accountants because they were wearing suits. Not the sort of garb you would expect farmers to wear. They were obviously city men. Were they Gestapo agents?

"Don't be afraid," the short man said. To our immense relief, he spoke unaccented Polish. We were even more relieved when he added, "We're here to help you."

We asked them who they were.

"That doesn't matter," answered the tall man. "The point is, we know who you are. And so do the Germans. Gestapo agents from Lvov are looking for you in Sambor. Soon they'll be coming here. You must leave this place at once if you don't want to get caught."

Mila and I needed no further convincing. We stood and made as if to go. Then I had a thought. Turning to the two men, I said, "My mother and sister are being held in the Sambor jail."

"Yes, we know this too," the tall man replied.

"Well, are they all right?" I asked, suddenly gripped by an almost frantic concern for their welfare.

They both shook their heads. "We don't have that kind of information," the tall man said. "We only know that they are still in the jail."

On an impulse, I reached into my purse and pulled out a small wad of paper zlotys, which represented all the money we had. I peeled off several bills and pressed them into the tall man's hand. He stared at the money uncomprehendingly. "What is this for?" he asked.

"To buy food for my mother and sister."

"The food I can buy, no problem," he told me. "But getting it to them, in a German jail—I do not think this is possible."

"Please," I said. "Just try, I beg of you. That's all I ask—to try."

"As you wish." The tall man pocketed my money. "I'll do whatever I can, I promise."

"I know you will," I said. "And I thank you for it."

"Yes, thank you," Mila chimed in. "Thank you so very much for everything." Whereupon she leaned forward and kissed the short man on his cheek.

The short man grinned. "You're quite welcome."

I was too shy to kiss him, so I shook his hand and the hand of his companion.

With that the two men said good-bye and walked back around the corner of the house. Where they went I do not know. They simply disappeared into the open countryside. It was very strange: one moment they were there, the next, they were gone.

I said to Mila, "They were so nice—maybe I should have kissed them too." I felt guilty that I hadn't.

Mila laughed. "Forget about it," she said with a dismissive flip of her hand. "They know you're grateful."

I never learned who these men were. However, it is logical to assume that they were members of some faction of the Polish resistance, perhaps the Home Army itself, operating in and around Sambor. (Interestingly, neither man appeared to be armed, although they could have been carrying handguns under their coats.) I do not know how they knew about us. Had they seen us coming out of the Sambor jailhouse the previous morning? Maybe so, but we did not see them. Had they followed us all the way from Sambor, tracking us at a discreet distance through the fields? I doubt it—we were alone in those fields, of that I am certain.

Here is a possible explanation. On the evening of the day we fled Sambor, the two SS men would have come home in lustful anticipation of the carnal pleasures we were to provide them, only to find their house empty. Incensed that we had double-crossed them, and with sexual frustration stoking their rage, they launched an area-wide search to find us. Assisting them in this effort was the Gestapo, which sent some agents down from Lvov at their behest. Meanwhile, local resistance operatives were alerted to these goings-on by spies or informants, prompting them to send out their own search parties to find us before the Germans did. Somehow these operatives found out where we were staying. Perhaps they were contacted by the man of the house, who waited until we were asleep, then went out looking for resistance members to inform them of our presence.

It is a plausible scenario. But I prefer another explanation. There was something enigmatic about those two men. Their appearance in the garden was more like a materialization than an arrival, and their departure into the surrounding fields was too sudden and suspiciously complete, as if they had literally vanished into thin air. Perhaps they were not men at all. Perhaps they were divine beings, angels sent by God to help us. That is what I prefer to believe. Of course, they were probably flesh-and-blood men. But if they weren't angels then, I am sure that they are angels now.

We went into the hut to say good-bye to our hosts and to thank them for their hospitality. Curiously, they gave no indication of being aware of their most recent visitors, which reinforces my half-held belief that the two men in the garden were angels.

A few minutes later we were once again walking through fields of ripening crops. Once again we had no plans, no idea where we were going, where our next meal would come from, where we would spend the night. We didn't worry about these things. All that mattered was to keep moving.

We realized, though, that we could not go on like this forever. So we decided that we would find a railroad station and take the first train that came along to whatever destination it was going to, so long as that destination was not Lvov. Fortunately, I had enough money to buy train tickets for the two of us. Sometime around mid-afternoon we came across railroad tracks and followed them to a village whose name I cannot remember. We went to the village train station, which was nothing more than a platform sheltered by a wall with an overhanging roof. On the wall a schedule had been posted which listed Kraków as the final destination of the next train. We waited there for about an hour. When the train arrived, we boarded it, purchased tickets from the conductor, and settled into our seats. A few seconds later the train pulled out of the station and we were on our way, heading north and west to Kraków.

Kraków

I felt good about going to Kraków. It was a big city, one of the most populous in Poland, which meant that a person could easily get lost in the crowd there. This was our plan—we wanted to blend in, to be anonymous. Of course, I was aware that, before the war, Kraków had been home to a sizable number of Jews. I assumed that this was no longer the case. Surely the Jewish population of Kraków, like the Jews of Lvov, had been severely reduced if not entirely liquidated. But this did not trouble me. I had no intention of going anywhere near the Jewish ghetto or wherever Jews had been concentrated. And why should I? After all, I was Urszula Krzyzanowska, Catholic girl, and I had no business being among the Jews.

On the train to Kraków, Mila and I sat across from a young girl who appeared to be about our age. She had short, dark hair, thin lips, and brown eyes. The moment I saw her, it occurred to me that she might be Jewish; in fact, she looked more Jewish than Mila and I did. But I kept this thought to myself, and Mila and I did not speak to her, not at first. Engaging in conversation with strangers was dangerous, particularly if they looked Jewish; it was also a surefire way to draw attention to ourselves. But the girl seated opposite us evidently had no fear of strangers and began talking to us almost as soon as we sat down. As it turned out, she proved to be so open and affable that we could not resist her friendly overtures, and in no time at all the three of us were gabbing like old pals.

Her name was Stephanie Tartar, and despite her looks she

was not Jewish, but rather a Catholic girl from Kraków. We told her who we were, or rather who we were pretending to be; and, in a conspiratorial whisper, we informed her that we were Polish patriots who were politically sought by the Nazis. Upon hearing the words "politically sought," Stephanie fairly lit up with excitement. Leaning toward us and speaking in a low voice, she confessed that she, too, considered herself a patriot, and though she was not sought by the Nazis, she was entirely willing and eager to help anyone who was. In the next breath, she insisted that we stay with her in Kraków, in the apartment she shared with her family.

It was an attractive offer, but Mila and I hesitated to accept it. Stephanie seemed quite genuine, yet we knew nothing about her or her family. More to the point, they would know nothing about us. Therein lay the potential for disaster. Suppose they hated Jews. Suppose they guessed that Mila and I were Jewish. What then? We didn't want to find out. And yet, we didn't want to refuse a place to stay in Kraków, either.

We could not give Stephanie an answer. So we sat there in silence, tongue-tied by indecision.

Stephanie did not wait for our reply. She went on to tell us that her mother, who managed their building for its owner, had the authority and the connections to register us as long-time occupants. Having thus established our residency in Kraków, Stephanie said, we could straightaway obtain work papers from the local *Arbeitsamt* (labor office), which in turn would enable us to find jobs easily.

"So you see," she said with a grin, "you have no good reason to refuse me and every reason to take me up on my offer."

She was right, of course—more so than she could ever know. It sounded like the ideal setup for two Jewish fugitives like ourselves. So we said yes, despite our reservations.

We found the apartment to be a tiny place with one room and a minuscule kitchen off to the side. Stephanie lived here with her mother and father, two sisters, and a brother, all six of them sleeping together in that one room.

Given that the apartment was really too small for the Tartar family, I wondered how they could even think of accommodating two houseguests. But they didn't regard this as a problem, not after Stephanie introduced us as "politically sought" fugitives. These were the magic words. For the second time in two days, they had opened the doors of a Polish home to us. Upon their utterance, the Tartars practically demanded that we move in with them—they told us they would be honored by our presence. And so we moved in.

The Tartars made space for us in their kitchen, giving Mila and me a single narrow cot to sleep on. It would have been an intolerable arrangement if not for Stephanie's mother. She was a short, rotund woman with a cheerful disposition and a tender nature who was as caring and solicitous to us as she was to her own children. Stephanie's father, though also kind, was a sad case. He was officially the janitor of the building, but he did precious little work around the place on account of his addiction to alcohol. Scrawny and haggard, with the waxy complexion so common to alcoholics, he daily consumed huge quantities of vodka and spent most of his waking hours either drunk, hung over, or in transition between the two. But he was a harmless sort, friendly and docile even when he was in his deepest cups. So we put up with the crowded quarters and the father's boozing without complaint. We were sincerely grateful to the Tartars for taking us in. We recognized that in doing so they may have saved our lives even as they had knowingly placed their own in jeopardy.

At great personal risk, Stephanie's mother registered us with the authorities, thus procuring residence papers that "proved" we had lived in the building for several years. With these papers in hand, we went to the city hall to obtain our *Kennkartes* and then to the labor office to pick up our *Arbeitkartes*. That done, we went out hunting for jobs.

This wasn't easy. Jobs were hard to come by, even for people with legitimate work papers. Mila and I went out and pounded the pavement, going from door to door, asking the proprietors of various shops and businesses if they were hiring. We also checked the job listings in the newspapers and scanned the street-corner kiosks for help-wanted posters. We did a lot of walking, and it was hungry work. Once, we took a lunch break during our job search, purchasing an entire loaf of fresh black rye bread from a bakery in Kraków's outdoor market district. We wanted to divide the loaf evenly, but we didn't have a knife to cut it.

"Here's what we'll do," said Mila, hefting the loaf in her hand. "Either I'll break the bread and you choose which piece you want, or you break it, and I'll choose. That way, neither of us will feel cheated."

I told Mila to break the bread. She did, I chose my half, and we gobbled the bread down. Then we resumed our job search.

Finally, after a few days—success. Mila got herself hired as an office secretary, and I found employment as a bookkeeper at a grocery store on Długa Street. The store was owned and operated by a *Volkdeutscher*, an ethnic German who was born and raised in Poland. I was hired because I was good with figures and, more importantly, because I was fluent in German. Now all those dreary hours spent in the classroom trying to master the German language reaped dividends that I could not have foreseen at the time. I had not enjoyed learning German, but now I blessed my parents and my school for seeing to it that I had. For the truth is, the job came as something of a godsend, because it meant that I would not starve in the foreseeable future. Only Germans and *Volksdeutsch* were permitted to shop at the store, which was abundantly stocked with food that was either scarce or nonexistent at the stores where the Poles were allowed to shop.

When I arrived at the store to apply for the job, I was met by the owner, a thickset, bald-headed man in his early forties, a physically imposing but unappealing fellow. He wore what I soon learned was his standard garb, a white apron soiled with dirt and stained with food and grease. His name was Karl, and when he heard me speak German, he hired me on the spot and took me up a narrow staircase to the second-floor room that was to be my office. The room was a cubby hardly bigger than a closet, with one small window that looked down on the street below. I liked the room precisely because it was so small. It made me feel hidden and secure from the world outside.

Karl was a strong man and a hard worker who was always busy, always in motion, lugging crates, putting items up on the shelves, and performing the countless other menial chores his store demanded of him. Though taciturn and gruff, he was at heart a decent sort who was generous and fair to his employees. He required us to report for work at sunup, well before the store opened, but to compensate for coming in so early, he gave us breakfast. This consisted of a big stein of warmed-up beer mixed with a raw egg yolk. When he first offered me this concoction, I was revolted by it. For a moment I examined the stein's contents, which had a light, cloudy appearance; it looked vile, and the idea of drinking it almost made me gag. But I was hungry, and at his urging I gulped it down. It was delicious! And not only did it taste good, it was surprisingly filling. It was also nutritious and gave me a real energy boost that kept me going for several hours afterward. Plus, it made me slightly tipsy, which put a nice glow on the day! That rich beer on an empty stomach had a tonic effect, and I started looking forward to it.

Sometimes this was my only meal of the day. However, on most days Karl shared his midafternoon supper with me. This was real food, and it, too, was delicious. It was a veritable feast, usually consisting of soup, potatoes, and bread or rolls, and, maybe two or three times a week, a few slices of veal or roast beef as well. His sister—who lived nearby in an apartment with Karl, Karl's wife, and young son—prepared the food at their home and brought it to the store around three o'clock in the afternoon. Karl would give me a plate of food and a glass of milk, and I would take these upstairs to the privacy of my cubby, where I nibbled on my meal like a mouse in his hole. My portion was small compared to Karl's, but it was a sumptuous banquet so far as I was concerned. And I loved dining alone. The solitude of that room was glorious; it made me feel safe and thus afforded me a fleeting measure of tranquillity. Of course, my room wasn't safe, no place was, but at least it seemed that way. It gave me some peace of mind, something I craved and desperately needed. Karl also allowed me to take food home from the store—a couple of rolls, perhaps, or a hunk of bread. Such usually comprised my evening meal. It was enough; I didn't need or want much more.

A curious thing had happened to me: in a sort of perverse twist, I became indifferent to food, even though I was constantly around it. I was in the most enviable of positions and yet it hardly mattered to me. My breakfast beer-and-egg beverage and midafternoon meals were delicious but not essential. I could easily forgo the latter, and sometimes did, either because Karl didn't give me any food or because I was simply uninterested in eating. Not infrequently, a few slices of bread were all I had to eat.

The explanation for this is simple. Though outwardly I appeared to be calm and collected, in reality my nerves were worn to a frazzle; I was always on edge, always frightened. My emotional turmoil dulled my appetite and changed the way I thought about food. I took little pleasure in it: food was fuel and little else. Of course, I was hungry all the time, but the point is I didn't pay attention to my hunger. It was like having a headache or a lingering pain in your lower back; you just ignored it and got on with your life. If I got enough food to keep me going and healthy, I was satisfied.

To be sure, I needed food. The effort to be Urszula Krzyzanowska was exhausting work, like being an actor who was on stage in every scene in a play that never ended. It consumed a good deal of energy that only food could provide. Nevertheless, my overriding concern was to avoid getting arrested in an action while on my way to and from the store. I thought about this all the time. I thought about what I would do if I got caught up in an action. I made plans to fight, to run, to hunker down and hide. The only thing I did not plan to do was give up.

One day Karl asked me to take care of his five-year-old son for the afternoon. I said I would, although I really did not want to. Karl's son was a spoiled brat, unruly, disobedient, and impudent. But I could not say no to Karl and expect to keep my job.

Karl deposited the boy in my second-floor room and left

the two of us together. At first the boy was no problem at all. He sat quietly in an armchair behind me while I worked on the books. I was relieved he was behaving so well and ignored him while I did my calculations. Suddenly, I smelled smoke. I turned around. The armchair was burning. Somehow the boy had gotten hold of a pack of matches and set the chair on fire. I snatched my coat and threw it over the flames, smothering them. But the damage was done: there was a gaping hole edged by charred fabric in the cushion.

The boy looked at me with a frightened expression. As young as he was, as obnoxious as he had been, he realized that, for once, he had gone too far. I wanted to spank him. He richly deserved a paddling for this and countless other naughty deeds. But I stayed my hand. He was Karl's son after all.

"Don't worry," I assured him. "I won't tell your father."

The boy was both grateful and chastened. He behaved himself for the rest of the day.

At the end of the day, Karl came upstairs to retrieve his son. Immediately upon entering the room, he smelled the pungent odor of smoke and charred fabric. "Something was burning in here," he said, sniffing the air. "What was it?" Whereupon the boy dashed out of the room and ran downstairs. I wasn't about to be blamed for something I didn't do, so I went back on my pledge to the boy and explained what had happened.

Karl was quite pleased with what I had done, as well he should have been. By taking quick action to put out the fire, I had saved both his son and the store. To show his appreciation, he increased the size of the portions he gave me for my midday meal. From that day on and for as long as I worked at the store, I always had more than enough to eat. I ate as well as Karl or any member of his family. This form of compensation was better than money; it made taking care of his horrid little boy worth the trouble.

Karl did not punish his son for starting the fire. I don't think he even discussed the matter with him. This was typical of Karl. He never punished the boy for his many misdeeds. Consequently, the boy thought I had kept silent about his guilt, and regarded me as his special friend. He liked and trusted me now, and pretty much behaved himself when we were together. It was another unexpected benefit to be derived from a potentially disastrous incident.

Several weeks passed. Mila and I were settled in our jobs and getting along reasonably well. We had even managed to save a little money. The time was right for moving out of the Tartars' overcrowded apartment and into a place of our own.

We asked Mrs. Tartar whether there were any other residents in the same building who might want to share their apartment in exchange for rent. Mrs. Tartar knew of one such person. Her name was Zosia, and she was a single mother with three-year-old daughter, Christina, who had been born out of wedlock.

Zosia was a few years older than us, in her late twenties. She was tall and slinky and had long dark hair and blue eyes. She might have been pretty but for her pointy chin and nose, which gave her a shrewish, witchy look. In contrast, Christina, whom Zosia called her "love child," was a soft little angel with curly blond hair and big brown eyes.

Zosia's apartment had one room, and we all slept in it, Zosia and her daughter on one cot, Mila and I on another. At first, we were compatible and quickly established a routine for our household. Every morning Zosia purchased a bottle of milk and heated the contents on her stove. She would skim the cream off the top and give it to Christina, then pour herself a glass from the next layer. Mila and I received the watery part at the bottom. I didn't complain. Zosia had bought the milk with her own money, and anyway I would get my beer-and-egg concoction once I got to Karl's store.

In the evenings when I returned from work, the first thing I did was delouse myself. My hair had gotten infested with lice during my one-night stay in the Sambor jail, and try as I might, I could not get rid of them. To kill the lice one needed a special kind of soap, and there was none of that to be had in Kraków. Instead, I'd unbraid my hair and run a fine-toothed comb through it, catching hundreds of lice in the teeth. I would then squash the odious creatures between my thumb and index finger, and scrape them off the comb into the garbage can. For a few hours, my hair would be free of lice and the itching that accompanied their presence would be gone. But the lice had laid eggs in my hair and these soon hatched, so that by the next day I was itching again.

On Sundays the four of us would go to the ancient church that stood at the end of Długa Street, on the edge of a plaza with an outdoor vegetable market. Formally known as Kościół (church) Najswietczej Marii Panny, but popularly referred to as Kościół Mariacki, this was a huge and beautifully decorated church, one of the most famous in Poland. During the services Mila and I genuflected and prayed and crossed ourselves like born Catholics. But we never took Holy Communion; and, though I mouthed the words of Catholic prayer, in my thoughts I spoke to God in my own way, asking Him to watch over me and keep the Nazis off my trail.

(On one occasion we emerged from the church to find an action under way in the plaza, with German soldiers herding Jewish men, women, and children at bayonet point into trucks. Several churchgoers cheered the Germans, jeered the Jews.)

After Sunday services we came home and spent the rest of the day safely indoors. Zosia would usually scrub the floors with an ammonia cleaning solution while Mila and I would shampoo our hair in the small sink. Sometimes, I would mend the runs in my one pair of silk hose which I had purchased so long ago in Lvov.

We never left our apartment unless we absolutely had to. We went to work, we went to church, we went to the market to buy food. Other than that, we did not go out. The streets were very dangerous because the Germans were constantly conducting actions. I took a tram to work and Mila walked to her job, and neither of us knew when we left our apartment in the morning whether we would come home that night. In the morning as we went out the door, we would say good-bye to each other in an offhand manner as people normally do when they are going off to work. "See you later tonight," we might say, or "Be careful." We did not want to turn our daily leave-taking into a big deal. But it was a big deal, and we both knew that we might never see each other again.

It was, needless to say, a terrible way to live, and Mila finally reached a point where she could stand it no more. So, she took the only way out that was open to her. One day she came home from work and announced to me that she was getting married to a Polish Catholic man who worked at her office. She told me this in a flat, cheerless voice with her features composed in an impassive mask. In her eyes I detected an element of sadness, but I also saw an implacable hardness there as well. I had never met the man she was to marry, and she had never once spoken of him. She told me a little bit about him, but what she didn't tell I could easily guess: She wasn't in love with him, nor did she feel any sexual passion for him. This was to be a marriage of convenience or, more precisely, of desperation. It was a simple and pragmatic solution to an intractable problem. Marrying a Catholic would protect her true identity. She would have more freedom and someone to care for her.

I did not blame her for what she was about to do. I wished her well and said that I would miss her. And that was that. No celebration, no tears. Marriage was no big deal either. For Mila it was a survival tool, pure and simple.

Of course, the thought of finding a husband had also crossed my mind. I had one definite candidate for the job. This was Stephanie's younger brother, Maciek. He had become infatuated with me while I was living in the Tartars' apartment, where he had proved a most persistent suitor. It wasn't easy in that crowded place to find a way to be alone with me, but somehow he always did. Then he would pull me aside and profess his love for me in the most earnest terms. He often proposed marriage to me and promised a life of wedded bliss in which he would take care of me and see to it that I would want for nothing. Given that there was a war on, it was a reckless and ridiculous promise to make, but he was smitten and had thus lost all sense of perspective about the way things really were.

Maciek's devotion came in handy whenever I had to leave

the apartment to run an errand of some sort. For instance, if I was going to the market he would accompany me, and because he looked like a typical Pole—he had straw-colored hair, pale eyes, a little snub nose—people would naturally assume that I was Polish as well. So I was safer when he was with me.

But the truth is, he did not interest me at all, and despite the threatening circumstances of the Nazi occupation, I never once entertained the thought of marrying him. I rejected him gently but firmly—not once, not twice, but many times. Still the message did not get through. He would not take no for an answer. Eventually, he became a real pest. Even when we weren't talking, he would gaze at me with a moony expression that was sometimes accompanied by a tender but barely audible sigh. I was embarrassed for both of us and felt a strong urge to slap his face and make him snap out of it. But I didn't do it. I smiled and gently put him off; then one day I moved out.

The owner of the *Volksdeutsch* grocery store was also something of a problem, at least in the beginning of my employment. Although married with children, Karl had a roving eye that became fixed on me for a brief while. He found me attractive, which was doubtless one of the reasons he hired me in the first place. He treated me better than his other employees—I was his "pet." He constantly did little favors for me that he would do for no one else. For instance, he would often come to my room to give me a glass of hot milk, which I had not requested. It was obvious that he just wanted to be with me, and bringing a glass of milk to my room allowed him to do just that. In fairness to him, I must say that he always behaved correctly whenever we were alone together. He never forced himself on me or said anything that even hinted at an indecent proposal. But a girl can usually tell when a man is interested in her. However, his desire and availability were merely implied and not declared openly or directly. He wasn't going to make the first move, and neither was I.

Fortunately, Karl was a practical-minded man with thoroughly bourgeois sensibilities, which acted as a brake to his

philandering impulse. I was resolutely oblivious to his restrained flirtations and, unlike Maciek, he got the message. It
did not bother him. Once he understood that I had no intention of getting involved, he gave up on the idea. He was a busy
man with a store to run, and as long as I did my job, everything would be all right between us.

Mila got married and moved out of the apartment to live
with her new husband. I did not attend her wedding, which
was held in the groom's parish church, and I lost touch with
her until long after the war was over. She survived the war,
and in this sense her marriage could be deemed a success.
However, she paid a high price for survival, as I was eventually to discover.

Once Mila was gone, Zosia's daughter Christina began
sleeping with me in my bed. I would not have minded this if
not for the fact that the space Christina had previously occupied in Zosia's bed did not stay empty, but was instead filled
by an endless succession of male companions. Zosia evidently
did not like to sleep alone. More to the point, she often
seemed not much interested in sleeping at all. She entertained
lovers several nights a week, and was not at all shy about having sex with them while Christina and I were in the room.

I was appalled and embarrassed by her behavior. I could
not believe that she could be so immodest and indiscreet.
While she and her partner frolicked, Christina and I would lie
in my bed with the covers pulled over our heads. We would
try to fall asleep, but, of course, sleep was difficult what with
all that was going on in Zosia's bed.

Zosia tried to be unobtrusive. I'll give her that—she tried.
She and her visitor would tiptoe into the room late at night
and crawl into bed without turning on the light; then they
would go on about their business, always starting out quietly,
but invariably building to a noisy climax.

Zosia was an amateur prostitute. Her male companions
gave her money in exchange for sexual favors, and she used
this income to augment the wages she earned at her job. I
don't remember where she was employed or what she did, but

I do recall her admitting to me that she once had sex with her boss during their noonday break. I could not blame Zosia for selling herself because I knew she did so out of sheer desperation, as a way of keeping body and soul together at a time when the two could be so easily and violently separated. She was thus able to provide for her child, a praiseworthy achievement despite the means she used to attain it.

Her clientele was another matter entirely, however.

Most, if not all, of her visitors were German soldiers. Many were military policemen from the police station that was located just across the street from our building. This was what finally drove me out of the apartment: not my lack of sleep and resultant exhaustion, and not her shamelessly open promiscuity, but rather the presence of naked German soldiers grunting and groaning in the throes of copulatory ecstasy just a few feet from my bed.

I left a few weeks after Mila departed, renting a room in a house on Długa Street, a few blocks east of the *Volksdeutsch* grocery store. I found the room through an advertisement that was posted at the store. The house was owned by a husband and wife in their fifties. I later found out that they had a son in his early twenties, but he didn't live with them and I didn't meet him right away. I dealt mostly with the wife and only rarely saw her husband. They were both pleasant people and, like Mrs. Tartar, the wife was especially nice. She was always very solicitous about my welfare. She provided me with bedding and towels and such, and she often came to my room just to check up on me, to ask if I was all right and whether I needed anything. She saw that I was a young girl alone in the big city, and she wanted to take care of me. She became especially concerned when I told her that I was an orphan, that both my parents had died before the war. It was a useful lie which I had thought up in order to keep her from asking too many questions about my past. She did not want to press me for details about my family for fear that she would stir up sad memories of my deceased parents. I also intimated that I was politically sought, and this, too, earned me her sympathy and solicitude. Once again, the combination of being a young girl on my own and politically sought had made a Polish couple eager to help me.

I didn't have any cooking facilities in my room, nor a bathroom or a sink. The house had only one bathroom with a toilet, so I washed myself from a large basin. I would fill the basin in the bathroom and bring it to my room. The water was always very cold, but at least I was able to stay clean. I never ate with the family, although I am sure they would have welcomed me to their table if I had expressed a desire to join them. Sometimes I brought food to my room, but usually I ate in my office cubby at the grocery store.

The house was a good place to live because it was so close to the store. I could walk to work and thus save money that I would have spent on tram fare. Also, its proximity to the store cut my travel time to and from work. I was outside for shorter periods, which meant that I decreased the risk of being swept up in an action.

Unfortunately, I could not avoid going out altogether. Eventually, perhaps inevitably, this proved to be my undoing. There was another action and I was arrested. It happened about one month after I moved into the room; it was now the spring of 1944, March or maybe April. Once again, I was taken in the morning while on the way to work. I was walking down Długa Street when a dozen or so trucks pulled up next to the curb and disgorged a squad of shouting German soldiers. I kept walking and stared straight ahead. I maintained my pace even though I wanted to run away. No use. A frowning young German soldier armed with a bayonet-tipped rifle stepped in front of me and ordered me to halt. My heart began pounding and my stomach felt as if the bottom had dropped out of it. I was frightened but I was also very angry. You bastard, I thought, you rotten, miserable bastard. A murderous rage boiled up within me; I really wanted to kill that man. But there was nothing I could do except obey him. So I halted. I bowed my head and stared at the ground and said nothing. I adopted this humble attitude partly to mollify the German, but also because I couldn't stand the sight of him. I thought that if I looked at him my rage would make me lose control of myself and say or do something that would get me into a lot of trouble or even get me killed. I had been through this sort of thing before, and I knew how to comport myself. I also knew what was coming next. Even so, I thought perhaps this time I would be lucky; perhaps this time the Germans would let me go.

But the soldier did not let me go. Instead, he demanded to see my identification papers. I protested that I was a Christian Pole and that I had a job; but he either did not believe me or did not care to hear anything I had to say. Again, he demanded my papers and the angry and impatient rasp in his voice made it clear that I had better do as I was told, or else. I produced the papers from my purse and he looked them over. The papers were legitimate—my identity was the only thing about them that wasn't real—but he arrested me anyway. He gestured with his rifle toward the nearest truck. "Go on, get up there," he barked.

I climbed aboard the truck.

Within minutes, the back of the truck was packed with other young women, but no men. Several of the women were conversing in whispers, speculating about why they had been arrested. One of them said that she heard the Germans were arresting young women at random all over Kraków in an effort to ferret out Jewish girls with false identification papers. She said the Germans believed that many rich Jewish girls had used their money to purchase Aryan papers and were living among the Poles as Catholics. I listened to this and said nothing. I was acutely aware just then of being Jewish; I felt almost as if I were wearing a sign proclaiming in big letters that I was a Jew.

When all the trucks were filled, they drove in convoy to Kraków's most notorious prison. This was a four-story brick building with cell blocks arranged in a square around a courtyard. When we got there, we were herded inside to a corridor and instructed to sit on long wooden benches that were set against the wall. We sat there in silence, hardly daring to move while a single German soldier stood guard over us.

The guard paced slowly up and down. Suddenly a pretty

girl with blond hair and lovely features stood and turned to face the soldier. He cocked his head and watched her, saying nothing. The girl started walking slowly toward him. He lowered his rifle and pointed the weapon at her. Undaunted, she strutted down the corridor, swinging her hips and staring at him with a lewd smile. I gaped at her in amazement. We all did. We watched as she sashayed right up to the tip of the soldier's bayonet, then lifted her skirt above her waist with one hand and pulled her panties down with the other.

We all gasped.

The girl stared at the soldier, smiling her lewd smile, still holding her skirt up, with her panties down around her knees. The soldier was not amused. Nor was he interested in taking her up on her explicit if unspoken offer. Instead, he ordered her to pull up her panties. The girl's smile abruptly faded and she covered herself. Then the guard ordered her to sit and gave her a shove toward the bench. She sat down next to me.

A few minutes later, we were taken into a room where men dressed in white surgical gowns and masks poured a sticky white powder into our hair. The powder was laced with a DDT-based disinfectant that was supposed to kill head lice. We then trooped upstairs to the first floor where the women were incarcerated (men were housed on the top floor). We were put into a large cell, and once we were all inside, the guards slammed shut the cell's heavy wooden door, which closed with a resounding thud.

In all, there were about fifty women in the cell. There was a long wooden table in the middle of the cell, and in one corner a bucket that was to be used as a toilet. On the inside wall were four barred windows that looked out onto the courtyard. Mattresses made of rough burlap stuffed with straw lined the walls. I immediately staked my claim to a mattress beneath a window on the wall opposite the toilet bucket. I wanted to be as far from that bucket as I could get.

The girl who had exposed herself to our guard selected the mattress next to mine. We struck up a conversation and I found out that her name was Danuta. She was a nice person and not at all the wanton temptress I had thought her to be.

She did not look Jewish, and she told me later that she was really a Christian and had no business being in prison. I neither believed her nor doubted her word. I didn't care who or what she really was, and I didn't want to know. The less one knew in a place like this, the better.

In a sheepish tone, Danuta explained the reason why she had bared herself to the guard. She said she had intended to offer the guard sex in exchange for her freedom. "I'd do anything to get away to get away from the Nazis," she said ruefully.

I nodded in sympathy. I shared her sentiment even if I did not agree with her tactics.

While I was chatting with Danuta, a group of girls seated on a mattress across the room suddenly began singing a Hebrew song. I recognized it as "Ani Ma'amin," which means "I Believe." A slow and solemn dirge, its words are taken from the *Thirteen Principles of Faith* by Maimonides, the renowned Spanish-born rabbi and theologian who lived at the end of the twelfth century: "I believe in the coming of the Messiah. / Even though he tarry / I still believe." It is at once an affirmation of faith and a proclamation of defiance in the face of death, a song of martyrdom, made tragic by the circumstances for which it is meant, yet profoundly uplifting for what it signifies. Danuta and I stared at the girls for a moment. They clung to each other as they sang, and I thought it terribly brave of them to proclaim their faith in such a fashion, in such a dismal place as this. They must have known that they were baiting the Nazi lion in his den and that, unlike Daniel, there would be no miracle to deliver them from his jaws. Death would soon come to them and probably many torments as well, yet still they sang. I listened to them but I did not let on to Danuta that I was familiar with their song. I would keep my Jewishness a secret from my fellow prisoners. I was sure that there were German spies in the cell; I thought there may have been spies even among the singers. And though I admired and respected the singers for their courage and solidarity and religious steadfastness, I had no intention of emulating them, for I had no desire to be a martyr. I thought that if they believed in God, then why didn't they believe in life? Why didn't they fight for life instead of accepting, through song, their impending deaths?

Of course, I was aware that singing "Ani Ma'amin" constituted what was really the only form of resistance available to them. The Germans already knew those girls were Jews, which meant they were as good as dead; their time was fast running out. Let them sing, I thought; let them meet their end with dignity and heroism. As for me—well, my time might be running out too. Perhaps this prison would be the place where Urszula Krzyzanowska would finally be unmasked as Lala Weintraub. But until that happened, I would keep my disguise. I was determined to play the role of Urszula Krzyzanowska to the last. I would not go to my execution singing Hebrew songs of martyrdom but rather protesting my Catholicism right up to the instant that the bullets penetrated my flesh. One never knew: at the last second before the order to fire was given, the Germans might decide that I was indeed telling the truth and stay my sentence. It was a slim reed to grasp at, but grasp it I most certainly would if I thought it would keep me alive.

The Germans did not come for those Jewish girls right away. So I got to hear "Ani Ma'amin" over and over again in the days that followed. It was sung to the accompaniment of bloodcurdling screams and anguished moans emanating from the floor above. This was the sound of Jewish men being tortured by the Germans, a sound that rang throughout the prison at all hours of the day and night like some agonized threnody of damned souls.

In this respect the men had it worse than the women: being circumcised, they could not conceal their Jewishness. If there was any doubt about their identity, the Germans simply made them lower their trousers for inspection. Once that was done, the game was up, and even the most artfully contrived Aryan papers were of no use to Jewish men. So the mark of God's covenant with the Jewish people served to betray the men to their enemies. Jewish women were more fortunate. We had no comparable mark on our bodies, no telltale sacred scars. Thus, we were given a choice: we could lie or die. I chose to lie.

I was in prison for seven days, and I spent much of that time sleeping. It was easy to sleep because I was depressed. Sleep was a way to escape both my depression and the prison cell. The mattresses, I soon discovered, were infested with lice, so I slept on one of the benches that were next to the table in the middle of the cell.

For the most part, my cellmates passed the time conversing in hushed voices or just sitting on their mattresses and staring off into space like catatonic mental patients. Others, who were too restless to sit still and uninterested in conversation, would drift aimlessly around the cell or stand at the windows and peer through the bars into the courtyard. At first, I did not talk to any of the girls except Danuta. I would curl up on the bench, close my eyes, and put myself to sleep. I got to where I could make myself fall asleep in a matter of seconds. Then I would make myself dream. I would just close my eyes and be transported into a different world. I dreamed profusely and my dreams were always pleasant; in a very short time I became an expert at manufacturing dreams of surpassing beauty and tranquillity.

I usually dreamed of being outside the prison. Sometimes I dreamed that I was in an office, working as a secretary, or that I was back home in my family's apartment in Lvov or in my apartment in Kraków. But as time went by, my dreams were increasingly about food.

These were the best dreams. The food I dreamed about most often was eggs. Scrambled eggs and fried eggs, cooked sunny side up with potatoes on the side. I could almost taste those eggs and smell their aroma. Ah, how wonderful they smelled, how delicious!

The Germans didn't give us much to eat. We were fed once a day by two women guards who brought us a kettle of soup and a couple of loaves of black bread. The soup was turbid and watery, with maybe a few small pieces of potato floating on the surface. We were given bowls and spoons to eat the soup, but the bread we had to pull apart and eat with our hands; the Germans didn't trust us with knives, even dull bread knives. This was the only meal we had, and we very much looked forward to getting it. It was the one bright spot in the day. Of course, in my dreams the food was tastier, and more varied and plentiful. But the soup and bread were real, whereas my dream food was not. So I wolfed down my meal ration and thanked God for every bite.

Once, I decided to save half of my bread ration for an evening snack. I slipped the piece of bread into my sweater pocket and lay down on the bench to sleep. I awoke a few hours later and reached into my pocket only to find that someone had filched the bread while I was asleep. From then on I ate all my food at mealtime.

After a day or two, I was so bored and despondent and lonely that I could no longer stand to hold myself aloof from my cellmates. I needed companionship and conversation. And so, little by little, I began to fraternize with the other girls. I even talked with the Jewish girls, although I let it be known that I was not one of them, that I was a Gentile.

Our conversations were usually about food. We were always hungry—my God we were hungry!—and we talked about food incessantly to allay our cravings. We would spend hours together describing our favorite meals in exquisite, mouth-watering detail. As one might expect, such talk only exacerbated our hunger by stimulating our appetites with visions of food we could not have. But the conversation was enjoyable nonetheless.

Sometimes, though, it got to be too much. Then I would stand by one of the windows for a few minutes and gaze into the courtyard or up at the sky just to remind myself that there was indeed a world beyond the walls of the prison. But that world could be a terrible place. Too often I saw trucks parked in the courtyard with men and woman prisoners climbing aboard them. The prisoners would do so prodded by the bayonets of Germans guards, all the while weeping and moaning in fear and anguish. When the loading was completed, the trucks would drive off, only to return empty a few hours later. Those prisoners were never seen or heard from again, and we were never told what happened to them. But I could guess.

My cellmates and I tried not to let their presumed fate discourage us. Being young, we still had hope, and hope fostered an "it can't happen to me" mentality. Even so, we were well aware that "it" could, and probably would, happen. It was so difficult to think that we might die. But we were realistic enough to know that there was little probability that we would ever leave the prison alive; or, if we did leave it alive, we would be put in trucks and hauled off to a place where we would be killed. And so, faced with certain death, we simply refused to accept the finality of it. We often talked about the possibility of reincarnation. Several girls believed, or wanted to believe, that we had many lives to live and that death was merely a transition from one existence to the next. The belief in reincarnation became more widespread and fervent the longer we were incarcerated. We used to discuss what form we would take in our next life. We assumed that we would not be reincarnated as human beings but would instead come back as some species of plant or animal. We all preferred to be something other than human. One of the girls said she wanted to come back as a poodle in a Jewish home. When I asked her why, she said that Jews treated their poodles better than most people treated their own children. The dogs were pampered and petted and, most importantly, well fed. But the majority of girls, I think, wanted to come back as birds. The ability to fly exercised a strong hold on our imaginations. Many of us, myself included, fantasized about sprouting wings that would enable us to jump out the window and fly far away from the prison, from Poland, from the war itself.

The one thing all of us stipulated for the next life was food: good food, and plenty of it. This was a hard and fast rule, a fantasy we all shared.

We discussed our dreams with each other. In the fashion of Jungian analysts, we tried to interpret our dreams, to assign meaning to the images, to find messages and clues that might reveal the future to us. We began to look upon the surreal dramas enacted in our dreams as prophetic visions that would point out a path from the prison cell to freedom. The general consensus was that if you dreamed of new shoes, broken glass, or anything green, it was a positive sign. Green was acknowledged to be the color of hope because it was the color of the grass and trees outside the prison. Dreaming of shoes meant that you would be set free and walk out of the prison. The Jewish girls asserted that broken glass was a sign of luck, because when you get married the groom always stamps on a glass to break it. The Christian girls liked the sound of this and adopted the Jewish superstition. Whether Jew or Gentile, we all agreed that dreaming of broken glass betokened good things.

Time passed slowly in prison, and the slow-motion pace of events was excruciating. Most people think seven days is not a long time, but they have never been in prison; the truth is, when you are a locked up in a cell, seven days can seem like a century. After a while, time virtually ceased to exist. I am sure my frequent sleeping contributed to this feeling, but I blamed it on the Germans. It seemed to me that the Germans had not only become proficient at destroying human beings, they could destroy time as well.

The small amenities of life one normally takes for granted became matters of overriding importance, the more so because they were either scarce or entirely absent. For example, performing one's bodily functions became a very big deal, and a very noxious and humiliating one at that. With only that one bucket in the corner for fifty girls to relieve themselves in, hygiene and privacy were nonexistent. By mid-morning the bucket was always overflowing with excrement, which spilled onto the floor around it. I will leave it to the imagination of the reader to imagine how unsanitary conditions were, how loathsome was the stench that permeated the cell, or what an ordeal using the bucket became. I actually became wistful and nostalgic about the old way of having a bowel movement. Sometimes I would lie on my bench, not dreaming about food, not fantasizing about flying away from the prison, but thinking: Oh, how luxurious it would be just to sit on a toilet once again.

The stinking contents of the toilet bucket were not the only source of malodorous smells in the cell. The reek of our own unwashed bodies also fouled the air. It was spring and the guards allowed us to open the windows to let in fresh air from outside, but this did not help much. There was no running water, and so we got filthier as the days went by. Lice proliferated and infested our mattresses and hair. Upon waking up in the morning, we spent the first few minutes of the day picking the lice out of our hair and scratching the bites these parasites had left on our bodies.

The Germans were not entirely indifferent to our squalid conditions. Every morning the women guards would bring us a pail of water and two brushes, which we used to wash down the floor and the table. We took turns performing this task. I had never cleaned a floor in my life, since my parents always hired an au-pair girl to come to our apartment for that purpose. But I watched how the other girls cleaned the floor and table, and when my turn came I followed their example.

After the third or fourth day in prison, the Germans began to hold hearings to determine who we were, where we worked, and whether or not we were Jews. One by one, the girls were summoned from the cell to another room for interrogation. They were taken away by the woman guards and were usually gone for several hours. Many returned with their faces swollen and discolored by bruises from the beatings the Germans had administered. Inevitably, the girls who had been beaten most severely were Jews who had tried, unsuccessfully, to pass themselves off as Poles. Once the Germans ascertained a girl's Jewish identity, she was subjected to a fierce battering and then returned to the cell to await further punishment. One girl who came back with a black eye and various other bruises and welts recounted in a choked voice—she was sobbing and in considerable pain—how the Germans had found out she was Jewish. They had asked her, "How do you say 'eyes' in German?" In German the word for eye is "augen," pronounced *owgen*. In Yiddish the same word is used but is pronounced *oygen*. She had given the Yiddish pronunciation and was duly beaten. Soon she would be executed. I listened raptly to her story and said nothing. But I filed the information away in the back of my mind for the time when I would be interrogated.

The night before I was interrogated, I had an extraordinary dream. I dreamed that I awoke in prison on a Sunday morning. I got off my bench and went over to the window and looked out to behold a beautiful autumn day. There were no trucks in the courtyard and no prisoners were screaming. One of the woman guards was walking across the courtyard. She was dressed like a nurse in a white uniform instead of her usual navy outfit. She was carrying a pair of green lace-up boots in her left hand and a white porcelain plate in her right hand. Suddenly, she dropped the plate on the courtyard's cobblestoned surface and it shattered.

This was a lucky dream! When I told my cellmates about it, they became very excited. They said the dream meant that not only was I going to get out of prison, but that I would also go to America. I wondered, where did they get that from? What were they talking about? It was just a dream after all. I didn't believe the dream meant anything.

Finally, my turn came. The woman guard called out my name, and I left with her, following her through the empty corridor of the prison. The corridors were like subway tunnels, dimly lit, deserted, cavernous. Our footsteps echoed on the floor, and I could hear occasional screams and mournful howls from other hapless prisoners shut away deep in the prison. We walked down a corridor until we came to a door. The woman guard opened the door and nodded with her head to indicate that I should go inside.

I went in and found myself in a huge room with high ceilings. There were no furnishings except for a long wooden conference table set nearly against the wall that was opposite the door. Behind the table sat ten or twelve uniformed SS officers. I looked at them and they stared back at me impassively. They reminded me of savage beasts that might suddenly pounce on me and rip me apart. No one spoke. I didn't know what to do. Then the woman guard shut the door behind me. The heavy thud of the door as it shut had a galvanizing effect. Without thinking, I marched across the room to the table and planted myself in front of the officer in charge, who was sitting in the center of the group.

"How dare you keep me here!" I shouted, shaking my finger at him. "Don't you know that I have an important job? Don't you know that I have a lot of work to do? But instead of letting me work, you make me sit here for seven days. I've been wasting my time for an entire week!"

I paused to catch my breath. Incredibly, the Germans did nothing, said nothing. They just stared at me. But on the face of each man, beneath the veneer of hard imperturbability that SS officers assiduously cultivated, I thought I detected traces of befuddlement and doubt. My outburst had surprised them; it was not the sort of behavior they expected from a young girl about to be interrogated by the mighty SS. They were accustomed to cringing and fear from their captives, not the brazen display I had just put on for them. It had brought them up short, and in doing so, control of the situation had momentarily passed into my hands. Without thinking, I hurtled on, resuming my tirade at full blast.

"Can't you see that I'm a Pole?" I yelled, working myself into a fine lather. "Just look at me. Do I look like a Jew? No, of course not. That's because I'm not a Jew. I'm a Christian, just like you. If you don't believe me, call the Labor Office. They'll tell you who I am. They'll tell you that I've lived in the city for a long time, that I have job, that I'm not a Jew. Go ahead, call them!"

And with that I fell silent. There was nothing more to say, and in any case I did not have the energy to continue. I had shot my bolt and it remained to be seen whether I had hit the mark. I stood there gasping for breath. The Germans let a few seconds pass. Then one of the officers said, "I think we should call."

The officer in charge nodded and said, "All right, I will."

There was a telephone on the table in front of him. He

snatched the receiver off the cradle and spoke in German to
the operator, asking to be put through to the Labor Office.
While we waited for the connection to be made, I stood there
frowning, with my hands held stiffly at my sides, fists
clenched. I may have even tapped one foot impatiently on the
floor. I was trying my level best to appear outraged. This was
not difficult. I really was livid because I hated the Germans so
much.

With the receiver held to his ear, the officer in charge studied me with eyes as cold and penetrating as an arctic wind. An
eternity went by. The men behind the table hardly stirred, said
nothing. Someone coughed. Another man scribbled something on a tablet of paper, his pen making a scratching sound
as he wrote. Once again I saw the Germans as ravening wolves
clothed in fancy military uniforms. It was almost as if I were
hallucinating. It was a weird and unsettling vision that made
me feel dizzy and disoriented.

A voice, distant and tinny, spoke out of the telephone's earpiece. I could not make out what it was saying. The SS officer
began talking, asking questions in a clipped businesslike tone.
He mentioned my name several times. Then he quit talking
and waited for answers. Another eternity passed, seconds
ticking slowly by. Then I heard the voice in the earpiece again.
The SS officer punctuated his interlocutor's report with nods
and grunts and maddeningly truncated comments and questions: "Yes. Yes, I see. She did? When? Where? How long?"
And so on. At length he thanked the man on the other end of
the line. "*Vielen dank. Wiederhören.*" He replaced the receiver in its cradle and looked at me.

I waited for his verdict, trying not to show my anxiety.

"*Raus!*" he snapped. He gestured toward the door. "*Raus!*"
Out.

That was all he said: Out. At first I couldn't believe my
ears. Was he really telling me to leave?

"*Raus!*" More emphatically this time. It was true: I was free
to go. Evidently my name had checked out.

With my heart in my mouth and my knees shaking, I
turned and strode to the door. When I got there, the woman

guard opened it and I went into the hall. Then I walked out of the prison without looking back. I didn't look at the guard at the main entrance as I walked past him, and I didn't look at the soldier who opened the gate for me in front of the building. I kept my eyes fixed straight ahead, and I walked at a steady, even pace. I didn't want to run and thus show the Germans that I was anxious to get away from them. I didn't want to provoke the beasts into chasing me now that I had gotten out of their lair.

At some point before I left the building, someone handed me my identification papers and I may have even signed a receipt for them. But I don't remember this. I was in a daze. What I remember next is strolling down the sidewalks of Kraków. Suddenly I was conscious of my surroundings, suddenly I was aware. It was as if I were awakening from a deep coma. I was awake and I was on the move! The city was unusually peaceful; the streets were quiet, nearly deserted, and I remembered that it was Sunday, and most of the people were either in church or having supper with their families. The sun was shining, birds were singing, the air was warm and fragrant with the smell of flowers and greenery. It was glorious! I was alive and free and the world was glorious!

Later that evening, I would replay the whole incident in my thoughts. It was only then that I realized what had happened, what I had unwittingly accomplished. I say "unwittingly" because there had been nothing premeditated about my actions. I wish I could say that standing up to the Nazis and rebuking them was a calculated ploy, because then I could congratulate myself for being a very brave and clever girl. But this would be dishonest. The truth is, I had formulated no plan for this latest encounter with the Germans. I didn't know what to do, and I really don't know what possessed me once I entered the interrogation room. Perhaps I was so fully immersed in playing the part of Urszula Krzyzanowska as to temporarily merge my identity with that of this fictitious woman. The fact that this happened spontaneously in response to being under extreme duress only made me more convincing as Urszula. I had become the perfect actress, at once completely inhabiting, and inhabited by, a spirit of my own invention. My performance was not stilted or obvious because I was not acting; for the few minutes I was in the interrogation room, I really was the woman I claimed to be. Thus, my indignation that the Germans might think otherwise was authentic.

I like to think that my performance was inspired by chutzpah—Jewish guts. It was madness, but it worked. And under the circumstances, it was the best thing I could have done, as the Germans seemed predisposed to be favorably impressed by people who spoke harshly and comported themselves with arrogant self-confidence. Had they known I was a Jew, they probably would have shot me out of hand for showing such unpardonable effrontery to the devoted servants of the Third Reich. But that was the point: they did not know I was a Jew, and after I had finished haranguing them, they did not suspect it, either. To their way of thinking, Jews were a cowardly race, and I had been anything but cowardly. Since I had confronted them in a high and righteous dudgeon, they simply had to assume I was a Gentile, otherwise where and how would I have gotten the nerve to give them such a tongue-lashing? Significantly, then, it was not the content of my tirade that convinced them I was a Gentile, so much as it was the hauteur with which I delivered it. The bureaucrat at the Labor Office had only confirmed what they already believed to be the case.

I went back to my room. My landlady made a huge fuss over me when I walked in the front door of her house. My sudden and prolonged absence had greatly troubled her—she was worried that I had come to a bad and violent end, a commonplace occurrence in Poland. "Where were you, what happened to you?" she asked in a strained voice. "What have you been doing all this time?" I told her that I had gone to Lvov to attend the funeral of a relative. It was a lie I made up on the spot, something I had gotten very good at. She believed me. I could see that she wanted to talk some more, but I begged off and went upstairs to my room. She followed me up, however, and came into the room behind me. She told me that her son had come for a visit. "He's twenty years old," she said, "and I would like for him to meet you."

I opened my mouth to tell her that I didn't want to meet anyone just now, but she left the room before I could speak. In the next second, her son came in, walked over to the bed, and sat down beside me.

I had never seen him before; I didn't even know my landlady had a son. I think he was a student somewhere and had come home from school for the weekend. He was a handsome young man with fair hair and regular features, and normally I would have been delighted to make his acquaintance and talk with him for a while. But not that day. I was in no condition, either physically or emotionally, to be around other people. My confrontation with the SS officers had completely unnerved me—I was still so frightened by the experience that my hands were shaking and I felt sick to my stomach. Also, I was exhausted and dirty, I was covered with lice, and my clothes smelled. I just wanted to be alone; I wanted to get cleaned up and then crawl into bed and go to sleep.

"You know," I told him, "I'm sure you're a nice boy, but this is not a good time for me. A member of my family died a few days ago and I've just returned from his funeral. I've been traveling all day, and I'm really tired and upset. I think it would be better for both of us if you would leave."

Incredibly, he did not leave. Instead, he started talking to me. I wanted to scream. I couldn't believe he would stay after what I had told him. I was supposedly grieving, which called for an immediate exit on his part, yet here he was trying to chat me up! Although annoyed, I had to marvel at his persistence and that he found me at all attractive, given how filthy and unkempt I was.

I didn't want to get on his bad side for fear that he might then go to his mother and turn her against me. So I just sat there and let him prattle on. I don't remember what he said; he was just making small talk, and it went in one ear and out the other. I listened impassively and said nothing, hoping that he would quickly grow as tired of me as I was of him. I thought that he had better go in the next few minutes, before the lice I had brought back from prison discovered his presence. It would serve him right if they did!

I was giving him the cold shoulder, but he either didn't care or was oblivious to it. Finally, I could stand him no more. So I got up, stomped over to the door, held it wide open, and frowned at him. "Please," I said in an icy tone, "do me a favor, and go."

That did the trick. He got up off my bed and slouched dejectedly out of the room. I waited until he had gone downstairs, then fetched my washbasin, took it to the bathroom, and filled it with cold water. I found a bar of soap and put it in the water and carried the basin back to my room. Once inside, I shut and locked my door and peeled off my lice-infested clothes and threw them in a heap on the floor, then kicked them to one side. I could not get out of those clothes fast enough. I hated them and how they made me feel. I was disgusted by my filthiness and revolted by the lice that inhabited my itching flesh. I stood there naked in the middle of my room and washed myself with a soapy wet washcloth. I did not care that the water was cold and that I was shivering; getting clean was all that mattered to me. My stomach was covered with raw red bites, and I had several open sores which stung when the soap got into them. But I ignored the pain and scrubbed myself hard for an hour or so. When I was finished, I washed my hair, then combed it while it was still wet, running the comb through my hair over and over again to get the lice out. Finally, after toweling myself off, I put on a skirt and blouse, which were the only other clothes I had. Then I gingerly carried my prison clothes outside and tossed them down into the trash can. I never gave a second thought to washing those clothes. I could never wear them again even if they could be made clean. They would remind me of the prison, and that was a place I wanted only to forget. It was better that I should wear my other clothes until they were rags than let those prison clothes touch my skin again.

I returned to work at the grocery store the next day. On the way there, I had to fight back waves of panic brought on by the terrifying realization that I might at any moment be swept up in another action. When I finally got inside the store, I felt a tremendous sense of relief, as if I had entered a place of sanctuary. Like my landlady, Karl was also disturbed by my absence, and not a little angry as well. "Where have you been all week?" he asked in irate tone. "What have you been doing?" I didn't dare admit that I had been arrested on suspicion of being a Jew—he would have fired me at once. So I gave him the same excuse I gave to my landlady: a sudden death in the family, a funeral to attend. It was a credible explanation; Poland was filled with death and there were a lot of funerals. He nodded in sympathy, muttered something in the way of condolences, and said he was glad to have me back. I went upstairs to my office and resumed work on his books.

Around noon I heard the tread of footsteps coming slowly up the stairs. A man in a threadbare gray suit appeared at my door. He was short, in his thirties. His face was unshaven and he had a hunchback. An ugly little fellow. I did not know who he was. But he didn't look like anybody I wanted to know. He looked like trouble.

The hunchback entered the room without waiting for me to invite him in and seated himself in the chair next to my desk. I calmly asked him what he wanted. He leaned forward and flashed a malevolent smile, showing a mouthful of rotten snaggled teeth that were stained yellow and brown. It took an act of will on my part not to recoil from this repulsive man. He told me that he worked at the prison and had seen me there. He said he knew that I was Jewish and that he would destroy my file—he had access to the prison records, he said—if I gave him a certain amount of money. I listened to him without losing my composure, but inwardly I was in turmoil. I asked him how much he wanted. He named a sum, and I said that it was more than I had. He told me I could give him whatever cash I had and make up the difference with food from the store below.

"That's fine with me," I said; "I'll give you what you want, food as well as money. But I can't get all of it today. Can you come back tomorrow? I'll have everything for you by then."

This was agreeable to him. He stood, saying that he would return at the same time tomorrow. Then he was gone.

Left unsaid in our exchange was what would happen to me

if I did not meet his demands. But I knew what he would do, and he knew that I knew. He had me over a barrel. If I refused to pay him off, he would denounce me to the Nazis.

I could not concentrate on my work after the hunchback's departure. I was scared and perplexed; how, I wondered, did that little creep know I was Jewish? I spent the rest of the afternoon mulling over this question. Certainly my identification papers could not have given me away; except for the name on them, they were absolutely legitimate, having been issued by the right government agencies with all the requisite stamps and certifications. It occurred to me, therefore, that the hunchback didn't really know that I was a Jew; perhaps he only suspected that I was Jewish and had come to the store on a fishing expedition. It also occurred to me that he had made a regular practice of extorting money from girls who had been released from the Kraków prison.

But all that was beside the point. The point was, he had guessed correctly about me. He might not yet be aware of this. But he would recognize it for a fact if and when I gave him his food and money, which would constitute a de facto admission that I was a Jew. Would he then destroy my file, as he had said? Or would he demand more money, only to denounce me to the Nazis when I had finally run out of cash?

I could not take the chance that he would keep up his end of the bargain. Blackmailers are never satisfied, and they are by definition treacherous. And, anyway, I did not want to give in to his threats. His scheme was despicable, and the very idea that he might profit from it made my blood boil. I vowed not to hand over a single zloty to him. There was only one course of action open to me. I would have to run away . . . again.

After work I went back to my room and stuffed my few belongings—a toothbrush and a comb, a sweater, and various other items—into a paper bag. Then I sneaked out the front door of the house without saying good-bye to my landlady. By then it was late afternoon. I went to the nearest tram stop and boarded a tram, which I rode all the way to the other side of the city. An hour later I had found a studio apartment to rent. It wasn't at all difficult to find a place. The war in general and the destruction of Kraków's Jewish population in particular had depopulated the city and produced an abundance of housing.

The next morning I went out to find another job. Of course, I could not return to the *Volksdeutsch* grocery store, but neither could I seek employment through the Labor Office. Very soon my name—Urszula Krzyzanowska—would become as dangerous to me in Kraków as the name of Lala Weintraub had been in Lvov. It all depended on when the hunchback informed on me, when my landlady reported me missing to the authorities, when Karl notified the Labor Office that I had failed to show up for work. It could take days or weeks before I was tabbed for rearrest and questioning, but that it would happen I did not doubt. I would have to get a job on my own, through informal channels. And that is what I did. I found work as a secretary at a small Polish-owned company located near my room. I don't remember the name of the company or the nature of its business, but I do recall that the man who hired me, a Pole, agreed not to register my name with the Labor Office. He would keep me off the books and pay me "over the counter," as it were, to avoid paying employee's taxes to the German government.

While looking for work, I discovered a public bathhouse for women, a so-called Turkish bath, just down the block from my room. I went there after my first day on the job and on the following two evenings as well. For the price of a few zlotys, I would lie for an hour or so in a pool of steaming hot water, which was said to have medicinal properties due to its high mineral content. As it turned out, the baths did indeed have a marvelously healing effect on the louse-bite sores that covered my stomach. The combination of hot water and steam alleviated some of the pain and also helped to sooth my frayed nerves. And I could relax in near privacy, as the clouds of steam were so dense that you could hardly see the person next to you. It was sheer heaven, a luxuriant if brief respite from the war, and when I came out of the bathhouse, I felt refreshed and invigorated and maybe even a little optimistic too.

But I lasted less than three days in that neighborhood. On

the third day, at noon, I had returned to my room for lunch, and I was spreading beet jam on a slice of bread when there came a pounding on my door. How often I had heard that sound since the war began! It made me feel as if a freezing cold knife had been thrust into my vitals. I got to my feet and went to the door, knowing that when I opened it I would find a German soldier standing in the hallway. I was right. This time my captor was fat and middle-aged, an oafish fellow with a big belly and a double chin and a uniform that somehow managed to be at once too tight and too baggy on his blubbery body. He was certainly a noncommissioned officer, probably a sergeant, and definitely a slob—a soldier with a decidedly unsoldierly bearing and, therefore, not an officer. In my experience, German officers were almost obsessive about their neat appearance. Standing next to and a little behind him was the building's Polish janitor, a skinny little man with shifty eyes, a pinched ratlike face, and a pencil moustache. "That's her," he said, and the German sergeant announced that I was under arrest and that I should come with him.

It was the rat-faced janitor who had turned me in. Like the hunchback who came to the grocery store, he could not have known that I was a Jew; but he must have assumed that I was and had denounced me to the Germans in order to collect the bounty that was awarded to anyone who gave information leading to the arrest of Jews.

I tried to tell the sergeant that I was "legitimate," that I had an identification card and a work card that would confirm this. I showed him these papers but he waved them aside. "You're coming with me," he growled.

My heart sank. Now what? I thought. How will I get away this time? I was terrified by the prospect of going back to prison where, I thought, I would certainly be killed.

I followed the German soldier down the stairs and out onto the sidewalk. The janitor trailed along behind us. When we got outside, the janitor pointed to a shop across the street. It was an ice cream parlor with a banner hanging over the entrance announcing that today was its "Grand Opening."

The janitor had already been to the place and sampled its wares, and he praised the quality of the ice cream, telling the soldier how rich and creamy it was. The fat soldier licked his lips and grinned. "Ice cream!" he exclaimed, sounding like a little boy. His bloated face took on a dopey expression, at once nostalgic and avid. He had to have ice cream now, and my journey to prison could wait. So we scurried across the street together, the soldier waddling like some monstrously overweight duck and me sort of skipping along beside him. When we got to the door of the shop, he told me to stay put until he came out. I nodded and said I would. He went inside. The moment the door closed on him, I took off running.

I took an evasive course through the streets of Kraków, describing a zigzag pattern as I darted up one block, down another, up another, and so on. At first I had no idea where I was going. And I paid no attention to the people who stared at me as I raced by. I only wanted to get away from the fat soldier, to put distance between us in case he decided to chase after me. I didn't think he would, however; he was too fat to run very far or fast. And besides, he would have wanted to eat his ice cream before it melted.

At some point in my headlong flight, I veered toward the railroad station. I realized that I had to leave Kraków; the city had become too hot for me. If I stayed, sooner or later I would be arrested again. So I went to the railroad station and bought a ticket for the next train out.

The train was bound for Warsaw. I did not want to go to the capital, which had acquired a sinister reputation for Jews. I recalled that in the spring of the previous year (1943), a revolt by Warsaw's Jews had been brutally crushed and the ghetto there liquidated. I had heard about the uprising around the time it ended, but didn't give it much thought, even though my Aunt Nadia and Uncle Broder and Cousin Marcus had lived in the city. I realized that they may have been slain in the fighting, but this did not upset me, as I had assumed that they were by then already dead, having been killed in an action or a death camp. In any case, it seemed to me that Warsaw was just about one of the worst places to try to hide out if you were a Jew. Any Jews still alive in the city were no doubt being vigorously hunted down. So I decided that I would get off at the town of Radom, which was a stop along the line.

❖

To War's End

The journey by train was blissfully uneventful. After a couple hours or so, the train chugged into the station in Radom, a medium-sized city located just northeast of Kielce, about two-thirds of the way to Warsaw. As the train slowed I scanned the platform, looking for German soldiers. Two or three soldiers were standing guard; they appeared bored and uninterested in the train and its passengers. When the train halted I opened the door of my compartment, stepped down onto the platform, and walked briskly—but not too briskly— through the station and into the street beyond. No one stopped me.

I had never been to Radom, and I knew nothing about it. All I had with me were the clothes on my back and my purse, which contained my documents and some money. It was now late afternoon, and I knew that I had to find lodging quickly; otherwise, I would be spending the night outdoors, huddled in some doorway, perhaps, or curled up under a clump of bushes in the park, where I would be vulnerable to arrest by the police or an army patrol. Outside the station's entrance, I asked a passerby for the location of the Labor Office and was directed to a building a few blocks away.

I went there and registered for a job. I spoke in German to the man who recorded my name, and he was favorably impressed by my grasp of the language. He told me about an immediate opening for a dishwasher at a restaurant that catered to an exclusively German clientele; in addition to a job, the man said, the restaurant would also provide me with

a place to stay on the premises . . . was I interested? I smiled
and said I was very interested. Oh, how earnest and enthusiastic I made myself sound! The man smiled back at me.
"Good," he said. "The job is yours—you start tonight." Then
he called the restaurant to let them know I was coming. After
which he gave me directions to the restaurant and sent me on
my way.

I reported to the restaurant within the hour. Before putting
me to work, the manager took me to a room in the back of
the building and showed me where I would be sleeping. The
room had several beds for other indigent employees; the bed
assigned to me was in a corner alcove that was partitioned
from the rest of the room by a curtain. Then he took me to
the kitchen and I began washing dishes.

Everything had fallen into place quite nicely. The manager
had even said that I could eat the leftovers when my work
was done. There was only one drawback to the place, and it
was a major one. The restaurant's clientele was not merely
German: it was, as far as I could tell, almost entirely composed of SS officers. I had determined this after poking my
head through the kitchen door into the dining area for a quick
look around. I had done so out of curiosity, but when I saw
that most of the patrons were attired in SS uniforms, I jerked
my head back into the kitchen and silently upbraided myself
for letting my curiosity get the best of me.

I slept soundly that night, as I was utterly exhausted from
the events of that long and difficult day. There was nothing
fancy about my bed; it was simply a mattress on a narrow
frame with two sheets, a rough wool blanket, and a small,
hard pillow. But it was comfortable and, better still, completely devoid of lice!

But there remained the problem of the restaurant's SS-
dominated clientele. I tried to persuade myself that I would
be safer working here than almost anywhere else—because I
was in the belly of the beast, the beast would not notice me. I
reasoned that the Germans would never think that a Jew
might choose to live and work among them; thus, my proximity to the Germans would be my salvation.

There was probably some truth to this, but it did little to make me feel less afraid. Since Kraków, I had come to regard the men of the SS as demoniacal creatures who were not of this world—creatures of pure evil, made of flesh yet imbued with awesome strength and hideous powers. They inspired in me the same sort of paralyzing, spine-chilling fear that some people feel toward ghosts and other preternatural phenomena.

At night when I lay in bed, I prayed to God and talked to Him in my thoughts, and this considerably eased my fear. I always recited "Shma Yisrael" in Hebrew: "Hear, Oh Israel, the Lord is our God, the Lord is One." Then I would recite a Hebrew children's prayer called "Mode Ani," which my grandmother had taught me when I was a little girl. The title means "I Thank You," and this is what the prayer says: "I thank You, ever-living God, for reawakening my soul; great is Your mercy and faithfulness."

At the time I did not know what the Hebrew words meant; I had learned them by rote and never bothered to ask for a translation. But Pesha had told me that it was a prayer for the morning, and back in Lvov I used to recite it just before breakfast while standing next to a window with my face uplifted to God. In Radom I said it at night because it calmed me and helped me get to sleep. As time went on, that prayer became to me what a holy mantra is to a Hindu or a Buddhist. In my moments of deepest despair, it was always on my lips and it always lifted my spirits, giving me the courage and the determination to keep going, to continue my struggle to survive. I still recite it, not because I am in despair, but because it makes me feel good; it gives me hope. I recite it when something special is happening in my family, as a way of interceding with God on my family's behalf. Somehow, it seems to help. It helped me during the war and it helps me now.

Despite all my prayers and other efforts, I could not get over my fear of the SS men in the dining room. And so, just three days after starting work at the restaurant, I went back to

the Labor Office to apply for another job. I told the people at
the Labor Office that I was seeking a position with more
responsibility, something that would make better use of my
education and skills. I was in luck. A farm located a few miles
outside Radom needed an experienced bookkeeper who
could speak German and Polish. I got the job and was told to
report back to the Labor Office on the morrow for transport
to the farm, where I would also be provided with a place
to live.

I returned to the restaurant, notified the manager that I
would be leaving the next day, and worked one final shift in
the kitchen. The following morning I went to the Labor
Office at the appointed hour and waited outside for my new
employer to arrive. He showed up at midmorning driving a
horse-drawn wagon. He was an older man with coarse, leath-
ery features and a sturdy physique—a typical peasant. We
went through the motions of introducing ourselves—his
name was Janek—and then I climbed into the back of the
wagon and tried to make myself comfortable on the straw
that was piled there. Janek gave the reins a shake and made a
clucking sound at the horse, and the wagon rolled forward. A
few minutes later, we passed the town limits and went
trundling into the Polish countryside.

I was going to a farm that had previously been owned by a
wealthy Polish aristocrat but had been confiscated by the
Germans and put under Janek's supervision. The journey
lasted several hours over unpaved roads, and in that time we
said very little to each other: a few words about the weather,
the condition of the crops, and my upcoming duties and
responsibilities. The course of the war, the German occupation, my background—these were subjects we did not discuss. His rare and brief utterances found expression in an
inelegant vernacular, and I surmised that he was a man of limited formal education, one with whom I had little in common
and even less to talk about. It was just as well, I thought, as I
was not keen on talking to anyone, educated or not.

So we traveled mostly in silence. We rolled past vast fields
of newly planted wheat and pastures populated by herds of

grazing cattle; and we went through tiny settlements with no more than a half-dozen huts. The terrain was flat and trees were scarce, and the fields seemed to stretch endlessly to a distant and indeterminate horizon where heat haze obscured the boundary between earth and sky. In the villages nothing much stirred other than a few clucking hens, which strutted about the dusty lanes as if they owned the place; most of the human inhabitants were out working in the fields—their huts were hushed and shuttered and thus appeared to be sleeping in the hot noonday sun. The dirt roads on which we traveled were gouged and creased by ruts and studded with large stones, all of which made for a bumpy ride, even though our horse was clopping along at the pace of a slow walk. I bounced and swayed with the motion of the wagon as it negotiated the road corrugations, and despite the softening effect of straw piled on the wagon bed, I knew that I would be very sore and tired by the time we reached our destination.

The journey was uncomfortable and boring, and yet I was content. It felt wonderful to be bored for a change. And though the landscape suffered from a lack of eye-catching features, it was redeemed beyond measure by the absence of Germans. So far as I could see (and I could see very far indeed), there were no Germans in the vicinity. Apart from the topography itself, it was the principal reason for the countryside's prevailing dullness. No Germans meant no excitement of a kind that I had too often experienced in the cities and could well do without. There is a certain energizing thrill to being hunted and threatened with death, but it is an ugly and painful emotion that is both exhausting and destructive to one's character, and ultimately to one's sanity as well. I wanted to get away from that peculiar form of madness and the men that caused it, and I began to think I could do just that out here in the Polish hinterland.

Finally, we arrived at Janek's farmstead. We pulled into a complex of buildings that included the main house, a number of thatch-roofed huts for the field hands and their families, barns with adjoining fenced-in yards and animal pens, grain-storage silos, and sheds. It was evident from all this construction that the farm was a large-scale operation. How large would be revealed to me during the next few days as I familiarized myself with its business affairs. This I did by going over the books, which told me that the farm was a diverse and thriving enterprise engaged in raising livestock (cattle, pigs, chickens), as well as in cultivating wheat, corn, rye, and various other crops. The sheer size of the farm was another indicator of operational scale. The number of square acres it encompassed escapes me, but I remember that you could look in any direction from the building complex and not see the end of it even on a clear day. Of course, this was in a region where immense holdings were the norm, so the limitless vista was nothing too unusual. Moreover, the land's uncompromising flatness no doubt made distances appear greater than they actually were. But I was a city girl and easily impressed by wide-open spaces.

I was not impressed by the main house, however. It was not the palatial manor one might have thought it would be. This I discovered upon being told by Janek that I was to live there with him and his family. He took me inside to show me around and get me settled. I was mildly surprised by what I found. A single-story structure, its dimensions were modest and its furnishings spartan. The layout was simple. On the left as you went in through the front door were the living quarters for the manager and his family; on the right was a study which would serve as my combination bedroom and office. Further back were more rooms, including the dining room and kitchen. The house was wired for electricity, but electrical outlets were few, as were light fixtures. There was no running water unless you counted the hand pump in the kitchen sink. This meant that there was no bathroom and no toilet either: when nature called one answered her in a detached privy behind the house. Overall, it was a rather primitive dwelling, and it made me wonder about the aristocrat who had previously owned it. Evidently he had not enjoyed the enormous wealth that is usually the signal feature of the noble-born; either that, or he was a man of exceedingly austere tastes.

My room was small but it had two big windows looking out on the fields, which made it seem airy and spacious. A padded bench stood underneath the windows and next to the wall opposite the windows there was a narrow bed with a wrought-iron frame. I was provided with a desk and a chair, but I had no chest of drawers in which to store my personal effects. I asked Janek if he had something I might use for that purpose, and he gave me a straight-backed chair that I placed next to the bed. On the chair I put my belongings—a few articles of clothing, a toothbrush, a comb, and other such items. I owned almost nothing, and certainly nothing valuable, which was a good thing, since the room was also used as a parlor by everyone else who lived in the house. Throughout the day, people were constantly entering and leaving the room, and as a result, I had very little time to myself. But I had grown used to a lack of privacy and did not mind it too much. In fact, I liked my quarters and I liked the farm as well. I thought it would be a good place to live until the war came to an end.

My job was to keep the books, audit expenditures, make cash disbursements, and generally maintain financial records of all the business activities of the farm. In essence, I functioned as the farm's comptroller, although this is a glorified term for what I did. As such, I was entrusted with all the money the farm made in its various transactions. The money was held in a locked strongbox that was kept in a metal file cabinet next to my desk. Only Janek and I had keys to the strongbox. Once a week or so, Janek would take the money into town and deposit it in a bank or use it to purchase supplies. Sometimes he sent me into Radom to do the shopping. He would give me a list of things to buy and I would be driven into town by one of the field hands.

There were five men employed by the farm as field hands. They lived in the thatch-roofed huts with their wives and children, who also labored in the fields or wherever else there was work to be done. In all the farm supported and was home to about twenty-five or thirty people. Among them, I was the only one with any sort of education and probably one of few who were literate. They were peasants and, as with Janek, I had little in common with them. They were different from me in so many ways. The way they talked, the clothes they wore, their customs and beliefs, their social conventions and deportment, their outlook on life—all different. Theirs was a rural upbringing with all that implies: little or no schooling, an insular mind-set, a roughness of speech and manner, a hardness of mind and body. They were taciturn, stoic, hardy, staunchly Catholic, often reflexively anti-Semitic. My background and life experiences were so at variance with theirs that we had no basis for any meaningful conversation. Yet, I got along with them very well. They were nice people, friendly and refreshingly unpretentious. They actually might have been a little in awe of me because I was a city girl with an education—they regarded me as something of a big shot.

My status was further enhanced by the fact that I was exempted from field work. But not because I was "too good" to soil my hands at manual labor. In the first place, my bookkeeping duties kept me fully occupied. In the second place, I had no idea what to do in a field or barnyard. Educated I might have been, but when it came to farming, I was a complete ignoramus. Janek recognized this and wisely elected to have me devote myself to accountancy and financial matters. Anyway, I didn't act like a big shot. I liked these people and I wanted them to like me. I didn't want to make any waves. I just wanted to fit in, do my job, and survive the war.

As it turned out I had no problem fitting in. Not that my relationship with Janek and his family was especially close. I scrupulously maintained a certain distance from them, on the grounds that too much familiarity was dangerous for my health. I was afraid of what I might reveal about myself during a moment of friendly but incautious conversation. It is hard to be at once friendly and secretive, particularly with people one likes, and I had to tell myself repeatedly that, if I was not careful, it would be an easy thing to relax and let slip some incriminating fact about my true identity. I had to guard against this, and the only way of doing so was to hold myself somewhat aloof from everyone. The trick was not to be excessively aloof, not to make people think that I was a snob. There was a fine line here and I trod it carefully, never once stumbling along the way. I managed to convey the impression that my aloofness was not to be interpreted as snobbery, but rather as the polite and eminently proper formality a young unattached girl should cultivate when she is out on her own in the world. Nevertheless, I grew less aloof with the passage of time. It was unavoidable; I was around these people too much to stay detached. I worked all day in the main house, and in the evening I took my meals with them at a large table in the dining room. We lived together, we ate together, we talked and laughed together. Conviviality has a kind of gravitational pull, and unless you are made of stone, it is difficult to resist being drawn in. And I was not made of stone.

Those meals, by the way, were hearty and the food was plentiful. This was the advantage of living on a farm in 1944, perhaps the most terrible year in human history. How many millions of people in the world were malnourished or starving as direct result of war? How many millions of lives already had been lost due to famine? How many more would eventually sicken and die because they had too little food or none at all? Whatever their numbers—and they are surely beyond counting—we would not be among them. In our isolated corner of Poland, we were spared this particular scourge. There were no shortages here; we always had an abundance of meat—pork, chicken, and beef—as well as milk, bread, cheese, potatoes, corn, tomatoes, cabbage, and other greens. The only problem was that the farm had no refrigerated storage facilities. As I recall, we did not have a smokehouse either. Consequently, the meat on our dinner table was never more than a few hours removed from the butcher's gibbet—what was slaughtered in the morning was generally consumed that evening, before it could spoil. Once, I remember, the cook showed me some day-old pork chops. At a glance they looked appetizing, but upon closer inspection I saw that they were crawling with worms. The cook had to throw them out and order the slaughter of another pig.

This cook was a portly middle-aged woman. If I don't

recall whether she was married with children of her own, it is perhaps because I seemed to be the sole object of all her motherly affection. She was a sweet and generous soul, and I think she felt sorry for me because I struck her as lonely and vulnerable. I was a single girl, without family, adrift in a land ravaged by war, and she was compelled by her kindly nature to befriend and watch over me. Thus, in the kitchen, where she reigned supreme, I enjoyed privileged treatment. For example, she always made sure that I had a place and the privacy in which to wash up, an important consideration in a house with no bathroom or plumbing. In the morning she would heat up a big basin of hot water, chase all the men away from the kitchen, draw the curtains on the windows and shut the door, then set the basin out on the counter. I would then strip down to my underwear and wash myself with a bar of soap and a washcloth, which she also provided.

It felt so good to be clean, and I appreciated what she did for me in that regard; I think maybe that I liked being clean more than I liked being well fed. That is what a week spent in the squalid confines of a Nazi prison had done to me: it had made me desire cleanliness over food. On the farm I could have as much to eat as I wanted, but the fact is I still couldn't bring myself to eat much. I was still indifferent to food, and on occasion I might even skip a meal. But I would never skip an opportunity to wash myself.

The days went by peacefully, and after a few weeks I began to notice that I was less fearful and anxious than I had been in a very long while. The war seemed far away, almost nonexistent. Of course, it was neither, and was in fact drawing closer almost by the hour. It was the spring of 1944, and though I did not know it then, the Red Army was making tremendous strides in its ongoing efforts to reconquer the Soviet motherland. The Russians would later call 1944 the "Year of Ten Victories," and by the time I came to Radom, they had already scored two triumphs, the first in January when they broke the siege of Leningrad, and the second in March when they annihilated a German army in the Korsun region, southeast of

Kiev. By May, after the Russian spring offensive was halted, the Red Army had recaptured the Ukraine—including my ancestral home of Kamenets-Podolski—and had driven to the pre-1939 border with Poland.

But I was either unaware of these developments or had steadfastly refused to acknowledge them, even to myself. The truth is, I was not interested in the course of the war, because whatever was happening on the battlefronts had no real impact on my life. People might tell me that the news was good, that the Allies were beginning to gain the upper hand, but it was irrelevant to my circumstances, which remained fundamentally unchanged: the Germans still ruled Poland and I was still a Jew in hiding. Besides, I did not trust good news. A lot of it, I thought, was false, the product of wishful thinking. Everyone, myself included, wanted so desperately to believe that liberation was just around the corner. But this was a dangerous belief, and I refused to put my faith in it. I could not allow myself to entertain optimistic thoughts. It was a matter of preserving both my physical and mental well-being. If I let myself believe that the Germans were on the run, that the Red Army would soon boot them out Poland, I might become lax in my vigilance; I might let down my guard and let Lala Weintraub emerge from the identity of Urszula Krzyzanowska, which would be a catastrophe if things once again went sour for the Allies. The Germans might be experiencing difficulties now, but there was always the possibility that they would recover and beat the Soviets back into Russia. Then where would I be? If I were Lala Weintraub, I would be in big trouble. More to the point, even if I were still Urszula Krzyzanowska, I would be emotionally devastated by such a turn of events. I could not stand that. So I did not permit myself to hope, and I did not listen to any talk about supposed Red Army advances in the Ukraine.

My life settled into a routine, dull but safe. Nothing much happened on the farm. The only real excitement occurred when neighboring farmers brought around their cows to mate with our bull. The bovine tryst was conducted in a corral with all the field hands watching from behind the fence, lewd and expectant grins plastered on their rough faces. I did not join in the fun only because I would have been out of place among all those guffawing men. But I sometimes watched through the windows of my office, which looked out on the corral. I admit that what I saw made me smile as well. However, I don't know which I found more amusing — the sight of those two huge animals doing what comes naturally, or the boisterous naughty-boy behavior of the field hands. Anyway, afterward I would collect the stud fee from the owner of the cow and write out a receipt for him. The show was over for the day.

Every few weeks my books were audited by a German officer who drove to the farm in a battered old automobile. He was an overweight man in his fifties who looked like an albino, with white hair, white eyebrows, white eyelashes, and skin the color of white glue. A really ugly fellow. He was decked out in a uniform consisting of a white short-sleeve dress shirt, black riding pants, and black boots, but he wore it as if it were a costume for a theatrical role he was ill disposed to play. I got the distinct impression that he was really just an accountant in soldierly garb. He drove the back roads of Poland alone, traveling from farm to farm to have a go at their books. Presumably, he reported his findings to some central economic planning authority, which used the information to determine how the yield of the farms was to be allocated. If so, and if there were many like him, it was no wonder Germany was losing the war. He had the tired dispirited air of a traveling salesman who can't make a sale, and he usually arrived at our farm in various stages of inebriation, his breath reeking of schnapps. He must have packed a bottle in his car, and it was obvious from his condition that he had no qualms about drinking and driving. It was also plain to see that he took no pride or interest in his work. We sat together at my desk, and I would try to show him the books, but he hardly glanced at them. Sometimes, for the sake of appearances, he would take one of the ledgers and leaf through it in an apathetic manner, giving it only the most perfunctory reading because he was too intoxicated to do the required arithmetic and too massively indifferent to his job to care whether my calculations were correct. I suspect he wouldn't have checked my figures even if he had been sober.

Occasionally, he would make an off-color comment of some sort, which was his way of testing the waters with me. It was no mystery what he was after; in Poland, when a man talked dirty to a woman, he wanted only one thing from her, and it wasn't love. If the woman responded favorably, it meant she wanted the same thing he did. I dealt with the problem by not responding at all. I simply ignored him, and he never pressed the issue. He was as perfunctory and feckless at making amorous advances as he was in the performance of his job. When we had finished going over the final ledger, he would say, "All right, everything is in order," and that was the end of the audit. He would then drive off to the next farm. During one visit, however, the audit ended prematurely when he fell sound asleep right next to me while sitting up in his chair. I had been explaining the fine points of some transaction when he suddenly nodded off and began snoring with his chin on his chest. I looked at him and it was then I noticed that he had previously unbuttoned his fly and opened his trousers to make himself more comfortable. As I stared at him, he unconsciously fumbled with trousers and in doing so managed to expose himself. It was a revolting sight: A fat old man with a white-glue complexion and his private parts hanging out. I got up and left the room.

Master race, indeed.

In addition to that repugnant German bureaucrat, there were two boys living on the farm who showed an interest in me. They were the sons of field hands, and both were about my age. One of them I didn't much care for, but the other I became rather fond of for a while. He developed a mild crush on me, but in spite of that our relationship remained casual and chaste—we were friends, nothing more. Sometimes, in the evenings after work, we would sit out on the veranda of the main house and talk until after dark. Or we would ride bicycles together in the countryside around the farm. He was

an uncomplicated boy with an easy way about him, and I
enjoyed his company because of it. But as time went on, I
began to find him a little too uncomplicated. The fact is, we
really didn't have much to talk about. We were very different,
and because we were different our conversations didn't go
very far or deep. As a result, neither did our friendship. It was
a pleasant thing for both of us, but it wasn't enough for me. I
was lonely and bored. I needed to be with someone more like
me—someone of my own kind.

A person matching that description turned up in May. I
learned about this individual from one of the field hands. He
told me about a building site located a few miles down the
road to Radom. The construction company that was doing
the work employed a secretary who lived near the site in a little hut. According to the field hand—who was evidently
something of a snoop—the secretary was "just like you," by
which he meant that she was young and well educated.

This was exciting news. I decided I wanted to meet this
girl. That same evening after supper, I borrowed a bicycle
from Janek and pedaled off in search of her.

I found her hut and knocked on the door. It was opened by
a pretty girl with reddish blond hair, clear blue eyes, and delicate features. She gave me a tentative smile, and I introduced
myself, explaining who I was, where I came from, and why I
had come calling on her: "I'm lonely, and I thought we might
get to know each other, that we might be friends."

She told me that her name was Wanda and invited me
inside. We hit it off at once, and within a few minutes we were
gabbing like schoolgirls. Wanda, I discovered, was also lonely
and bored. She was born and raised on a farm in Silesia, and
her parents had somehow scraped together enough money to
send her to a good school in nearby Katowice. But her education had been acquired at the expense of any skills that might
be useful on her family's farm. There the knowledge imparted
to her in the classroom was of no practical value and she was
just another mouth to feed. Not wanting to be a burden to
her parents, she had left home a few months previous to seek
work elsewhere. She had found employment with the con-

struction company, but until now she hadn't found anyone to talk to. She said that she felt lucky that I had come along.

I felt lucky too. Wanda was a lovely girl in every sense of the word: she was physically attractive, she was smart, and she had a sweet disposition. Girls like her are often stuck up, but not Wanda; she was modest and unpretentious despite all she had going for her. We became fast friends and spent a lot of time with each other, as much time as we both could spare. Usually we got together in the evenings. I would ride my bicycle to her hut or she would bicycle over to my farm. We didn't do all that much; mostly we just sat around and talked, or we sat and said nothing. We were kindred spirits for whom talking was not really necessary; the pleasure of sharing a few hours with each other was by itself a wonderful thing, serving as kind of palliative—like meat and drink for souls that had been too long starved for companionship.

Wanda and I grew very close, but even so I didn't dare reveal to her the truth about who I was. When first we met she had asked me about my family, and I had told her that I was an orphan, that my parents had died when I was very young and were buried in the Catholic cemetery in Kraków. It was just the sort of story a person would invent if he or she had something to hide, and I don't think it convinced her. But she had the decency not to ask any further questions about my personal history, nor did she reproach me for not being more forthcoming. She understood that there was probably a good reason for my reticence and made no effort to find out what that might be.

Though we never discussed the fate of the Jews in Poland, I am certain that Wanda didn't have an anti-Semitic bone in her body. She was simply not the type to harbor such hateful prejudices. The same could not be said for her family, however. I found this to be the case when I went with Wanda to spend a weekend with her on her family's farm.

She had wanted to visit her family for quite some time, and when the opportunity arose, she asked me to accompany her. I readily accepted her invitation, since I was eager for a change of scenery. I asked Janek for a couple of days off, and he said that I could have them. Wanda and I took a train to the outskirts of Katowice. The train let us off at a rural siding that was within walking distance of her family's farm. I was happy to be there—I thought this brief vacation would be fun. Little did I know what I was getting myself into.

Her family's farm was small and devoted chiefly to raising sheep. Her father and mother lived there with her older brother. I liked her mother, a typically plump farmer's wife with a ready smile and a warm disposition. It was plain to see that Wanda had inherited her personality from this woman. She certainly did not take after her father, a hulking, red-faced man who was aggressively crude in his speech and manners. Her brother was much the same—he was very definitely his father's child. Only twenty-five years old, the brother was already well on his way to becoming the lout his father was. In fact, he surpassed his father in at least one aspect that was especially pertinent to my own concerns: he was a vicious anti-Semite, and a very vocal one at that.

On the afternoon of our arrival, Wanda and I were sitting on the porch of her family's house, enjoying the warm spring sun, when her brother sat down beside us and, apropos of nothing, started haranguing us about the perfidy of the Jews.

He said, "Hitler must win. The Jews are trying to take over the world. They take all the good jobs from us. They control all the money. They don't work the land like we do—they think they're too good to get their hands dirty. Instead, they lend us money at usurious rates. That's how they've gotten rich. They drive us into debt, then take our property when we can't pay them back. I'm glad that the Germans are killing them. They deserve to die."

I did not respond to his diatribe. It would have been the height of folly to disagree with him. Had I done so, he would surely have regarded me with suspicion. Catholic girls did not go about rebutting anti-Jewish tirades. But by the same token, I was not about to say anything that would lead him to think that I shared his views. So I took the middle path and said nothing. It was a new experience for me, however. I knew that some Poles felt as he did, but in my short life I had never heard anyone express these sentiments in so many words and with such vehemence. He had bared his hatred for the Jews in much the same way that a rabid dog will bare its teeth. Compared to him, even the SS men I had encountered had been models of decorum. Beneath their civilized veneer, the SS men were monsters, but the point is they had a veneer, whereas Wanda's brother did not. The Germans tended to refrain from Jew-baiting language because it was uncouth, but Wanda's brother had no such qualms. His bigotry was unvarnished, and he was proud to put it on display. I wasn't particularly offended by his performance. He was obviously a moron, and it would have been a waste of energy to take offense. I could no more be angry with him than I would be with a mad dog. But as with a mad dog, I wouldn't have objected to putting him out of his misery.

A few minutes later, after Wanda's brother had quieted down, the door of the house swung open and Wanda's father came out on the porch brandishing a huge butcher's knife.

"I'm going to kill a sheep," he announced. "Anyone want to watch?"

I hemmed and hawed. It was not a question I was accustomed to answering.

Wanda saw that I didn't know what to say. "Have you ever seen a sheep killed?" she asked.

I admitted that I hadn't. But I didn't want these people to think that I was a complete novice to rural life, so I hastened to add that we had pigs on the farm. "They squeal and run around when they see the knife," I said in a nonchalant tone, trying to convey the impression that the slaughter of animals was old hat to me.

"Sheep are different," the father said with a smirk.

We walked over to the pasture where the sheep were grazing. Wanda's father selected a sheep from the flock, put a rope around its neck, and led it back to the farmyard, where he had placed two wooden chairs side by side. He picked up the sheep and put its head on one chair and its body on the other. The sheep didn't struggle. It lay meekly on the chairs, and when Wanda's father began cutting its throat, it didn't move and it didn't utter a sound. It didn't even blink. It just lay there mute and motionless with calmly staring eyes while Wanda's father slashed its throat.

The sheep's docility amazed me, to the extent that I was not sickened by the method of its dispatch. Even more amazing was what Wanda's father did next. He lay down on his back beneath the sheep and positioned himself with his mouth open to catch the blood that was gushing from the animal's severed jugular. The blood pumped into his mouth and he gulped it down.

Now I suddenly felt faint. I didn't throw up, but I wanted to. When Wanda's father had drunk his fill, he stood and wiped the blood from his face with his shirtsleeve. "Umm, good!" he exclaimed, smacking his lips. "That's the best thing!" He looked at me and grinned. Blood dribbled from the corners of his mouth. "If you want some, go ahead and drink," he said.

I just about keeled over. "No, thank you," I stammered. "If it's all the same to you, I'd rather not."

The father and brother laughed and made fun of me for being so squeamish. I frowned at them. I was not a good sport about it. And that evening at supper, I could barely bring myself to eat. On our plates were mutton chops carved from the sheep whose death I had witnessed. I picked at my food without enthusiasm. It was really quite savory—Wanda's mother was a terrific cook—but even so, it made me want to gag. The image of Wanda's father guzzling the sheep's blood was still fresh in my mind. To say the least, it had a dampening effect on my appetite.

After that I couldn't bring myself to look directly at Wanda's father and brother. I found it hard to believe that Wanda could be related to those two. She was their complete opposite, gracious where they were boorish, graceful where they were repulsive. It was with considerable relief that I finally said good-bye to them and returned to my farm.

The weekend with Wanda's family was the most memorable event of my rural sojourn. The rest of the summer passed without incident, at least around Radom. Not far to the east, however, the war was raging with unprecedented fury. On June 22—the third anniversary of the German invasion of Russia—the Red Army started a mighty offensive aimed at driving the Germans out of Belorussia. In the weeks that followed, the Germans suffered a series of catastrophic defeats culminating in the destruction of an entire army group. Toward the end of July, the Soviets, having cleared Belorussia, stormed across the 1939 Polish border, capturing Lublin on July 24, Lvov on July 27, and Brest Litovsk on July 28. They had crossed the Vistula, establishing bridgeheads north and south of Radom, and were advancing on Warsaw, when, on August 1, the Polish Home Army started an uprising in the capital city. The Home Army aimed to drive the Germans out of Warsaw before the Red Army got there, and at first it seemed they would. It also seemed that Radom would soon fall to the Soviets.

Sadly, neither Warsaw nor Radom would be rid of the Germans for nearly six months. The Soviets would be contained in their Vistula bridgeheads and the Home Army would be defeated. But we could not know this. At the time, on our farm, there was the feeling that the Armageddon of the Third Reich was well under way. We thought Soviet tanks would be showing up any day. The mood of the field hands became increasingly tense and expectant. Their job performance plummeted accordingly. With the millennium just beyond the horizon—it seemed almost within sight—they were disinclined to exert themselves overly much. They were equally disinclined to submit to authority. They became indolent, insolent, immune to censure. Duties were shirked, responsibilities evaded, chores neglected. News of the D-Day landings in Normandy in June, followed by the advance of Anglo-American armies through northern France in July and August, further encouraged them in their misbehavior.

This all transpired gradually, over a period of weeks, and the process was irreversible. Rankled by their attitude, Janek remonstrated with them, and they more or less told him to go to hell. He might then remind them that he was an agent of the German government—and they would just shrug and go about their business, which now seemed to involve a whole lot of goofing off and loafing about. And even when the Soviets resolutely failed to appear—they remained stalled before Warsaw while the Home Army fought it out with the Germans—the field hands did not mend their malingering ways. The spell of terror and brute force that had kept the Poles in thrall to the Germans was almost broken. It was a development that caused Janek much anxiety and consternation. The Germans were not yet gone and he had quotas to meet.

He was never able to solve this problem. And like any manager who can't deliver the goods, he lost his job. But it wasn't the Germans who got rid of him, and it wasn't the Russians either. There was a third force operating in the area, and there came a day when its members served notice to us that the farm was under their control and that they would no longer tolerate Janek in the role of overseer.

It happened on a quiet, balmy evening in late September. We were relaxing on the veranda of the main house—Janek, his wife, the cook, and me—when there was a stirring in the bushes beside the house. A hand appeared to part the branches, and four men emerged from the hole made in the wall of foliage. They were dressed in civilian clothes but were heavily armed with an assortment of pistols, rifles, and submachine guns. We all stood in anticipation of what they might do. They had dark hair, dark complexions, and what could be regarded as Semitic features—no Slavic towheads among them. I thought they looked Jewish. They also looked tough and dangerous. Were they partisans or bandits?

We didn't ask, and they didn't tell us. But at first they acted like bandits. They pointed their weapons at us. "Hands up!" one of them barked.

We raised our hands.

"Inside the house!"

We filed in through the front door.

We stood in the dining room, hands over our heads. The man who was doing all the talking—presumably the leader of the band—bullied up to Janek. "Where's the money?" he shouted.

Janek made a limp gesture in my direction. "She's in charge of the money," he said in a quavering voice.

The leader came over to me. "Is that true?"

I nodded.

"Get it."

"Follow me," I told him.

We went into my room, and I fetched the strongbox from the file cabinet and opened it. On the removable top tray of the strongbox, there were a few cash notes and some coins mixed in with a number of receipts. The man grabbed it all and stuffed it into his pants pocket. Then, gesturing with a pistol, he ushered me out of the room. I realized that he hadn't lifted the top tray to look into the bottom compartment of the strongbox, where most of the cash was stored. I didn't mention this oversight to him. I figured that if he didn't know his way around a strongbox, why should I be the one to enlighten him?

Just then, the man said to me in a low voice, "We know who you are and we know what you are. But don't worry—your secret is safe with us."

I was stunned, rooted to the spot, unable to move or speak. Was I to interpret his utterance as a veiled threat or reassurance? I stared at him. He had a stern, tired expression, but there was no hostility in his face. Reassurance.

We went back into the dining room. The leader pointed his gun at Janek. "You," he snapped. "You're coming with us."

Two of the partisans—for that is what they were, otherwise they would not have been so mindful of my security—seized Janek by either arm and forced him out the door. Janek didn't protest; he was powerless in their grasp and must have known that protest would only make matters worse for him.

The leader warned us to remain in the house for at least five minutes after they were gone. Then the partisans slipped into the bushes whence they came, and that was the last we saw of them. And it was the last we saw of Janek, too.

After their departure, several questions sprang immediately to my mind. How did the partisans know who I was? Had they been keeping me under surveillance? And if so, for how long? I shivered at the realization that they must have been watching me, even if only occasionally and probably from afar. Then again, they may have gotten quite close to me. I thought about all the times I had bicycled over to Wanda's place. How many times had their eyes followed me from the shadows of some roadside clump of bushes while I pedaled by? It gave me the creeps—I felt that I had been somehow violated, even though they had never touched me. And yet, I was also heartened by the knowledge that these men had been hovering in the background of my life. The whole episode was eerily reminiscent of my encounter with the two mysterious strangers outside Sambor, the "angels" who had suddenly appeared in the yard of the peasant hut where Mila and I had spent the night, who had warned us that the Gestapo was coming. I should have been annoyed and frustrated—not to mention thoroughly unsettled—by the fact that, despite strenuous efforts to keep my identity a secret, there were still people out there who knew that I was Jewish, and perhaps knew as well that my real name was Lala Weintraub. But I couldn't get upset, for in both instances the men involved had demonstrated that they were allies in my struggle to survive. I just wish I knew where and how the partisans had gotten their information about me. But this was a riddle I never solved.

The partisans' existence and actions seemed to indicate a divine power at work on my behalf; but to poor Janek they must have seemed like demons in the flesh as they carried him off at gunpoint to an unknown and probably unpleasant fate. I believe they took Janek hostage to guarantee their escape. Or maybe they kidnapped him because he was collaborating with the Germans and eventually executed him for his treasonable acts. In any event, after thirty minutes or so, when we had gotten over the shock of what had happened, the men on the farm fanned out in every direction through the fields to look for Janek. Notwithstanding their chronic insubordination, they didn't dislike Janek—he was, after all, one of them—and so they did their best to find him, searching all that night and into the next day, and the day after that as well. They combed the fields and the surrounding countryside like hunters beating the bush for prey, but to no avail. Janek did not turn up. There was no sign of him anywhere. He had vanished.

His wife went wild with grief and anxiety, and in the days that followed, she was often convulsed by fits of hysterical weeping and wailing. The cook tried to comfort her during these episodes, but she would not be comforted and did not cease her lamentations until she had exhausted herself. At length the poor woman calmed down, but for as long as I remained on the farm, her countenance was disfigured by a stricken expression, and she walked aimlessly about with the bleak and haunted detachment of a ghost that does not know it is dead.

Somebody—presumably one of the field hands—contacted the authorities, and two men belonging to the Polish constabulary in Radom subsequently showed up at the farm. The Germans didn't send anyone; they couldn't have cared less about Janek. They were resigned to the fact that they had lost control of the countryside and were only concerned with maintaining their dominion over Radom and other cities and population centers. The Polish policeman were similarly indifferent to Janek's kidnapping and conducted a most perfunctory investigation. They took a few notes and asked a few questions, but undertook no search of their own, thus making it plain that they were not going to pursue the matter any further. Perhaps they were afraid of the partisans. Or, more likely still, they belonged to, or were in sympathy with, the resistance movement.

Just before they left, the policemen told us what we already knew: the farm had been raided by one of the many partisan units known to be operating in the area. Among others, there were Home Army units, pro-Soviet Communist units, and units respectively composed of anti-Semitic Catholics, anti-Communist Socialists, members of the antigovernment Peasant and Labor Parties, and Soviet soldiers who had remained in Poland after the invasion of 1941 and took their orders directly from the Kremlin. Jews could and often did belong to most of these units (except, obviously, the anti-Semitic ones)

and to the parent organizations that sponsored them. However, there were also exclusively Jewish groups whose orga-
nizing principle might either be a particular ideology (Communism or Socialism) or a simple desire to band together in
common cause against a world intent on removing them from
it. In addition, there were also units with no political, ethnic,
or religious affiliations—essentially bandit gangs composed
of renegades of every stripe. Membership in the units could
be overlapping; for example, fighters in the so-called Peasant
Battalions, which had been spawned by the Peasant Party,
had been absorbed into the Home Army. Yet these units
sometimes battled with each other as well as with the Germans, and for reasons that included doctrinal differences, personal vendettas, and ethnic-religious hatred. The latter was
especially applicable to conflict arising between Jewish and
anti-Semitic groups. As a result, rural Poland was beset with
anarchy and factional violence from which no one, not even
the most patriotic Poles, was safe. Janek was only the latest
victim of this chaos and lawlessness. But, of course, the Germans were most apt to come to harm—all the underground
groups were out to get them—and so, by late 1944, they
rarely sent patrols into the countryside for fear of having
them ambushed and wiped out.

From the description we gave them, the policemen surmised that our visitors were Jews. "But who knows for sure?"
they said, shrugging their shoulders.

It was testimony to the increasingly tenuous grip the Germans had on Poland that numerous partisan units, even Jewish units, could operate so boldly and with such impunity.
Things were truly falling apart.

It is said that the most dangerous part of a war occurs right
before it ends, when rampant civil disorder combines with
the clash of armies to put everyone, especially civilians, at
risk. Janek's kidnapping bore this out. But such periods are
also a time of opportunity, if one knows where to look for it.
I found opportunity in the bottom compartment of the
strongbox. I was the only one who knew that most of the

farm's cash receipts were still in that compartment. My coworkers on the farm assumed that the partisans had robbed us of every zloty, and I didn't disabuse them of this notion. And as soon as the coast was clear—that is, when everybody was running around in circles, frantically looking for Janek—I returned to my room and took the money from the strongbox.

Later that night, when I was alone in bed and reasonably sure that no one would come into the room, I counted my loot. I had gotten the equivalent of maybe forty or fifty dollars—not a lot of money by today's reckoning, but a veritable fortune in the autumn of 1944. I had then, and still have, pangs of guilt about stealing that money. I thought that I should have turned it over to Janek's bereaved wife; she could have used it to feed and take care of her children now that her husband was gone. But I kept the money. I needed it, too. And, I reminded myself, Janek's wife wasn't the only person to have lost a family member in the war.

A few days later, when I went into Radom on my weekly shopping trip, I used some of the money to buy a skirt at the local fabric store. It was the first article of clothing I had purchased for myself since before leaving Lvov. I also bought a blouse for the cook and, in the following week, I bought her a skirt to go with it. I gave her these things in part to express my gratitude for the kindness she had always shown me and in part to assuage my guilty conscience. She thanked me profusely for the clothes and, in her wisdom, didn't ask how I could afford them.

I stayed on the farm for a few more weeks. The field hands also stayed and continued to work as if they were still laborers in Janek's employ. I don't know who was managing the farm—perhaps one of Janek's most trusted men. Not that the farm needed much in the way of management. It was running on automatic pilot, though with decreasing efficiency. The field hands kept it in operation for reasons of self-preservation. They had nowhere to go and they didn't want to go anywhere. The farm housed and fed them and provided them with sanctuary from the tumult beyond its borders. And they knew that they had to bring in the harvest or they would face a winter of starvation. So they continued to work the crops and perform all the other chores required of them, if somewhat less diligently than before.

I continued to keep the books, but I was getting antsy to move on. The cook and some of the field hands, the ones with whom I was most friendly, recognized my growing restiveness and advised me to stay with them through the winter. "You'll be safe here," they said. "Out there, things are rough."

Another important sign of just how rough things had gotten was the functional collapse of Nazi governance over the countryside. I guess I really became aware of this when the loathsome bureaucrat who audited my books disappeared. This happened in late summer, around the time of the partisan raid. He simply stopped coming to the farm. Nor did anyone else ever come in his place. We received no more visits from the Germans in Radom. And we received no messages from them: no explanations, no orders, no instructions, nothing. It was as if the Germans had forgotten that we even existed.

So Janek was gone and the Germans had absconded. Thus, I was under no one's supervision and called no man master. I could do pretty much as I pleased. So maybe the farmhands were right; maybe I should hold on to what had become a very pleasant sinecure. And yet . . . I didn't really like living and working in a place where no one was in charge. It was an unpredictable situation that might easily and swiftly go bad on me. In Eastern Europe, periods in which central authority had broken down were traditionally the times when the peasantry went on Jew-killing sprees. I didn't know if the field hands would succumb to this age-old temptation to spill Jewish blood, but I knew that I didn't want to be around to find out.

On top of that I began to worry about how the Germans might react to partisan raids in our area. What if the partisans had finally gotten too bold for the Germans to tolerate? What if the Germans overcame their aversion to venturing into the countryside and conducted an antipartisan sweep of the area? The very thought of this made me tremble with fear. I had been caught up in German dragnets before, and I didn't want to repeat the experience.

With that in mind, I went to see Wanda one day and told her that I was thinking about leaving the farm. Wanda said that she had also thought about leaving. That clinched it for me. I wasn't going to stay through the winter without Wanda to keep me company. I could just imagine myself snowed in on the farm, trapped in the house with Janek's distraught wife, unable to even go for solitary walks or bicycle rides to relieve the monotony. It would be unbearable!

I asked Wanda if she wanted to go to Katowice with me. I said that we could rent a room together and find jobs. She brightened at the idea. She had never lived on her own in a city and wanted to give it a try. It seemed like a terribly adult thing to do.

Living in a city once again appealed to me as well. An urban setting was my natural milieu. And Katowice would be a good choice. I could be anonymous there and lose myself in the crowd—no partisans would be watching me from afar. It didn't bother me too much that the Germans were still in Katowice. Ironically, the death of so many Jews, and their absence in Poland, made it safer for me to get around. By then the roundup of Jews was over. There were no more actions. For all intents and purposes, the Germans had succeeded in killing most of the Jews in Poland—which was, as the Germans would say, essentially *Judenfrei,* or "free of Jews."

I didn't notify the Labor Office in Radom that I would be leaving. There was no need to. The German administration there was disintegrating, and the Labor Office had all but ceased to function in anticipation of a Russian attack. There was no such attack immediately pending, but the Germans knew it was coming. The Russians were just across the Vistula and Radom was directly in their path.

I left the farm on a crisp autumn day—October, I think it was. I packed my few possessions—including the money I had stolen from the farm—and said good-bye to the cook and Janek's wife and some of the field hands. Then I went out the front gate of the farm and walked down the road to Wanda's place. Wanda was ready to go when I got there, and we went to the local railroad siding to catch the train to Katowice.

The train ride was, once again, uneventful. All the trains in this part of Poland were running and the lines were open, just like in peacetime. The Russians had made no effort to bomb the tracks or attack the trains that were using them. The skies were clear of warplanes bearing the telltale red-star insignia on their wings. This was really a curious thing, but I gave no thought to it. It didn't occur to me to wonder why the Russians weren't sending swarms of aircraft into the region to wreck its communications and transportation infrastructure, which would have hindered the ability of the Germans to deal with the next Red Army offensive. But it made sense for the Russians to leave well enough alone. They needed the road and rail systems intact. The valuable industries of Upper Silesia, where Katowice was located, could not continue to operate without them. It was true that these industries were presently in German hands. But the Russians were looking ahead to the inevitable day when they would own them.

I wasn't looking ahead to that day, however. It seemed too remote; it might as well have been light-years distant. Unless someone was shooting at me or otherwise trying to kill me, I didn't pay attention to what the men with the guns were doing. The ebb and flow of war, the battles that were fought, the tally of victories and defeats, the gains made and the losses suffered by the combatants—it was all too difficult to follow.

In fact, it was downright impossible to follow, at least with any degree of accuracy. There were no newspapers, and radios were scarce. Rumors were the main source of information. The air was filled with them: the Germans were losing the war and the Russians were coming. But when? Here the rumors differed. Soon was the word in some quarters, but many people took a dimmer view. "Don't hold your breath," they said. I was inclined to agree with them. I saw nothing to indicate that the Soviets were on the way. In Warsaw, the Germans had crushed the Home Army's uprising and the

Russians hadn't lifted a finger to help the Poles. The Red Army had stayed put while the Germans destroyed the city. But our unmolested passage to Katowice should have told me something about what the Russians really had in mind. Had I read the signs right, I might have stayed put too and been liberated at an earlier date. For Radom and its environs were captured by the Soviets on January 16, 1945—twelve days before the Germans withdrew from Katowice, where I then resided. Now, twelve days may not seem like much. But in a world ruled by the Germans, it could be a very long time indeed.

In any event, I went to Katowice with Wanda. I had never been there—I was coming into the city "cold." But this did not faze me. By then I was an old hand at this sort of thing.

Upon arriving at the train station, Wanda and I went straight to the Labor Office and registered for work. We obtained some referrals, and before the day was over, we had both found clerical jobs at different companies.

The Labor Office also provided us with a list of rooms for rent. There were a lot of places available. We went to a nearby address and took a room in a family-owned apartment building.

The room was small and we had to share a bed, but this was no problem for either of us. We got along just fine because we liked each other and were accustomed to cramped quarters. I may have benefited most from the arrangement in that Wanda was an excellent cook. She consistently prepared tasty meals for us, though she had little to work with. Her rural upbringing had taught her how to work wonders with even the most basic foods. She had a special skill with beets, which was fortunate, since beets were the only fare available on a daily basis. Her beet soup was delicious and nourishing, and I never grew tired of it.

One day we learned that the city had received a shipment of horse meat. People got very excited about this and rushed to the butcher shops to buy some before the supply ran out. Our landlady came to our room and proposed that we all go to the butcher's together. "Let's get some horse meat!" she happily exclaimed, and you would have thought she was talking about a prime cut of beef. We went and bought some of the meat, and Wanda made a soup of it. But when she served it to me, I pushed the bowl away. I am sure the soup was delicious, but the thought of eating horse meat made me sick to my stomach. Wanda just laughed at me. "You don't know what you're missing!" she said, and ate her soup with gusto.

I might have wished that the horse she was supping on had been turned into a good pair of shoes instead. I had been wearing the same pair for more than three years, and despite numerous repairs the shoes were worn out and ready to fall off my feet. But like everything else in Poland, there was a scarcity of leather, which meant that footwear of every kind was either too expensive or unavailable. Fortunately, Wanda had the same size feet as me, and her shoes were in good shape. She let me wear them whenever I had to go out, provided she didn't have to leave the room herself.

Wanda's taste for horse meat was not matched by her appetite for city life, which diminished considerably as the weeks went by. She disliked her clerical job, which she found mind-numbingly tedious, and she was much put off by the drabness of the city, which looked especially bleak with winter coming on. She began to think that she wanted more out of life than to live and work as an office girl amid the dreary landscape of close-set apartment buildings, concrete streets, and smokestack industries that typified Katowice. For her the urban experience was not all it was cracked up to be, and after about a month, she called it quits and returned to her family's farm. She invited me to go with her, saying that I could live with her in a room in her parents' house, but I said no and made up some excuse for declining the offer—I think I told her that, being a city girl through and through, I couldn't bring myself to leave Katowice. This was true, but it wasn't the whole truth. I didn't tell her that I couldn't live under the same roof with her crude father and her repulsive, anti-Semitic brother.

Incidentally, I have always thought that Wanda suspected I

was Jewish. Not that she ever said anything in this regard. The subject of the Jews never came up in our conversations and she did not discuss it with her brother. Whenever her brother launched into his Jew-hating tirades, she would listen without comment. I got the distinct impression that she was avoiding the subject because she thought I was Jewish. Anyway, that is what I choose to believe.

Wanda and I parted company unemotionally, with a brief hug and a peck on the cheek. It was no big deal; we had both been separated from friends and family many times before, and we just couldn't get worked up about it. We may have said something about getting together after the war—I don't remember. In any case, I never made the effort, and neither did she. When she walked out of our room in Katowice, she walked out of my life forever.

Shortly after that I found a slightly better-paying job as a secretary for a coal-mining company. The company's offices were located across town from where I had lived with Wanda, and I moved to another apartment to be closer to them. My new home was a room on the second floor of a two-flat building that was owned by an elderly couple. The couple lived alone. They had two grown children who lived elsewhere, and I was their only tenant.

A few weeks later, the Germans posted orders all over Katowice that everyone, men and women alike, between the ages of sixteen and thirty-five had to report for duty to dig entrenchments on the outskirts of the city. The orders further stipulated that no one was excused from this duty other than those with important jobs.

Nowhere in the text of these orders was there an explanation as to what constituted an important job. But I was pretty sure that whatever the criteria might be, I did not possess them. However, I knew that the company for which I now worked was absolutely vital to the German war effort. Having recently lost the Romanian oil fields to the Soviets, the Germans desperately needed the coal my company produced as an alternate fuel source. And if the company was vital,

could not the same be said for the employees who kept it running—even an employee who was only a lowly secretary? I
decided to put the matter to the test. Digging trenches as a
member of a *corvée en masse* was not an occupation that
appealed to me. For one thing, I was afraid of being around so
many people, any one of whom might recognize me from
Lvov or somehow discover that I was a Jew. Moreover, winter was now upon us, and I didn't want to trade my warm
office and relatively cushy job for backbreaking physical labor
out in the cold countryside. I knew the Germans would do
little if anything to ease our lot; we were their slaves, and our
creature comforts did not matter to them. They would work
us until we dropped or until those trenches got dug, whichever came first.

But I was not hopeful about my chances for obtaining an
exemption. The night before I was supposed to register for
trench-digging duty I went to bed in a black despair over
what I thought lay ahead of me. I realized that if I were a
German and a Polish secretary informed me that she was too
important to be released from her job, I might be tempted to
hand her a shovel and order her to start digging right then and
there. I fell asleep thinking that I might be better off just to
accept my fate rather than risk provoking the wrath of the
Germans with some ridiculous story about my supposed
value to the economy.

That night I dreamed I was a child back in Lvov. I was in
the big park near our apartment on 51 Zyblikiewicza Street,
where my mother used to take me as a toddler. There were
two circular promenades in the park, and one of them encompassed a large sandbox. There were several wooden benches
beside the sandbox where the mothers sat and talked while
their children played. Behind the sandbox the ground sloped
sharply upward into a wooded area where I had never been
and was forbidden to go. The top of this hill is perhaps as
high as a three-story building, but when I was a child it
seemed as lofty as a Himalayan peak. The trees that grew on
it were old and tall and thick, and the brush beneath them was
quite dense in spots, and as dark and mysterious as the troll-

infested thickets in a fairy-tale forest. In my dream I left the sandbox and walked purposefully over to the eaves of the forest and, though my parents had declared it off-limits to me, plunged without pause into the green and shadowy realm beyond. I immediately lost sight of my mother, but this did not deter me, for I was on a quest of some sort, though to what end I did not know. I continued upward, climbing the wooded slope until I reached the summit, whereupon I turned and looked down on the city below. I was at a tremendous height and the buildings seemed of matchbox size and the people were tiny figures almost imperceptible to the naked eye. Suddenly, I realized that I had come alone to a high place in the middle of a dark forest, and I sensed all around me the presence of something that was formless yet powerful and imbued with evil intent. Now I was afraid, and I looked for a way back down but could not find a traversable path. The slope was too steep and the forest was impenetrable: I was trapped on the summit. I searched the park for my mother, but she was nowhere to be seen. She had abandoned me—or so I thought. In a panic I whirled around and looked down the other side of the hill. Far below I saw my mother, and she was looking up at me. I reached out to her and she extended her hand to me, and though the distance between us was vast, our hands touched and she took hold of me. Her grasp was firm and it steadied me and banished my fear. Still holding her hand, I stepped off the summit into midair, and in the next instant, I was standing on the ground beside her.

I woke from that dream feeling restored and revitalized. The despair of the previous night had been purged from my being. Its place had been taken by courage, confidence, determination. I was filled with awe when I contemplated how I was thus transformed. The spirit of my dead mother had come to me from beyond the grave and strengthened me with her touch. She had given me the power to do what was necessary in order to survive. Now it was up to me to use that power.

An hour later I marched into the office where I was to register for trench-digging duty. There were no Germans at this facility, as it was run by the Polish civil administration. The Germans were too busy fighting the Russians to organize labor gangs; instead they presented their manpower demands to their Polish underlings and then stood aside to await delivery. The Poles were given wide latitude in the methods used for assembling a work force as long as the requisite numbers were produced on schedule. In particular, the Poles had the authority to dispense labor exemptions. This was done in a room with a sign over the door that said "Official Excuses."

I entered this room not knowing quite what I would say; I didn't have a story worked out beforehand. I was relying on chutzpah to inspire me. There were only three or four people in the room, and they were lined up in front of a desk behind which sat an elderly Polish woman. Evidently there were few Poles with jobs that were important enough to gain them an exemption. No doubt there were even fewer Poles with the temerity to claim importance where none existed. After the woman had dealt with those ahead of me, it was my turn, and I didn't hold back. As I presented her with my identity and labor cards, I launched into an improvised spiel about the critical work I was doing for a company whose smooth operation was crucial to the economy. There weren't too many people like me, I told her—a person who was fluent in both Polish and German. I then explained that I had important letters to send to various Nazi officials concerning shipments of coal to the front. I wanted her to think that I was in charge of drafting the letters. I didn't tell her that I was only responsible for typing them. I let her think whatever she wanted to think.

The woman listened to me without interrupting. When I had finished talking, she glanced through my papers. I got nervous, thinking that I had not convinced her of my importance, and started to restate my case. She cut me off with a wave of her hand. "No problem, no problem," she said. "You're excused from duty."

That was all she said to me. She did not ask any questions or demand more information about my job. She had granted me the exemption based on my word alone. I stood there flabbergasted as she rubber-stamped my papers with the signs and seals that released me from any obligation to wield a shovel. It had been so easy!

"Next," the woman said, looking over my shoulder at another applicant. She gestured briskly for the latter to step forward. I had been dismissed.

I walked out of the office in a daze. I would not be digging ditches any time soon. I gave silent thanks to God and my mother for this remarkable turn of events. I should have given thanks to the woman behind the desk as well. I don't think she granted me an exemption because my job was important but rather because she had been given a certain number of exemptions to issue at her discretion. I had gotten to her desk before her quota was filled. In other words I had been lucky—once again.

The winter of 1944–45 was a time of extremes with respect to both the weather and the war. The temperature was often bitterly cold, and heavy snowfalls were frequent. And though it was clear that the war was entering its final phases, the fighting was increasing in intensity and not subsiding as one might have hoped or expected. In the process Europe was being laid waste as never before, and its people were suffering and dying in untold numbers. Yet all was quiet in Katowice, which was spared the carnage and destruction that were visited on so many European cities. I was always cold because I did not have a heavy winter coat and boots, but other than that I was getting by well enough. I had a job and a place to live, and I usually had enough to eat. I even had something that resembled a social life. Through my work I had met and become friendly with several boys and girls about my age, and we often got together in the evenings.

There wasn't much for us to do as most of the places where people normally go for entertainment and fun—cafés, restaurants, movie theaters, nightclubs—had closed down. Besides, none of us had enough money to spend on leisure pursuits. Instead, we sat around in the rented rooms and apartments where various members of the group lived, and we talked, drank tea, and maybe listened to records if these and the phonograph to play them were available. Sometimes, when the weather was nice, we strolled around the city. I wasn't as afraid to be out and about as I had been in the preceding years, because now the Germans hardly bothered anyone. There were few arrests and fewer executions, because the Germans had already killed most of the people they wanted dead. They needed the rest of us alive to work in their factories or to dig trenches on what were soon to become the front lines of the war.

My best friend in Katowice after Wanda's departure was the girl I mentioned at the beginning of this account. Her parents had died early in the war, but she never told me precisely when and in what manner they had lost their lives. She sometimes implied that they had been killed during the 1939 invasion, but she would not elaborate on this topic out of respect, she said, for the married couple that had since adopted her. She lived with the couple in Katowice and often invited me to their apartment for dinner. Her foster parents were Polish Catholics and so was she; however, something about her told me she may have been Jewish. She had straight blond hair and blue eyes, but I was living proof that this did not necessarily mean you weren't Jewish. She was sociable and outgoing, but she had a certain elusiveness to her, a certain applied superficiality, as if she was trying to keep people from getting to know her too well. In other words, she was a lot like me. That is why I thought she was Jewish and, probably, it is also why I can't remember her name. I thought that her natural, Jewish parents had been murdered by the Nazis, and that she had obtained Aryan papers and a new identity to avoid the same fate. She could have done so either before she was adopted or afterward, in complicity with her foster parents. But I had no hard evidence that she was Jewish, and I never confronted her with my suspicion. My conversations with her usually went no deeper than discussions about what to wear when we went out with the boys. Since we both owned only a few articles of clothing, these discussions were mostly on the order of fantasy and wishful thinking, and the question of whether or not one of us was Jewish did not come up.

As for those boys—well, some of them were better friends than others, but forming close attachments with members of the opposite sex was not part of my plan to survive the war.

On January 12, 1945, the Soviets ended six months of inaction in Poland by launching a great offensive at Baran, a city on the Vistula River just west of Kraków. Two days later Soviet forces to the north joined in on the attack, capturing Warsaw on January 17 and driving deep into western Poland toward the old German frontier.

One day I arrived at work to find the other secretaries in my office talking excitedly about the Soviet offensive. The Red Army was advancing on Katowice. I don't know how my coworkers had come by this information; probably one or more of them owned radios (even though they were forbidden) and had been listening to BBC news broadcasts.

After the middle of the month, you didn't need a radio to tell you that the Soviets were coming. The constant and ever-approaching thunder of artillery just over the eastern horizon spoke volumes in this regard. I had mixed feelings about this. On the one hand, I was overjoyed; on the other hand, I was frightened that the arrival of the Red Army would precipitate a terrible battle. But that battle never took place. On January 28, in the midst of a blizzard, the Germans withdrew to the west and the Red Army took the city without a fight.

The Allies had more than three months of hard fighting ahead of them before they forced the Germans to surrender. But for me the war was finally over. I had survived. I was one of the victors. Yet I did not feel victorious. I felt nothing, for I had achieved nothing except my own survival. This was not an insignificant achievement. But it could not make me forget the fact that, aside from my life, I had lost everything that was important to me.

In the wake of liberation, I kept working at the offices of the coal-mining company. The company continued its operations uninterrupted in the service of our new Soviet masters. I held on to the identity of Urszula Krzyzanowska. It was too soon to give it up and too much trouble. However, at night, in the privacy of my room, I thought about being Lala Wein-traub again. It was not a happy thought. My family was dead and the idea of reclaiming my true identity only emphasized this fact. During this period I cried just about every night before going to bed. I was empty, adrift, desolate, and profoundly alone. I didn't know who I was or who I should be. I was not Urszula Krzyzanowska, but I could not stand to be Lala Weintraub. The former was a fiction; the latter was a casualty. I had a wound in my soul that hurt worse than any injury ever done to my body. And it was a wound that would not heal.

I was, as the Catholics might say, in limbo. The days went by one after the other, but time seemed to stand still. I was going nowhere in both the literal and the figurative sense. The liberation of Katowice had robbed my life of direction and purpose. During the war survival had been my overriding concern. Well, the war was over and I had survived. But what to do next? Should I stay in Katowice, or should I leave? And if I left, where should I go?

America.

I had family in America, or so I thought—my Uncle Isadore. I didn't know where he lived, or even if he was still alive; I didn't know whether he had any children, who would be my cousins. But I resolved to try and find him. I thought that if Isadore was alive, he could arrange for me to immigrate to America. This became my goal. It restored purpose in my life and became my reason to live. By going to America, I would fulfill the destiny established by my grandfather and for which my father had worked so hard but so futilely to accomplish. And I would get out of Poland to a place where Jews could be safe, where they could thrive and prosper, where they would not be hunted down and killed like dogs in the street.

In those days the road to America led through the offices of the International Red Cross. With the permission of the Soviets, that blessed organization had opened an office in Katowice to help displaced persons, Jews in particular, locate surviving family members and otherwise assist them in any way it could. One day in early spring I went there and registered my name—my *real* name, Lala Weintraub—in hopes that the Red Cross might somehow find and notify Uncle Isadore of my existence. This marked the first time in several years that I had revealed my real name to anyone, and I did so reluctantly, since I still had some residual fear of the Nazis.

That done, all I could do was cross my fingers and wait. Once a week I stopped by the office to check for news about my uncle. But, week after week, there was none. In the meantime, I had to go on living. I continued to work for the coal-mining company, I went out with friends in the evening, and I cried myself to sleep at night. I remember dreaming one night that Franklin Roosevelt had died. The next morning as I was walking to work, I passed a kiosk and saw newspaper headlines announcing this fact. "Roosevelt dies, Roosevelt dies," a newsboy called out. The date was April 13, 1945, and Roosevelt had died the previous day. I wasn't surprised. Nor did I think my dream was extraordinary. Having prescient dreams had practically become a habit with me.

I was unmoved by Roosevelt's death. I thought, why should I mourn for the American president? I couldn't see where he had done anything to help the Jews. People said that he was a friend to all those oppressed by the Nazis, but under his direction the mighty United States had stayed on the sidelines during the first two years of the war while the Germans butchered us. Some friend.

I know now that the reasons for what America did and did not do with reference to Germany and the Jews are complex and controversial. But at the time, all that mattered to me was the failure of America to save us from the Germans. This failure was incomprehensible to me then, and even today, even after all the aforesaid reasons have been explained to me, I have trouble understanding and accepting it.

At the end of the month, the world learned of the suicide of Adolf Hitler. The Devil was dead, and a few days later so, too, was his monstrous regime. May 8 was VE-Day, the end of the war in Europe, the fall of Nazi Germany. It was a momentous day, and this time the streets of Katowice rang with celebration. My friends and I took part in the merry-making; we went out in the streets, we cheered, we shouted for joy, we danced around and hugged each other. I felt safer now that the war was officially over and the Nazis were finished. But I still felt threatened—though by whom I could not say—and so I told no one my real name, except the people at the Red Cross office.

And life went on. I remember a young man in his twenties who was an announcer on the local Soviet-controlled radio station. He became a member of my circle of friends, and because he was educated and could speak some English, my friends held him in high regard. I wasn't at all interested in him, but evidently I wasn't clear about this, because he soon fell head over heels in love with me. And though I rejected him, politely, he nevertheless went all out to win my affections. One night he showed up beneath my window and began serenading me with a Polish love song. I was embarrassed both for myself and for him—he had an awful singing voice! I didn't dare appear at my window for fear of encouraging him. In different, better times I might have enjoyed his wooing and even consented to go out with him, but not now. He annoyed me, and I just wanted him to go away.

But he wouldn't leave. When he had finished his song, he began ringing the doorbell. My landlady answered the door and a few minutes later she came to my room.

"Lala," she said, "there is a very nice young man outside, and he would like to see you."

I told her, "Please say to him that I don't feel well, that I have a horrible toothache."

My landlady went downstairs to convey this message to my gentleman caller. She then returned to my room.

"The young man," she informed me, "has asked me to say that he is sorry that you are in pain, and he wishes that he could have your toothache for you."

One afternoon, while walking home from work, I ran into the sister of Petia, our Gloomy-Gus neighbor from Lvov. We recognized each other immediately and stopped to talk. I told her a little about my experiences over the past four years, and she did the same. She told me that she had survived the war on false papers. I could see that she would have been convincing as a Pole, for she was very fair, with honey-colored hair and blue eyes—she looked even more like a Pole than I did. But she had had a husband and son who were not as fair as she, and I asked about them, wondering whether they had also gotten through the war on false papers. She shook her head sadly and told me that her husband had died—she didn't say how—but added that her son was alive and living with her in Katowice. I asked about Petia. Again, she shook her head sadly. Petia had been arrested in one of the early actions in Lvov. She didn't know what became of him, but she assumed that he had been taken to the Janowska Camp and either executed or worked to death.

We looked at each other. There was nothing more to say. We walked away in opposite directions, without exchanging addresses or agreeing to meet again.

Around that time I had another chance encounter, this time with the wife of the lawyer who had also lived in our apartment on Zyblikiewicza Street. She invited me to their home for dinner that same evening, and I accepted the invitation. As we sat around talking before dinner, they revealed to me that they, too, had survived the war on false papers. The husband was a handsome man with sandy hair, blue eyes, and a straight nose—classic Slavic features. However, his wife and daughter were both very dark, and they looked Jewish to me. And if they looked Jewish to me, they must have looked Jewish to the Poles and the Germans. But despite this they had succeeded in passing themselves off as Gentiles throughout the war.

In addition to adopting Gentile identities, they had also converted to Catholicism. When they told me this, I at first assumed that their conversion had been made not out of any deep-seated religious conviction but rather to save their lives. They vehemently denied this, however. And when I told them that I wanted to immigrate to America because "in

America, Jews are safe," they informed me that the safety of
Jews did not concern them. I then realized that their conversion was wholehearted and sincere, to the extent that they
had completely renounced the Jewish faith while embracing
the anti-Semitism of some of their Polish and German coreli-
gionists. "We don't want anything more to do with Jews or
Judaism," they told me cuttingly. "We're finished with that
forever."

I understood why they felt this way and did not presume
to judge them. But I could never repudiate my faith as they
had. It wasn't an option for me; it wasn't even something I
thought about. Being Jewish was integral to who I was; it was
bred into my bones, it was wrapped into my genetic coding. I
could no more deny it than I could deny being human. Anyway, I did not believe that changing religions would count for
much when the Gentiles decided it was time to kill Jews
again. It certainly hadn't counted to the Nazis. They had been
as merciless to Christian converts as they were to Jews who
had kept their faith, demonstrating that a genuine and pas-
sionate commitment to Christianity was usually no protection from the gas chambers and the firing squads.

But it had protected my former neighbors, and that had
made all the difference in the world for them. They had taken
Christian names and they had gotten documents verifying
that they were Gentiles; and then, somewhere along the line,
they had gotten the Christian faith as well. All their friends
and acquaintances in Katowice thought they were Christians
by birth; they attended mass on a regular basis, and they had
named their little girl Christina and had had her baptized in a
Catholic church. "We're bringing her up as a Catholic," the
parents said. "That way, if this ever happens again, she won't
have to go through what we did."

One day, everything suddenly changed. I went to the Red
Cross office expecting to be disappointed once again. Instead,
one of the Red Cross workers handed me an envelope. The
return address gave the name of my Uncle Isadore as the
sender.

I ran home and locked myself in the bathroom. While seated on the toilet, I ripped off one end of the envelope and pulled out the folded sheet of paper inside. As I unfolded it, a photograph fell out and dropped to the floor. I picked it up. It was a photograph of Fima taken just before he was drafted into the Red Army. I held the photograph in one hand and stared at it for a few seconds. I didn't know what to think—I may not have been thinking at all. I was holding the letter in the other hand and now I turned away from the photograph to read it. In the letter, which was written in Polish, Isadore told me that he lived in New Jersey and would help me immigrate to America if that was what I desired. He told me that Fima had gotten in touch with him through the Red Cross; my brother, Isadore wrote, was alive and well and living in Palestine, and wanted very much to hear from me.

A brilliant light seemed to fill the bathroom and tears welled up in my eyes so that I could not see. I bowed my head and began to sob uncontrollably. But these were tears of joy, not sorrow.

Fima was alive!

✿

Afterward

The story of how my brother came to be in Palestine is a fascinating one and could fill a sizable book of its own. The following can only be a much abbreviated account of an odyssey that took him from the frozen environs of Leningrad to the warm and sunny climes of the Holy Land.

Wounded on the Finnish frontier by a bayonet thrust to his stomach, Fima had been sent to a hospital in Leningrad to recover. But the healing process was hindered by a poor diet that was hardly sufficient to keep him alive, much less enable his torn body to mend. The city was almost completely encircled by German and Finnish forces, and as a result only a trickle of foodstuffs and other supplies were reaching the soldiers and civilians defending it. Whatever food had been stockpiled in the city prior to the siege was soon gone, and in due course the populace began to sicken and die of starvation. The situation became increasingly desperate as the Russian winter descended on Leningrad with a cruelty and ferocity exceeded only by the unceasing battles and bombardments by which ownership of the city was meant to be decided. Fatally weakened by the lack of food, people were literally dropping dead in the streets. They died by the thousands, and there was no possibility of giving them a proper burial because the ground was deep in snow and frozen solid as iron. Instead, the corpses were hauled away to warehouses and other collection facilities, where they were stacked like cordwood to await the spring thaw. But those assigned to the corpse-hauling crews found that they could not keep up with the demand for their services. So many people were dying so fast that their bodies often lay where they fell for several days before anyone came to pick them up. Arctic temperatures effectively preserved the corpses, but did not protect them from ravages far more gruesome than those wrought by putrefaction. A growing number of corpses were discovered with their limbs and buttocks and other fleshy parts hacked off by people who had turned to cannibalism in order to stay alive. No one will ever know how many Leningraders resorted to this vile practice, but it is certain that the incidences of cannibalism increased as the winter wore on and tightening siege lines reduced still further the amount of food that was getting into the city. One thing was for sure, the cannibals would not starve. There was no shortage of corpses on which to feed. Nonetheless, most people did not avail themselves of this potential food source. But they ate just about anything else they could force down their throats and keep in their stomachs, including dogs, cats, rats, and bread leavened with sawdust. A special delicacy was wallpaper paste, which was made of flour and therefore edible. Crazed by hunger, Leningraders stripped the paper off their apartment walls and used the paste in the making of bread. They even ate the wallpaper, which added bulk and fiber if not nutrients to their diet. "It tasted good at the time," Fima once told me, and I am sure that it did. To people who are starving, just about any kind of food can taste good—even, perhaps, human flesh.

Fima got more food than most because his girlfriend, Zoya, was a nurse in the hospital where he was convalescing, and she had access to the hospital's food stores. Zoya was responsible for distributing the daily food ration to the patients in her care and was thus in a position to give my brother preferential treatment. The ration consisted of a hundred grams of black bread, vodka, and a lard compound called "speck." Zoya saw to it that he got a few extra grams of each item. In addition, Fima exchanged his vodka ration for more bread or speck—he had never been a drinking man and now his predilection for abstinence was paying dividends. It wasn't much, but it was enough to keep him going, and it probably saved his life.

The siege of Leningrad would not be lifted until January of 1944. It would last nine hundred days, but Fima would not see it through to the end or even close to the end. Unbeknownst to him while he was hospitalized, his deliverance, if not Leningrad's, was near at hand. In the halls of the Kremlin, a deal had been struck concerning the Poles. Shortly after the German invasion of the Soviet Union in June 1941, Stalin concluded a pact with General Władysław Sikorski, leader of Poland's government-in-exile in London, in which the formation of an independent Polish army on Soviet territory was stipulated. It was agreed that the army would be stocked by Polish soldiers then serving in the Red Army and by the tens of thousands of Polish military and political prisoners incarcerated in the Gulag system. In August 1941, General Władysław Anders was appointed to command the army, but first he had to be released from the Lubyanka Prison in Moscow in order to assume his new post. The Soviets then freed hundreds of thousands of Polish nationals from the Gulag camps and settlements where they had been interned since being deported from Poland in the preceding years. Among those released were young men of military age, but also old men, women, and children, sometimes entire families. All were turned loose with little means of support and were forced to fend for themselves and find their own way to the military installations where the Polish army was assembling. Many failed to arrive at their intended destinations, as they had either died en route or were redirected by Soviet authorities to settlements in Central Asia.

Initially, Polish Jews were allowed to enlist in this so-called Anders army. But then Stalin changed his mind and forbade Polish Jews, as well as Poland-born Ukrainians and Belorussians, from joining this force after November 1941. Thenceforward, it was to be Soviet policy to regard Jews and ethnic Ukrainians and Belorussians born in Poland as citizens of the Soviet Union. The logic in doing so was based on the Soviet claim to eastern Poland, which the Red Army had seized in September 1939. The Soviets reasoned that if eastern Poland belonged to the Soviet Union, then so, too, did those elements of its population who were not ethnic Poles. Fortunately for Fima, this policy was not officially announced until December and therefore not strictly enforced. When he heard about the formation of the Anders army, he eagerly volunteered for it. He was not immediately accepted because he was a Jew born into a family of refugees from the Ukraine. But the Anders army needed Polish officers, as there was an inexplicable scarcity of such men. (In point of fact, the Soviets had executed thousands of Polish officers captured in the 1939 invasion, but this was not generally known at the time.) And so, with the Soviets looking the other way, Fima was enrolled in the Anders army with the rank of lieutenant.

But his actual induction into the army had to wait until his wound had healed and his strength returned. In the meantime, General Anders established his headquarters in the town of Buzuluk on the Samara River, some forty kilometers southeast of Kuibyshev. Assembly areas for the army were also established in that vicinity. Living conditions in the army camps were appalling, as the Soviets were neither prompt nor generous in providing their former enemies with food, clothing, shelter, and other essentials. In a face-to-face meeting with Stalin, Sikorski and Anders complained about the inadequate provisioning of the army, and the Soviet dictator replied angrily that the Poles were receiving the same rations as the Red Army. In January 1942, the army and its huge civilian entourage were relocated to camps in the Uzbek and Kirgiz republics, with the headquarters established in Yangiyul just outside of Tashkent. The new camps were even less habitable than the old ones, and the plight of the Poles worsened accordingly. It was hoped that proximity to Iran would give the Poles access to British supplies (the British occupied most of Iran south of Tehran), but such proved not to be the case. Acting on the assumption that the Soviets either would not or could not provide for the Poles under his command, General Anders applied to Stalin for permission to evacuate several thousand Polish soldiers and civilians to the British-occupied zone in Iran. After some equivocation, Stalin decided to let Anders have his way in this matter. The evacuation was undertaken from March 24 through April 3, 1942, with the Poles traveling by rail from their camps to the port city of Krasnovodsk on the Caspian Sea, and then boarding ships that transported them to Bandar-e Pahlavī in Iran. Nearly forty-six thousand Poles were involved in this movement.

In February, meanwhile, Fima had at long last regained his health and was judged fit to travel. After bidding a fond and poignant farewell to Zoya—whom he never saw or communicated with again—he climbed aboard a truck that was part of one of the nightly convoys to leave Leningrad. The only way out the city was across the frozen surface of Lake Ladoga, where the ice was thick enough in midwinter to support an unending parade of vehicular traffic. Snowplow trucks had carved roads across the lake, and the convoys that used them brought replacements and munitions into the city and took out wounded soldiers, children, and other nonessential personnel. Near Leningrad the roads were within range of the German siege guns and were shelled constantly. Fima's convoy departed after dark and hadn't gotten very far before German artillery opened up on it. There were explosions all around him, and several trucks were hit and blown apart, while others careened wildly and plunged into shell holes blasted in the ice, where they sank instantly before their hapless passengers could escape. Fima was terrified. He had to remain seated on the back of that truck with no protection against the cascading shells and no way of predicting if or when one of them would hit his vehicle and blow him into eternity. To control his mounting panic, he put his head between his legs and shouted at the driver, "Go! Go! Go!" Somehow the truck made it to the safety of Lake Ladoga's eastern shore. From there, Fima continued east by truck to Kotlas, an industrial town and supply base located north of the sixtieth parallel, where he and several thousand other Polish volunteers were crammed into cattle cars for the train ride to Tashkent.

The journey south lasted six weeks. The rail line had but a single track, and priority of use was given to the supply trains headed north and not to one rather unimportant southbound

train loaded with Polish troops. The line was so heavily trafficked that Fima's train was often shunted to sidings where it
might remain for several days before being allowed back on
the main track. Of course, the Poles had not been given
rations for a six-week journey, and so they used these lengthy
stops to forage about for food. Nearby villages would soon be
swarming with gaunt Poles in tattered uniforms who were
willing to trade away anything, including their ragged clothes,
for something to eat. But it was winter and food was scarce in
the Russian hinterland, and the villagers were often unwilling
to part with what little they had. Thus, frustrated in their
attempt to acquire food by honest means, the Poles turned to
thievery. Fima became adept at sneaking into farmyards and
stealing chickens, which he learned how to kill by twisting
their heads off. They cooked the chickens, along with potatoes they had stolen from the fields, in their helmets. Once, he
and several companions stole a calf and slaughtered it in their
boxcar. For the next few days, they feasted like lords on fresh
cooked beef and knew the drowsy satisfaction of a stomach
filled with protein and animal fat.

In July, Stalin approved the evacuation to Iran of the balance of the Polish army and its civilian hangers-on. But not
everyone could go. On December 1, 1941, the Soviet government had formally stated its position on the issue of Polish
citizenship as it pertained to Jews, Ukrainians, and Belorussians born in Poland. If you weren't an ethnic Pole, the Soviets said, then you weren't a Polish citizen; you were a Soviet
citizen and therefore had to stay in the Soviet Union. How
rigorously this policy was actually enforced remains open to
question, at least with regard to the Belorussians and Ukrainians. But it seemed to Jews that they were unusually affected
by it, and deliberately so.

Fima believes to this day that the Polish high command was
responsible for what amounted to the de facto expulsion of
Jews from the Anders army. He will tell you that the Poles
used the Soviet citizenship rule as a legalistic tool to rid themselves of the Jews. Such was not the case, however; it is, rather,
a lie the Soviets promulgated out of spite for General Anders.

The truth is, Anders himself lobbied tirelessly and successfully to bring several thousand Jews to Iran.

In any event, Fima knew nothing of these developments when his train finally chugged into the Tashkent railroad station a full month and a half after leaving Kotlas. When he jumped down from his cattle car to the station platform, he did so thinking that Tashkent was just one more stop on the road to Iran. He was soon disabused of this notion. First, he was told that he would have to stay in the Soviet Union because he was Jewish; then he was told that he was to be sent back west to Kuibyshev to command a unit assigned to guard a foreign embassy. (Soviet government offices and foreign embassies had relocated to Kuibyshev in October 1941 in anticipation of the fall of Moscow, and they were still there in the spring of 1942.) Fima was dismayed. He knew he was in a fix, and he didn't know what to do about it. He went to a cafeteria to have some hot tea and think things over. Tea was all that he had put in his stomach in two days. But he was not hungry. He was too depressed to be hungry. But as he sat there morosely sipping his tea, he was approached by a young man with a humpback and a wan complexion. The man introduced himself as Stanislav Daszkewicz, and without waiting for an invitation, he took a seat at Fima's table. "Why so sad?" Daszkewicz asked as he sat down. Ignoring the man's effrontery and the likelihood that he was here for more than just tea and conversation, Fima explained his predicament. He needed to talk to someone, and Stanislav Daszkewicz had made himself available. Daszkewicz listened sympathetically, and when Fima had finished, he declared that he had the solution to my brother's problem.

Daszkewicz said that he was from western Poland. In September 1939, he had fled east ahead of the advancing German armies into what shortly became the Soviet zone of occupation. There he was arrested for the crime of being a refugee and deported into deep Russia. For more than two years and until quite recently, his home had been an internment camp in Siberia. When the Anders army was formed, he was booted out of the camp and put on a train to Tashkent with instructions to enlist in the army as soon as he got there. But upon arriving in the city and reporting to the army depot, the Polish recruiting officers took one look at his deformed back and sickly pallor and informed him that he was unfit for military service. Now he was stranded in Tashkent with no job, no money, and no place to stay. In the circumstances, the prospect of guarding an embassy in Kuibyshev sounded appealing. It was easy duty, and he would be getting fed and paid on a regular basis. He told Fima that he had a proposition to make. "How much money do you have?" he asked Fima. Fima told him. It was a fair amount, for he was receiving combat pay in addition to an officer's stipend; moreover, he was an expert poker player and had amassed a nice little wad of cash in card games on the trip down from Kotlas. "Look," said Daszkewicz, "I will sell you my identity papers—and my identity. You can become me, Stanislav Daszkewicz. But in return you have to give me your papers so I can become Yephim Vinogradov."

Now Fima understood why this man had approached him. He understood as well that Daszkewicz's scheme would give both men what they wanted: a way out of Russia for Fima, a way to stay in Russia for Daszkewicz. "I'll do it," said Fima, and they shook on it and exchanged the money and identity papers right then and there. A few hours later Stanislav Daszkewicz, alias Yephim Vinogradov, alias Fima Weintraub, was standing before the desk of a recruiting officer in a nearby army camp where he was not known. He produced the identity papers with his Gentile nom de guerre, informed the officer that he had been released from an internment camp in Siberia, and announced his intention to join the Anders army. The officer believed his story and enlisted him as a private soldier.

Fima's days of exercising command were over, at least for the time being. Naturally, he did not let on that he had been an officer in the Red Army. He went through basic training and tried to behave like a novice soldier with no previous military experience. He tried to pretend he was dull-witted and slow, like an illiterate Polish peasant. But he was not a good actor and did well in spite of himself. His officers were impressed by his performance. They marveled at what a quick study he was. Soldiering seemed to come easy to him. He seemed to have an almost instinctual grasp of the handling and use of weapons. They offered him a commission, but he turned it down. He told them he didn't want the responsibility that came with the job.

He was often assigned to night-sentry duty along with a group of Jewish soldiers. He didn't tell these men that he was a Jew, but they suspected as much. For one thing, he had wavy brown hair, a physical trait associated with Jews. For another, he was too friendly with the Jewish soldiers. He would stand around and talk with them in a congenial way, which was something no self-respecting anti-Semitic Pole would do. Once in a while, one of the Jewish soldiers would grin and give him a conspiratorial wink and say, "Daszkewicz, we know who you really are. But don't worry, we won't tell anybody." On another occasion, this same man sidled up to him and said, "You know, we have a saying: 'A Jew can smell a Jew.' I think you're one of us."

When confronted in this manner, Fima would smile blandly and say words to the effect that he didn't know what the man was talking about. "Sure, sure," the man would say. And again, he would give Fima a conspiratorial wink.

The second and final evacuation of Anders army soldiers and civilians began on August 10 and lasted through the month. This time around seventy thousand people, including four thousand Jews, made the trip to Bandar-e Pahlavī. Fima was among them, although, of course, he was not counted as one of the Jews. Just before they broke camp for the trains that would take them to Krasnovodsk, they were assembled on the parade ground of their respective camps to listen to a speech from a high-ranking Soviet officer. "Now you are leaving Russia," the officer told his audience. "Whatever money you have, whatever Russian documents you might possess, whatever you have on your person that belongs to Russia, you must now put on the ground in front of you. Soldiers of the Red Army will come by and collect these things that belong to Russia, and after that you will be free to go. However, you should know that you are liable to be searched at any time between now and when you board your ships. And if we find that you still have in your possession something that is the property of Russia, you will be arrested."

The Poles reacted with predictable dispatch to this warning. There was a sudden flurry of activity as they tossed the proscribed items on the ground. Fima didn't take any chances; he emptied his pockets of everything, including his money and even photos of his family. "Here, take it all," he muttered to no one in particular. "I just want to get out of here."

The voyage across the Caspian Sea was positively nightmarish. Fima's ship was an ancient rustbucket of a freighter that was lacking in every kind of amenity and only marginally seaworthy. It yawed and pitched violently in the rough seas, inflicting the miseries of seasickness on most of its passengers, many of whom were already stricken with dysentery and other debilitating maladies such as typhus and malaria. The plumbing didn't work, and there was no food, little drinking water, and no water for washing. There was no room. People seemed to occupy every square inch of the aptly named weather decks, where they were utterly exposed to the alternating torments of wind and rain and sun. The compartments below decks, as well as the connecting gangways and stairwells, were similarly overcrowded. They were also broiling hot and suffocatingly humid and befouled with the stench of unwashed bodies, vomit and intestinal bile, and excrement that spilled out of the vessel's chronically clogged and overflowing toilets.

One can only imagine how thankful the passengers on these ships were to set foot once again on dry land. They staggered onto the docks at Bandar-e Pahlavī harbor in a pitiable state. British military personnel sent to greet them were appalled by their condition and took them straightaway to a reception center to be registered, fed, and deloused. After that they were assigned to nearby camps to be housed in tents with the Poles of the first evacuation. Everyone—men, women, children—was given a British army uniform and two woolen blankets. After changing into the uniforms, they handed their Soviet-issue clothes over to the British, who burned them.

That night Fima bedded down among several other men on a cot in a big army tent. He slept soundly and woke the next morning to find Iranian peasants teeming about the camp selling oranges, bananas, eggs, dates, and other foodstuffs. He didn't have any money to make a purchase. Nobody did. It had all been given to the Soviets. But Fima didn't let this stop him. He took one of his blankets and traded it to an Iranian for two dozen eggs. Fima notes that both men thought they had gotten the best of the deal. The Iranian had a heavy woolen blanket which was worth far more, by the reckoning of traders in the bazaar, than two dozen eggs. But Fima was happy because the blanket had cost him nothing to begin with. In effect, he had gotten the eggs for free.

They almost did him in. They had to be eaten right away or they would spoil, so Fima built a small fire, broke all twenty-four eggs into the helmet the British had given him, and scrambled them into a giant omelet. Then he ate the omelet, every bite of it. He ate two dozen eggs in one sitting, in the space of a few minutes. They tasted very good. They also made him deathly ill. A few hours later he was rushed to a British army field hospital, where an Indian doctor treated him for acute dysentery. Fima says he almost died. This may be an exaggeration. But even so, there must have come a point in his suffering when he wished he were dead.

In general, the Poles were in poor health and required several weeks of rest and decent food, provided courtesy of the British army, before the Anders army began to take on even the semblance of a combat-capable formation. That it would eventually be committed to battle was the fervent desire of the Poles, who had many scores to settle with the Germans. The Western Allies were only too happy to oblige them. The Allies appreciated and respected the fighting qualities of the Poles, which had already been demonstrated on several battlefronts. In particular, Polish troops operating under British command (but not associated with the Anders army) had been involved in the fighting in North Africa and had given a good account of themselves. The British, therefore, viewed the Anders army as a potentially valuable addition to their order of battle. But first things first. In the autumn of 1942, the

Poles moved south to Qazvīn, whence the civilians were sent east to transit camps near Tehran, while the soldiers journeyed west to camps in Iraq for additional training and organization before deployment to a combat zone.

The coming months were relatively uneventful ones for Fima and the Anders army, whose units were reorganized into a formation which was officially designated II Polish Corps. Fima was stationed at Kirkuk. He was often assigned to drive a truck to Baghdad to pick up supplies, and while in that city he would visit the shops and bazaars to purchase various items—mainly coats and wristwatches—which he would sell, at a profit of course, to his comrades back in Kirkuk. The money he thus made, augmented by his poker winnings, ensured that his wallet always contained a least a few dinars, or whatever currency the Anders army happened to be using at the time.

In that same period, the Allies drove Axis forces out of North Africa and Sicily and invaded Italy. Plans were formulated to commit II Corps to the fighting in Italy, with preliminary maneuvers to be conducted in Palestine. A base camp was established near Gaza and II Corps took up residence there in September 1943—just in time for Rosh Hashanah. The Polish high command was well aware of the High Holidays. With over four thousand Jews serving in II Corps, the top Polish commanders had become extremely sensitive to Jewish holy days and their attendant rituals. In a gesture of respect to their Jewish troops—and, no doubt, to win their goodwill—the high command granted them leave to attend holiday services at the Beth Sefer BILU school on Rothschild Boulevard in Tel Aviv. The Jewish troops, more than three thousand of them, rode to Tel Aviv in a convoy of trucks. The soldiers driving the trucks were Gentiles who had volunteered for the duty. One of the drivers was a young private named Stanislav Daszkewicz.

When the Polish officers asked for volunteers to drive the Jews up to Tel Aviv, Fima had raised his hand without quite knowing why. He was impelled by a presentiment of things which he could not name or describe. Certainly, he had no intention of participating in the religious services. He did not want to blow his cover, as he believed that he would have to be Stanislav Daszkewicz for some time to come.

The trucks parked outside the front entrance of the school, and the Jewish soldiers went inside the building's assembly hall. The drivers now had three or four hours to kill, and most of them went sightseeing in the city. But not Fima. He ambled over to the doors of the school and, when he was sure none of the Polish drivers were looking, he ducked inside.

He positioned himself at the back of the assembly hall to watch the goings-on as the crowd got settled. Again, he did not know the reason for his actions. Some of the Jewish soldiers noticed his presence and gave him quizzical looks. Fima ignored them, said nothing, offered no explanation. He couldn't explain himself to the Jews; he couldn't explain himself to himself. He had no idea why he was in the school, no idea what to do next. He simply stood there and waited for the service to begin.

It never got started. Instead, a number of tough-looking men in khaki shirts and trousers entered the assembly hall through its front and back entrances and shut and bolted the doors behind them. After posting guards at the doors, three of the men strode through the congregation to the hall's *aron hakodesh*, the ark where the scrolls for the Torah were housed, and turned to face their audience. An expectant hush fell over the throng, and one of the civilians began speaking in Polish. "You're probably wondering why my companions and I are interrupting the start of the service," he said. "Well, we didn't come here to pray. No time for that. We're here to fight a war. We're soldiers of the Palmach, and we want you to join us."

Palmach is a contraction of *peluggot mahatz*, which translates as "assault companies." The Palmach was the elite strike force of the Haganah, the clandestine Jewish army that was dedicated to establishing a Jewish state in Palestine. It was originally composed of Jewish settlers who had previously served in commando units recruited and trained by the British in early 1941 in anticipation of a German invasion of the region.

Axis and British forces were then fighting for possession of northeast Africa, and it seemed not altogether unlikely, given the course of the war thus far, that the enemy might attempt to drive across Egypt and into Palestine on his way to seize the oil fields of the Middle East. If the British were expelled from Palestine, the commandos were to wage a guerrilla war against Axis forces. But in July 1942, the Germans and their Italian allies were permanently removed as a threat to Palestine when they were decisively beaten at the Battle of El Alamein in Egypt. Whereupon the commandos had formed the Palmach and turned their guns, as well as their considerable skills in irregular warfare, against the British.

The Palmach spokesman told the members of the audience that they had a choice: they could fight for Poland or they could fight for the as-yet-unborn state of Israel. The spokesman said that the only really compelling reason for a Jew to fight for Poland was because he had, or thought he had, family in that country. "But this reason no longer exists," the spokesman pointed out, "because the Germans are killing all the Jews in Poland. In fact, they're killing all the Jews in Europe. By the time this war is over, most of them will be dead. So if you're thinking of being reunited with your family after the war, you might as well forget it. Odds are, you won't find a single member of your family left alive, because the Germans will have killed your loved ones down to the last man, woman, and child."

The spokesman went on to describe the death camps with their gas chambers, the actions, the depredations of the *Einsatzgruppen,* and the other methods of mass murder the Germans were employing against the Jews. This was the first definite news the Jewish soldiers had heard about what was happening to the Jews of occupied Europe. Fima, like everyone else, listened raptly to the spokesman. The man's account contained no real surprises. Rumors about a systematized campaign to exterminate the Jews had been circulating for a long time. Nevertheless, Fima was shocked and horrified. His thoughts turned to his own family, and he could not help but wonder whether it, too, had been wiped out by the Germans.

The Palmach spokesman more or less assured him that it had. "So you see," he said, "you shouldn't think that you can simply go back to Poland after the war and pick up where you left off. That world is gone forever. It can never be recovered." The spokesman then observed that it would be replaced by a world that was no less hostile to the Jews. So why, he asked, even think about returning? "You know very well that the Poles don't want you back. They hate you just as much as the Germans do, they're just as anti-Semitic as the Germans. Why fight and die for people who hate you? Why fight and die for a country that doesn't want you as a citizen? Your future is here. Your future is to fight for the creation of Israel."

The spokesman concluded by saying, "We need you for this struggle. You will be the backbone of the Haganah because you are trained for military service—some of you, many of you perhaps, have already seen combat. Soon our army will fight to defend ourselves and our land. For a Jew, this the only cause worth fighting and dying for."

The spokesman paused for a reaction. A stir ran through the crowd. His speech had had the desired effect; it had cut them to the quick of their emotional sensibilities. When he asked who among them would follow him to become a member of the Haganah, virtually every man in the hall raised his hand.

Fima was one of them. The time had come, he realized, to shed the identity of Stanislav Daszkewicz.

"Form yourself into groups of eight to twelve men," the spokesman told his new volunteers. "We will take you to a place where you will be safe."

Fima approached one of the groups that was forming. All but one of the men in that group stared at him with bewilderment. Wasn't he a Gentile?

"No, no," Fima told them. "I'm really a Jew."

The one man in the group who wasn't startled by this disclosure had been among those with whom Fima had pulled sentry duty back in Tashkent. He grinned at Fima. "Well, well, Daszkewicz," he said, "it looks like we were right about you after all."

"Not Daszkewicz," Fima said with a smile. "Weintraub."
The Palmach men directed the volunteers out the back
doors of the hall to the adjoining street, where dozens of
trucks, taxicabs, and cars were waiting to whisk them away.
They piled into the vehicles and drove off into the countryside.

The volunteers were subsequently dispersed to kibbutzes
throughout Palestine. Fima was taken to Kibbutz Golan outside Rishon Le-Zion. When they arrived there, Fima and his
fellow volunteers were ordered to strip naked and hand over
their Polish uniforms and identity papers. They were then
ushered into a communal shower, and while they washed
themselves, their uniforms and identity papers were burned.
Upon emerging from the shower, they were given sandals,
underwear, white short-sleeved shirts, and khaki shorts to
wear. It was the ensemble that men and women alike wore on
a kibbutz. Fima got dressed, and in a twinkling he was transformed from a deserter from the Polish army into a proper
kibbutznik.

The volunteers were also given new names and identity
cards to go with them. My brother Fima took the name
Chaim Carmi, which is the Hebrew rendition of Fima Weintraub. It was his fourth name in as many years!

More than three thousand Jews deserted to the Haganah
that day, the equivalent of three regiments. The Poles made
little effort to find them. The II Corps was about to be
shipped to Italy to fight the Germans, and the Poles had neither the time nor the inclination to hunt down men who would
no doubt offer armed resistance to anyone who attempted to
arrest them.

Fima spent the rest of the war on Kibbutz Golan engaged
in various agricultural pursuits. Shortly after the war in
Europe ended, he left the kibbutz and went to Haifa, where
he found work in a pottery factory. Like so many other Jewish immigrants to Palestine, he had left behind family members in Europe; he now undertook to find them, or at least to
learn of their fate. But this was no easy task, and he wasn't
quite sure how to go about it. He thought that he should start

with Uncle Isadore, the only trouble being that he didn't know Isadore's address in America or even whether Isadore was still alive. He thought that Isadore lived in the vicinity of New York City, perhaps Brooklyn; the question was, how to locate him? New York City and its immediate environs had the largest Jewish population in the world, and trying to find Isadore there would be like looking for the proverbial needle in a haystack.

Around this time, Fima renewed his friendship with one Elyakim Ben-Shir, a former classmate from his technical school in Lvov. Told by mutual acquaintances that Ben-Shir was living in Tel Aviv (where he owned a gift shop on Shenken Street), Fima got in touch with the man and, soon thereafter, moved in with him. For the next six months or so, Fima and Ben-Shir shared a tiny, one-room apartment that was really nothing more than an oversized closet. Notwithstanding the minuscule size of their quarters, the move proved to be a blessing for Fima in that it was Ben-Shir who helped him locate Isadore. Ben-Shir knew that there were two ways to search for our uncle, both involving the New York media: radio station WOR and a newspaper called *Forward*. The latter was a Yiddish publication (it now publishes in English) with a substantial circulation in the New York area. Since the surrender of Germany, it had devoted a section to personal ads by people seeking to learn the whereabouts of family members caught up in the Holocaust. Ben-Shir placed a Yiddish-language ad in *Forward* which said that Fima Weintraub, son of Ilya and Olga Weintraub of Lvov, Poland, was seeking Isadore Rosenwald, brother of Olga Weintraub, son of Moses Rosenwald, who was last known to be living in Brooklyn. The ad also provided a brief history of our family, including the names of Isadore's sisters.

A shortened version of the ad was placed with WOR, which broadcast a weekly program called the "Jewish Hour" when such messages were read on the air.

Now, at that time *Forward* and WOR were receiving thousands of missing persons inquiries every month. But Isadore did not listen to the "Jewish Hour," nor did he read *Forward*.

He lived in Perth Amboy, New Jersey, where the newspaper was not widely read or distributed. Fortunately, he had a friend who read it. The friend saw the ad, and called my uncle and told him about it.

The last time Isadore had seen or talked with Fima was back in 1932 on a trip to Lvov with my grandfather. But no matter—he was overjoyed to learn that Fima was alive, as he had assumed that his entire family in Europe had been killed during the war. He immediately sent a telegram to Fima, after which the two began corresponding by mail. In his first letter to Isadore, my brother stated his desire to come to America. In his reply Isadore said that this really wasn't a good time to try to gain entry to the United States. The country was still at war with Japan, and severe restrictions on immigration were in place and would likely remain so until that war had been won. But he promised to send Fima the necessary paperwork, affidavits and such attesting to the fact that my brother had a relative in the United States who would sponsor him and see to it that he would not be a burden to the community upon his arrival. Receipt of these papers would at least enable Fima to set the immigration process in motion.

The war with Japan ended, however, and Isadore still had not sent the papers to Fima. My brother tried to be stoic about this. He resigned himself to the fact that he would be living in Palestine for awhile. By then he was also resigned to the fact that he had no family left except those relatives who lived in America. Then I got in touch with Isadore through the Red Cross. When Isadore learned I had survived the war and was living in Katowice, he passed this information on to Fima in a telegram. Fima was elated. He immediately sat down and wrote me a letter, then mailed it to Isadore along with his photograph.

The letter reached me not long after that. And that was how I came to be sitting in a bathroom in Katowice, with a photograph of my brother in my hand and tears of joy streaming down my face.

Fima went right to work on my behalf. He wrote to Uncle

Isadore and asked that the affidavits Isadore had prepared for him be changed to my name. He felt it was more important for me to get out of Poland than for him to leave Israel. He also sent me money, which was not then an easy thing to do as Palestinian banks were not making money transfers to European banks. Fima found a way around this problem. One of his army buddies in Palestine had a sister who had survived the Holocaust and lived in Katowice, of all places. The man's sister was relatively well off: their family had been wealthy before the war, and she had managed to hold on to some of their material assets, diamonds and such, throughout the war. She often sent money to her brother, who, like so many immigrants to Palestine, was partially dependent on outside sources to make ends meet. Fima proposed that she should instead give that money to me, and he would pay his friend the same amount. The friend was agreeable to this and wrote a letter to his sister giving her the particulars of the scheme. In the meantime, I received a similar letter of instruction from Fima, which included the name and address of the friend's sister. A short time thereafter, I called on the woman at her apartment, and the cash transfer was made. It wasn't a lot of money—Fima didn't have all that much to spare—but it seemed like a fortune to me! I wasted little time in spending it. Mostly, I used it to buy clothes, a sorely needed commodity in the autumn of 1945. I purchased a warm winter coat, shoes, underwear, and a real dress, my first dress in years.

At the time, Fima was employed at another pottery factory in Tel Aviv. One Saturday afternoon, he decided to take a walk along the main street. The shops were closed for Shabbat and the streets were empty. He stopped by a window to admire a menorah in the Bezalel Israeli arts and crafts shop. Suddenly, a man tapped his shoulder.

"Fima Weintraub, right?"

Fima was startled. He hadn't been addressed by that name for several years. He turned and found himself staring at a man who looked vaguely familiar. The man introduced himself. His name was Lemberg, and he was a dear friend of my parents who had immigrated to Palestine before the war. As

Fima would learn in conversation with the man, it was Mr. Lemberg to whom our father had written a letter inquiring about the possibility of bringing our family to Palestine. In his reply, Mr. Lemberg had discouraged my father from pursuing this course. Life was very hard in Palestine, Mr. Lemberg had said, due to miserable economic conditions and sporadic warfare with the Arabs. Moreover, it was difficult to get into Palestine—the British were doing their utmost to keep European Jews out. My father was thus persuaded to forget about Palestine and concentrate instead on immigrating to America.

Subsequent events have shown that this was the wrong decision to make. But Fima did not blame Mr. Lemberg for proffering advice that led, indirectly, to the death of our parents. On the contrary, he was glad to meet someone, anyone, who had known us in Lvov. Such people were few and far between. Most everyone who had known us in Lvov was dead.

Mr. Lemberg invited Fima to his home in Tel Aviv for dinner. They became friends, and later Mr. Lemberg introduced Fima to another friend of our father's, a man who had also emigrated to Palestine before the war. This man was a successful architect, and he hired Fima as a draftsman in his firm. Fima was finally doing the sort of work he had always wanted and trained for.

Not long after that, Mr. Lemberg's wife invited Fima to a party given by their friends, the Lakritzes. The party was a welcome-home celebration for their daughter, Myra, who had just returned to Palestine after graduating from Columbia University in New York City. The intent here was to introduce Myra, who was single, to suitable candidates for marriage, so several bachelors, Fima among them, were in attendance. Fima and Myra met and were instantly taken with each other. They dated only three months before announcing their engagement, and they were married shortly thereafter.

I was at the office one day when I happened to look up from my work to see a stocky, middle-aged man with a ruddy face and silver hair standing in the doorway. He was looking around the room, and when our eyes met, he grinned and waved at me. I put my hand to my breast and gasped in surprise and recognition. It was my Uncle Herman! I leapt up out of my chair and rushed over to him. We embraced right there in front of my coworkers, and it was all I could do to keep from bursting into tears. I had assumed that Herman had been killed, and his sudden appearance was tantamount to his being raised from the dead.

After we had hugged, Uncle Herman bent to my ear and whispered, "Can you get away from this place?"

I said that I could.

"Let's go, then," he said. He turned and walked back outside.

I stammered something to my coworkers about how this was my uncle and that I had not seen him since before the war. Then I excused myself, telling them that I was taking the rest of the day off, and followed Herman into the street.

Parked at the curb was a large flatbed truck with side rails and a rear gate. I recognized the type. I had ridden on several such trucks, always after I had been arrested by the Germans. Herman, who had owned a farm outside Borszczów, had gotten rid of his property and purchased the truck for reasons he would not divulge in public. We climbed into the cab and drove to my apartment. On the way there, Herman told me how he had survived the war. The campaign to round up Jews in the rural areas and resettle them in urban ghettos had been slow in getting under way around Borszczów. German murder squads composed of SS *Einsatzgruppen* and Order Police units were scouring the countryside, arresting and shooting Jews en masse, but somehow they didn't make it to Herman's farm. In the brief respite thus given him, Herman made preparations to go to ground—literally. He dug a secret bunker beneath the floorboards of his barn, then arranged to give his farm and most of his money to his Polish field hand, provided that the latter would hide Herman's family until the Germans were gone. Herman, his son Moishe, his daughters Lea and Nuscia, and Lea's husband and small child spent most of the war in that hole in the ground. In the meantime, the field hand

and his wife had worked the farm as though they owned it. The Polish couple had made sure that Herman and his family got enough to eat and revealed their existence to no one. When the war ended, Herman kept his end of the bargain and turned the farm over to his erstwhile servant. He then purchased the truck and went with his family to live with friends on a farm outside Katowice.

They had registered with the Red Cross in Katowice, and that was how Herman had learned that I, too, lived in the city. They had no intention of staying in Katowice, however; in fact, they had no intention of staying in Poland.

"We're going to the West, to the American zone of occupation in Germany," he said. Stalin was letting Jews and other displaced people in the Soviet zone move freely across the borders to the West, where the Allies had set up camps for the refugees. Herman wanted to take advantage of this situation while it lasted. He figured that his family could stay in a displaced persons camp in the American zone until Isadore—with whom they had also been in touch—provided them with the documents needed to emigrate to the United States.

Herman asked me whether I wanted to go with them.

"Yes, of course, more than anything!" I exclaimed.

"Then pack up your things and let's go."

"Now?" I asked.

"Right this instant!" Herman said. "Hurry! And don't tell anyone you're leaving!"

I was an expert at sudden departures and disappearances—I knew exactly what to do. I threw my clothes into a paper bag, and we walked out of the building, got into the truck, and drove off. I didn't tell my employers that I had quit. I didn't even say good-bye to my landlady.

We embarked on our journey that same day. Initially, there were eight passengers in our truck: Herman, Moishe, Nuscia, a Mr. and Mrs. Goldberg (acquaintances of Herman, also Jews, who were sharing in the cost of the journey), the Goldberg's two sons, and me. Our trip across Poland was a rollicking good time, a kind of party on wheels. Except for the driver (usually Herman) and a passenger in the cab, we all rode in the back of the truck and had great fun with each other despite the discomforts this entailed. We were all giddy with excitement about going to the American zone and the prospect this held of continuing on to the United States. We were no less elated to be leaving Poland with all its hardships and oppressions, its dreadful experiences, its painful memories. There was a sense of shared adventure, of new beginnings and happy endings, of a better life in between. I know that I was filled to bursting with hope and optimism: I was genuinely happy for the first time in years and felt as if a huge weight had been lifted from my back. I didn't concern myself with the particulars of where we were going or how we would get there; I let Herman handle the details. I was just along for the ride. I felt carefree, lighthearted, even mirthful. I remember that we laughed a lot. This was a novel experience for me. I had thought that I had forgotten how to laugh. But we had all been through so much, and as a result we were primed and ready to laugh at the slightest pretext.

Much of our laughter was caused by Mrs. Goldberg, a natural-born comedienne with a happy-go-lucky personality who kept us in stitches with an endless stream of jokes, wry comments, amusing stories, and general silliness. She was at her hilarious best when it came to dealing with Russian soldiers. We encountered the soldiers at checkpoints where our papers were inspected and we were searched and subjected to other petty harassments. There were many such checkpoints spaced at irregular intervals along the road, and one might think that they would not have offered much occasion for humor. But this is not to reckon with the comedic gifts of Mrs. Goldberg, who had a way of turning these encounters into something on the order of high farce. She did so by making sport of the soldiers in Yiddish, a language they did not speak or understand. She would make smart-alecky remarks and wisecracks at the soldiers, and they would listen to her with dull, uncomprehending expressions while the rest of us were convulsed in laughter. She mocked them even as they were gesturing at us with their rifles and roughly pawing at us and shoving us around. And I must say they richly deserved our ridicule, because they were bullies and thieves who invariably shook us down for money or valuables before allowing us to go on our way. However, they didn't get much out of us, partly because we didn't have much to give and partly because they didn't know where to look. Mrs. Goldberg, who was as clever as she was funny, carried on her person a handful of diamonds which no Russian soldier ever found. She put the diamonds into a condom which she inserted into her vagina. This was the one place the Russians never thought to search. They were thorough, but not *that* thorough.

Once, we drove up to a checkpoint before Mrs. Goldberg was able to prepare herself for a search. As we were rolling to a stop, she jumped off the back of the truck and ran toward the bushes at the side of the road. The soldiers shouted at her to halt, but she shouted back that she had to relieve herself and pushed on into the foliage. The soldiers just shrugged — they did not want to interrupt nature's call. When she did not return after several minutes, we grew worried and got permission from the soldiers to look for her. But to no avail — she seemed to have vanished. The soldiers were unconcerned. They just stood there waiting for her to rejoin us. After a while she emerged from the bushes, whereupon the soldiers searched her. But while she was in the bushes, she had put the condom inside her, and they did not find it. She had her fun with them: "Look at these idiots," she said in Yiddish. "What fools they are!" We guffawed; the soldiers frowned. But they didn't understand her, thank God. Finally, her husband gave them some money, and they let us go.

Just before we got out of Poland, we stopped in a small town to pick up Herman's oldest daughter Lea and her husband and baby boy. They had moved to that town just after the war ended. Lea had instructed Herman to meet them at a certain street corner. Herman would know that he had come to the right corner, Lea had said somewhat facetiously, because he would see two "Jews standing there and talking." Mrs. Goldberg was greatly amused by this: the very idea that any Jews in Poland would at this late date be recognizable as such was really absurd. If they were Jews, Mrs. Goldberg pointed out, and they were alive, you wouldn't know them as Jews: they would have the appearance of Gentiles, because those were the only sort of Jews who had survived. So we picked up Lea and her family, and drove on. The journey lasted about two weeks, and the going was made slow not only by frequent stops at Red Army checkpoints but also by the condition of the roads, which were devastated by over five years of war. We spent the night in barns and purchased food from the farmers who owned them. After crossing the German frontier, we drove across the Soviet-occupied zone of Germany to the border of the American zone, which later became part of the Federal German Republic, or West Germany. Just before we entered the American zone, those of us who possessed forged identity papers burned them. We had been told back in Katowice that it would go badly for us if the Americans caught us with false papers: they would send us back to the Soviet zone. So I put a match to my papers, and in a little puff of smoke and flame, I put an end to Urszula Krzyzanowska and became Lala Weintraub again.

At a checkpoint on the border between the two zones, American soldiers directed us to a displaced persons camp in the city of Kassel a few miles further west. Like so many cities in Germany, Kassel was a grim and desolate place that had been demolished by the Allied bombing campaign. Where buildings had once stood, there remained only huge piles of scorched brick and concrete rubble. The streets were strewn with debris and cratered by bomb explosions. The inhabitants were gaunt, forlorn, in tatters, and they scuttled furtively in and out of the ruins of their city like rats.

We drove through this urban wasteland to the displaced persons camp, which had been established at the Hasenecke barracks complex. Our first glimpse of the camp was almost enough to make us turn the truck around and drive back to Poland. The camp was enclosed by barbed-wire fences, and there were guard towers with searchlights overlooking the compound within. Inside were dozens of long buildings made of wood with corrugated metal roofs. The place reminded me of the Janowska Camp, and we all feared that it would be put to a similar use. We were filled with dismay and alarm. It seemed that the whole thing was starting all over again: the Americans had replaced the Germans but the victims, Jews, remained the same. I thought, what the hell are we doing here in this prison? We're free, aren't we? We've been liberated, haven't we?

But we entered the camp despite our fears and registered at the main office. This was a memorable event for me, as it was the first time since I had left Lvov that I signed my name as Lala Weintraub. Well, not really the first time. I had given my real name to the Red Cross in Katowice. But somehow this seemed different. Having previously consigned the identity of Urszula Krzyzanowska to permanent oblivion, it seemed as if I was now announcing to the world once and for all that I was Lala Weintraub and no one else, and that I was no longer on the run from anyone. So it was a heady moment when I wrote out my name on the registration forms. I also gave the names of my parents and my brother and sister. In doing so I felt as if I were reclaiming not only my identity, but my family as well.

We were assigned to rooms in one of the barracks. I was put in a room with Herman, Nuscia, and Moishe; Lea and her husband and baby were given a room of their own across the hall. The Goldbergs also got their own room. In my room there were only three cots for the four of us. It was agreed that Herman and Moishe would each have his own cot, and I would share a cot with Nuscia. We had a table in the middle of the room and a cooking stove next to the wall beneath the room's one window. There was a communal shower and toilet at the end of the hall, which we shared with everyone in the building.

When I went into my room, I felt as if I were going back into a Nazi prison cell. I sat on the edge of my cot and began to cry. "I don't want to be here," I sobbed. "I want to get away from this place. I just want to go to America."

Herman tried to reassure me. "Don't worry, Lala," he said, patting me on the shoulder. "We'll figure something out." But I wasn't convinced. Everyone, Herman included, seemed just as downcast and disheartened as I was. That night I cried myself to sleep.

Life in Hasenecke was not physically hard, nor was it dangerous. Even so, I was miserable there. The worst part about it was the boredom. There wasn't anything to do except stand in endless lines for our food rations. We stood in line, we got our food, and we went back to our rooms to eat. That was the sum of a normal day's activity. Upon our arrival in the camp, we had applied for permission to emigrate to America, but the weeks went by and we heard nothing in that regard. There were tens of thousands like us who wanted to go to the United States, and the authorities had their hands full processing all the applications. We were told that several months could pass before our names even came up for consideration. We were also given to believe that in all likelihood we would be denied entry until the following year. America had an annual immigration quota, which was quickly filled. It made little difference that we had relatives in America; so did everyone else, it seemed.

It was all very frustrating, and I grew impatient waiting for our situation to change. Then at some point I heard about the American Joint Distribution Committee, or JDC, which was a charitable organization founded by American Jews after the First World War to help Jewish refugees in Europe. Along with several other charitable agencies, it operated under the auspices of the United Nations Relief and Rehabilitation Administration, or UNRRA. I learned that the JDC had an office on the other side of Kassel, and one day I resolved to take matters into my own hands and pay it a visit. Without telling anyone of my plans, and with the affidavits Isadore had sent me stuffed into my purse, I set out early in the morning on a laborious trek across Kassel's ravaged landscape. I spent the entire morning climbing up and down piles of rubble before I reached my destination. The office was located in one of the few buildings still left standing in Kassel, and by the time I arrived there, its lobby was jammed with displaced persons like me. They had come there in hopes of meeting with the head of the office—Morris Fishman—the "Herr Direktor" of the JDC, Kassel Region. Everyone had some sort of request to make, a complaint to lodge, a tale of woe to tell to the Herr Direktor, and I was no different. It was just past noon, and I was told that the wait was several hours long and there was no guarantee that the Herr Direktor would see me before his office was closed for the day. I wondered, where do I go now, what should I do? Should I get in line, or return to Hasenecke and try again another day? There was a secretary who sat behind a desk, but I dared not approach her; she was busy writing and paid no attention to me.

While I was standing there looking around and trying to figure out what to do, the door to the inner office opened and a man in an American army uniform came out into the lobby. A handsome man in his early thirties, with thinning hair and wearing wire-rim glasses, he was obviously very self-assured, very much in charge of things. It was the Herr Direktor himself. He scanned the room, saw me, and smiled. Then he walked over to me.

"Can I help you?" he asked in German.

"I certainly hope so," I said.

"Please, come into my office."

While everyone in the lobby glared daggers at me, I went into the office with Herr Direktor Fishman. I had been jumped to the front of a very long line, and everyone was angry about that. Morris ignored them, and so did I.

Why had Morris accorded me special treatment? He once told me that when he saw me standing there in the lobby, I looked like a breath of fresh air to him. He had spent the whole day listening to one sob story after another, and he was tired of it all. The stories were all beginning to sound the same to him and they seemed endless. People would come into his office with a big sheaf of papers, affidavits attesting to the fact that they had relatives in the United States who would support them. But such papers were quite useless. The United States wasn't giving out any more visas to Eastern Europeans even if they did have sponsors. Morris had to explain this to one person after another, and it was getting him down. The crestfallen look on their faces when he told them that their papers were of little value ripped him up inside. These people had all suffered the torments of the damned, and now he was adding to their misery. So he had stepped out into his lobby to stretch his legs and take a break from what had become a really onerous task. It was then he saw me. He thought it would be refreshing to talk to a young girl for a change, and so he invited me into his inner sanctum.

We sat down—me in front of his desk, Morris behind it—and he asked, "So what brings you here?" I told him that I was seeking a way to speed up the immigration process. He asked me for some background information, and when I began to tell him about my experiences in the war, he became very interested. Speaking in a mixture of German and Yiddish, he asked me to tell him everything—where I had been, what I had done, what had happened to my family, the whole story. We talked for a while, and then I asked him about the possibility of my going to America. I showed him the affidavit and other papers I had gotten from Isadore. I thought to myself, I bet my papers are good. Morris glanced at them briefly and said, "Your papers are in order, and you have an excellent chance of getting a visa."

Now, I knew other people with papers better than my own had been refused a visa. So I was somewhat taken aback by what he said. I asked him, "How is it that these papers are so good, and others just like them are not?"

He replied, "They've been filled out correctly, they've been certified by the proper authorities, and they confirm that you have a sponsor in America. But you know, all that is beside the point. Your papers are not going to get you a visa."

"How can I get a visa, then?"

Morris gave me a mischievous look. "You are a pretty young lady," he said, "and because you're so pretty, it won't take you long to get to America. You'll meet an American officer, he'll marry you, and you'll go to the United States as his bride."

I knew he was joking with me, just teasing me a little, and I didn't mind what he was doing. I found him quite charming. I smiled and said, "Getting married to an American officer may work for some girls. But that is not how I plan to go to the United States."

"Well, we'll see," said Morris. Neither of us could know that he had just foretold my destiny—and his as well.

We talked for a little while longer. Finally, Morris said that he had other people to see. As I got up to go, he asked where I lived in Hasenecke. I told him my address. "I'll see what I can do to help you with your problem," he said. "And I'll get back in touch with you."

I left his office feeling as if I had made a new friend.

That evening a circus was scheduled to put on a show in Kassel. Morris decided that he wanted to go to the circus. He summoned his driver, who could speak German and often helped Morris with the transport and distribution of rations and other supplies to the camps. Morris asked him, "Do you know anything about the Hasenecke camp?"

"Of course," the driver answered. "I go there every day to deliver food parcels. I know it well."

"There's a young lady staying there," Morris said. "Her name is Lala Weintraub." He told the driver my address. "I want you to look her up and tell her that the director would very much like to have her accompany him to a circus that is in town."

He sent his driver over to Hasenecke to fetch me. The driver arrived at my barracks just a few minutes after I had returned from Morris's office. It had taken me that long to walk back through the ruins of Kassel. Herman was cooking dinner when I arrived. No sooner had we sat down to eat than there came a knock at our door.

I opened the door to find the driver standing there. He asked if I was Lala Weintraub, and I said I was. The driver said, "Herr Direktor Morris Fishman would like you to go with him to a circus."

I was flabbergasted. I couldn't answer him at first. I didn't know what to think. But Herman did. "Go, by all means, go," he said, giving me a gentle push toward the door.

So I climbed aboard the Jeep with the driver and went to the circus with the Herr Direktor. And the rest, as they say, is history.

Who was this man?

In the weeks to come, I would learn that Morris was an ordained rabbi who was born and raised in Brooklyn. His father was from Poland, his mother from Romania; both had emigrated to the United States as teenagers. Morris's family was observant of Jewish rituals and traditions, but only to a point. For although his father had come from a strict religious background, he had to make compromises when he came to the United States, concessions, as it were, to the iron laws of economics. For example, he could no longer go to the synagogue every morning, as he had in Poland, because he had to report to his job (he was a coppersmith). And since he had to work on Saturdays, he could not observe the Sabbath in the Orthodox manner.

Nevertheless, Morris was imbued with a religious sensibility, so much so that at age eleven he transferred from the New York public school system to a yeshiva in Brooklyn. In his final year at this school, he decided to go to Poland and study at a famous yeshiva in the town of Mir, located just west of Minsk, about fifteen miles from what was then the border of Poland and the Soviet Union. (It is now in Belarus.) He did so on the recommendation of a respected rabbi and teacher at the Brooklyn yeshiva. The teacher had extolled the spiritual life at the Mir yeshiva, telling Morris that it offered a more authentic and intensive way of living in accordance with Jewish law and tradition.

Morris's father supported his son's decision to study in Poland and gave him as much money as he could spare to cover travel costs. To this amount Morris added the money he had saved by serving as a Torah reader at a neighborhood synagogue. Morris had become fluent in Hebrew at an early age, and when he was thirteen his father had gotten wind of a small congregation that needed a reader and was willing to pay a small sum for his services. His father arranged for Morris to get the job, which he held until he went to Poland. With the money he had saved, he was able to purchase a steamship ticket and pay for many ancillary expenses as well.

He was sixteen years old when his ship weighed anchor in July of 1932. The five-day voyage across the Atlantic Ocean was a tremendously exciting experience for a boy of his age, especially since he had never been outside the New York City area. However, although he was on his own, he was not without adult guidance. Several of the Mir yeshiva's alumni were also making the trip back to Poland, having completed fundraising activities in the United States on behalf of their alma mater. Morris was befriended by one of these men, a rabbi who represented a number of institutions in Poland that depended for existence largely on American contributions. There were several other important rabbis on the trip, but this one in particular took Morris under his wing. They all watched out for him, however, even though he was not officially attached to their group.

These men were serious about their religion. Just how serious was demonstrated to Morris at dinner, when the steward set a tub of margarine down in front of them. Margarine was a new invention, and nobody knew what it was. But it looked like butter. The rabbis were aghast. The ship served a kosher cuisine, and this was supposed to be a kosher meal. But the dietary laws dictate that butter cannot be served with meat. "There must be some mistake," one of the rabbis told the steward. "This is a kosher table."

"No mistake," the steward replied, "we have authorization from the rabbinate in London to serve this." The waiter then explained that margarine had been developed by the Germans and that no dairy derivative had been used in its making. This came as a revelation to that company. Nonetheless, there ensued a big debate about whether margarine could be considered a nondairy food. It was finally agreed that it was; however, they banned it anyway, for appearance's sake!

Morris studied at Mir for four and a half years, returning to the United States in January 1937. The final months of his stay were spent learning the trade of the *shochet*, a kosher slaughterer. It was not an occupation he had wanted or found in any way appealing. His goal was to become a working rabbi, and he was ordained as such when he completed his schooling at Mir. But his father knew that the older members of most congregations would be disinclined to entrust their spiritual upkeep to one so young as he. Consequently, his father thought, it was doubtful that he would be employed as a rabbi any time soon. So his father advised him to acquire a skill which might provide a more dependable source of income in that Depression-strapped decade. Morris, a dutiful son, had heeded this advice despite his aversion to the bloody business of the *shochet*. In Poland, where keeping kosher was a widespread practice, it was also a thriving business; there was a big demand for *shochets*. Morris availed himself of the opportunity to obtain the necessary instruction, enrolling in a course with an inexpensive tuition and an exhaustive curriculum. He started small, on chickens, then graduated to larger animals, slaughtering lambs and sheep, and finally, cattle. (It is interesting to note that Jews had traditionally controlled the meat business in Poland; Jewish meat purveyors would sell the forbidden hindquarters to the Poles, keeping the forequarters for sale to Jews. But in 1935, the Polish government established quotas limiting the amount of kosher meat that could be slaughtered, and the bulk of the meat business passed into the hands of Gentiles.)

Morris's stay in Poland was rewarding and for the most part enjoyable. But his last two years in Mir were marred by a significant increase in anti-Semitic sentiment, as well as by ominous developments in neighboring Germany. He saw how the Poles often accused Jewish merchants of overcharging them and being deceitful; he heard the Poles say, "One day we'll have Hitler here and he'll take care of you Yids once and for all." Morris himself became a target of physical attack while visiting his grandparents in a town called Łomża. Morris had cultivated a scholarly goatee, and one day while he was out and about in the town, a young man came over to him and grabbed his beard. "Such a pretty little beard, such a cute beard," the man said mockingly. No doubt he intended to abuse Morris further, but he should have chosen another victim. He was probably accustomed to bullying European rabbinical students, who tended to be passive when confronted with aggressively anti-Semitic behavior. But Morris was an American, and he behaved as an American would in such circumstances: he hauled off and struck the Pole squarely in the face with a roundhouse punch that sent him sprawling!

By the time Morris left Poland, he was sure that another war was brewing in Europe and that something horrible would happen to the Jews. He kept up with events in Poland by corresponding with his uncle, his grandparents, and other relatives, as well as with various acquaintances he had made during his stay in that country.

In the United States, Morris found that, contrary to what his father had thought, there was little demand for his skills as a kosher slaughterer. However, his standing as a *shochet* did gain him an interview with a small congregation in Northampton, Massachusetts, that was searching for a rabbi. Morris hit it off well with the congregation. The older members wanted an authentic rabbi from the old country; the younger members wanted a rabbi who could speak English without an accent—a rarity in strict Orthodox congregations in the 1930s. Morris fit the bill on both counts. So, he was hired.

As it happened, the old folks usually got their kosher meat in Springfield, which was only twenty miles distant. Once in a while, Morris was called upon to slaughter chickens and, more infrequently, a calf. But he always found the job quite distasteful. The task of slaughtering larger animals became downright repellant, and for several weeks afterward he could not bring himself to eat meat of any kind.

Morris was living in Northampton when the Germans invaded Poland. Immediately upon the outbreak of war, the letters from his family and friends in Poland ceased to come. He never heard from any of them again. Like most of the Jews of Poland, they were wiped off the face of the earth.

Morris stayed in Northampton for five years. In 1938, following the Munich accord, which resulted in Germany absorbing Czechoslovakia, many Czech Jews emigrated to America. A number of these Jews ended up in Northampton, and some of them joined Morris's congregation. Among the émigrés who began attending services in Morris's synagogue was Dr. Richard Karpe, a well-known psychiatrist from Prague who had studied under Dr. Otto Fenichel, who had studied under the master himself, Dr. Sigmund Freud. Morris, who had been suffering from chronic migraines, asked Dr.

Karpe for advice on what to do about his headaches. Dr. Karpe suggested analysis, and Morris, intrigued by the psychotherapeutic process, decided to give it try. He spent the next three years undergoing analysis, with Dr. Karpe as his therapist and guide in what Morris later termed a "voyage of self-discovery." Analysis led Morris to reexamine his religious views, which, he discovered, were at variance with Orthodox beliefs. He began a gradual shift toward a more liberal interpretation of Judaism, and this put him at odds with his congregation. At length, he began to feel that he was being dishonest to his flock. He had quit the meticulous observance of many Orthodox rituals; he literally was not practicing what he preached. In 1942, he resigned his post. He was then twenty-seven years old.

Morris left Northampton and enrolled at the Jewish Theological Seminary in Manhattan on a full scholarship. He was attracted to the seminary in part because it offered a more progressive approach to religion. More importantly, it gave him the opportunity to study under Mordecai Kaplan, the founder of Reconstructionism, a movement which is philosophically situated between Conservative and Reform Judaism. He also took courses at the New School for Social Research, where he earned a degree in sociology, and worked part time as a rabbi for a small congregation on Long Island.

Morris stayed at the seminary through the war, graduating in 1946. While the war was still being fought, he gave considerable thought to joining the military, even though he was exempted from the draft because he was a rabbi. In this matter, he sought the counsel of the chancellor, Dr. Louis Finkelstein, of the seminary. The chancellor urged him to continue his studies. He told Morris that as there was a sufficient number of Jewish chaplains already serving in the field, it was unlikely that he would receive an overseas posting. "You will do more good for the Jews here," the chancellor told him, and Morris was persuaded. However, he closely followed war news, particularly as it pertained to the fate of the Jews in occupied Europe. Well before the Final Solution became widely known, he was aware that a mass extermination of

Jews was under way. He lived next door to a rabbi and jour-
nalist named Philip Alstat, who summed up the news from the
Yiddish press in a newspaper column that appeared in an
Anglo-Jewish publication. Alstat would leave clippings under
Morris's door almost every night, and this was how Morris
learned about the Holocaust.

Morris graduated in 1946 and was ordained for the second
time. He then applied for a rabbinical post in Albany and was
elected to it. But he turned it down, for he had also applied to
the American Joint Distribution Committee, which was then
advertising for people to send to Europe to work in the displaced persons camps. The JDC was impressed by his qualifi-
cations: a background of living and studying in Poland; fluen-
cy in Yiddish and a workable knowledge of German and Polish;
rabbinic ordination; and a sociology degree. Morris was
offered a job running DP camps in Europe, and he accepted it.
After a short training course, he was sent to Germany as a
civilian attached to the U.S. Army, with the equivalent rank of
colonel and the uniform to go with it.

He arrived in Europe in the summer of 1946 at the height
of a mass influx of refugees to the West from the Soviet zone
of occupation. He flew into Frankfurt and attended a briefing
that made him feel quite unequal to the responsibilities he was
to assume. Furthering his sense of inadequacy was the ability
of the secretary at the Frankfurt office to speak five languages.
(The secretary, a Hungarian girl, was also the wife of Morris's
driver.) But he quickly adjusted to the situation. He was put
in charge of all the camps in the Kassel area, which included
the Hasenecke camp. His first job was to conduct an inspection tour of the camp at Babenhausen, outside Frankfurt. The
camp had formerly housed a German cavalry regiment, and
the refugees lived in the troop barracks. These were ram-
shackle structures that had not been subdivided into rooms
and were thus unsuitable for housing the refugee families that
were assigned to them. Several families would share a barrack
room, where they lived in alcoves created by hanging blankets
on ropes that were strung from one wall to another. These
cloth barriers afforded very little privacy to the dozens of

men, women, and children who occupied each building, and virtually no one was satisfied with the arrangement.

Most of the occupants were Polish Jews who had escaped to the Soviet Union in 1939, only to be deported to camps in Central Asia. After the war, the Soviet Union decided it did not want them anymore and dumped them on the Western Allies. They had come to the West with great expectations, which were quickly dashed by the realities of Babenhausen. The state of the barracks, plus chronic and serious shortages of food and other supplies, convinced them that the Americans were plotting their annihilation. The fact that the camp was encircled by a barbed-wire fence reinforced this conviction. Morris was sent to assuage their fears, and he did so in a speech he delivered from atop a railroad cattle car that was parked on a siding at the edge of the camp. To the thousands gathered to hear his speech, he said in Yiddish, "Here, you are among friends. I represent the Jewish community of America reaching its hands out to you in love and friendship, and promising you that you are going to get settled in a decent area where you will have proper housing and more than sufficient rations and clothing." Afterward, he went into the barracks and met with the people individually, thereby establishing an excellent rapport with them. All of which had the desired effect: the people trusted him and were persuaded to believe that the Americans were not intent on doing them harm.

After Babenhausen, Morris inspected several other camps in the area. One of them was Wetzlar, also on the outskirts of Kassel. This camp was initially occupied by Polish-Christian displaced persons who were due to vacate the place and resettle in another camp. It was now autumn, and as the weather was getting colder, Morris was most interested in finding out whether the barracks were built to withstand the rigors of winter. He ascertained that they were, and decided to move the occupants of Babenhausen to Wetzlar.

At Kassel, he commandeered a villa that had belonged to a Nazi *Gauleiter,* or governor. Upon moving in, Morris found a large photograph in the basement showing the *Gauleiter* resplendent in an SS dress uniform. One day the *Gauleiter* came to Morris asking for permission to remove some of his personal effects from the villa. Morris said that he could not grant such permission because everything in the house had been inventoried by the U.S. Army. "I don't have the authority to give anything to you," he told the man. "For that, you must speak to the United States Army." Morris could have made it easy for the *Gauleiter* to get his things. But he didn't want to do any favors for this man, who had had a reputation during the war as being a very tough and ideologically committed Nazi.

One of the first things Morris did when he became the director of the Kassel camps was to reorganize the system by which food rations were packaged and distributed. Previously, the ration parcels had been distributed by refugee committees whose members invariably gave the largest amounts to their own families and friends. Morris changed all this, making sure that the parcels were portioned out equitably, with priority given to children and nursing mothers.

In his capacity as a rabbi, he also performed many marriages. Weddings were frequent because unmarried couples were getting pregnant in numbers that suggested that sex was the chief activity of a majority of the young men and women in the camps. As indeed it might have been. And who could blame them? Now that the war was over, people were allowing themselves to fall in love and to experience all the pleasures that love can offer, including the physical ones. Nature took its course: children were conceived and born, families were started or expanded. All this—love, sex, conception, childbirth—constituted a response to the horrors these people had so recently put behind them; it was a life-affirming gesture that told the world of their triumph over evil even as it served notice of their desire and determination to live fully and completely in the way God had intended. My cousin Lea, incidentally, was one of those who had a baby in the Hasenecke camp, giving birth to her second child, a boy, just a few months after arriving there. I remember how, just a few hours after he was born, she cradled him in her arms—he was squalling lustily, but not, it seemed, because he was unhappy, but rather because he was such a strong and healthy baby, one determined to announce his presence to the world, to tell the world that he was alive and here to stay. We all laughed at the sight and sound of him, and we cried too—tears of joy ran down our cheeks as we gazed upon this tiny boy with the beet-red face and the mighty voice. As Lea drew him to her breast—he was making such a fuss, after all, because he was hungry—she grinned and told me, "Hitler thought he beat us, but he didn't! My son is living proof of that!"

Many couples who got married did so not only because the woman was pregnant but also because they thought that this would enable them to obtain a visa to enter the United States. In this they were mistaken, which was why Morris usually advised them to try for Palestine instead. In the immediate postwar period, it was also very difficult to gain legal entrance to Palestine, as the British government there had instituted a ban on Jewish emigration. But Morris circumvented this ban by working through illegal channels, which included the B'richa, a sort of Jewish underground railway.

The illegal outflow of people to Palestine also made it possible to bring more people into the DP camps. This became a matter of paramount importance when a large number of Czech Jews sought entrance to the American zone after the doors to Germany had officially been closed to refugees from the East. Morris got around this problem by taking the identification cards of those who had escaped to Palestine via the B'richa and giving them to the Czech Jews. This secured for the latter admittance to the camps, but it also meant they would no longer be known by their real names. The loss of their names proved most distressing to the Czech Jews, and they appealed to Morris for ID cards that would restore to them their true identities. "We beg of you this one thing," a leader of the Czech Jews said. "We have been through so much. We have been running from pillar to post for so many years. Now we are in the American zone and we have our freedom. Just do us this one favor—just give us back our names."

Morris was somewhat annoyed by this attitude. Having been accorded the official status of displaced persons—albeit under false pretenses—the Czechs were receiving food rations in the camps to which they had been assigned. Morris thought this a pretty good deal, especially in light of the fact that they had been on the brink of starvation before coming to the American zone. So he told the leader, "If I give you back your names, you will have nothing to eat. So which do you want: your old name and no food, or to eat under a new name?" The leader laughed at this and said they would keep their false names for the time being.

But Morris was not insensitive to their plaint. He understood why they attached such importance to having their real names: it was a matter of preserving for posterity the names of families that had been all but annihilated during the war. But he didn't do anything about it until one day a directive was issued by the U.S. Army ordering new ID cards to be made for all displaced persons and issued in exchange for the old cards. This meant trouble for the Czech refugees because the physical descriptions on the old cards didn't match the cardholders. The Czechs asked Morris for help, and Morris said he would do whatever he could. He went to the district office of UNRRA in Enberg, where he met the man in charge, an Englishman who was formerly a renowned Shakespearean actor in the British theater. He laid the whole problem out for the Englishman. There were many Jews in his camps who had taken the cards, and hence the names, of former inhabitants, and they wanted their real names restored; however, they were afraid that this would cause them to lose their DP status, whereupon they would be kicked out of the camps and thus cut off from their only food source. They would be thrown on the untender mercies of the German economy, which was hardly sufficient to support the Germans themselves. Since they are totally stateless, Morris observed, they wouldn't be able to get work visas—which meant they couldn't get jobs to make money with which to buy food.

The Englishman was sympathetic to their plight. In his view the Czech Jews were to be regarded as legitimate displaced persons, and the fact that they had not gotten out of Czechoslovakia before the official cutoff date should not have disqualified them from aid. "What do you suggest we do?" he asked. Morris asked him if he could get hold of the original ID cards of the people who had escaped to Palestine. The Englishman saw what he was getting at and told Morris that he should get in touch with a certain Madame Solange, a former member of the French Resistance who now kept the files where the cards were stored. Morris asked whether she could be trusted, and the Englishman replied, "100 percent."

Madame Solange was duly contacted and enlisted as a willing co-conspirator in their budding scheme. She arranged for the cards in her central file to be entrusted to the camp committee charged with registering the new arrivals. The committee members were also provided with a set of blank ID cards. They worked all night to fill out the blank cards with the real names and physical descriptions of the Czechs. The next day these cards were traded in for the new cards. In the process, the Czechs became legitimate DPs and got back their real names. Thus Morris and his partners in crime were able to get upward of two thousand refugees settled in the American zone.

Some months later, Morris inspected a DP camp in Bavaria. The director of the camp complained that for some reason there was an acute shortage of blank ID cards and that this was causing a problem with the registration and feeding of his new arrivals. He told Morris that he planned to ask the JDC to provide him with rations for those people in his camp who didn't have ID cards and who were thus not recognized as displaced persons entitled to receive Allied aid. Morris gave the pro forma answer that this was quite impossible—no ID cards, no rations, that was the rule. To which the director replied, "I know you JDC guys can do it. I heard there was a JDC man in the Passau area who got all the cards he wanted, whenever he wanted them. I heard he sold the cards and made a fortune off them. You wouldn't happen to know the name of this man, would you?"

"No, I don't," Morris said with a straight face.

"I'm told he was a real manipulator," the director said.

"Sounds like it," said Morris.

"Too bad you don't know him," the director sighed. "We could use a man of his expertise. I can only hope and pray we've got such a man here."

Naturally, I was unaware of the full scope of Morris's activities, legal and otherwise. What I did know was that I felt very comfortable with this man and that I liked being with him. He felt the same way about me, and as a result our relationship blossomed. We spent more and more evenings together, and I became the envy of the young, single women in the camp. They thought I was quite the lucky one to be dating an American with so much power and influence. By the same token, Morris became the envy of the camp's bachelors, at least those who had been flirting with me before the Herr Direktor began showing up in his Jeep. They couldn't compete with Morris and they knew it. So they gave up on me. From then on, Morris had me all to himself.

My own family was amused by the situation and teased me often about it. Whenever Morris drove up in his Jeep, Uncle Herman and my cousins would joke, "Oh, here he is again. The Prince of Hasenecke has come to see you."

One evening Morris popped in unexpectedly while I was out running an errand. Herman told Morris, "Lala isn't here. But you can take out my daughter, Nuscia." To the embarrassment of everyone but himself, Herman practically pushed Nuscia into Morris's arms. Morris gracefully refused the offer of Herman's daughter and said he would wait until I returned.

Once, Morris took me to the local American officers club, my first time there. A band was playing, and Morris asked if I wanted to dance. I declined his invitation. When Morris asked why, I told him that I had on the same pair of stockings I had worn through most of the war—they were full of runs, and I didn't want anyone to see them. The next day Morris took me to the PX and bought me new stockings, and lipstick and mascara as well. Finally, I could wear makeup again! Morris didn't like to see me all made up—he said I was too pretty to paint my face, and in any case I always put too much on. He also bought me sanitary napkins made in America—the greatest luxury of all. I don't know whether Morris really knew how much these seemingly trifling items meant to me. But he was considerate enough to buy them for me whether he understood this or not, and that was one of many reasons to like him and, eventually, to fall in love with him.

There was a downside to dating Morris, however. I was very conscious that he was a big shot while I was just a DP girl, and therefore almost a nonperson in the hierarchy of official being. This wasn't Morris's view. It was mine. My self-esteem was very low. To bring it back up, I decided that I had to get a job. I also wanted a job because I was going crazy with boredom. There was nothing to do in the camp but sit around or stand in line for food. I told Morris of my desire to work, and he said, "I can get you a job, but first you have to learn English."

Nuscia had an English/Polish textbook, and I buried myself in it. I studied the book all day, every day, and well into the night until I couldn't stay awake to read. So hard did I study that I began to get a functional grasp of the language in just two weeks' time. Morris was amazed by my progress. Previously, we hadn't been able to communicate at all in English. When he spoke to me in that language, I would just nod and say, "Yes, yes." Now I could actually begin to carry on something resembling a conversation with him.

Morris got me a job in the office at a DP camp in nearby Muncheberg. This camp was an improvement over Hasenecke in that the buildings were in better shape and there was no barbed-wire fence. I left Hasenecke and moved into a room above the office at Muncheberg. I was a secretary, and I worked very hard to improve my language skills by setting a goal to type a few more sentences in English than the day before. There were two Hungarian girls who worked in the office, and we became friends. I couldn't speak Hungarian and they couldn't speak Polish, but it was just as well since we were all more intent on speaking English. All in all, it was great to be working again and to be making money and living on my own; it was great to be making new friends. As a result, I felt very good about myself and the course my life was taking.

While I was at Muncheberg, Morris and I saw a lot of each other. He frequently dropped by my room, and we went out several evenings a week. Our relationship was growing stronger by the day, and I thought it was headed in a very obvious direction. Then, without warning, Morris stopped calling on me. He simply disappeared. He didn't even show up at work. I wondered what had happened to him. I remembered how I used to disappear from towns without telling anyone that I was leaving. But I did not ask anyone in the office where he had gone. After five days had passed, however, my curiosity and concern got the best of me, and I put the question to his driver. He told me that Morris was in Paris on a furlough. I felt as if a bucket of ice water had been dumped over my head. My boyfriend was having himself a nice little vacation in the most romantic city in the world, and he didn't even have the courtesy to tell me in advance that he was going there. To say the least, I was furious! I imagined that he might have a girlfriend in Paris, and this made me more furious still. I fumed and fretted, and worked myself into a fine indignation. "Okay," I told myself, "if that's the way he wants it to be, then it's finished between us." I decided to break off our relationship and resolved not to talk to him when he got back.

I did talk to him when he returned, but only to tell him that we were through. He asked me why—as if he didn't know— and I spelled it out to him in no uncertain terms. "Taking a trip to Paris by yourself was bad enough," I said. "Not telling me that you were taking such a trip was infinitely worse—it showed that you had no respect for me." Admittedly, I was being a bit melodramatic. But he got the message. Now it was his turn to be upset. He realized that he had been taking me for granted and that he might lose me if he didn't make amends. In the days that followed, he did just that. He came calling with gifts he had bought for me in Paris, perfume and earrings. He soothed my hurt feelings with words of apology and affection. It wasn't long before he won me over. The truth is, I wanted to be won over. But he obliged me, however unwittingly, by coming to this conclusion on his own.

Not long after the resolution of this "crisis," Morris received orders transferring him to Passau on the Danube, by the border with Austria. He asked me to go with him. He also asked me to marry him. I said yes to both questions. And that was how we became engaged.

We stayed in Passau for several months. At first, before the wedding, we lived in separate quarters, as was only right and proper for a single girl to do. I didn't have a job there and felt no need to have one. Almost every weekend we went sightseeing somewhere in Europe. We went to music festivals in Salzburg. We took a train into Czechoslovakia and bought crystal, and we went skiing at Berchtesgaden, where Adolf Hitler had had a vacation home. We socialized with the other officers and their wives. We went dining and dancing at the officers clubs, and we went to parties with our friends. I felt as if I were on top of the world. Life was good, never better.

Morris wrote his family in Brooklyn to tell them about our engagement. His sisters, Lilly and Gussie, sent me skirts, blouses, and underwear. He also undertook to get new identification papers for me, a necessary requirement for getting married and getting into America as well. Even though I was nominally a Polish citizen, in Germany I was officially a stateless person and was thus ineligible for a passport as well as a marriage license. It all entailed much scrambling about from one office to another, proving that the Germans were capable of maintaining a formidable civil bureaucracy even in the depths of their ruin and defeat. Fortunately, Morris was good friends with the director of the local department of vital statistics, the *Standesamt*. This individual got me the necessary documents, which enabled me to get a Polish passport. The way was cleared for marriage in a German civil court and for travel outside Germany.

We set a date for the wedding and got the word out about it to all our friends and various associates. The people at the

UNRRA office were very happy for us and insisted on hosting the wedding at their headquarters building in Passau. I borrowed a wedding dress from a young German peasant woman who lived on a nearby farm. We often bought fresh produce from her farm and had gotten to be friendly with her. When we told her that we were getting married, she asked whether I had already purchased a dress. When I told her that I had not, she offered me the dress she had worn at her own wedding. She showed me the dress, and it was beautiful; I tried it on, and it fit perfectly. I accepted her offer!

We were married on November 30, 1947. It was an auspicious time: the day before, the UN General Assembly voted to partition Palestine into Jewish and Arab states. First, we went through a civil ceremony at the city hall; the ceremony was conducted by the director of the *Standesamt*. Then we went to the headquarters building for the religious ceremony, which took place under a lovely *chupah* (canopy) adorned with fragrant flowers. We were married by Rabbi Abraham Klausner, an army chaplain and former classmate of Morris's at the Yeshiva Torah Vada'ath in Brooklyn. Herman and his family came to the wedding, and it was Herman who gave me away. Standing there under the *chupah*, wearing that beautiful dress, I felt as if I had truly gone from rags to riches.

After the ceremony, we had a sumptuous banquet with two entrees, goose and veal, prepared by the army sergeant who ran the food service at UNRRA. The sergeant had also married a Polish girl, and we had gotten to be good friends with them. Our wedding cake was another one of his creations, a towering confection made with some three dozen eggs. Among our guests was the army colonel who commanded the regional occupation forces, and he lent us his ceremonial sword for the cake cutting.

The whole affair cost Morris a carton of cigarettes in payment. Almost everything—the *chupah*, the banquet—was provided courtesy of the United States Army.

We couldn't go on a honeymoon right away, though we moved in together. Almost immediately after the wedding, Morris was transferred to Regensburg, where he was to finish his tour of duty with the JDC. There, we were assigned a large apartment in a villa. The apartment had its own kitchen, and Morris hired a maid to do the cooking and cleaning. He also leased a piano, which I learned how to play. And he hired a language tutor, a middle-aged German man, who taught me how to speak everyday English from back issues of *Reader's Digest* magazines. Once he pointed to a word in one of the magazines and said, "This says 'voluptuous.' Do you know what that word means?" I said I didn't. He said, "Well, you are voluptuous."

I rather liked this man. He seemed nice. One night, though, I had a strange dream in which he figured prominently. I dreamed that I walked into a local *bierstube*, where I found my tutor, Morris, and Adolf Hitler sitting at the same table, drinking beer and talking. I sat down next to them, but I couldn't understand what they were saying—they were talking in English. I became very angry: I felt that they were speaking English as a means of excluding me from their conversation. A few days later during one of our sessions, the tutor mentioned that he had been in the German army during the war. At first I thought, so what? Almost every German male above the age of sixteen had served in the German military. Then he showed me a snapshot with him wearing an SS uniform. That ended the lesson for the day. It also ended his employment as my tutor. I had Morris fire him. Morris got me another tutor, a woman this time.

Morris would later say that I had always known, on a subconscious level, that the man was a Nazi, and my dream was proof of this.

I enjoyed our stay in Regensburg. But I really didn't want to be there. I wanted to get out of Europe and put its terrible history behind me. I wanted to go to the United States and start life anew as an American. Morris kept postponing the date of our departure, even after his contractual obligations with the JDC had been fulfilled. He felt that he still had much work to do on behalf of the Czechoslovakian Jews and displaced persons from other Eastern European nations. But I was adamant and, finally, in the spring of 1948, he agreed that it was time to leave.

We did not go straight to the United States. We owed ourselves a honeymoon, and now we took it. We first went to Italy, visiting Venice, Florence, and Rome. I liked all three cities, but I was looking forward even more to the next leg of our trip, a visit to Tel Aviv to be reunited with my long-lost brother. It was now August, and though we had previously written to tell Fima that we were coming, we could not be specific about an arrival date because our itinerary was open-ended. Much of it was dependent on whim, but also on the availability of flights to Tel Aviv. Recent political developments had made travel to that city problematic. On May 15, the British Mandate in Palestine was officially terminated and, in Tel Aviv, Jewish leader David Ben Gurion proclaimed the existence of Israel. The reaction of Arab nations in the region was swift. The next day armies from Egypt, Transjordan, Iraq, Syria, and Lebanon invaded the fledgling state. Israel was born in battle. And Fima was right in the thick of it.

May 15 was not the beginning of the war for possession of what is now Israel. There had been heavy if intermittent fighting since December of 1947, particularly in and around Jerusalem, but also in Tel Aviv, Haifa, and a number of other towns and settlements. But Independence Day marked a dramatic expansion and intensification of the conflict. Only a few hours old, Israel was already in danger of being snuffed out of existence.

As a soldier in the Palmach, Fima was in the forefront of the fighting around Tel Aviv and Jaffa. He was not an eager warrior. Myra was seven months pregnant with their first child, and it troubled him to think that death might take him before he ever had a chance to be a father. But he went to war just the same. It was his duty, and he was no shirker. Anyway, he had no real choice in the matter. The war was coming to him. Israel is a small country now, but it was smaller then. Five Arab armies were on the march, and they didn't have far to go before they overran the whole region.

Fima was an especially valued member of the Palmach by virtue of his stint as a Red Army artillery officer. Seeking the best possible employment for a man of his knowledge and experience, the army had offered him a commissioned officer's rank. But Fima turned it down because it meant committing to several years of active-duty service. Instead, he was made a sergeant and put in command of an artillery battery. But this battery was unlike any that Fima had ever before served with or seen. Instead of modern high-velocity rifled cannon, it was equipped with four 150-year-old guns left over from Napoleon Bonaparte's abortive expedition to Egypt and the Holy Land at the end of the eighteenth century! These were muzzle loaders cast in bronze with smooth bores, and they had been plucked from the display cases of a Tel Aviv museum, where they had stood as seemingly permanent memorials to the wars of a bygone era. It was almost inconceivable that they would have been pressed into service, and it is a measure of the crisis confronting Israel that they were. Fima and the men under his command had only the vaguest notion of how to operate them, and they had to learn on the job, while under fire, how to load, aim, and shoot them. Though the guns were inaccurate and their range was limited, they were quite deadly enough to make the Arabs dive for cover when Fima and his men opened fire. Fima and his men increased their effectiveness by mounting them on the back of trucks, thus creating self-propelled artillery carriers that could dash as needed from one sector of the battlefront to another. In this fashion they were able to fool the Arabs into thinking that the Jews had more big guns at their disposal than was actually the case.

One of Fima's men, Menachem Lichterman, the owner of an electronics store in Tel Aviv, hit upon the idea of wiring the battery's weapons for sound to enhance their frightfulness, if not their killing power. Lichterman often attached microphones to the muzzles of the battery's cannons and machine guns and strung them to loudspeakers that were placed close to the Arab positions. When the guns were fired, the noise was amplified to apocalyptic levels. To an unsophisticated Arab soldier, it could seem as if the Jews had loosed a barrage of almighty proportions in his direction. Some could not take it. Fima once saw several Arab soldiers flee headlong from their positions in their bare feet. They were peasants and they did not like the boots they were forced to wear, so they had taken the boots off. They had felt safe in doing so because the Jews in the trenches opposite theirs were supposed to be too few and too poorly armed to launch an attack. Then the store owner from Tel Aviv went to work, and the loudspeakers began blasting. The Arabs didn't know what had hit them. They didn't realize that nothing had hit them, and they didn't stay to find this out. They left their boots behind. They could run faster without them.

Fima was involved in another ruse which surpassed the microphones-and-speakers trick for sheer chutzpah. Came the dawn, and the battlefield was blanketed with a ghostly fog. After draping white sheets over their heads, Fima and his mates leaped out of their trenches and began howling and capering wildly about in full view of the enemy. The Arabs were terrified. They thought the spirits of dead soldiers had risen from the ground to haunt them. Again, they ran away.

The fighting abated in mid-June when the United Nations brokered a truce between the warring factions. The Israelis took the opportunity to reorganize their forces. Up until then the Israeli army was really just a collection of independent brigades. Some of these units were fielded by paramilitary groups—notably the Irgun and the Lehi—which were ideologically at odds with the Haganah's high command and the Ben Gurion government. The reorganization process was undertaken to meld the disparate brigades into a cohesive army, which was henceforth known as the Zahal, or Defense Force. But the Irgun resisted incorporation into the Zahal even though the law now forbade the establishment and maintenance of autonomous forces. A showdown between the two was forced on June 21 when a ship called the *Altalena* anchored off the beach at Tel Aviv with a cargo of weapons earmarked for the Irgun. Among those on board the *Altalena* was Menachem Begin, the leader of the Irgun and no friend of Ben Gurion. The latter correctly saw Begin's intent to distribute the weapons to his men as a challenge to the authority of his government, and he ordered the Zahal into action against the ship and its crew.

Fima was in a unit that was ordered to fire on the vessel. Fima balked; he found the Irgun an unsavory group, but not to the extent of killing its members. Yet he did not refuse the order. He was a good soldier, and good soldiers do not disobey their superiors. He had his men fire their cannons, first taking care to aim the weapons himself. Somehow, every round missed. The rounds overshot, fell short, or flew wide of their target. His inaccuracy was extraordinary—or would have been, were it not so deliberate. "I didn't care what they had done. There was no way I was going to shoot at other Jews," he later told me.

His officers knew what he was up to, but there was little they could do about it. When they asked Fima why his marksmanship was so poor, my brother shrugged and said, "I don't know. I must be having a bad day." His officers chose not to press the issue. Seen in the dual context of the Holocaust and Israel's War of Independence, his logic for deliberately missing the *Altalena* was really unassailable and eminently forgivable. Besides, his participation in the pending assault was not needed. There were plenty of soldiers willing to follow orders to the letter. So the *Altalena* was attacked and set afire. Fifteen men were killed in the subsequent fighting, most of them members of the Irgun.

Morris and I flew into Tel Aviv's Lod airport, which was really not much more than a dirt strip, in mid-August. By then Fima and Myra were the proud parents of a six-week-old girl, Leora. They lived in an apartment in Tel Aviv with Myra's parents.

The truce was still holding when we arrived. As we got off our plane, we noticed a Quonset hut above which flew the powder blue flag of the United Nations. Several men, mostly Israeli officers, were standing in front of the hut, and we went over to talk to them and find out what was going on with respect to the cease-fire. One of the men was Count Folke Bernadotte, the Swedish representative of the United Nations, who served as a mediator between the Arabs and the Jews. Morris introduced himself and me to Bernadotte, and we chatted with him for a few minutes.

(Later that evening, Morris told me that he was appalled at the lack of security for the UN mediator. We had approached him without a single member of his entourage making a move to stop us. "My God, the man was totally unprotected!" Morris exclaimed. If Bernadotte failed to take appropriate measures to ensure his personal safety, Morris believed, there was no telling what might happen to him. The man had many enemies, particularly among the Israelis, who viewed him and the UN as de facto allies of the Arabs. Morris predicted an attempt on his life. It was made on September 17. The perpetrators were members of the outlawed Lohame Herut Israel, better known as the Lehi, better known as the Stern gang. They gunned him down while he was on an inspection tour of the truce line in Jerusalem. Hit by six bullets, he died in the hospital where he was taken after the attack.)

From Lod airport we took a taxi into Tel Aviv. We knew Fima's address: 7 Hagilboa Street. But we could only hope that he would be there and not out in the field with his army unit. We couldn't call him; he didn't have a telephone. Fortunately, Fima was home on leave from the army that day.

It was dusk when our taxi pulled up in front of his building. Morris waited on the sidewalk while I bounded up the steps to the front door and rang the bell. The door was opened by Fima's father-in-law. The old man looked me up and down. In the years to come, he often joked that, upon first laying eyes on me, he thought I was a woman from Fima's past, a woman with some sort of claim on his son-in-law—perhaps a former mistress and the mother of his "love child," or, worse still, the wife he had left behind in the Soviet Union and never legally divorced. He was just kidding, though. He had a pretty good idea who I was without having to be told.

Nevertheless, he stared at me for a few seconds and said nothing. I said, "Is this where Fima Weintraub lives?" The old man replied that it was. Just then, Fima came walking up the hall behind his father-in-law. We saw each other in the same instant, and we both cried out in the next instant. I pushed past his surprised father-in-law as Fima rushed forward. We collided, we embraced, we shouted for joy. We remained in that embrace for several minutes, laughing and crying all the while. It was all we could do. We could not talk. We did not want to talk, nor did we need to. After seven years, we were together again. There was nothing that we could possibly say that would add to the euphoria of that reunion.

I should note that Morris has a different memory of my reunion with Fima. He says that he went to the door first while I waited a few steps back; and, upon ascertaining that Fima lived there, he waved me forward. We have often argued over whose interpretation is the correct one. I stand by my interpretation, and Fima agrees with me. But who can say for sure? Memory plays tricks on us all. Anyway, the precise ordering of events is unimportant. All that really mattered is that Fima and I were together.

We spent the rest of the evening at the apartment catching each other up on the years we had spent apart. Naturally, the fate of our family was the major topic of conversation. I told Fima everything I knew. Fima was saddened by what he heard, but not so much that the evening was ruined. That evening could not be ruined. Fima had long suspected that most of his family members were dead. What mattered was that we were both alive. Against all odds we had survived. Now we were here, in this room, talking to each other. I was in his life again and he was in mine. And we were happy because of it.

Finally, we left the apartment to check into our hotel. We got a room with no fans and no air-conditioning. The night was suffocatingly hot and humid. I opened the balcony door to let in some fresh air.

The next morning we awoke to discover that my purse and Morris's watch, which we had left on the nightstand beside the open doors, were gone. They had been snatched by a cat burglar who came into the room from the balcony while we were asleep. My visa had been in the purse. Without it I could not get into America. And I could not get a replacement visa in Israel. I began to panic.

We ran downstairs to report the theft to the concierge. He offered us little help and no consolation. It seemed to him that we were astounded that one Jew would rob another. Perhaps we were. Perhaps we thought Jews, particularly Israeli Jews, were above committing such petty crimes. As if the suffering of the Jewish people in the war had ennobled us, had somehow made us more honest and law-abiding. The concierge set us straight on that score. Israel was not perfect, he told us; it had thieves just like any other country.

We reported the incident at the local police station. The police were as blasé about the theft as the concierge. "We're sorry you've been robbed," they said. "But, you know, these things happen." They expressed little hope that the thief would be caught or that we would recover our stolen items. "But we'll do what we can," they said, making it quite clear by their decidedly indifferent attitude that they would probably do nothing at all.

Trying to stay calm, we walked back to the hotel.

When we arrived, the concierge handed me my purse and my visa.

"I found them in the bushes," he said. "You see, Jewish thieves have hearts. He took your money and the watch, but he left you your papers."

A few days later, Morris decided to hazard a trip to Jerusalem to see for himself what was going on there. This was not such an easy thing to do. Travel to the Holy City was restricted to those with special permits. And to get a special permit, you had to be someone special. Morris approached the people who operated the bus that went to Jerusalem and asked to buy a ticket. They demanded to know who he was. He told them: Rabbi Fishman. The people who operated the bus were impressed. They thought he was THE Rabbi Fishman, the head of the Jerusalem rabbinate, who had recently changed his name to Maimon after the great Hebrew scholar Maimonides. Morris did not disabuse them of this notion. They issued him the permit, and he went to Jerusalem.

The way to Jerusalem was a rugged dirt track through the Judean Mountains known as the "Burma Road." The mountains were disputed territory where fighting sometimes broke out, but this was really the least of the travelers' worries. More threatening to their well-being was the road itself, which was in awful condition. There were stretches where the road barely existed, where the bus was in danger of rolling off the edge into the valley below. The passengers would then get out and walk behind the vehicle until they reached safe ground.

In Jerusalem, Morris found a room in a small hotel, after which he explored what he could of the city. In the middle of the night, a firefight broke out near his hotel, and he dove under his bed and stayed there until the shooting stopped. He went back to Tel Aviv the next day. When he walked into the lobby of our hotel the concierge pulled him aside. "Did you know your wife went out alone last night?" he said in a conspiratorial whisper. "Oh, did she?" Morris said with barely concealed amusement. "Yes, I'm afraid so," the concierge said solemnly, "and she didn't return to her room until very late." He thought that I had been up to no good, and wanted Morris to know about my behavior. Morris told him that I had been visiting with my brother, and the concierge slouched back behind his desk in a chastened state.

After a few days in Tel Aviv, we went to Carmel and then to Haifa to visit with a psychiatrist who had been on Morris's staff in Germany, then back to Tel Aviv for one final visit with Fima. My brother's furlough had expired; the time had come for him to rejoin his army unit. As we were saying our good-byes, Fima made me promise him that, once in the United States, we would do everything we could to bring his family to America. He loved Israel but, like me—like our father before us—America remained his ultimate goal.

Morris accompanied Fima to the army camp where he was to report for duty. The next day Morris and I boarded a plane for the next leg of our honeymoon, a stopover in Paris. For me, the French city was like a dream come true. I had yearned to see Paris since I was a little girl, and when my father promised to send me to school there, I had spent many hours fantasizing about what it would be like to live in the most beautiful and intellectually stimulating city in the world. But the Paris of my imaginings was nothing compared to the reality of the city. Here, I once again experienced that rags-to-riches feeling when Morris bought me a custom-made suit and I had my hair done at a salon on the Champs-Élysées. And he showed me all the sights; we strolled around the Left Bank, took a boat ride on the Seine, ate in fashionable restaurants in St. Germaine and Montparnasse, and danced the nights away in the Latin Quarter. It was wonderful. There was one sad note, however. It was while we were in Paris that Count Bernadotte was killed. We learned of his death from newspaper headlines, which proclaimed: *Bernadotte Assasiné!*

The war in Israel started up again in mid-October and Fima was involved in the fighting. Near Beersheba, his battery was firing its guns in support of an infantry unit when the latter's radio conked out. Unable to receive firing coordinates from the unit, Fima jumped into his Jeep and drove to the front to plot the numbers himself. There he was caught in an enemy artillery barrage, and a shell exploded next to his Jeep, killing or wounding everyone around him. His windshield was shattered by the blast and shrapnel, and his passenger seat was demolished. Somehow, though, he was left completely unscathed. He did not have so much as a scratch upon him. Once again, death had looked his way and continued on.

From Paris, we flew to New York and were greeted at the terminal gate by Morris's parents, Albert and Rebecca. I sat beside Rebecca in the cab that took us to Brooklyn. She looked me over. I was wearing my custom-made Parisian suit and my Parisian hairdo, and I thought I looked pretty good. I smiled and said nothing. After a minute or two, Rebecca nodded her head approvingly. In letters to his parents, Morris had said that I was pretty, but Rebecca figured that her son wouldn't have married me solely for my looks—I would have to be intelligent as well. At any rate, though she did not know me at all, she assumed this was the case. "You must be a smart girl to marry my Moishele," she said.

We moved into an apartment in Brooklyn. One of my first

impressions of America was how many clothes people owned. Morris's sister, for example, had a closet full of clothes. I remember how, in the morning before going to work, she would open her closet door, look inside, and complain, "I don't have a thing to wear." And I would think back to Poland and how I wore the same old clothes every day, how I had patched and mended them because I could not afford to buy new clothes. America is a strange place, I thought, a place where you can have a closet full of clothes and still complain that you have nothing to wear.

We lived in Brooklyn less than a year, moving to Missouri when Morris's rabbinic placement committee found him a job with the B'nai Brith Hillel Foundation at the University of Missouri in Columbia. I was pregnant when we arrived in Columbia. In 1949, I gave birth to a son, named Eli in honor of my father, Ilya. Two years later, in 1951, we had another child, a daughter. We named her Ora after Olga and Rysia (we added the *a* to make the feminine form of the name).

Moving to Missouri was a difficult transition for me. I was a Polish Jewish girl in the American heartland, and you can be sure that there were few people even remotely like me for hundreds of miles in any direction. My grasp of the English language was improving but still left a lot to be desired. Hence, I was unable to make any close friends. So I was alone much of the time—alone, but with my children.

Having children only added to my difficulties. I was really unprepared to be a mother. I hardly knew what to do. Like Fima with his antiquated cannon, I had to learn the rudiments of parenting "under fire." I had no one to go to for advice. The only person I could talk to was our pediatrician, a woman doctor. I called her often, usually at the slightest sign of trouble, sometimes when there was no trouble at all. If Eli cried too loud and too long, I was on the phone to her. Fortunately, the woman was blessed with infinite reserves of patience; she always talked to me, always went out of her way to reassure me and calm me down.

I also had to learn how to be a rabbi's wife, which meant learning how to be a gracious host and an adept socializer.

Our door was always open to members of Morris's flock— people were constantly coming and going. I had to make them feel welcome and comfortable. But everyone in Missouri was so different from me! How could I make them feel comfortable when I felt so uncomfortable myself?

Finally, I had to learn how to be an American. More hard work. I took courses in English at the university. I studied the Constitution while nursing Eli. After two years of residence in the United States, I was eligible for citizenship. I took the required test and passed it. Then I took the oath of citizenship in Kansas City. Naturally, I was pleased and proud to be an American. It made me feel secure. But I was an American in name only. I had yet to feel assimilated. I had yet to *be* an American.

Curiously, it was while I lived in Missouri that I quit having bad dreams. Since the end of the war, I had tried to banish the memory of my war experiences to the deepest and remotest corner of my mind. I didn't want to think about the war, and I didn't want to talk about it either. But such memories have a way of making their presence felt. They clamor for attention if you don't acknowledge them. And if you don't deal with them on a conscious level, they will confront you an unconscious level. They will get into your dreams and raise all kinds of hell. That is what happened to me. I was plagued by bad dreams for quite some time. Many was the night when I would be jolted awake by vivid nightmares about the war. I would find myself lying in bed next to my peacefully sleeping husband, terrified and drenched with sweat. But Eli and Ora made the nightmares go away. I was too busy caring for my babies to dream about Nazis. I got on with my life and, more significantly, the life of my children—and the nightmares went away forever.

In 1953, we received the news that Fima and Myra had had a baby boy, Eliot, also named after our father. We were thrilled. But Eliot was born with a heart defect that Israeli physicians were unable to repair. The physicians told Fima that only in America could he get the treatment his son needed. So Fima asked us to help him bring his family to the United States. As both his sister and an American citizen, I was now in a position to help him. I could get him in on a family quota. But first he had to have a guarantee of employment. Morris arranged with Myra's uncle, Willie Lakritz, to provide this guarantee. Fima and his family obtained visas, and they immigrated to America in 1954. They came over on a ship that docked in New York harbor. Morris and I and several other family members were there to greet them. When they got off the boat, we enacted another happy reunion, and I like to think that the spirit of our dear departed father was watching over us and smiling at this fulfillment of his dream.

Fima and his family moved to the Bronx, and he attended night school at Columbia University, where he studied chemistry. Morris asked his seminary to recommend him for a post on the East Coast so that we could be closer to my family. He was subsequently elected to the pulpit of the Community Synagogue in Atlantic City, New Jersey, and we moved there in May 1954. We were thus able to see a lot of my brother, my Uncle Isadore, my Aunt Esther, and their respective families.

But Morris was never really happy at the Community Synagogue. The members of his congregation were mostly middle-aged or older, pretty much set in their ways, and rather casual in their approach to religion. He was bored with them. He wanted more of a challenge. And he got it by starting a new congregation in Margate, a suburb of Atlantic City, where young married couples with small children were the norm. Morris felt that it was important to reach out to the younger generation of Jews, because without a religious commitment by the younger generation, Judaism would not survive. This was a period of financial struggle for us, as it was for the members of Morris's congregation. These people were just getting started in their professional lives, earning low wages in entry-level jobs. They couldn't afford to pay Morris much, and sometimes they couldn't afford to pay him at all. We were always strapped for cash. We often raided Eli's and Ora's piggy banks for grocery money. Nevertheless, life was good. And it got even better in 1961, when we were blessed with the birth of our youngest daughter, Abbey Gail, named after Morris's father, who had died the year before.

In 1964, we moved again, this time to the Rogers Park neighborhood on the north side of Chicago, where Morris assumed the pulpit of Congregation B'nai Zion. After four years there, however, Morris decided that a career change was in order. As a result of having undergone analysis with Dr. Karpe, he had developed an interest in psychology and psychotherapy, and now the time seemed right to enter that field. Accordingly, he started courses in clinical pastoral education and psychotherapy at Chicago State Hospital (now known as Chicago-Read Mental Health Center), studying under Reverend Karl Rankin, the director of the hospital's chaplaincy and training department. He was soon earning a modest income as a pastoral counselor. Two years later Reverend Rankin retired, and Morris was appointed to his post.

Morris had been well paid at Congregation B'nai Zion, and his departure entailed a significant drop in our income, which his paycheck from the state hospital did not cover. To help make ends meet, Morris became a sort of roving rabbi, which suited him better than a permanent post. He liked to joke that he was the rabbinical equivalent of a hired gun: "Have tallis, will travel," he used to say when describing what he did. Morris's specialty was to serve new congregations that were struggling to build up their membership and were unable to afford a full-time rabbi. Every Saturday found him with one or more congregations, which he served on a kind of pay-as-you-go basis.

Around this time as well, Morris was becoming interested in a more ecumenical approach to religion, particularly with respect to forging closer ties between Jewish and Christian denominations. This led to his being appointed as an adjunct professor of religion at Chicago's Loyola University, teaching the Old Testament. He was the first Jew hired for the faculty of Loyola's theology department.

This was a period of transition for Morris, and not only on a professional level. It was, for him, another "voyage of self-discovery," one where he recast many of his views toward life and matters of the spirit. I was not unaffected by these changes. In fact, I was going through changes of my own. Previously, I had felt trapped in the role of a rabbi's wife—it was too rigid and confining. I wanted to do something more meaningful with my life and, inspired and encouraged by Morris's example—and by Morris himself—I resolved to pursue my long-delayed dream of becoming a designer. In 1969, I enrolled in the Chicago Academy of Fine Arts, attending classes with students who were mostly thirty years younger than I was! I was a bit apprehensive about going to school, not least because of all the work involved—homework in addition to the work of a housewife and a mother. But I stuck with it, graduating in 1974 with a degree in interior design. I was then fifty-two years old, and when I stepped up to the podium to receive my diploma, it was as if I was taking the final steps of a long and arduous, but ultimately worthwhile, journey. I felt twenty feet tall.

Here's why. The diploma and the knowledge it represents, this is mine forever. I can lose all my material possessions, and all my money too—people can take these from me, but they can never take away my education. I will always have my education, and thus I will always be able to work and make a living. This is what it means to have a "Holocaust mentality": you are always preparing for the day when you might once again be cast out on your own, when you might have to fall back on whatever skills and knowledge you have in order to survive one more month, one more week, one more day or hour. Getting an education means acquiring survival skills. You never know when you may need them. You just never know.

I started my career as an interior designer almost immediately upon graduating. And though I am now past retirement age, I still take occasional design jobs. I enjoy the work. But I also do it to remind myself that I have a skill that people will pay me to use. Because . . . you just never know.

❊

Epilogue

Morris retired from both the Chicago-Read chaplaincy and Loyola University in December 1991. We now live in Skokie, Illinois, where we remain active in the Jewish community.

Fima and his family lived for several years in the Bronx. Upon graduating from Columbia, he became involved in the flavor industry, making scents for perfumes and flavor extracts for soft drinks. He eventually changed his name from Chaim to Frank Carmi—another name change!—and moved to Los Angeles, where he lives today.

Uncle Herman and his family emigrated to Canada. I stayed in touch with Nuscia and Lea in the years immediately following the war, but distance and the passage of time caused us to drift apart. I haven't heard from them in years.

Aunt Esther, bless her soul, died in 1993, while I was writing this book. Herman and Isadore have also passed on.

The war still affects me in many ways. For instance, I tend not to trust people. As a child I felt that the world was a good place, that life was good, that most people were decent. I trusted everybody. The war changed that about me. In the years immediately following the war, I trusted almost no one. I also had little concern for anyone aside from myself and my family. I was emotionally numb to other people, and it took a while for the "feeling" to return. But even today, I keep a certain emotional distance from people, and I am extremely suspicious of strangers.

I judge people quickly and harshly if anything about them, even the most superficial thing, rubs me the wrong way.

I cry more readily now. Funny thing is, I didn't cry at all during the war. Nowadays, a compliment, a pleasant word, a kind gesture is all it takes to bring on the tears.

I have learned to cherish the freedom that is considered a birthright in America. So many Americans seem to take this freedom for granted. I don't. And when I hear of people struggling in other parts of the world for their independence from some dictatorial regime, my heart aches for them. Perhaps it's only when you lose your freedom that you realize how precious it really is. And only then can you understand why people are willing to fight to the death to have it.

I am very grateful to be an American and to live in the United States. When I first came to America, I knew that my children would have a chance in this country. That much I could bequeath them: a chance. It was more than my parents could give to me. In Poland before the war, it was possible to believe that Jews could live well, could better their condition, could enjoy long and happy lives. But it was an illusory belief. They never had a chance.

I am told that many Holocaust survivors feel guilty for having survived. They ask, "Why me?" I've never yet heard a satisfactory answer to that question. Maybe there is no answer. In any event, I stopped asking it when I realized it only led to more despair. I made a conscious decision not to feel guilt for anything that happened to my family during that time, not even when I left my mother and sister behind in Sambor. I knew then, and I know now, that there was absolutely nothing I could do for them.

Sometimes people ask me what the Holocaust was like. As if I could answer that question in just a few words. As if I could answer that question with all the words in all the languages in the world. But I tell them that it was a form of hell. But not just any kind of hell. An organized hell. That's because the Germans are masters of organization. They can organize anything; it figures that they could organize hell.

And while I am on the subject of the Germans—I never

speak their language anymore, even though I am fluent in it. I hate the language. I never want to speak it, or hear it spoken, again.

I am still angry that the Western Allies did not do more to help the Jews. It seemed that everyone in the West was silent while the Jews were being annihilated. Where were the Americans? Where were the British? I am not talking about military action here; I am well aware that the Allies were incapable of invading Continental Europe in the early and middle years of the war. But why didn't they speak out against the Holocaust? Their leaders, their newspapers, and their radio programs should have screamed bloody murder, but they didn't. And where was the Pope? Why didn't he cry out for all the world to hear? Why didn't he publicly bring the full weight of his moral authority to bear against the Germans?

No voices were raised. The world at large was silent and indifferent. That is the worst thing. Indifference is worse than hate. To be ignored by people—that is the ultimate insult.

When I am around people my age, there is sometimes talk of the war. I usually keep my mouth shut. They talk about what America did in the war, but they rarely talk about what America didn't do. I don't want to have to be the one to tell them. I don't want to insult them. But I hurt inside. The indifference of America, my adopted country, a country I love—when I think of its indifference to the Jews during World War II, it still hurts.

I like to watch National Geographic specials on public television. I find them mesmerizing, especially the ones that show predators hunting prey on the African veld. I always identify with the hunted animals—the springbok and the zebra, the wide-eyed antelopes. I watch as the lions stalk them and, in my thoughts, I urge them to run away and hide. I feel sorry for them. They spend most of their lives trying to find food and avoid being killed by predators. It is a way of life I know well. I once lived it.

In June 1988, I went to Poland for the first time since the war. Morris and Abbey went with me. The primary purpose of the trip was to make contact with "refuseniks" in the Soviet Union. We did so as representatives of the Friends of Soviet Jewry, an organization dedicated to helping Soviet Jews in their struggle for religious freedom. We spent five days in Moscow meeting with the dissidents, providing them with writing materials, books about Judaism, and kosher food we had brought from America. Then we flew to Lvov, which was then (and is now) in the Ukraine, not Poland. As the plane descended toward the city, I thought that I would be crying all the time we were there. Instead, I was elated. The moment we landed I felt excited and happy. We stayed five days. We walked around the city, visiting all my childhood haunts. I took them to the park where I used to play, to my school and Fima's school as well. We went into the neighborhood where the ghetto used to be. We went to the opera house, and we strolled down Akademicka Street.

The climactic moment of the trip came when we went to my family's apartment on 51 Zbyliewicza Street. I knocked on the door with great anticipation. A young man and woman opened the door together. I introduced myself and explained my connection to the place, and I asked to see the apartment. They told us that they were also Jewish and invited us inside. We explored the apartment and the memories came flooding back. I pointed things out to Morris and Abbey: the alcove where my grandmother tried to hide from the Nazis, the tile stove in the kitchen (still there!), the place where my bed had stood.

The apartment was sparsely furnished, and the lack of furniture called to mind my mother's breakfront; I remembered how she had sold it to the janitor, Wacław, for a loaf of bread. I went downstairs to the janitor's apartment to see if it was still there. The janitor told me that the breakfront was gone, but he let me into his apartment so that I would know he was telling the truth. I wanted to visit my grandmother's apartment, but the young couple advised against even trying. They said the occupant of that apartment was an alcoholic, a very nasty fellow. So we went out on the balcony of my former apartment, the same balcony where I had stood with my father to watch German planes bombing the city, and gazed at the scenery for a few minutes. After touring the apartment, we sat and chatted with the young man and his wife. They were very polite and friendly, and we genuinely liked them. We learned that they were also dissidents. At the end of the day, as we were leaving, they invited us back to their apartment, and we did return, two or three times. Once they cooked us dinner, and I had my first meal in forty-six years in that kitchen! We had them over to our hotel room and took them out to dinner as well. When we returned to the United States, we worked on their behalf to bring them here. They now live in Brooklyn; the young woman is an educator and her husband is an engineer.

We didn't go to the site of the Janowska Camp. I wanted to save that for another trip. We thought about going to Kamenets-Podolski, only to discover that travel arrangements from Lvov to Podolia had to be made in the United States. We considered hiring a car to take us there, but we were told that it would take at least two days to reach Kamenets because the roads were so bad. This sounded very unappealing, and we didn't have two days to spare. So we decided against it.

On the flight back to America, I basked in the warm glow I felt from being in Lvov and seeing my childhood home again. I was surprised at how happy I was. I had expected to be sad; I thought I should have been sad. I actually felt guilty about this and subsequently talked about it with a friend, a woman who is also a psychotherapist. "You know, something must be wrong with me," I said. "I didn't shed a tear while I was there. I was just so happy to show Abbey and Morris my background, where I grew up, where my mother and I used to shop for groceries, where I played and went to school. Of course, nothing is the same, except the layout of the streets. But I remembered everything. And I was so happy."

And my friend said, "Lala, you know why? Because your memories are happy. You had a happy childhood."

That made sense. I realized that I had seen Lvov through

the eyes of the child I had once been. I did not think about the war and I did not feel sad, because the war and the sadness of war came after my childhood. I was relieved to know this. I had thought that I was some sort of emotional cripple.

I took my second and last trip to Lvov in the spring of 1992. This time I went with Fima.

My brother had wanted to go with us on the first trip, but he had just undergone multiple bypass surgery, and his doctor had ordered him to stay home. The powerful emotions that he would surely feel in Lvov might just as surely kill him, the doctor warned.

But he yearned to go. He didn't want to go by himself, and his wife couldn't accompany him—she had had a stroke and was ill with leukemia, and therefore unable to travel. So one day I told Fima that we could go together, just the two of us.

By then the Ukraine was a sovereign nation. But first Fima wanted to go to Poland. He had arranged to meet with a business contact in Warsaw, someone who was interested in marketing his perfume scents and soft-drink flavors. But there was something else. He also wanted to get in touch with Mila.

Mila still lived in Kraków. We had gotten her address from her brother, Henry, a childhood friend of Fima's. Henry had immigrated to the United States before the war. He had lost track of Mila during the war and assumed she was dead. Then he found out through the Red Cross that she was alive and well in Kraków. He resolved to visit her there. He went to Kraków with two thousand dollars in twenty-dollar bills, at the time a lot of money in the United States and a veritable fortune in Poland. He found Mila's apartment and rang her doorbell. She opened the door, looked at him for a second or two, and slammed the door in his face. Henry was stunned. He thought that she had recognized him. But just to make sure, he called out, "Mila, I am your brother Henry. I came here to help you. I came all the way from America."

But Mila wouldn't open the door. Henry pleaded with her for thirty minutes or more. Finally, she relented and opened the door and invited him in, reluctantly. Henry was saddened by her appearance. She looked older than her years; she was sick and walked with a cane. She was fat, she lived alone, and she was obviously unhappy.

Henry offered her the money. He showed her a wad of twenty-dollar bills and told her the amount. She wouldn't take it. "I don't want your Jewish money," she spat. "I don't want anything to do with the Jews anymore."

Henry came home absolutely heartbroken. He told Fima about the visit. He asked Fima to get in touch with Mila. Perhaps his sister would be more responsive to a former boyfriend than a brother. Fima wrote her a letter. She never replied.

When Henry found out that we were going to Poland in 1992, he pleaded with Fima to make another attempt. "Please, give her a call," he said. "Or have Lala call her. Maybe she'll talk to Lala. After all, the two of them went through so much together during the war."

I was willing to give it a try. I loved Mila. We had once been friends. As Henry had said, we had been through so much together. And I felt so very sorry for her. Henry had since learned that her husband was dead, and her children—she had two daughters—had gotten married and gone their separate ways. I suspected that she didn't have any friends, either. She was a lonely old woman, tired, sick, and angry. I wanted to help her.

So we formulated a plan: while Fima met with his business contact in Warsaw, I would telephone Mila. I placed the call, and when Mila answered the phone, I said, "Mila, this is Lala Weintraub—Urszula Krzyzanowska, remember? We were in the war together." I told her, "I am here with Fima, and we would like to visit you."

And she said, "I don't know you!"

I said, "Mila, don't you remember? You came to our apartment in Lvov and we were together; we got Aryan papers—don't you remember me?"

She said, "I don't know such a person!" Then—bang! She hung up. Slammed the phone down. I was shocked and mystified. I told Fima what had happened.

"Well, that's that," he said. "If she won't even talk to us, there's nothing we can do for her."

That was it for Mila as far as he was concerned. And as far as I was concerned too. We didn't try to contact her again.

While in Warsaw, I looked for some trace of Aunt Haika and Uncle Yossi. The wife of Fima's business contact showed me a plaque that had been set up in what was once the ghetto. Their names were not on it. Later, we went to a Holocaust museum. Same thing: their names were absent.

Then Fima and I went to Lvov. The city, like the Ukraine itself, had deteriorated. It seemed dirty and unkempt. Fima's business contact in Warsaw had told him that it would be like this. And he had warned him about doing business there. "Watch yourself," he said. "Right now, everybody is out for themselves. There are no set prices; there are no rules. It's every man for himself."

We went to all the childhood places. I took Fima to our apartment. Now it was occupied by an old Polish lady. She let us in and Fima poked around the place. I watched him and I could see that he was moved. There were tears in his eyes, and seeing them brought tears to my eyes as well.

After a while, we sat down to talk with the Polish lady. She was a sad case. She told us a tale of misery and woe—and I don't remember a word of it. The truth is, I really didn't listen to her story. I just wasn't interested. I thought, I have enough sad stories of my own. When we left, we gave her some money.

Then we took a taxi to the site of the Janowska Camp. The site is now a park surrounded by an apartment complex, constructed in the area where the barracks once stood. Nearby, on the Janowska Road, an organization called the International Memorial Fund Janiski Camp has erected a block of gray granite, slanted backward, about six feet square and three feet deep. Cut into the rough surface is a smooth part, at the top of which is carved a Star of David and, centered on the star, the figure 200,000, representing the number of Jews thought to have perished in the camp. Below the star are inscriptions in English, Hebrew, and Ukrainian. The English inscription says, "Let the memory of all the Nazi Genocide Victims in Janowska Death Camp remain forever." We soon left the camp site. Transformed from a place of hellish torments into an ordinary and unthreatening neighborhood of family housing, it lacked the power to evoke strong feelings of the past. But it was an altogether different story at our next stop. This was a memorial located approximately one mile from the center of what was once the Jewish ghetto. It is situated in a lovely little park, about one acre in size, encompassed by a low wrought-iron fence. Entering the park through a gate in the southwest corner, you are immediately confronted by a black iron menorah perhaps seven feet high. The menorah is set in the middle of a divided pathway about one hundred feet long, reached by two steps. In front of the menorah is a black marble stone, polished to a gloss and inscribed in Ukrainian with the words "Remember and Save in Your Heart." To the right of the menorah, just in front of the steps and parallel to the walkway, are three more stones of polished black marble, each bearing the same inscription in a different language—English, Hebrew, and Ukrainian. The English stone is a mostly successful translation of the Ukrainian original. It proclaims, with one misspelling and a couple of unintended reversions to Slavic syntax: "Through this road of death in 1941–1943 were passing 136,800 Jewish victims martyred by German Nazi-Fascist occupiers in L'viv geto" [*sic*].

The right side of the walkway is flanked by a series of commemorative gray granite plaques inscribed with the names of Lvov Jews slain by the Nazis. Though there are many such plaques, substantial space has been allotted for more, signaling with depressing surety that the number of those killed has not yet been fully tabulated and that many names can and will be added to this sad registry of mass murder. My family's name, however, has not gone unrecorded. Among the plaques is one with "Weintraub" carved into it. The question of whether this refers to my father or another Weintraub is unimportant to me: the point is, the Weintraubs who died, all of them, are here remembered in that inscription.

Toward the back of the park, a huge black metal statue of a bearded man, garbed in biblical robes, stands on a pedestal of rough stone with his head thrown back and his arms upraised to heaven in a gesture of supplication. The pedestal is about six feet high; the entire monument rises to a height of about thirty feet or so. In front of the pedestal is a small pit studded with broken rocks and large chunks of glass of the sort produced by a blast furnace after a pour has been completed. In front of the pit is slab of gray marble carved in the shape of two pages from an open Bible. The Hebrew inscription on the marble slab paraphrases verses 11–14 from chapter 37 of the Book of Ezekiel (King James version), which reads:

> 11. Then he said unto me, Son of man, these bones are the whole house of Israel: behold, they say, Our bones are dried, and our hope is lost: we are cut off.
>
> 12. Therefore prophesy and say unto them, Thus saith the Lord God; Behold, O my people, I will open your graves, and cause you to come up out of your graves, and bring you into the land of Israel.
>
> 13. And ye shall know that I *am* the Lord, when I have opened your graves, O my people, and brought you up out of your graves.
>
> 14. And shall put my spirit in you, and ye shall live, and I shall place you in your own land: then shall ye know that I the Lord have spoken it, and performed it, saith the Lord.

Fima and I read this together, tears welling up in our eyes. We were both thinking about our father. And I was thinking about my own experience in the Janowska Camp. But we wept softly and quietly. There were other people there, and we didn't want them to know that we were crying.

Fima was shaken by the trip to Lvov. The city made him sad. He felt none of the happiness I had experienced on my first trip. Neither did I. This time I came away from Lvov feeling depressed. I understood why. On the first trip, I wanted to show Morris and Abbey where I grew up, where I had been a child, and in doing so, a part of me had become a child again, a very happy child. But on this second trip to Lvov, my childhood was gone. Being with Fima made me think about the war, not my childhood. So the second trip to Lvov was a trip back to the war. And this was a place to which I never wanted to return.

We were both glad to have made the trip. But on the plane to America, we agreed: that's it, no more, forget it. The circle had been closed. I will never go back to Lvov again.

In 1993, Morris and I went to Washington, D.C., for the opening of the Holocaust Museum and to attend a conference of retired rabbis. We weren't involved in the museum's opening-day ceremonies; we went there on the second day. I found it a very gloomy place: it reminded me of a Nazi prison. I came away from it with very mixed feelings. I believe it to be a worthy undertaking. It is a good thing for Americans to see; perhaps they can learn from it. The victims are remembered there; names are listed, photographs displayed. That's good, too. Americans should know that those who died once existed in the fullness of their being. They should be reminded that the dead were once something other than victims. But I don't need to be reminded of that. I have my own photos, my own collection of names. All I could think was, this museum doesn't change anything. All the photographs, the plaques with the names on them, the displays and memorials—none of it can bring my family back.

When you enter the museum, one of the first things you see is a display that describes America's role in the war and what America did for the Jews. It seemed to glorify America, and I found this irritating. I thought, where was America when I needed it? The Americans did nothing to help me.

I saw a display on Auschwitz. More ambivalent feelings. There was a photograph of the entrance to the camp with the infamous gate and the sign overhead: *Arbeit Macht Frei*. I stared at the photograph for a few seconds and then moved on. What reaction should I have? I thought. What reaction can I have?

Then we sat down to watch a short documentary film

about the Holocaust. What a strange feeling came over me then. I thought, here I am, sitting in a comfortable chair, watching a movie about the extermination of the Jews. It was as if I were in my local movie theater watching the Saturday matinee. Today's feature: a second-rate horror movie about genocide. Lots of frightened faces, strutting Nazis, dead bodies. Mass shootings, gas chambers, ovens. Bulldozers plowing skeletal corpses into a ditch. It was all so very unreal, as movies always are. The big problem: our seats were too comfortable. They were padded, soft, easy on the lower back. So we could sit there in our nice comfortable chairs and watch a horror movie about Nazis and Jews, and when it was over we could go out for a nice lunch, then back to our nice homes and our nice lives. What a difference from the real thing. There were no comfortable chairs in the Holocaust. But how can a movie show what it was really like? How can a museum?

There was another film in the museum that I found quite interesting. It was shown as part of a display dedicated to Lvov. The Germans filmed it while conducting an action in Lvov. One sequence shows men hanging from a balcony. I recognized the scene. I was there when it was filmed. It was the action I had witnessed on the day I went to our apartment in the ghetto to get Fima's clothes.

Outside the Holocaust Museum, there were demonstrators from a group that claimed the Holocaust never happened, that the whole thing was some sort of Jewish conspiracy. A woman about my age went over to them and rolled up her sleeve, showing them the numbers that the Nazis had tattooed on her arm. "Where do you think I got this?" she asked. The demonstrators were unfazed. They said that she was part of the conspiracy.

That incident, I think, is the best reason I know for building and maintaining a museum about the Holocaust.

Yad Vashem is an organization that searches out the fate of people who disappeared in the Holocaust. A few years ago, I contacted the people there in the hope that they could find out what happened to my parents and Rysia. I filled out a questionnaire listing all the information they needed to start a search: names, birth dates, physical descriptions, where they were last seen, etc. I was told that it might take years before their research turned up any information. I am still waiting to hear from them.

The Holocaust Museum has a room dedicated to the children. Hundreds of photographs of children are posted on the walls. I looked at every one, searching for Rysia. I always do this. I look for her in films, and I look for her in photos. I'll pick up a book about the Holocaust, turn to the photo section, and look for her there.

Rysia would be in her sixties if she were alive today. On both my trips to Poland and Ukraine, I always made a point of looking closely at every woman I saw who seemed to be in her age group. Fima did the same thing. We didn't talk about this with each other; we just did it. It is second nature to us. He looks, and I look. Maybe, maybe, maybe, we think. You always have that hope. Some part of me even hopes that my parents are still alive. Of course, this is impossible. My parents are long dead, and I can accept that. But not Rysia. Fima and I still have a feeling that Rysia is alive.

If we could only find her, we both tell ourselves. If only we could find Rysia, what wouldn't we do for her. . . .

❖

Jewish Lives